THE B █████████ OOL

THE BIRTH OF COOL

Style Narratives of the African Diaspora

Carol Tulloch

Bloomsbury Academic
An imprint of Bloomsbury Publishing Plc

B L O O M S B U R Y
LONDON · OXFORD · NEW YORK · NEW DELHI · SYDNEY

Bloomsbury Academic

An imprint of Bloomsbury Publishing Plc

50 Bedford Square	1385 Broadway
London	New York
WC1B 3DP	NY 10018
UK	USA

www.bloomsbury.com

BLOOMSBURY and the Diana logo are trademarks of Bloomsbury Publishing Plc

First published 2016

© Carol Tulloch, 2016

Carol Tulloch has asserted her right under the Copyright, Designs and Patents Act, 1988,
to be identified as Author of this work.

British Library Cataloguing-in-Publication Data

A catalogue record for this book is available from the British Library.

ISBN:	HB:	978-1-8597-3465-0
	PB:	978-1-8597-3470-4
	ePDF:	978-1-4742-6286-6
	ePub:	978-1-4742-6287-3

Library of Congress Cataloging-in-Publication Data

A catalog record for this book is available from the Library of Congress.

Typeset by RefineCatch Limited, Bungay, Suffolk
Printed and bound in Great Britain

For
my mother Cetira Emmeline (1924–2010)
my grandmother Roselyn Agatha (1905–1993)
my sister Elaine Tulloch
my daughter Lucy Shelton

CONTENTS

LIST OF ILLUSTRATIONS

LIST OF PLATES

ACKNOWLEDGMENTS

This book has been a very long time in the making. It began with an invitation from Kathryn Earle of Bloomsbury Publishing to write about black style. I am incredibly grateful to Kathryn's belief in the subject and support. Hannah Crump and Ariadne Godwin, also at Bloomsbury, have helped to steer this project to its end, thank you both for your encouragement and professionalism.

The project that has emerged has been shaped and developed over the years through the development of ideas through the publication of articles and chapters in books, curatorial projects, discussions with colleagues, the presentation of papers at conferences, workshops and as a guest speaker. I am indebted to: Paul Antick, Rebecca Arnold; Elke Aus dem Moore, Jeremy Aynsley, Oriana Baddeley, Bakri Bakhit, Robert Barker, Dipti Bhaghat, Geraldine Biddle-Perry, Sonia Boyce, Jamie Brassett, Christopher Breward, Ethel Brooks, Barbara Burman, Avis Charles, Sarah Cheang, Janice Cheddie, Shirley Chubb, Judith Clark, Hazel Clark, Gill Clarke, Shaun Cole, Jane Collins, Gen Doy, Edwina Ehrman, Amy de la Haye, Madeleine Ginsburg, Fiona Hackney, Stuart Hall, Mark Haworth-Booth, Heike Jenss, Susan Kaiser, Hope Kingsly, Sara Chong Kwan, Marius Kwint, Van Dyk Lewis, MA Fashion Studies and Fashion Design Students Parsons New School of Design Lecture Series "The Fashion Body Politic"; MA and PhD students of the Transnational Art, Identity and Nation Research Centre (TrAIN), Chris McHugh, Sandrine Micossé-Aikins, Liz Miller, Christina Moon, Renée Mussai, Mica Nava, Alistair O'Neil, Kwesi Owusu, Adam Phillips, Susan Pritchard, Malcolm Quinn, Leslie Rabine, Clare Rose, Mark Sealy MBE, Alison Slater, Penny Sparke, Valerie Steele; Andrew Stephenson, Nicola Stylianou, Shehnaz Sutterwalla, Lou Taylor, Joanne Turney, Melanie Unwin, Benjamin Whyman, Val Wilmer, Elizabeth Wilson. A special thank you to Lynda Dyson, Caroline Evans, Joanne Lacey and Toshio Watanabe for reading early versions of chapters, and to Stella Bruzzie and Pamela Church-Gibson for allowing an earlier version of "'My Man Let Me Pull Your Coat to Something': Malcolm X" to be included here.

The administrative staff at Chelsea College of Art and University of the Arts London have been exemplary in their support: Alice Clarke, Laura Lanceley, Claire Mokrauer-Madden, Eleanor Pitkin, Nick Tatchell, Prema Mundiandy.

Through the support of the following organizations I was able to conduct research in England and overseas, to purchase the illustrations that feature in this book, and the necessary completion of the color pages and administration of the book. Arts and Humanities Research Board provided funding for research study in New York and Washington; The Basil Taylor Travel Bursary enabled research in Jamaica; The British Academy granted funding for research in England, many of the images in this publication, and made it possible for the book to have color pages; Chelsea College of Arts supplied funding for indexing, research materials and additional images; TrAIN and The Research Department of the Victoria and Albert Museum (V&A) for jointly funding the *Dress as Auto/Biography Workshop* held at the V&A in 2013. An incredible thank you to all the institutions and individuals who have given permission to use images and text featured here: Autograph Abp, Denise Lawrence, Carlin Music, Getty Images, The Gordon Parks Foundation, Magnum Photos Ltd, Cynthia Sesso, National Library of Jamaica, Sony Music Entertainment Inc., Topham Partners, Historic England Archive.

I drew on a wide range of expertise from the staff of several libraries, archives and museums: Peter James and Emma at West Birmingham Central Library; Fashion Institute of Technology, New York; Staff at the National Art Library of Jamaica, Staff at the Jamaica Archives; Pat Jones, North Carolina Central University Art Museum; Lucy McCann and the staff of the Bodleian Library, University of Oxford; Lynette Morris and the staff at Spanish Town Archives, Jamaica; Terry Barringer, Royal Commonwealth Society Library Collections. Ellen Conlon and Merv Honeywood guided my manuscript through its production and editorial process. Judy Tither has been meticulous as copy-editor. A special thank you goes to this team.

Friends and family have been unflinching in their generosity of encouragement, from providing accommodation on research visits to just calling to support my endeavor to complete this book: Elaine Tulloch, Jane Collins, Veronica, Miguel and Denver Williams; Lucy Shelton, Elizabeth Le Bas, Carol Blank, Radha Blank, Roshi Naidoo, Norma Linton; Victoria Loughren and Katrina Royalle.

Importantly, my husband Syd Shelton. He has listened to early morning musings on every aspect of this research, he has read every chapter many times over, as a graphic designer he scanned and refined images for the price of a meal. When I could not see the end he could. Thank you Syd.

PREFACE

This book has been inspired by a range of images—photographs, paintings and text that form portraits, biographies and autobiographies of black women and men from different parts of the African diaspora. They have engendered a need in me to seek out the possible cultural meanings and contributions that the style narratives featured in the images of the lives of individuals and groups as a contributory factor in, and comment on, the societies and cultures they inhabit. The work considers how moments in history and an associated image can lend alternative perspectives of black identities, aesthetics and history across the African diaspora. Some of the individuals and groups discussed here are world-famous, others are part of the underrated everyday existence of so called ordinary people.

This study has also been informed by images of my subconscious, memories of the myriad styles worn by black men, women and children that have been part of my life. I was born in the 1950s in Doncaster, South Yorkshire, England and was fortunate to grow up with the so called "first generation" of post-World War II migrants and immigrants who travelled from different parts of the then British Empire and Commonwealth. From childhood through to adulthood I witnessed amongst this group, and their descendants, how deftly they marked out their lives through the styling of their bodies that consequently became part of the holistic making of themselves, if often in contentious and potentially debilitating contexts. For some cool was and is a necessary goal and a palpable achievement. Those spectral images and existentialist endeavours are always with me and have been the major inspiration to write this book.

INTRODUCTION

This time it's personal

I once asked my father if it became compulsory for all men to wear flared trousers, what would he do? He replied, "Go in the nuddy [nude]". I laughed at his response, thinking he was just old fashioned. I must have been about eleven or twelve and my idea of a well-dressed man came in the form of Jimi Hendrix who reigned supreme in such pants. This was the period of revolutionary dress for the young.

My dad was fastidious about his clothing. His suits were always bespoke, he believed in the best quality fabrics you could afford. His ties were the area in which he could really demonstrate some flair. I remember he had a plain black silk one knitted in garter stitch, the epitome of the modernist ethic, with its angular shape of square ends and straight sides. Another was made of cream silk, with pointed ends and gossamer threads of shimmery red, silver and gold pulled sporadically through the fine weave. He also wore tie pins. One had a jockey riding a horse, indicative of his fondness for horseracing. I cannot remember the shirts he wore with his suits, and I think he always wore black shoes, but his ties and his suits are what stick in my mind.

These items contrasted dramatically with my father's weekday clothing that he wore when he was first a coal miner and then a power station construction worker. What I can remember were his checked, lumberjack-style shirt, and a pale blue rib-knit V-necked jumper. This latter item is indelibly printed on my mind as it remained hanging on my parents' wardrobe door for days after my father was killed in a car accident in 1971. This "aesthetics of absence" (Ash 1996: 219) that is lodged in the style memories of my father, have stayed with me these forty-five years.

The image of my father well dressed in a two-piece suit and tie (plate 1) is how I want to preserve the visual memory of him. This version of Alfred Valentine Tulloch (1930–1971) is reinforced in the only photograph that exists of him taken in Birmingham in the mid-1950s following his arrival from Jamaica, a print of which was sent to relations back home.[1] I will never know what prompted my father to have the photograph taken, why he chose that composition of garments to have his photograph taken in. What were the colors of his suit, shirt, tie and shoes? Was that jacket his, as it seems a little big around the neck? Was it ready- or tailor-made, purchased in England or brought over from Jamaica?[2] Where was the tie pin from? Why was his hair natural rather than conked, African-American vernacular for straightened hair, as this was an acceptable alternative hairstyle-choice for black men at the time? So many questions that will go unanswered as the people who could provide the answers have passed away. Of course, as Stuart Hall has said, from the moment the photograph was taken to my looking at it numerous times over the many years, layer upon layer of "meaning [slides] across the frame. It is difficult, if not by now impossible, to recapture some of its earlier, historical meanings ... the search for an 'essential, true original' meaning is an illusion. No such previously natural moment of true meaning, untouched by the codes and social relations production and reading, exists" (Hall 1984: 2–3).

Essentially, what the studio portrait does provide for me is an image of my father as a young man, before the period of having a family and the consequent patriarchal responsibility. At the time of his death in 1971 my father was just one of the millions of people in Britain who were still "hidden from history"—people of difference based on "race", class, gender and sexuality. What his styled body in this photograph does for me is to place Alf, as he was also known, as part of his fellow generation of Jamaicans and other Caribbeans who migrated to Britain in the first half of the 1950s, and situates him squarely as part of that celebrated moment of British history.[3] Therefore this photograph joins the "body of evidence"—both in terms of styled bodies and the wealth of photographs of Caribbean and African men, women and children during the period of post-war migration held in archives such as the Ernest Dyche Collection at Birmingham Central Library, and the Harry Jacobs Archive at Lambeth Archives, London, "where people were, at a certain stage of life and how they imagined themselves, how they became 'persons'" (Hall 1984: 5).

Indeed, my father may well have had his photograph taken at the Ernest Dyche Studios, as it was taken in Birmingham, the city he chose as his first place to live on migrating to England. Unlike the usual scenario of the anonymity of the sitter in images held in the Dyche and other collections, there is a biography attached to my father's photograph, the life he lived with my mother after the photograph was taken (plate 2). The photographs of my parents were obviously taken at the same studio in Birmingham—the backdrop and table are the same, the vase in each portrait is of similar design. Did my parents go separately before they met or did they go to the photographic studio together once they became a couple? Another question that will never be answered. The photograph of my mother as a young woman is, nonetheless, enlightening. It reaffirms qualities that came to define the styled self of Cetira Emmeline Thomas (née Green, born 1924) until her death in 2010. In this photograph, my mother is incredibly smart. All the elements of her style are in harmony. Her belted dress, with its ruched sleeve detail and demure length, reverberates respectability, which is echoed by her neat shell-shaped hat. A desire for ornamentation is expressed through my mother's handbag and the use of what appears to be a handkerchief that hangs from it. This detail lends an air of leisured time.

Regardless of these speculations, the information that is missing from my father's and my mother's photographic documentation is, as mentioned above, why did they choose what they wore for this photographic sitting? Again, questions that cannot be answered categorically, like the range of styles worn by the women and men in this book. In the spirit of one of the aims of *The Birth of Cool: Style Narratives of the African Diaspora*, to *read* the identities and style narratives of visual and textual images of black people, my mother's handbag is a significant marker of her desire for adventure and agency; she travelled alone to England, and the accessory acts as a hinge between her past and future. As Adam Phillips has said: "It is in the gap between the life she has and the life she wants that a woman chooses a bag . . . a bag always links her to her history in an uncanny way. Bags are useful because they are evocative . . . they remind us of many things . . . What these psychoanalytic stories want us to wonder is how a handbag fits into the pattern and the project of a woman's life. The stories warn us away from trivializing these objects. Indeed, they want us to believe that 'What's in a bag?' is the most urgent question we ever ask" (2012: 30). An urgent question I ask, what do the style narratives of the African diaspora mean?

I am in agreement with Tina C. Campt that, regardless of whether the sitter in a photograph is known or not, "it is equally important to theorize how such photographs function as images and as practices of social and cultural enunciation that exceed their biographical details" (Campt 2012: 196). What is fundamental here, as illustrated in the photographs of my mother and father, and a key thread that runs through this book is the aesthetic of presence, a technique of *being* to counter the aesthetics of invisibility that people of the African diaspora have had to overcome since slavery. It is a further aim of this publication to engage with moments of articulation in the aesthetics of presence in different parts of the African diaspora through style narratives.

Cool: an aesthetic of presence across the African diaspora

The growing number of books on the history and cultural meaning of cool, which ranges from sunglasses, architecture and capitalism, has cool originating in the USA.[4] Indeed Peter N. Stearns declares that "[C]ool. The concept is distinctly American, and it permeates almost every aspect of contemporary American Culture" (1994: 1). Robert Farris Thompson is a leading academic on cool with his seminal texts of the 1960s and 1970s: "An Aesthetic of the Cool: West African Dance" (1966), "An Aesthetic of the Cool" (1973), and "An Introduction to Transatlantic Black Art History: Remarks in Anticipation of a Coming Golden Age of Afro-Americana" (1974). Thompson links the articulation of cool amongst African-Americans to Africa in order to provide what he calls cool as "historical depth" (Thompson [1973] 2011: 19).[5] He defined an aesthetic of the cool as "in the sense of a deeply and complexly motivated, consciously artistic, interweaving of elements serious and pleasurable, of responsibility and of play" (Thompson [1973] 2011: 16), and that the "mask" of coolness is worn in times of stress and pleasure "in fields of expressive performance [and dance]" (Thompson [1973] 2011: 16). Of particular note in this context is Thompson's elaboration that cool in some West, Central and East African languages means newness, rebirth (Thompson [1973] 2011: 16), that is part of the heritage that Thompson believes informs the multi-dimensional interpretations of what he categorized as "black cool": "Black Cool is an idiom of *social balance* . . . and *internal* or *spiritual balance*, the sign of clear conscience . . . when one returns to oneself in an ideal sense, achieving or rediscovering character, when what one does and what one ought to be are one" (Thompson 1974: 196).

Rebecca Walker sees "Black Cool" as captivation (2012: xi–xvi). This concept was crystallized for her in Barack Obama during the 2008 USA presidential elections. She was "captivated" by his style of dress and his poise: "Obama emerges from a sleek, black Town Car wearing dark sunglasses, a suit, and a red tie. This is all, and yet, in this picture, Obama is indisputably cool. He is so, so cool I cannot turn away from the image . . . It is Black Cool. It is made up of elements that can be traced back to a place, a people, and a culture" (Walker 2012: xiv–xv). Apparently this "captivation" of cool was something that the jazz artist Thelonius Monk experienced whilst "staring up at a picture of Billie Holiday tacked to the ceiling praying for the essence of cool" (MacAdams 2001: 61). Walker asks that a "periodic table of Black Cool, element by element" be developed (Walker 2012: xvi).

An aim of *The Birth of Cool: Style Narratives of the African Diaspora* is to provide other possible meanings of cool as expressed across the African diaspora at different times. The book is an acknowledgement of cool as an expansive diasporic act of black aesthetics, as well as cool being a critical tool in the projection of the aesthetic of presence.

The mechanics of style narratives and the African diaspora: a methodology

I use the term "style" as agency—in the construction of self through the assemblage of garments and accessories, hairstyles and beauty regimes that may, or may not, be "in fashion" at the time of use. I see the styling practices of a layperson's articulation of everyday life through their styled body as exercising that agency. This is part of the process of self-telling, that is to expound an aspect of autobiography through the clothing choices an individual makes—what I have come to call style narratives (Tulloch 2010: 276). This has derived from my argument that in the study of black people and the African diaspora, the concept of style-fashion-dress (Tulloch 2010) encompasses myriad routes and connections, flows and tensions that originate from the analytical frame of Africa and its diaspora. Style-fashion-dress is a term that constitutes a system of concepts that signifies the multitude of meanings and frameworks that are always "whole-and-part" (Picht and Draskau 1985: 80–1) of dress studies. But in the issue of black people and their construction of self, and/or the use or production of garments and accessories in that process, there is a need (as it would be for any close study of a specific group or subject area) to appropriate the correct term from this triumvirate to explore this.

When applied to the African diaspora, I still stand by my plea made in 2010 in the argument for and agreement with George Shepperson (1968) that the African diaspora means Africa and the groups that formed outside Africa following the Atlantic slave trade, colonialism and imperialism. What needs to be considered is how, when and where these separate entities of the triumvirate of style-fashion-dress come into play in this area of study (Tulloch 2010: 296). A further impetus is Eyal Sivan's proposition that we consider a site, a geographical space, as an archive, that the de-archiving and re-archiving of a site delivers a new narrative. Such an approach enables a more expansive reading of individual and group identities of the people across the African diaspora through the network of things, details and ideas.[6] The site being considered here is the African diaspora. This effectively merges diaspora and transnational as concepts, a strength of combination that, according to Thomas Faist, fuels "reflexivity of agency and processes, also needs to be brought to bear upon the understanding of broader issues of social change and transformation". (Faist 2010: 33). Such an approach, I believe, can lead to a more balanced understanding of the style-fashion-dress practices of black people as a comment on a sense of self in contested situations and contested spaces, the consideration of this form of self-presentation across the African diaspora leads to a dynamic profile of black people that undercuts misrepresentations and ethnic absolutism.

Together, these elements have provided me with a specific methodology that I can apply to the study of the style-fashion-dressed bodies—the umbrella term I call dress and the African diaspora which was the title of a special issue of *Fashion Theory: The Journal of Dress, Body & Culture* (2010) where I first explored the terms style, style narratives and style-fashion-dress. The elements that construct my methodology of dress and the African diaspora are: to challenge so-called historical truths, difference, entangled experiences, entangled identities, networks, narratives, cross-cultural connections, social, cultural and political issues (figure 0.1). I am encouraged by the definition of methodology as: "*method*s refer

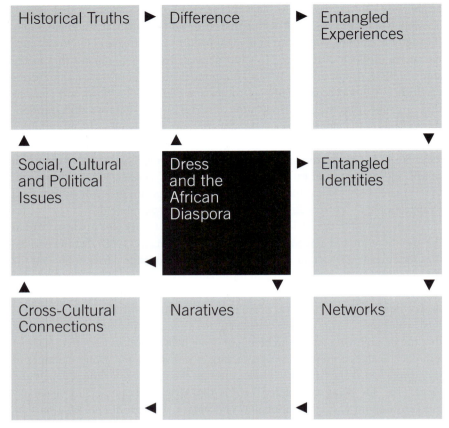

Historical Truths ▶	Difference ▶	Entangled Experiences
Social, Cultural and Political Issues	**Dress and the African Diaspora** ▶	Entangled Identities
Cross-Cultural Connections	Naratives	Networks

FIGURE 0.1 Dress and the African diaspora: A methodology diagram. Composed by Carol Tulloch. Designed by Syd Shelton.

specifically to individual techniques … where as *methodology* can be construed broadly to suggest both the presuppositions of methods, as well as their link to theory and implications for society" (Morrow & Brown 1994: 36), and I would add culture and its practices. Equally, Gillian Rose advises in *Visual Methodologies*, "Successful interpretation depends on a passionate engagement with what you see. Use your methodology to discipline your passion, not to deaden it" (Rose 2001: 4).

The Birth of Cool: Style Narratives of the African Diaspora is a look at a series of case studies that have been cherry-picked from the USA, Jamaica, England and South Africa and different time frames, from the late nineteenth century to 2006. This is done to illustrate that through individuals, cultural groups and where there are transnational and transcultural connections across historical time zones of the African diaspora. My decision to do this was the twinned responses of "falling for" particular objects and images and the narrative urgency to provide detailed exploration. I found it impossible to resist James VanDerZee's photograph of an African-American couple in raccoon fur coats that I discuss in chapter two, or having a personal connection with a subject, as in the African-Jamaican higgler, as my maternal aunt told me that my great grandmother was a higgler, whilst other subjects drew me into the debate set by others to attend to the profile of a cultural icon, such as Billie Holiday. Therefore *The Birth of Cool: Style Narratives of the African Diaspora* wants to convey that objects-people-geographies-histories are intertwined, and often interdependent in the contributions that style-fashion-dress practices have made to the articulation of these diasporic relationships and their place in dress studies.

Style narratives and auto/biography

In light of the personal memories and connections detailed above, I acknowledge Sheila Rowbotham's warning to researchers of the dangers of being part of something as well as a chronicler of it, as this kind of relationship with history may "give you insights; it does not, however, give rise to any easy overview" (Rowbotham 1999: 73). The academic framework of auto/biography can help address this. Liz Stanley's early treatise on the auto/biographical has been a driver for this book, as she has argued for the academic validity of the autobiographical self of the researcher in the research text. Stanley pointed out that the research a researcher undertakes becomes part of their autobiography, and in turn the autobiography of the researcher can impact on the research (Stanley 1992: 17). Auto/biography now has an established presence in narrative studies, which Linda Anderson explains is a term coined:

> to denote the way autobiographical and biographical narratives are related and to suggest how the boundary between them is fluid. This can be manifested in the way autobiographies may contain biographical information about the lives of others, or be read for the biographical information they contain about the subject. Biographies also may include personal revelations about their authors or a personal narrative of their own quest for information or their relation to the biographical subject.
>
> **ANDERSON** 2011: 140

Elspeth Probyn (1993), Jan Campbell and Janet Harbord (2002) have also considered the intellectual relevance of the inclusion and recognition of the academic self in one's research. This so-called "autobiographical turn" of academic auto/biographical writing in texts is present in design history and material culture (Sparke 1995, Ryan 1999, Attfield 2000) and no less in the study of dress, fashion and style (Ash 1996, Fawcett, 2002, Tulloch 2010). The subject of dress as auto/

biography is of growing interest,[7] the ways in which bodies are fundamental to life experiences, which in turn reflects everyday life. Therefore, how individuals "design", their lives and bodies for day-to-day living ultimately informs an individual's biography or autobiography. So if "narrative is a type of inquiry, an analytical process in which researchers engage" (Stanley 2011) then what impact does this line of subjectivity have on the development of style-fashion-dress studies? This is an aspect that is explored in this publication.

The book, of course, is inspired by the Miles Davis Nonet jazz album *Birth of the Cool*, the genesis of which began in 1947 and has had continued worldwide influence across musical and art genres. Davis and his band explored complex emotions and experiences through improvisation, composition and the performance of ensemble jazz. A line of enquiry I also explore in *The Birth of Cool: Style Narratives of the African Diaspora*.

1 ANGEL IN THE MARKET PLACE: THE AFRICAN-JAMAICAN HIGGLER 1880–1907

This chapter looks at the style narrative of the Jamaican female market trader, colloquially known as a higgler, between 1880 and 1907. I focus on this period to provide a broader understanding of African-Jamaican higgler style at this time. There have been numerous studies on the history, practice and significance of the higgler in Jamaica, some of which refer to higgler practices in other parts of the Caribbean.[1] With regards to the style practices of the African-Jamaican higgler, there is detailed thinking of this from slavery to the early 1960s by Winnifred Brown-Glaude, who focuses, primarily, on paintings and textual portraits of the marketeer (2011: 91–118). Steve O. Buckridge includes the African-Jamaican higgler in his study *The Language of Dress: Resistance and Accommodation in Jamaica, 1760–1890* with reference to the "pull-skirt," her headdress and apron (2004: 47, 161–4). A more recent history of the higgler is given by Gina A. Ulysse, who relates style practices and transference between higgler, purchaser and her own experiences in late-twentieth-century Jamaica (2007: 219–55).

Additionally, the late nineteenth- to early twentieth-century saw a concerted development of tourism on the island and consequently of the Jamaican postcard. Together, these systems were seen as part of the economic restoration of the British West Indies desired by the crown colony government (Thompson 2006: 256). The ubiquitous presence of the higgler at this time was one example of Jamaica's ties to its British slave past since 1655,[2] and the pursuit of freedom of its black inhabitants since the emancipation of slaves in 1834. The higgler emerged within that "catastrophic history" (Hezekiah 2012: 6) of British slavery on the island of Jamaica.[3] Within that system, plantation owners granted "permission" (Edwards 1979: 8) to enslaved women and men to sell produce grown by them on their provision grounds at public markets. The higgler's trade as a marketeer has continued, uninterrupted, to the present day (Ulysse 2007, Brown-Glaude 2011).[4] This case study considers the higgler's style narrative as a comment on this fact of cultural continuity, focusing on the period of 1880 to 1907, a period of the marketeer's practice that is under represented. In light of this, I refer to the higgler as the African-Jamaican higgler. Such an epithet gives a pronounced definition and challenges the issue of discontinuity in the lineage and cultural identity of enslaved Africans and their descendants on the island. I use the term higgler, as Sidney W. Mintz has clarified, that it is "the term specific to Jamaica" and "most commonly used and tends to be applied indiscriminately to people filling roles at every step in the marketing process" (Mintz 1955: 98).

I have chosen as the visual entry point for this discussion the photographic postcard, "A Jamaica Lady" (figure 1.1), published in 1903[5] by the white-Jamaican entrepreneur Aston W. Gardner. For me, the postcard stands at the vanguard of the past-present-future juncture of the higgler's identity in Jamaica, and consequently her contribution to Jamaica's identities from slavery onwards.

The critical draw of the postcard "A Jamaica Lady"

Like many other African-Jamaicans featured on postcards during the late nineteenth and early twentieth century, this woman's personal details are lost to us. There is no way of knowing her age. She could be anywhere between forty and sixty. What is suggested that if she was closer to sixty, she was an ex-slave, and if nearer to forty, then her parents were enslaved. Either way, this woman had a direct link to the pre-emancipation period in which the higgler trade was established in Jamaica. This makes the postcard all the more fascinating. Furthermore, who exactly is it a portrait of? Was the woman actually a higgler or a model for "character studies"? (Boxer 2013: 18). Was she wearing her own clothes or items provided by the photographer? A statement that is communicated here in the production of the postcard is that this is an image of a woman clothed and accessorized in the properties that are associated with the African-Jamaican higgler: uncorseted garments protected by an apron; a headtie, which prompted some observers to call African-Jamaican higglers "bandanna women" (Caffin 1899),[6] a nomenclature that categorized an accessory with a specific female trade of work; and the head-portage, the use of a vessel to carry produce on the head, a key tool for the higgler in which to transport goods to market.

To undertake such a study of a photographic portrait is to enter a web of issues that includes, as Graham Clarke has pointed out, "what, and who, is being photographed" (Clarke 1997: 101), the choice of objects that surround the

COPYRIGHT   A JAMAICA LADY.   GARDNER'S SERIES

FIGURE 1.1 "A Jamaica Lady," Gardner's Series, 1903, Jamaica. Courtesy of the
National Library of Jamaica.

individual to communicate what is being said in the representation of that individual in a particular context (Clarke 1997: 101–3). Regardless of the authenticity of the sitter, whether she was a higgler or not, her "anonymity is poignant, offering a Proust-like savouring of memory, as if a postcard could act as the smell or taste of a past to be recovered" (Nairne 2004: 9). I am drawn to this image because of its potential circulation as a postcard depicting the performativity of the African-Jamaican higgler, in the sense the performativity of her trade and its distinctive style has made "a difference in the world" (Loxley 2007: 2).[7]

Others have referenced the image "A Jamaica Lady". For example, Victoria Durant-Gonzalez used the postcard, without the caption, in her study "The Occupation of Higglering" (1983). The aim of the study was to legitimate the practice of the higgler, to give it respectability, and focused on the 1970s to the early 1980s, but the article is supported by numerous historical images of higgler practice, the earliest being 1806. Buckridge included the postcard "A Jamaica Lady," again without the caption, alongside two photographs of African-Jamaican higglers on their way to market, to discuss the dress of "peasant women who were market traders" (Buckridge 2004: 161–4). Rosemary Crill references the image, without the caption, in her detailed study of the local and global journey and use of Madras cloth and handkerchief (Crill 2015: 146–149, 165).

The artist Roberta Stoddart drew on the image as inspiration for a central figure in her 1996 painting *Tools of the Trade* (plate 3) which "symbolises the journey from a dystopian past into what is still, for many, a dystopian present" (Stoddart 2014).[8] Poignantly, Stoddart painted the work at Good Hope Estate, in Trelawny, Jamaica. Originally a slave plantation that began in 1774 as a sugar estate, Good Hope was owned by John Tharp, at the time "the largest land and slave owner in Jamaica." The woman in "A Jamaica Lady" embodied numerous cultural, personal and metaphysical references for Stoddart:

> I have created a clear visual reference to the image "Jamaica Lady" from the Institute of Jamaica. She is a symbol of dignity, and she is the shipmaster of this long, perilous journey. She is my late helper Ma Lou, our Mother, our Grandmother. She is a higgler, a market lady, a labourer. She is a helper, a maid. She is a heroic symbol of female survival against the horrors of slavery, and the numbing, crippling indignities of poverty. In her own quiet way, she is triumphant.
>
> **STODDART** 2014[9]

But why did I choose this image of all the possible alternative photographs, painted and photographic postcards of the African-Jamaican higgler produced between 1880 and 1907 as the lead into understanding the style narratives of the African-Jamaican higgler at this time in Jamaica's history? My decision was partially based on what Elizabeth Edwards explains as "the inexplicable point of incisive clarity" (Edwards 2001: 1). Edwards is building on Roland Barthes' renowned term the *punctum*: the "sting, speck, cut, little hole—and also a cast of the dice. A photograph's *punctum* is that accident which pricks me (but also bruises me, is poignant to me)" (Barthes 1993: 27).

This image is "poignant" for me because the idea of the African-Jamaican higgler is allowed to fill the entire space of the photograph, thereby giving this distinctively African-Jamaican female trade undoubted, glorious presence and importance.[10] The unknown photographer's magnification of the details that compose the African-Jamaican higgler's identity, in sum, quantifies and conveys to potential tourists to the island, and possible recipients of the postcard abroad, what it means to *be* a higgler in Jamaica. It also, of course, elevates the centrality of objects in the construction of the styled body as a narrative on, in this instance, slavery and personal freedom, colonialism and autonomy. The elevation of the African-Jamaican higgler to iconic status by Gardner reflects how he believed Jamaica should be represented to the outside world. In 1900, for example, Gardner made a public protest in the correspondence section of *The Daily Gleaner* newspaper with regard to the use of "Llandovery Falls, in St. Ann" chosen to represent the island on the "New Jamaica Penny Stamp" which Gardner believed to have been a mistake and "a view of Wales has been copied" (Gardner 1900: 7) and used instead. Gardner made his case for a more Jamaican alternative: to the editor of *The Gleaner* he wrote:

> Sir, The new postage stamp is now issued. Can you say why a really typical view of our island is not given . . . If changes are contemplated in the other issues, then in the name of common honesty alone, let us have one thing at least representative. Banana groves are numerous, as are natives and amateur photographers, . . . of whom could, I feel sure, supply something infinitely more handsome than that the adhesive in question.
>
> **GARDNER** 1900: 7

The photographic portrait concentrates on the top half of her body, which is presented in such a voluminous gesture that it seems "as if those parts . . . were the truth" (Tagg 1988: 35). From the late 1880s in Britain, the composition of photographic poses were subjected to the categorization of social status. A direct, facial pose was common amongst the lower orders, whilst side-views were preserved for the bourgeoisie, systems that were understood within British society (Tagg 1988: 35–7). The use of the higgler in profile formed part of the indexical properties in the intended reference of "A Jamaican Lady." I would argue that the postcard is more a portrait of the garments and accessories associated with the higgler, than of an individual. The body merely acts as an indexical peg. All the symbolic motifs of higgler dress are heightened: the brightness of her apron and other garments are made more striking by the stark contrast of her "black"[11] skin; the exaggerated tie of the madras check handkerchief makes use of its meter square diameter, providing additional definition to the woman's head; the gargantuan market basket draws the viewer's eye to it as a crucial piece of higgler machinery, and similarly to all the other grand gestures of the portrait. The composition may send out signals of a woman in working dress, but the finishing touches of the single strand of beads and an earring strike a chord of overall pride in the presentation of self. Therefore:

> Like any visual art, the art of dress has its own autonomous history, a self-perpetuating flow of images derived from other images. But any living image of a clothed body derives essentially from a picture or, rather, from an ongoing, known tradition of pictures of clothed bodies ... Dressing is always picture making, with reference to actual pictures that indicate how the clothes are to be perceived.
>
> **HOLLANDER** 1975: 311

These are the details of the photograph that drew me in (Barthes 1993 [1980]: 42–3) and provided the critical framework I want to use to understand the style narrative of the African-Jamaican higgler.

The critical possibilities of the postcard "A Jamaica Lady"

The critical framework derived from the photographic postcard "A Jamaica Lady" for this chapter is constructed of seven elements. Firstly, the complexities of time. To return to Barthes and the *punctum* in photography as an expression of time, "*that-has-been*" for "in historical photographs: there is always a defeat of Time in them: *that* is dead and *that* is going to die" (Barthes 1993 [1980]: 96). Could this point be expanded upon to see the *punctum* in the example of the photographic postcard "A Jamaica Lady" not as a "defeat of Time" but the possibilities of time as a testimony to the African-Jamaican higgler's connection with the emergence of higgler practice during slavery, *and* as a marked disconnection with the practices of slavery?

The possibilities of time are marked by presence. I am inspired by Eelco Runia's work *Moved by the Past: Discontinuity and Historical Mutation* (2014) where time is a significant factor in the "presence in absence" (Runia 2014: 55) and "the presence of the past" (Runia 2014: 104) in relation to photographs and history. In such considerations, Runia remarks that "time is created anew, in which—so to speak—a new linearity is rolled out" (Runia 2014: xiv) in order to understand "how, in an endless series of metamorphoses, we have transformed and continue to transform ourselves into who we are" (Runia 2014: xv). He goes onto explain that the presence–absence–past tangram runs alongside metonymy and metaphor to unravel the connection between continuity and discontinuity. Contributory to this is Runia's concept of *stowaway*, "what is absently and unintentionally present on the plane of time, metonymy is a metaphor for discontinuity or, rather, for the entwinement of continuity and discontinuity" (Runia 2014: 81). The stowaways of history, this "presence of the past" (99) comes, according to Runia:

> [I]n the form of "common knowledge"—or ... "public secrets" it resides right in front of us, but in places that coincide with our blind spots. Presence succeeds in going unnoticed not because it is hidden from view, but because it coincides with our culture. In a sense it is our culture. Culture, after all, is the set of things we do not have to talk about, our private collection of public secrets.
>
> **RUNIA** 2014: 99

Secondly, the choice of caption used, "A Jamaica Lady" under a sensitive portrait of one of the custodian's of Jamaica's peasant culture. Why name her so when postcards were one of the principle ways in which images of black, working-class Jamaican identities during this period was categorized by white-Jamaicans, Europeans and Americans for their potential white viewers in derogatory terms such as "nigger" (Gilmore 1995: 19)[12] or "Negro Washerwoman"? (Lucie-Smith 2013: 230–45). The naming of portraits is an "essential aspect of portraiture because names so precisely identify the reference at the core of the genre" (Brilliant 1991: 29). This form of labelling is significant as it is dependent upon who initiated the naming. Crucially, to name is to exercise power, and to do so is to exercise one's agenda. This point is particularly poignant when one remembers that the denotation of "lady" was denied enslaved women in the British West Indies (Beckles 1998: 36).

Captions, then, have a rhetoric; they have meaning and time can influence and change that meaning. As a leitmotif laid bare for analysis, the caption can assist in the unveiling of hidden aesthetics of the intended impact and responsibility of the photograph by its author. The issue is how to get at the inherent significance of the indexical properties of the African-Jamaican higgler, and the higgler community as a whole, which constituted in the representation of the African-Jamaican higgler such relatively complementary thinking from the white-Jamaican Gardner? Therefore, this study will also address the coupling of image and text, the publisher and the subject of the postcard. An extended dimension of this relationship is the display of the higgler on a genre of imperial communication, the colonial postcard, which situated her as a commodity spectacle in the touristic culture of the British colony of Jamaica, and consequently of the British Empire.

Thirdly, Krista A. Thompson warns of falling into the trap of using colonial postcards as "unbiased" and "typical" representations, as they are "[T]he contrived touristic image" (Thompson 2006: 275). Thompson wonders, "[C]an postcards, the very representations that denied historicity to the black population, ever unproblematically yield 'black history'? Can black histories ever be built on fragile postcard infrastructures?" (2004: 274–5). This concern was also raised by Malek Alloula (1986) and Annelies Moors (2003) around how to confront the problematic politics of colonial postcards of Algerian women in the early twentieth century and picture postcards of "Palestinian Women in Palestine/Israel" respectively (Moors 2003: 23). Both acknowledge that the use of clothing and jewellery within the postcards, while representative of the identities of the women being depicted, was an attempt "to reflect a part of reality" (Alloula 1986: 62, Moors 2004: 35), but were nonetheless constructions from the perspective of the photographer and/or postcard producer (Alloula 1986: 62; Moors 2004: 35), that result in such postcards as myth (Il Pai 2013: 311). In the case of the colonial postcard, Alloula is adamant: "It is the fertilizer of the colonial vision" (Alloula 1986: 4).

In essence, all photographs are contrived. What is imperative is to unpack that contrivance. I am not trying to construct a style narrative and associated history of the African-Jamaican higgler that "one can be proud of " through the uncritical use of postcards (Thompson 2004: 278), but I want to use the postcard "A Jamaica Lady," "as postcards as intervention" (Kennard 1980: 13), to use it as a critical tool on the historical relevance of the styled body of the African-Jamaican higgler. As Runia's persuasive treatise on pushing for a new perspective on history outlines, to "think" about the past, to blend theory and history, in Runia's words, "taking things apart . . . wilfully making a mess" to understand the past. For me, "A Jamaica Lady" is what Benjamin called "thought-images" where "the dialectic of image and thought is unfolded and becomes visible" (Weigel 1996: 51). Such images inform the production of texts "in which the act of thinking is performed and in which history, reality and experience find their structure and expression: *representations of ideas*" (Weigel 1996: 51–2). Therefore, regardless of the original impetus for the production of this postcard, it remains a connection between past thoughts on African-Jamaican identities and the need to reassess that earlier thinking. It is, to quote Olu Oguibe, "a gesture of semblance" (Oguibe 2004: 83). I am further inspired in this direction by the exhibition and publication *Art and Emancipation in Jamaica: Isaac Mendes Belisario and His Worlds* (2007).[13] The contributors to the publication made use of a range of references—paintings, drawings, sculpture, photographs, maps, costumes and musical instruments—to bring fresh perspective on Jamaica's history and culture from 1655 to emancipation.

A fourth consideration is a flipside to the cultural meaning of postcards. Within epistolary studies, the postcard has a valued place as it is a form of letter, that is it has "letterness" (Poustie 2010: 39). In the special *Life Writing* issue "To the Letter" (2011) Rosslyn Prosser's contribution is written in the voice of the postcard so the object can clarify what it is:

I am a visual image and made on paper. I embody the intention of the sender and the pleasure of the receiver. I tell small stories to travel . . . the stories of cities with their own peculiar rhythm. I register the spectacle of the viewer, held in place by the click and aim of cameras . . . I reveal fragments of stories that are personal representations of places and people, and I accumulate in a range of storage containers and in displays. I become a collection, which resembles elements of narrative. I constitute a memory archive and can prevent forgetting. I can be read in different ways by the interested and the disinterested. As a tourist souvenir I am bought and sent or unsent and kept, and for advertising purposes I am free. I am both museum artifact and personal souvenir, and can be kept in the domestic and the institutional space.

PROSSER 2011: 219

Therefore, the postcard is also a pleasurable "object of desire" (Prosser 2011: 221) that connects people in different geographical spaces, and time-scapes. The postcard indicates intimacy of connection and conversation between the sender and receiver, clearly "a technique of sociality" (Cardell and Haggis 2011: 130). For Prosser, the fragmented, miniature character of the postcard, what Jacque Derrida refers to as the "snapshot post cards [sic]" (1987 [1980]: 22), holds within its demure size personal and pictorial narratives, which act "as memory triggers, and activates fragments of stories and allow reflection on places they refer to . . . an attenuation of a longer story . . . fragments that provide keys to broader narratives" (Prosser 2011: 221). All of which applies to the postcard "A Jamaica Lady." To date, I have no evidence that this postcard was sent and therefore cannot discuss it in terms of being a souvenir sent as validation of someone's journey to Jamaica, but this postcard is in the collection of the National Library of Jamaica. It is an historical document that is a contributory fragment to the maze of meaning that is Jamaica's history since slavery.

Edwards has looked at the postcard in expansive terms as a material and visual object that connects a society, a culture and a history as "an appreciation of the historical density of these unassuming images . . . reveal not a single truth about a person or an age but work as powerful, and perhaps inexhaustible, starting points for the multiple realities from which people constructed their worlds" (Edwards 2004: 27). Therefore, a fifth role of the photographic postcard "A Jamaica Lady" is the added impetus for critical thinking on style-fashion-dress in this context, as "stories are not told by photographs but by the different readings brought to them. Their signs, despite the best efforts of their makers and sitters, are endlessly recordable" (Edwards 2004: 35). As Derrida has said: "my post card [sic] naively overturns everything . . . it allegorizes the catastrophic unknown of the order. Finally one begins no longer to understand what to come . . . to come before . . . to come after . . . to foresee . . . to come back . . . all mean—along with the difference of the generations, and then to inherit, to write one's will, to dictate, to speak" (Derrida 1987 [1980]: 21). The supposed innocence of this postcard belies its political content and context. This genre of postcard does not radiate "Wish You Were Here" but "If we are not here we are nevertheless implicated" (Kennard 1980: 13) in the activities of the place depicted. Hence the categorization of "A Jamaica

Lady" as a colonial postcard and all that this means during the period of production and the postcolonial. This study of a colonial postcard through its style narrative of the African-Jamaican higgler is "a translation between different kinds of otherness and as a relationship between differences which come into contact" (Fortunati et al 2001: 5).

Obviously, then, viewpoint is a sixth critical driver here. On the one hand, according to the *Oxford English Dictionary*, viewpoint is "a mental position or attitude from which subjects or questions are considered." For photographers, viewpoint is how they take a photograph, about where the photographer is standing when the photograph is taken and how one "sees" the subject (Edwards 2014). The viewpoint I want to consider here is the positioning of the colonial postcard "A Jamaica Lady" as symbolic of the past-present-future tangram that locks the coupling of the white-Jamaican publisher Gardner and the subject, the African-Jamaican higgler, as both carry the burden of Jamaica's history, in different contexts, into the future.

The seventh area of consideration is my suggestion that the styled body of the higgler was a graphic symbol of the colonial discourse practiced in the British colony of Jamaica. I therefore contest Quentin Bell's treatise on the "workman's" inability to be represented by art as a graphic symbol of the heroism of labor:

> The antithetical figure is the workman, the socially useful person, but the dignity of labour is a concept for which we cannot easily find a graphic symbol, because the workman is not socially reputable and therefore has no place in the mythology of art. In fact we usually feel some misgivings when, in an attempt to create an iconography of labour, ... a Millet or a Brangwyn invests the manual worker with the agonised grandeur of Michelangelo's slaves; such corporeal splendours seem rather to be an attempt to ennoble the subject by means of an artistic disguise, than the actual discovery of some unperceived beauty in the worker. In fact the dignity of labour is a purely moral quality and one not easily expressed in terms of physical excellence ... it would be hard to express his moral excellence in visual terms, harder still if it were necessary to do so by showing him with the tools of his trade.
>
> **BELL** 1992: 32–3

"A Jamaica Lady": portraiture, captions and "the intellectual space" of a postcard

> To select and put forward any item for display, as something worth looking at as interesting, is a statement not only about the object but about the culture it comes from.
>
> **BAXANDALL** 1991: 34.

Michael Baxandall's reference to the display of objects in an exhibition setting is a useful analogy in the analysis of the postcard "A Jamaica Lady" and its visible and hidden narratives. Baxandall suggests that the viewer becomes the reader of the object and initiates the process of dissemination—to give meaning to the object. This allows space for the viewer to express and profit from that evaluation. Effectively, the viewer situates themself in that space between the object and the caption, what Baxandall calls the "intellectual space" (1991: 38). This train of thought is fuelled by the framing of the caption "A Jamaica Lady" between two terms of authorial accreditation featured on the front of the postcard; "copyright" and "Gardner's Series." These markers, I argue, indicate the publisher's, or to keep in line with Baxandall's analogy, the exhibitor's, way of "thinking about the object" and consequently "his interest in the pieces of information may well have been because they locate the object as an effect, or sign, of this or that cultural fact, one item in the larger pattern of culture he is charged with exhibiting" (Baxandall 1991: 38).

The democratization of visual imagery was partially undertaken by the phenomenal success of the picture postcard, or "view-card" (Gilmore 1995: v) as it was known in the Caribbean. The height of its popularity, which culminated in the picture postcard "collecting craze," spanned from 1898 to 1918,[14] and cemented its universal language of communication worldwide. In keeping with Baxandall's thesis, one could say that regardless of its destination, the picture postcard was always on public or private display: whether in transit as a greeting or general means of communication, or as a decoration in the home. For the discerning collectors in Jamaica and abroad, an archive of postcards could be displayed in a specifically designed collection cabinet or album (Robertson 1985: 13–14; Gilmore 1995: viii; Goldsmith 1997: 92–3; Thompson 2006: 259–8).[15] The Cousins-Hereward Collection, which was established by Jamaica's first Director of Agriculture, H.H. Cousins, who originally came to the island as a British colonial officer in 1900, is indicative of this.

The collection is a useful insight into the collective view of Jamaica harbored by the various publishers of postcards who were based on and off the island.[16] The collection comprises some 200 photographic, oilette and illustrative depictions of Jamaica, published between 1899 and 1907.[17] Aston W. Gardner & Co. has the most substantial presence with sixty-six postcards that includes his "Alphabet" and "Proverbs Household Series" produced between 1902 and 1906, in which the latter included "marketing" and the African-Jamaican higgler. The impression conveyed is of an extraordinarily beautiful country that was inhabited by two distinct social groups. The middle and upper classes were represented as civilized and cultivated, and comprised the white and "colored" (mixed heritage) groups. They were a strata of Jamaican society who enjoyed the comforts of beautiful town houses enveloped in palms trees, with access to developed parks and gardens. An island where these women could walk alone in the lush beauty of the Fern Gully (figure 1.2).

FIGURE 1.2 Fern Gully, Jamaica, postcard early 1900. Author's collection.

The second group were the so-called "natives" and "coolie girls" as labelled on postcards held in the collection. These referred to the African-Jamaican and East Indian working and peasant class who resided, according to the images of them, in huts and worked as laborers, agricultural workers, higglers, washer-women and domestic servants. Interestingly, Maureen Kerr-Campbell and Frances Salmon view this aspect of the collection as being "the largest collection of illustrations that show the life of ordinary folk in their daily activities" (2013: 195). Unlike the plutocratic group, their everyday dress was not fashionable, but work clothes that had absorbed the detritus of their labor. Fashionable dress was reserved for such leisure activities as a wedding celebration or to attend church. Both genres of postcard subject matter were caressed by the wonders of the Blue Mountains, intoxicating waterfalls and rivers and the city delights of the island's capital, Kingston. Gilmore has asserted that in the telling of the social history of the Caribbean, the picture postcard gives:

> plenty of evidence to suggest that middle and upper-class West Indians were frequently just as indifferent to the well-being of their poorer compatriots. Not surprisingly, postcards provide a reflection of this. Local as well as metropolitan publishers produced postcards of Black and East Indian people which referred to them in the captions as "natives"—a word never used of the local white population. Many cards suggest that the photographer viewed working-class subjects as "types," rather than individuals ... there is a visible class bias in the

choice of postcard subjects—the entertainments of the rich figure more prominently than those of the poor.

GILMORE 1995: viii–ix

Thompson lodges such postcards, particularly those of working and peasant class African-Jamaicans and East Indians, as a treatise on tropicalization of the island "and to steer the meaning of the postcards" (Thompson 2006: 257), which is one way of "reading" the Cousins-Hereward Collection. Therefore, as a pawn in Jamaica's tourist industry, the picture postcard was several things. As a souvenir it was a "marker" of the tourists' experience, which achieves what D. MacCannell calls the singularization of a sight and "elevates it" (MacCannell 1975: 143). But in the proliferation of publications of these singularizations of an unequal view of Jamaica outlined above, then the picture postcard was "an ideological framing of history, nature, and tradition; a framing that has the power to reshape culture and nature to its own needs" (MacCannell 1992: 1).

The postcard "A Jamaica Lady," then, was just one of hundreds of postcards available on Jamaica in circulation within the interior and exterior of the island.[18] In light of the above, the flurry of picture postcard dissemination effectively created a fragmented touring exhibition of the people and culture of Jamaica. The picture postcard, in turn, which featured pictorial depictions of the colonized lands of the Empire—the colonial postcard—was "the supreme expression of control through a particular type of slanted visual understanding ... showing the whole range of indigenous people under imperial rule ... Picture postcards were a great deal more than a means of communicating a quick message" (MacKenzie 1984: 23). The imperial value of the colonial picture postcard was expanded beyond aesthetic pleasure and archival merit, to an educational aid in the knowledge of the empire. Beside this kind of evidence, the exalted tone and sensitive portrayal of the African-Jamaican higgler in workwear on the colonial picture postcard "A Jamaica Lady," stands out as an anomaly.

The colonial picture postcard, then, is a paradox, and this is the basis of its fetishistic value alongside other picture postcards. According to McClintock, although the colonial picture postcard intends to present "the world exactly as it is, the camera ironically proliferates the world. Instead of producing a finite catalogue of the real, photography expands the territory of surface reality to infinity. The camera thus lures imperial modernity deeper and deeper into consumerism" (McClintock 1995: 125).

Benedict Anderson is resolute as to the importance of the visual and the aural in the creation of an imagined community. For Anderson, visual representation is indicative of national identity and the occupational dress of that country, and its presentation of it to the world (Anderson 1991: 22–23). In the case of Jamaica in the early twentieth century and the postcard "A Jamaica Lady," the caption makes a literal and seemingly indelible point. The published word, in the form of the newspaper and the novel, are for Anderson at the root of this endeavor (Anderson 1991: 37–40). I would extend Anderson's argument to incorporate photography as the ubiquitous form of image reproduction to chronicle and categorize "new people," that is those freed from slavery and subjects of the British Empire. To bring this into line with this postcard, technology underscored the advancement of spectacle within a culture, in the spirit of "technology of representation"—the process and method of producing the spectacle becomes the spectacle itself (Richards 1991: 57). Within the spectrum of Jamaica's touristic spectacles, the photographic postcard was a comprehensive spectacle in itself as a colonial picture postcard. In the visual and textual indexation of the African-Jamaican higgler and her styled body as an iconic symbol of African-Jamaican womanhood, and historical continuity, then:

> In colonial postcards, primitive icons and atavistic relics were arranged around [or on] the sitters to metonymically signify an anachronistic relation to the technological time of modernity. In the colonial postcard, time is reorganized as spectacle; through the choreographing of fetish icons, history is organized into a single, linear narrative of progress. Photography became the servant of imperial progress.
>
> **McCLINTOCK** 1995: 125

The portrait is conspicuous in the portrayal of the African-Jamaican higgler in a non-specified area, rather than the usual visual depictions of her group of either being on the road walking to market, or selling in the marketplace. Instead, the higgler was photographed against a plain background in an outdoor setting.[19] The portrait may omit the "picturesque" insignia of this distant tropical land that was being touted as the "New Jamaica" (Thompson 2006: 27–91) yet it still brims with "auratic ambience" (Goldsmith 1997: 89). Through the magnification of the markers of African-Jamaican higgler style and market practice, neither "primitive" nor "atavistic," but as will be discussed later, are iconic pieces that connect with the past and harbors stowaways. Nonetheless, it informs viewers of what an African-Jamaican higgler *is*, and what she usually wore.

George Hughes' reading of the overwhelming influence of the tourist machine to reframe a geographical space as a place of destination, heightens the experience of difference for the visitor, and is one way to understand the naming of the African-Jamaican higgler as "A Jamaica Lady" by Gardner:

> Heritage attractions ... must be safe, clean and pleasing. In fulfilling such conditions, each artifact is displaced from its historical moorings and effectively becomes a different object ... Even if based on authentic historical precedents, heritage objects tend to acquire new meanings, which "overwrite" their original significance. In this process the complexities of social life are washed out and replaced with promotional gestures that fuse with the evocative expectations of

the visitor. They acquire, in other words, a different reality. Judgementally, this reality is likely to be evaluated aesthetically rather than scientifically or morally. As a priority it must "look right" irrespective of historical verisimilitude, cultural validity or moral probity. It must be "pretty as a picture".

HUGHES 1998: 210

On one level, the postcard "A Jamaica Lady," as a system of Jamaican tourism, illustrates what Thompson views as the need to stress to potential tourists and possible settlers how "ordered and orderly . . . its black inhabitants particularly, as civilized" British subjects (Thompson 2006: 67–8) to allay the island's profile of black resistance as in the Morant Bay rebellion of 1865 and the Montego Bay riots of 1902 (Thompson 2006: 67). Thompson lodges the postcard, in general, as a primary example of this, but which trapped aspects of the island, notably its working class black inhabitants, in the past (Thompson 2006: 257). On another level, this sensitive portrayal of the African-Jamaican higgler and her workwear was, I suggest, Gardner's ratification of the higgler's long existence on the island. The central importance of her garments and accessories to the picture postcard cemented the iconic status of higglerdom in Jamaican culture. They acted as a reminder of the pursuit of autonomy, despite the colonization of the body that they adorned. Gardner's choice of caption indicated the African-Jamaican higgler's other role in Jamaica as an historical entity, as the higgler was integral to the development of a black Jamaica, and the island's economy since slavery. Unquestionably, she was an important touristic feature of the island. By naming the African-Jamaican higgler "A Jamaica Lady," Gardner exercised his power as a plutocratic Anglo-Jamaican to shape how Jamaica and its inhabitants should be viewed, as mentioned earlier. By doing so he positioned the African-Jamaican higgler as part of Jamaica's heritage, effectively elevating her status from "simply" being a market trader, to a cultural treasure, with historical longevity.

I do not believe that Gardner employed the noun "Lady" to reference a woman with refined manners and instincts, but rather its other meaning of, according to the *Oxford English Dictionary*, "a woman who performs a certain job." In Jamaica, as elsewhere, the dress of a lady was the mark of respectability and status, pecuniary and leisured. A social position to pursue. Miss May Jeffrey-Smith, born in Jamaica in 1882, recounted that in 1891 she heard a Jamaican street vendor say: "When a lick on me silk frock and fling on me parasol over me shoulder and drop into Exhibition ground den you will know weder [whether] I is a lady or not" (*Jamaican Memories* 1959: 7/12/261). Whether at the age of nine Jeffrey-Smith could recall this declaration word for word is debatable. Nonetheless, the circumstantial argument is the positioning of silk, historically a mark of luxury, as the fabric and mark of a lady, and the importance of wearing it for such an occasion as the 1891 Jamaica International Exhibition which the vendor referred to.[20] Thus, for this working class street vendor, fine clothes represented a desire for transformation and glamor.

In the use of the word "lady" under the image of a styled African-Jamaican higgler, one has to remember that the denotation of "lady" was, as mentioned earlier, denied enslaved women in the British West Indies. Hilary Beckles recounts: "[E]lite white females in slave society sought to exclude, on the basis of race, black and brown females from the membership of the ideological institutions of womanhood and feminity—and, by extension, access to socially empowering designations such as 'lady' and 'miss'" (Beckles 1998: 36). Beckles looked to the published texts by English women living on the Caribbean islands of St Vincent, Trinidad and Jamaica during the 1820s and 1840s, who positioned black women as "masculine, brutish and lacking feminine sensitivities" (Beckles 1998: 36). She argues that within the slave system, "White women used their caste and class power to support the patriarchal pro-slavery argument that black females were not 'women' in the sense that they were, and certainly not feminine in the way that they wished to be. For the black woman, the scars of centuries of denial went deep; with the onset of free society the raw wounds remained, sending tensions down the spine of all recuperative socio-political strategies" (Beckles 1998: 37). Beckles' latter remark is significant—the lasting traumatic impact of the denial of feminine categorization to enslaved black women. Can this be seen in photographic postcards of the female descendents of enslaved women, or does it need the validation of a white male, as in Gardner? The ratification of the African-Jamaican higgler as "A Jamaica Lady" trumps the usual position of femininity as a debilitating aspect of womanhood. Here, the ethereal qualities of the light-colored white clothing and the elaborate expanse of flowing cotton fabric of her headtie, reflect the "soft"[21] qualities associated with femininity at this time. A reclamation that this quality has been part of the African-Jamaican higgler, and by extension the black woman, since slavery.

The African-Jamaican higgler, then, held a complex position on the island: as a commodified object, revered for her contribution to the country's economy through her market trading and as a tourist attraction which fetishized her voluptuously styled physique. To understand the range of narratives that was conveyed on a single colonial postcard in 1903, and to get at some semblance of the cultural and graphic significance of the African-Jamaican higgler and her higgler style, one has to understand the complex social and political history of Jamaica from which the African-Jamaican higgler and Gardner emerged.

The emergence of the higgler

There is consensus amongst researchers of the history of the higgler and the internal market system of Jamaica, that women were a prominent feature in its establishment during British slavery and that their business acumen in this field was central to its development.[22] Plantation owners experienced difficulty in providing food for the enslaved. This was for a number of reasons, for example, the haphazard nature of the import of goods that was affected by warfare. Enslaved women and men were encouraged to produce their own food stuffs (Mintz 1989[1974]: 181). This was done through the introduction of "provision grounds" provided by their owners, where the enslaved could grow their own food and raise livestock, and this was practiced across sugar plantations and other sites. The 1792 Consolidated Slave Act stipulated the supply of "provision grounds for the enslaved in the ratio of one acre for every ten enslaved laborers" (Shepherd 2007: 34).

The division of labor practised amongst men, women and children on plantations was also applied to the familial tending of a provision ground. A surprising anomaly of slavery was that the enslaved were allowed to sell surplus produce at markets. This was extended to the sale of handicrafts also produced by the enslaved. Mintz remarks that the emergence of trade in extra produce cultivated by the enslaved on their provision grounds was the basis for the development of "slaves as marketers": "The unsupervised production of food crops by slaves provided the very basis of an open market system ... The Jamaican higgler, or middleman, also finds his prototype in the slave society" (Mintz 1989 [1974]: 194–5) as the "intermediary" between different kinds of provision ground producers and crafts people, which Barbara Bush posits was a particular skill of urban enslaved higglers (Bush 1990: 49). Roderick A. McDonald supports this in his extensive study of the material culture of slaves in Jamaica and Louisiana. He argues that this aspect of the provision ground industry became the principal duty of the women; that enslaved women were given this role due to their established place on the Guinea Coast as being at the center of economic activities, especially in the planting and the marketing of produce (McDonald 1993: 26).

Exactly when enslaved marketers began selling at markets is unknown, but there is evidence that they did so in 1685.[23] From 1711, enslaved women and men had the legal right to sell "provision, fruits and other enumerated articles ... baskets, ropes of bark, earthern pots and such like" at market once they received "a ticket from their owner or employer" (Long 1774, 2: 486–7, 492). The markets took place on Sundays. They were also known as "Negro Markets" due to being "dominated by rural slave provision producers and urban slave hucksters" (Simmonds 1987: 32). By the late eighteenth century, Edward Long recounted a description of a Kingston market where the "vegetables, fruit and meat from different parrishes of the island," were for Long "In short, the most luxurious epicure cannot fail of meeting here with sufficient in quantity, variety, and excellence" (Long 1774, 2: 105). Some enslaved people would trade at market on behalf of their owner, sometimes the owner would engage them in a variety of jobs as part-time higgler and domestic within their home, and/or hiring out enslaved women as domestics (Simmonds 1987: 33).

These Sunday markets became integral to Jamaica's economy. It was the principal cash route for the internal economy of the enslaved, planters or their representatives. The involvement of the enslaved placed them in a pivotal position to the commerce of Jamaica, as they were the main suppliers of fresh food on the island to all, regardless of status and skin color: "Marketing activities by this population became so essential to the stability of the island that some stringent laws restricting slaves' mobility were actually relaxed for Sunday marketing activities, with masters granting slave permission to participate in markets even during the most tense times" (Ulysse 2007: 63, referencing Momsen 1988: 218).

The markets were a magnet for the various ethnic groups of the island, a bustling hive of selling and bartering, posturing and socializing, "Jews with shops and standings as at a fair, selling old and new clothes, trinkets, and small wares at a cent . . . to adorn the Negro person; there were some low Frenchmen and Spaniards, and [free] people of coloure, in petty shops and with stalls, some selling their bad rum, gin, tobacco, etc.; others sold provisions, and small articles of dress; and many bartering with the slave or purchasing his surplus provisions to retain again" (Bickell 1825: 66). The presence of enslaved women in these markets pushed the limits of "white colonial imagination" about who these women were (Brown-Glaude 2011: 92). This thinking extended to observations made by visitors to the island of the enslaved women on their way to market as they transported produce for sale became a visual feature of Jamaican life worthy of documentation. In the introduction of *A Picturesque Tour of Jamaica from Drawings Made in the Years 1820 and 1821* by the English artist James Hakewill, presents the argument that the enslaved in Jamaica were so well treated that they were making large earnings and savings due to their out-of-hours marketing (1825: 3–5). He makes no mention of market women, but his collection of color drawings depicts several enslaved women in understated clothing, barefoot, carrying baskets on their heads. One evocative painting included in Hakewill's publication, *Waterfall on the Windward Road* (plate 4), was actually painted by Thomas Sutherland (Barringer 2007: 349). It includes a black woman in a sheath-like sleeveless white dress and head-portage, walking along the curve of a road that cuts through a mountain. Her erect body in white mirrors the dense flow of the cascade to her left; together, the water and the higgler with her head-portage sweep effortlessly through the mountain.

It must be remembered that this chink of freedom experienced by enslaved women was to be managed alongside their social position as "the property" of a master or mistress. Igor Kopytoff reminds us that the act of enslavement was a process of commoditization, the singularization and possible future recommoditization as a platform from which to think about the "cultural biography of things" (Kopytoff 1986: 64–85). Kopytoff's explanation of this process is useful to situate the commoditization of the "free" colonized higgler in the late nineteenth and early twentieth century as an historical genre of Jamaica's culture (Simmonds 1987: 38). As "the property," the enslaved augmented the socio-economic identity and status of the slave owner, making the actual body of the slave the legislative and personal focus of the power relationship between them. Demonstrative of this unequal relationship was the presentation of the dressed-body of the enslaved within the plantation. I say dressed-body as the enslaved were clothed according to how the slave owner managed their work dress. The 1792 Consolidated Slave Act of Jamaica legislated that slave owners must supply, annually, their slaves with work clothing:

> The labouring Negroes are all allowed, by their masters, a frock and trowsers for the men, and the women a jacket and petticoate of osabrig (osnaburgh), besides woollen stuff; but tradesmen, and the better fort, are generally supplied likewise with checks, handkerchiefs, hats and caps; and the laws of the island oblige every owner to give his Negroes proper cloathing. What they receive annually in this matter composes their working-dress.
>
> **LONG** 1774: 426

McDonald clarifies that although there may have been a spirit of generosity amongst some slave owners in their supply of clothing to their enslaved—in an attempt to respond to criticism of the poor quality of cloth provided, or the recognition of requests from slave women for blue, rather than striped, woollens (McDonald 1993: 120)—did not override the fact that in the hands of the slave owner, work-dress and styling techniques was a fool-proof power structure sanctioned by law:

> The style and material derived from the heritage of the slaveholding Europeans, but at the same time the cut immediately identified the wearer's status. The men wore trousers and a loose shirtlike frock or smock covering the upper body; the women wore a full-length shift and a half- to three-quarter length coat. Headgear consisted of woollen caps, glazed or felt hats, and kerchiefs. Men wore hats or caps; women usually wore kerchiefs ... But although the material and style were European, the osnaburg trousers, frocks, shifts, and coats were the clothing of slaves and slaves alone.
>
> **McDONALD** 1993: 126[24]

In this way, slave owners consolidated the weekday individual identity of the enslaved into a homogeneous one through designated dress. That group identity was further substantiated by the styling of the various "slave gangs" in different colors to "encourage an *esprit de corps*" (Levitt 1991: 39). Here was an example of styling as an indicator of powerful restrictions and possession by one section of society on another, an uncomfortable twist on styling as agency for black people of the African diaspora. Inspite of this, the space of the Sunday market represented a level of autonomy for enslaved female higglers. As well as a place of possible profit, it was also a space of socialization (Bush 1990: 49). Yet even here, enslaved women were subjected to constant regulations and legislations on their trade

(Simmonds 1987: 37; Mintz 1989: 205; Brown-Glaude 2011: 71), as well as the continued legal stipulation of the Laws of Jamaica, 1826, that "no slave except when going to market shall travel about without a ticket, specially worded and signed by his owner" (Bush 1990: 49).

The aforementioned profits enabled the purchase and/or bartering of clothing, such as garments made of bark-cloth or lace-bark; accessories from handkerchiefs to jewellery (Buckridge 2004: 53; Brown-Glaude 2011: 93). As Long remarked in the late eighteenth century: "there are few of them who do not acquire sufficient profit, by their huckstering traffic, to furnish themselves with a wardrobe of better cloathes for holidaywear; upon these they bestow as much finery as their circumstances will permit, invariably preferring the gaudiest colours" (Long 1774, 2: 426). Through this elemental act of individualization enslaved female higglers were able to create, Brown-Glaude suggests, "alternate–feminine–identities, thus engaging in nonverbal resistance to colonial ideologies that discursively constructed them as unfeminine" (Brown-Glaude 2011: 93). Her thinking continues the assessment by Bush of the enslaved female higgler and the internal marketing system as being "a valuable contribution on her part to the creation, in the midst of hardship and oppression, of a positive underlife for herself and her fellow slaves" (Bush 1990: 50).

Therefore, to return to the drawing *Waterfall on the Windward Road* by Sutherland, to read this representation within the context of the legislated dress, and as outlined above, then, this drawing, regardless of authenticity, fuels the insistence suggested by historians of the role of the enslaved in the internal marketing system of Jamaica as a demarcation between two definitive realms of time for these women through their styled bodies: what I will call "enslaved time" on the plantation and the "freetime" on their way to and at the market, their access to and their revelry in freedom style-fashion-dress.

The internal marketing system of Jamaica continued after the momentous act of emancipation that began in 1834. In this period, markets were now held on Saturdays. Kingston had two major markets. Victoria Market was built on the original site of the Sunday/"Negro Market." It was named in honor of the island's monarch, Queen Victoria, and opened in 1872, on her birthday, May 24. Victoria Market was based at the end of King Street, near the capital's harbor, an area that was a hub of shopping activity. It was a grand space that housed 246 stalls within a space of some 1,840 feet (*Handbook of Jamaica* 1898: 440). Its entrance was decorated with a fountain and clock tower. The other market was Jubilee Market which was situated at the upper end of Orange Street, originally known as the Sollas Market.[25] In the *Tourist Guide to the Island of Jamaica,* published by Gardner in 1893, a description of the markets of Kingston reiterates the riches produced:

The Markets of Kingston are excellent institutions always well stocked with poultry, vegetables, fish, fruits and grains . . . The market on a Saturday morning is one of the sights of the city and perhaps unique in the world. The outer market is then a bustling good humored crowd of country women with enormous head loads of luscious looking pines, bananas or mangoes in their season, and on the stalls within, may be temporarily displayed ... an infinite variety of other fruit probably new to the tourist. The market buildings are elegant and airy iron structures and all due care is taken to secure their perfect sanitation.

GARDNER 1893: 51

Mintz has surmised that the development of a Jamaican peasantry post full emancipation in 1838 was an important transformation due to the long established provision ground and marketing system maintained by enslaved women and men. It provided them, in theory, with an economic skill to draw on in this free phase of their lives (Mintz 1989 [1974]: 204, 209–10). In reality, the transition to freedom was fraught with tension between the ex-enslaved and their ex-owners—low wages were offered for plantation labor, it was difficult for the ex-enslaved to acquire land, as well as the fundamental issue of civil rights (Satchell 1995: 213–14; Ulysse 2007: 65). The draw of small farming and higglering provided an independent route to counter this situation. Ex-enslaved men and women acquired land "as freeholders through purchases, gifts, leaseholders or renters" (Satchell 1995: 216) as well as squatting (Ulysse 2007: 65). The peasantry was dependent on the system of land transfers between other groups in Jamaica's society. British missionaries were strident in the liberation of slaves. In the wake of their freedom, the missionaries pursued this course in the complete separation of the ex-slaves from their previous owners.[26] They bought land to create "free villages" as an alternative to the plantation system on offer. Plots were sold mainly to Christian ex-enslaved. Catherine Hall recounts that, in the establishment of these villages, it was the missionaries' intention to fulfil the vision of a missionary utopia, to reconstruct the ex-enslaved and their respective villages into "a more ordered England in the Caribbean" (Hall 1992: 243–4).

Economic historian, Veront M. Satchell, has studied the presence of women landowners, conveyors and conveyees in Jamaica and states that "[W]omen constituted one of the most important of these groups in peasant development during this period" (Satchell 1995: 214). Satchell notes that the information available to assess which class members acquired what portions of land is difficult, but assumes that larger landholdings were the preserve of upper- and middle-class women, whilst the smaller rural holdings were acquired by the laboring and peasant classes (Satchell 1995: 214). According to Satchell, in the 1890s women acquired their land primarily from tradesmen and merchants, not planters, many purchasing from East Indians.[27] Women also acquired a large portion of holdings from among themselves and from small landholders. Satchell claims that women were amongst the top three groups of conveyors, as conveyees they were among the bottom four (Satchell 224–7).[28] Therefore, during the period of study, there was a fair sized percentage of women, including African-Jamaican women, of an independent position.

This new juncture in the formation of modern Jamaica was made more spectacular by its matriarchal character as in the female domination of the market trade. The 1881 census of Jamaica recorded 1,095 higglers across the island. There is no indication as to the proportion of women and men in this figure. The subsequent 1891 census registered that there were 1,011 female higglers and 11 men across the whole country. As these figures indicate, the role of the African-Jamaican higgler in this post-emancipation era was central to the economy of the island. Their role ranged from being the middle person between small farmers and buyers, as well as possibly being a division of labor between wife and husband small holders, where the woman of the home acted as the seller of their produce at market or even in the bartering of unsold produce (Bryan 1991: 133–4). African-Jamaican women contributed to the familial peasant economy as higglers, agricultural workers, domestics, washer-women, and it was not unusual for African-Jamaican women to conduct several of these duties simultaneously (Benn 1893, 1897). The figures of the census support observers' views that the post-emancipation domination of the higgler trade by black women to "control their own bodies and labor, and devoted most of their labor to their own peasant cultivation and marketing" (Brown-Glaude 2011: 77).

The female domination of the market place gave these women a prominent visibility, on *their* terms in *their* world: "In squeezing your way through that realm of women—a Jamaican market ... You may think sometimes that you are not observed. It is not the truth. The rolling eyes have been upon you, and your movements are being discussed already by half a dozen tongues" (Bellows 1907: 11). The market place is fundamentally the domain of the unofficial world, an autonomous and free space where traders, namely of the peasant small holder and working class, can express themselves. The market, then, is symbolic of the heart of the unofficial world (Bakhtin 1968: 154), yet unquestionably vital during and post-slavery. The female African-Jamaican higgler had represented this culture since slavery and the continuation of this strand of Jamaica's cultural and economic history. Marketing provided them with some semblance of tradition and psychological reassurance of the establishment of roots (Hobsbawm 1992: 1),[29] thereby creating a new facet to the character and history of Jamaica, and significantly the history of the African diaspora. The styling of the garments that transformed a peasant woman or female small-holder into a higgler, is a mark of continuity of that African diaspora history.

The soil of Jamaica was a symbol of good and evil. It was the source of interminable subjection for the enslaved and, simultaneously, provided them with a modicum of release. Emancipation exacerbated this duplicitous tether to land. If the soil in the post-emancipation period was the substance on which the African-Jamaican peasantry established their existence and their *becoming*, then the African-Jamaican higgler, in her identifiable higgler style, embodied that *becoming*—the uncorseted garments styled in a particular way by the African-Jamaican higgler—the roll at the hips of her skirt or dress into a "pull skirt" (Buckridge 2004: 47) which shortened its length, and when worn, her blouse, these in turn were protected by an apron, and the headtie used as the base for her head-portage of basket and goods for sale—was in effect *being* a higgler (Butler 1990: 32).

To possess and work the land, as the black peasantry achieved, equated with the formation of a solid identity and garnered respect as a significant social and cultural group. The plots of land owned by peasant families were seen as the major source of inheritance for their children, and thereby established family lines. Their attempt to become a self-generating community—founding villages, markets, churches, schools and local co-operatives, for example—earned them the description of "emancipation in action" (Bryan 1991: 132). Hall compares the development of the peasantry with the rise of England's new middle class in the eighteenth century. They, too, sought independence from a landed oligarchy and based their character on religious belief. Individuality, she argues, was at the crux of their new identity (Hall 1992: 256–8). Mintz summarizes this well:

> it is hypothesized here that the Jamaican marketing system . . . and the Jamaican pattern of small-farm cultivation are wedded not only historically, but functionally and psychologically as well, and that changes in either of these parts of Jamaican culture would almost certainly result in changes in the other. Had it not been for the pattern of subsistence-plot cultivation under slavery, and the perpetuation of subsistence cultivation by the growth of a rural peasantry after emancipation, the Jamaican economy would have taken on a very different character.
>
> **MINTZ** 1955: 99

A defining character was the African-Jamaican higgler in her established styled body.

African-Jamaican higgler style: a study through images

As proposed above, the representation of the African-Jamaican higgler in the postcard "A Jamaica Lady," is a depiction of an ideal higgler. When one recounts that an *Oxford English Dictionary* definition of ideal is: "Existing as an idea or archetype; relating to or consisting of ideas"; whilst the "ideal type" is: "a hypothetical construct made up of the salient features or elements of a social phenomenon, or generalized concept, in order to facilitate comparison and classification of what is found in operation," then if "A Jamaica Lady" is the "ideal" African-Jamaican higgler, how closely does this image actually represent the African-Jamaican higgler between the 1880s to 1907? To some extent "A Jamaica Lady" is accurate as the key elements of African-Jamaican higgler style are present: head-portage, headtie and apron but, unsurprisingly, this is by no means the only interpretation of African-Jamaican higgler style. As "A Jamaica Lady" is a partial portrait of this African-Jamaican as higgler, we cannot see the length of her garments or her feet. Therefore a study of photographs and photographic postcards of African-Jamaican higglers is presented here.

Since 1996 I have developed a collection of photographic, drawn and painted postcards, and photographs of the African-Jamaican higgler, as well as other aspects of Jamaica dating from 1880 onwards. This was done to gauge the range of representations and style possibilities of this cultural group to "create knowledge and steer discourse" (Neely 2008: 100), and to help to provide some answers (Edwards 2004: 26) to supplement material I researched at the National Library of Jamaica, the Cousins-Hereward Collection held at the Library of the University of the West Indies, Mona, Getty Images, and images featured in publications such as *Glimpses of the Our Past: A Social History of the Caribbean in Postcards* (Gilmore 1995) and *Jamaica in Black and White: Photography in Jamaica c. 1845–c. 1920, The David Boxer Collection* (Boxer and Lucie-Smith 2013).

What follows is an assessment of the various elements of African-Jamaican higgler style worn by higgler women on the road while walking or riding to market, higglers who have paused by the roadside on their way to market who have been photographed with or without their knowledge, images of others who have clearly "posed" for photographs, as well as images of higglers mingling and selling at market. It is a summary of a catalog of details that define African-Jamaican higgler style that appear on the bodies of higgler women featured in these images.

Head-portage

The head-portage of the African-Jamaican higgler was a defining feature of her trade. As indicated above, it is an image that dates back to slavery (Long 1774, 2: 413). As the market women made their way to market, the contents of the head-portage was overflowing with produce such as yams, bananas, plantain or sugar cane as well as baked goods. A variety of vessels were used as head-portage. One of the most popular was the "bankra," the colloqual Jamaican name for a basket, mostly associated with the market basket which is defined by its round form and concave base which helps it to balance well when carried on the head by the higgler.[30] Olive Senior explains that in Jamaica it was the main form of transportation of produce from the countryside to the towns before the expansion of other forms of transport (Senior 1983: 15).

FIGURE 1.3 "Market Women, Jamaica," postcard, post dated May 19, 1904. Author's collection.

Market baskets have been present on the island since slavery due to the skill of basketwork honed by enslaved people. The size of the baskets varied from the modest to large, deep bowled and shallow basin shapes, picnic-style baskets, whilst there were bale-shaped versions with lids and side handles (figure 1.3). The enormous bankra basket featured in "A Jamaica Lady" was not unusual. The decoration of the baskets ranged from undecorated, which seemed to be the most popular, to intricate woven designs as depicted in "A Jamaica Lady." In 1901, *The Bulletin of the Educational Supply Company* informed the teachers in Jamaica that "bankras," priced from 4½d upwards, were made from palmetto palm: "The distinguishing feature of the 'bankra plait' is its close, square, even appearance. The brown and the green straws, which are introduced by way of ornament and form borders and chequered patterns, are merely the palmetto in its early spring growth and its sere autumn condition. The colour often used is obtained by red ochre dye" (*Educational Supply Company* 1901: 3). Senior adds that market baskets were also made of bamboo and wicker (1983: 15).

Other forms of head-portage were oblong wooden trays with deep plain or scalloped frames. In one postcard, a tray was decorated in a form of folk art of hand-painted hearts, nine-petal flowers and dots (figure 1.4). Some higglers used pales in what appears to be enamel, with and without handles. For those who traveled by donkey, panier baskets were used which were connected by a rod. In some cases, African-Jamaican higglers concealed and protected their produce carried in the head-portage. Some examples show produce wrapped in a cloth tied

FIGURE 1.4 "No. 16 Market Women, Jamaica," postcard, A. Duperly, Kingston Jamaica, early 1900s. Author's collection.

with a single or double knot which was placed in the basket; or the whole head-portage, container and produce, was enveloped in a tied cloth (figure 1.5). Some higglers piled their wares in a bankra basket which was then secured by a band or strip of cloth. Photographs and postcards depict produce placed in a container covered with fabric with or without something to keep the cloth in place. Alternatively the cloth was tucked into the carrier.

At the market, the higglers would sell their "stall of wares" from a container placed in front of them or a cloth was placed on the ground on which to place items for sale (figure 1.6). There are photographic examples where the bankra was used as a prop or a seat for the higgler.

Headwear

The African-Jamaican higgler's hair was always covered. This was primarily done with a cloth wrapped and tied around the head in a variety of styles, and known by a range of names: turban, headwrap, bandanna, headrag, head handkerhief, tie head and headtie. For this study I will use the latter term.[31] It is a styling system that has continued since slavery (Long 1774, 2: 412–13, Tulloch 1999). The headtie provided extra padding for the head-portage. This was supported by a cotta, another item that was used by the enslaved in Jamaica,[32] a piece of cloth twisted and shaped into a flat coil and placed on the head to support the carrying of a head-portage. In visual representations of the African-Jamaican higgler, the

FIGURE 1.5 "On the Way to Market," Jamaica, 1900–03. Courtesy of the National Library of Jamaica.

FIGURE 1.6 No. 19 Jubilee Square Market, Kingston, Jamaica, early 1900s, postcard, A. Duperly & Sons. Author's collection.

headtie was usually the only form of headcovering, but it was not unusual to see a hat worn on top of a headtie.

There was a range of styles used to create the headtie[33] as indicated in postcard "No. 16 Market Women, Jamaica" (see figure 1.4). One young woman wears an elaborate construction with a tight band that extends from above her eyebrows to the top of her forehead, the knots of the headtie are brought from the back of her head and tucked into the headtie band, leaving short ends to fall from a large knot at the nape of her neck. Another woman wears a headtie with a smooth front and high crown, the cloth is tied above her ears and knotted at the back of her head leaving long cloth strands, which balances the high crown feature. A third young African-Jamaican higgler wears a headtie which shows a small amount of her hair at the front of her headwear. The headtie is fastened to slope across the top of her forehead, down across the top of her ear and is secured at the back of her head which creates a small amount of fullness towards the back of the crown.

According to Buckridge the headtie worn by the sitter in "A Jamaica Lady" is a design known as a "cock's tail" and the "peacock." This is created out of starched fabric using "cassava juice boiled for a long time ... The cock's tail was usually reserved for married women" (Buckridge 2004: 164). Buckridge also remarks that a particular style of headtie worn by "single and younger women in the market" was tied "tightly, with the knot or bow to the side of the head, without hanging folds" that signalled their availability for marriage (Buckridge 2004: 164).

The fabrics used varied from plain cottons to real or imitation madras check. The latter is a significant detail as the madras check has become the foundation of Jamaica's national dress and that of other Caribbean islands.[34] As I have argued previously, the history of the fabric has particular resonance to the relationship between Indian-Jamaican and African-Jamaican peasantry (Tulloch 1999: 70–71). The real madras handkerchief was a currency of slavery, associated with the triangle slave trade. It was manufactured in southern Indian villages, then transported to London to be auctioned to either the Royal Africa Company or private traders, and finally the cloth was used to barter for slaves in West Africa, as well as to clothe enslaved Africans in the West Indies. This system of trading continued following abolition. The real madras handkerchief, defined as a "prohibited good" by Britain, benefited from the practice of rescinding duties on re-exports from London. The West Indies remained one of the markets where the cloth was sold alongside the British-produced imitation madras handkerchiefs (Evenson 1994: 11; Tulloch 1999: 70–1; Faiers 2008: 262–5).[35] Senior, who refers to this checked fabric as "plaid cotton" or "Native Woman's plaid", views it as the "Occupational badge of higglers" (Senior 1983: 14–15).

Garments

It is difficult to assess whether the African-Jamaican higglers are wearing a blouse and skirt or a dress as the majority wore an apron, primarily a half-apron, that covered their clothing from the waist down. But there is evidence of both styles from the contrasting fabrics of the upper and lower half of an outfit being visible beneath the apron. There is also an example of a woman wearing a loose tunic-style blouse over the top of her apron (see figure 1.5).

Jewellery

Jewellery was present amongst the African-Jamaican higglers work style. This included beads, a detail that was observed as a staple style statement of enslaved higglers and women generally (Buckridge 2004: 59–60). Photographs of African-Jamaican higglers show them wearing a single strand of beads worn tight around the neck on top of the collar of a garment, which is just visible, others wear double strands of fine beads along the edge of the neckline, or a thick strand of beads hanging loosely around the neck. Earrings such as plain, small loops were also worn (see figure 1.1) as we can see in the postcard "A Jamaica Lady." Wedding rings can be seen clearly in photographs. Another visible piece of jewellery was a slim open bracelet with a ball detail on both ends of the band[36] (figure 1.7).

Furbelow

A ubiquitous detail associated with the African-Jamaican higgler that is not present in the postcard "A Jamaica Lady" is the pulling up and tying of an expanse of fabric

FIGURE 1.7 "'Greetings from Jamaica,' Going to Market with Yams and Canes." Constant Spring Road, postcard, 1900–03, A. Duperly & Son. Author's collection.

around the waist to hip area of the higgler's clothing to create what is variously known as a roll, furbelow, hold and pull-up or pull-skirt. A feature that was part of enslaved women's dress across the British Caribbean (Buckridge 2004: 47, 164, 209). Essentially, the overall effect was a thickening of the waist to hip area in volumes of fabric ranging from slim to bulbous versions that created a pillow effect (see figure 1.3). During the period under discussion, this detail was widespread amongst African-Jamaican higglers. Some wore the detail with more fullness at the back, others created the detail with it partially hidden by an apron at the front, whilst some constructed the roll to incorporate the apron, dress or skirt. The tie used to secure the furbelow, depending on the style of pull, would be visible, barely visible or invisible from under the roll, with the ends of the tie showing. It has been suggested that shortening the skirts of their garments into this detail was done by peasant women to make walking easier and to undertake work more effectively (Buckridge 2004: 47). Glory Robertson has noted that observers of higglers in the late nineteenth century stated that the shortening of garments was so high that it left "their legs bare as high as the knee" (Robertson 1995: 112). In the images I studied, only the ankles could be seen. In some cases, the pull detail did not shorten the length of the garment at all, and seems purely to be a styling feature (Boxer & Lucie-Smith 2013: 272).

Feet

The women were generally barefoot, although there are examples of higglers wearing laced boots. Thompson has argued that the ubiquitous presence of black people with bare feet in postcards was to signify the idea of "barely civilized natives" (Thompson 2006: 274).

The apron of the African-Jamaican higgler: an accessory to freedom

The apron, as worn by the African-Jamaican higgler, deserves detailed scrutiny. I propose that the apron worn by the higgler, "the badge of her calling" (Clarke 1966: 152–3), was a symbol of autonomy and the vestiges of freedom in the constrained frame of colonialism.

The apron was not the preserve of the African-Jamaican higgler. It was a staple accessory across Jamaica's laboring class as in domestic servants and agricultural workers, male and female. African-Jamaican female agricultural workers wore their aprons in a variety of styles—straight on, covering the entire front of their dress or skirt, and in some examples one corner of the apron is brought up across the front of the apron and tucked into the waist band to create a draped version (figure 1.8). Therefore, alongside the madras handkerchief headtie, the apron was a defining feature of the African-Jamaican peasantry and working

FIGURE 1.8 No. 7 Banana Carriers, Jamaica, postcard, A. Duperly & Sons, post dated March 14, 1907. Author's collection.

class; one could say that this was Jamaica's "aproned" group, a term which was "formerly used for: Of the working class" (*OED*).[37] This specific identifier of a section of Jamaica's society was recognized through British imperial eyes to such an extent that the apron was part of the "traditional dress" worn by the four female members of the Kingston Choral Union of Jamaica, a group that toured England, Ireland, Scotland and Wales between 1906 and 1908. Their first performance was at the Colonial Products Exhibition in Liverpool. During their tour of England, the choir of ten were renamed the Native Choir from Jamaica (Green 1998: 89–92). As part of their performance the choir wore "native costume" that included an apron as well as evening dress (Green 1998: 9).[38]

The blurring of who wore the apron when comes across in *The Jamaican Memories*.[39] Recollections here placed the apron amongst African-Jamaicans as a garment that marked an older generation and earlier dress practices. Mrs Una Wilson, for example, recalled: "The real old-timers were a joy to behold in their voluminous skirts and calico aprons. These aprons often had a text on at [sic] the hem in red cross-stitch. On their heads were bandana handkerchiefs, on top of which a whey-fe-do hat was often worn. These old ladies had dignity, charming manners and a ready smile" (Wilson 1959: 3–4/*Jamaican Memories* 7/12/265: 3–4). Wilson does not mention when this outfit was worn, whether everyday or specifically for market. As a child, Wilson also recalls seeing African-Jamaican higglers "sleeping on the piazzas of the city, on a Friday night, their heads on their hampers, or baskets to be ready for Saturday's market" (Wilson 1959: *Jamaican*

Memories 7/12/265: 3) and also seeing "the peasantry … walking barefoot to Church" (Wilson 1959: *Jamaican Memories* 7/12/265: 3).

A study of the aprons in the collection of photographic postcards and photographs of African-Jamaican higglers mentioned above, shows that the range of apron styles and customization varied considerably amongst the women, making clear individualization within a group identity. In the photographs of African-Jamaican higglers that I researched, all of them wore an apron. The most popular design was the half-apron, that is without a bib. The shape of the apron was A-line with a smooth line at the waist. Other versions of this have gathers at the waist with a deep frill at the hem with two to three rows of horizontal tucks. The tuck detail is a frequent embellishment ranging from simple to elaborate rows of two to five sequences, or a blend of tucks and pleats that make up twelve rows of detailing that is half the length of the apron from the middle of the garment to the hem. This is finished with a picoted edge (figure 1.9).

The length of aprons ranged from being the same length of a skirt or dress to being shorter than the clothes the apron was to shield. Some half-aprons completely covered the front of the dress or skirt, whilst others were narrower in width and revealed a kind of frame-within-a-frame between the apron and the skirt underneath.

The condition of the aprons veered from pristine to well-used and stained, torn and patched. Pattern and design was another major variant. As the collection of images studied are in black and white, it is impossible to recount the color range of

FIGURE 1.9 "People at/or going to market," Jamaica, early 1900. Courtesy of the National Library of Jamaica.

the aprons represented. There are tones of color which range from what appears to be bright white to light and dark versions. There were plain aprons and examples with a light polka dot pattern on a dark background, while striped versions make use of vertical and horizantal detailing (see figure 1.3).

Pockets were a popular feature, although not all aprons at this time had pockets. This detail fits with the development of the apron, as the addition of pockets onto the garment in the nineteenth century was seen as a major change to the apron's form (Gau 2011 : 86). The pockets on an apron varied in number, proportion and position. The tie-on pocket is visible in numerous photographs and ranges from a single pocket, dangling from the waist at the side of the body as an independent receptical, to a detachable pair of tie-on pockets worn on top of the apron secured by what appears to be string (figure 1.10). Interestingly, this version is a continuation of the tie-on pockets popular amongst women across the classes in the eighteenth and nineteenth century. Barbara Burman and Seth Denbo have documented a history of tie-on pockets, primarily in the United Kingdom. They explain that "tie-on pockets were probably the most personal and widely used over the longest period of time. It is remarkable that they were in use for well over 200 years" (Burman & Denbo 2007: 5). One or two pockets were stitched onto the front of the

Wayside Shop, Jamaica

FIGURE 1.10 Wayside Shop, Jamaica, postcard, undated, Aston W. Gardner & Co. Author's collection.

apron in either small or generous proportions (See figures 1.8 and 1.10). In later postcards and photographs of around 1908, market women wore aprons with piped pockets. Buckridge posits that the African-Jamaican higgler aprons that had two pockets were used to keep silver coins in one and copper coins in the other (Buckridge 2004: 164).

The images show personal individualization of how the apron was worn. For example, how it was tied around the waist by some and above the waist by others. Customization came in the different forms of "rolling up" the apron along with the skirt or dress, as mentioned earlier. Some of the higglers wore the apron with a roll of fabric above the waist of the apron. Others placed the apron over the front of the furbelow, with its shape being fuller at the back. In some examples, the apron and under garment were pulled up together at the hip and secured with a dark "ribbon."

The apron worn by the African-Jamaican higgler featured on the postcard "A Jamaica Lady" can only be partially assessed as she is photographed in profile and the mid- to lower-half of the apron is not shown. In comparison with the range of photographs of African-Jamaican higglers I have studied, this sitter is wearing a pinafore.[40] What is intriguing to me is that in the wealth of photographs of African-Jamaican higglers I have studied, the half-apron is the most popular design, but with some examples of the pinafore being worn by non-higglers.[41] Nonetheless, the sitter in "A Jamaica Lady" is wearing a pinafore. The lower section of the pinafore is gathered into a band, which connects the two main elements of the apron. The bib appears to be attached to the woman's clothing, not by straps, which reflects the definition of a pinafore in the *Dictionary of Etymology* "an apronlike covering over a dress . . . pin + afore on the front; so called because it was originally pinned to the dress front." This upper section of the apron, as seen in "A Jamaica Lady," is decorated with horizontal tucks that are secured by a vertical band on the side of the bib that does not extend to the full width of the bib section.

The use of the apron by the African-Jamaican higgler, and her fellow working class women, as a signifier of social status and occupation, connects with similar women in other parts of the world. Alma Oakes and Margaret Hamilton Hill's (1970) study of rural costume in Western Europe and Britain, makes reference to the "rural apron" of the fifteenth to nineteenth centuries (Oakes and Hamilton 1970: 160), which "together with the coif and corset-bodice, were the most distinctive garments of the countrywomen" (ibid: 160). By extension, Colleen Gau recognizes the longevity of the apron, and places it as part of "conventional work dress," regardless of gender, worn across a myriad of trades (Gau 2011: 85).

Therefore the apron is a definitive marker of an official form of work dress. On a prosaic level, the apron is a barrier worn on top of clothing to protect the wearer from dirt or injury. Overall, the apron is a conduit of engagement in work. The concept of the apron as a protective coverage of the front of the body dates back to Adam and Eve (Furlong 2014: 1). As stated in Genesis of the King James Bible "And the eyes of them both were opened, and they knew that they *were* naked; and they sewed fig leaves together, and made themselves aprons" (The Bible, Genesis: 3: 7). The napron, apron, half-apron, pinafore, "bib," cover cloth (Buckridge 2004: 164) or barm cloth (Lester and Oerke 2004 [1940]: 502) has been part of world dress for women and men of all ages ever since. It has always been part of the workwear of the lower classes and trades, and of course worn by professional and amateur artists and makers, a practice that has seen a resurgence in the twenty-first century partly due to the renaissance of domestic crafts and the draw of a return to a slower-paced and sustainable way of living. The apron's historical longevity broadens its cultural and social meaning: from the shendyt as worn by Egyptian pharoahs "as a sign of social status" (Furlong 2014: 1) to the fashionable elite of the West in the eighteenth century which took the apron into the realm of "an object of display, a demonstration of embroidery skills and sometimes a garment of not very practical nature" (Furlong 2014: 4; Styles 2007: 182). Although the apron had a contentious place on the body of elite women. Contemporary eighteenth-century observers saw it as "plebian, menial and vulgar in its associations, and therefore potentially impolite" (Styles 2007: 182).

In the early twentieth century, the apron became an activist tool as employed, for example, by Suffragettes in Britain who wore aprons emblazoned with Suffragette-related protest or information (Pankhurst 1979 [1914]; Furlong 2014: 6).[42] In contrast to this period of feminist action, in the 1950s women in Britain were encourged to have a "wardrobe of aprons," as inspired by the American trend, to maintain a diktat for the 1950s housewife of "looking your best" at all times. (*Picture Post* 1954: 39). Therefore, the apron's longevity is an essential element of working dress, the form of which deserved detailed attention if it was to be a "practical apron" (Anon. 1913: 302),[43] where form and function equate. This included the quality of the fabric to be used in its making, and consideration of its co-ordination with the garment(s) the apron was to protect. Additionally, the length of the apron was another important consideration in order to allow unimpeded movement of the wearer (Anon 1913: 302).

As already intimated, the apron can be a mark of difference.[44] Within the African diaspora it was a tool of segregation. The Hollywood film industry is reknowned for its stereotyped characterization of black womanhood in the USA through the figure of the housemaid. There are numerous representations, but three famous examples of those who tried to raise the bar on this black screen presence before the effects of the Civil Rights and Black Power Movement of the 1960s onwards, was Hattie McDaniels' Academy Award performance as the sassy "mammy" in *Gone with the Wind* of 1939, the jazz icon Billie Holiday as the singing maid, Endie, in *New Orleans* in 1947, and the mammy housemaid in the MGM *Tom and Jerry* cartoons who was defined by her frilly half-apron and broad girth as her face was rarely seen. Beyond the cinema screen the image of the black mammy, wide of girth, swathed in an apron was a popular figure in Britain used for the advertisement of such products as Sunlight and Lux (figure 1.11). It is

FIGURE 1.11 Sunlight Soap advertisement, 1898–1914, Lever Brothers, England. Author's collection.

historically correct that, since slavery, black women were domestic servants across the African diaspora. Within this context, the apron was also represented as being worn with pride by black women in the position of domestic servant as in this portrait by Hellis & Sons of London[45] (figure 1.12). The black South African artist, Mary Sibande, has recognized this in her long-standing work *Sophie*, about a larger than life domestic maid who always wore an apron as one of the defining motifs of her working status. Sibande created *Sophie* in 2008 "as a celebration of the women in my family, who were all maids—from my great-grandmother up to my mother"[46] in troubled, apartheid South Africa. The artist sees this as "a line of very strong women."[47] Joyce Bidouzo-Coudray views Sibande's trademark use of a white apron, blue uniform and white headscarf as worn by Sophie as "a gateway to unchartered elsewheres" (2014), which can be applied to black women's use of the apron across the African diaspora throughout history.

Thomas Carlyle's nineteenth-century treaty on the apron is still relevant, particularly in relation to the African-Jamaican higgler. He identified the apron's symbolism as a badge of protest and revolt, a plane that absorbs the hopes and actions of an individual or group: "[as] the royal standard of that country . . . How much has been concealed, how much has been defended in aprons." The apron, for Carlyle then, was not only a shield from danger, but a symbol of a people (Carlyle 1837: 47–8).

When worn by the African-Jamaican higgler, as illustrated in "A Jamaica Lady," initially the apron was there in its recognized capacity as the protector of garments. Metaphorically, in light of the issues raised above, the apron was a barrier against the elements that could sully the freedom-style of the higgler, and by extension the peasantry. It was a badge of the higgler being perpetually in free-time, and I suggest that, metaphorically, the apron protected that achievement.

The apron, then, is about function and emotion, socialization and racial stereotyping, activism and agency style-fashion-dress. From a phenomenological perspective, it is about the centering of the self. In the putting on of an apron it helps to center the wearer for the task at hand. In the act of securing the apron onto the body, of drawing it too and securing it there, tying its strings around the waist into a bow or knot and whilst wearing it, the apron becomes the symbol of the duties, profession and professionalism, craft and work the invididaul is engaged in. As a verb, the *Oxford English Dictionary* explains, to apron is "to cover with, or as with an apron," that is to cover or wrap in a particular way by tying, as with and in an apron. This action contributes to the act of the wearing and centering the self in work or craft. Additionally, the apron is a specific surface that absorbs fragments of life such as food, dust and dirt, the products and detritus of life, and can act as a shield between the body of the wearer and the world. Therefore I position the apron here as a buffer. This thinking is partly inspired by the aprons created by eighteen artists featured in the exhibition "Pinnies from Heaven"[48] where they produced their interpretation of what an apron means to them. As a body of

FIGURE 1.12 Studio portrait, London, undated, Hellis & Sons. Author's collection.

creative thinking, the apron artworks provided space to think about the broader cultural and personal meanings of this ubiquitous garment worn worldwide. The thinking behind Pauline Hearn's apron "Beneath the Surface" is particularly evocative:

> My pinnie protects me, whilst I try to protect my family. I have created two pinnies the purpose of which is to hold a narrative between myself and them. One is my working pinnie that I allow to become stained during my daily life. The other is fragile, white, clean and only for show. Bold statements have been hand-stitched onto it for all to see, the use of other stitching is not so visible. My fragile pinnie is used to cover the things I would rather hide. Life can twist and turn and throw up the unexpected. Things are best left between me and my pinnie.
>
> **MAKERS GUILD IN WALES** 2014: 17

Hearn's artistic response to the apron as an absorber of personal and familial conversations and emotions, complements Outi Sipila's historical study of the apron in Finland in the early twentieth century (2012). Sipila likens the apron to a "passepartout mounting" to position the wearer within a framework (2012: v). She suggests that to consider the apron within this context enables one to examine the apron as a piece of clothing that frames a person similarly to a passepartout around a picture, and defines the wearer within the framework of a certain space or situation. An apron as a passepartout mounting also has the opposite effect: "a person has had an opportunity to influence the way she is seen and experienced by the choices she makes when using and making an apron" (Sipila 2012: v).

This supposedly humble, yet essential, functional accessory for the working classes as exemplified in its use by the African-Jamaican higgler, is worthy as a critical tool to interpret the historical resonance and importance of the African-Jamaican higgler and her definitive style and practice. As part of the elements of African-Jamaican higgler style, the apron contributes to the synergy of this style and its historical place and meaning in Jamaica. To help consider this, I draw on Petrine Archer's article "Accessories/Accessaries; or, What's in Your Closet?" (2010). Archer's thinking is useful when considering the aproned image of the African-Jamaican higgler published on a postcard by a white Jamaican man. The impetus for the article is the legacy of slavery "in which we are all accessaries and all complicit, whether we recognize ourselves as actors, agents, chaperones, or voyeurs" (Archer 2010: 98). Archer seeks ways, primarily through what she calls "colonial history images," to "learn from this past. Returning to such pictures and rereading them, it is possible to reengage and reimagine our collective relationship to history, piecing together lost identities and challenging the hierarchies that dispel historical stereotypes and take responsibility of our present realities" (Archer 2010: 98). Archer argues that theory can be used to unpack the new circumstance in modern and post-modern Jamaica. Archer links the twenty first-century situation of dance-hall culture where black males who style themselves with feminine traits and accessories, to include the bleaching of their skin to redefine their identity. This form of unmasking, Archer argues, linked with the gaudy masks used by African-Jamaican men in the nineteenth century depicted by Isaac Mendes Belisario, in works such as *Koo, Koo, or Actor-Boy* (Belisario 1838). Archer demonstrats the complexity of fluidity—the push and pull need for change and fixity—the pulling together of history and its legacy that is part of the collective psyche of black men in Jamaica. I would add this applies to African-Jamaican women too. Archer states that, "Images of blackness proliferate in the public domain of Jamaica, and despite their sometimes pejorative nature, we need to track and reread them" (Archer 2010: 99), that is part of "two hundred years of masquerades and street performances . . . The legacy I have described here is one that speaks of costumes as a signifier of identity. For a people transported to the New World without possessions, clothes became an important marker of freedom and dignity" (Archer 2010: 99, 106).

Archer's thinking on "fluidity and fixity" connects with the African-Jamaican higgler as the need for change—that is adaptation from operating within a society defined by enslavement to the post-emancipation period—and fixity in the continuation of African-Jamaican higgler style that emerged during slavery. A style that came to be an "image of blackness" as autonomy. Therefore, the African-Jamaican higgler, through her styled body and the solid historical trait of her trade, did not need to question her place in emancipated society. She knew who she was. There was precedence of autonomy and agency of her trade: the African-Jamaican higgler. The freedom I see in the higgler is personal freedom. Toni Morrison has said that "all of us at some point are 'victims of something' . . . In a world like that, how does one remain whole—is it just impossible to do that?" (Bakerman 1978: 60). The thing, of course, is not to become a victim, to overcome external issues that impact our lives. If one considers the combination of personal freedom, the independent self and Erich Fromm's concept of "postive freedom" (Fromm 2004 [1942]: ix). I believe wholeness can be achieved, making—metaphorically and literally—the different parts of ourselves, the different parts of our lives, good to live with, to *be*. I draw on Fromm's thinking of positive freedom as it provides individuals with the agency to engage in original thinking, to seek truths to better understand the world, themselves, and themselves in the world. Although Fromm states that positive freedom develops within a democracy to: "imbue people with a faith that is the strongest the human mind is capable of: faith in life and in truth, and in freedom as the active and spontaneous realization of the individual self" (Fromm 2004 [1942]: 237).[49]

My use of positive freedom in connection with the African-Jamaican higgler may appear displaced, as they were British colonial subjects who were descendents of slaves who had, relatively recently, been emancipated, and the impact of the restrictions and trauma of these regimes had not dissipated. The idea of positive freedom is proposed in the knowledge that the peasantry at the dawn of the new twentieth century endured poverty. What I do see in the African-Jamaican higgler, if one considers the higgler as a generic group, is a concrete example in Jamaica of the persistant pursuit of personal freedom since slavery through the act of higglering—the period of time devoted to traveling to and selling at markets. I want to push Fromm's thinking of positive freedom in relation to the African-Jamaican higgler, to be one where the higgler as an individual and a group has earned an established social-cultural place in Jamaica's emancipated society that developed out of the "permission" to act freely during a period of extreme personal restriction—enslavement. Higglers were just one group that carved out mediated agency for themselves in Jamaica. As mentioned earlier, the issue of the freedom of movement amongst enslaved women, which was augmented by the same soil that had enslaved them, is marked by the freedom clothing these women wore. The basis of which was retained after liberation and came to consummate, visually, their "complete liberation" and autonomy as a peasant community.

One of the ways to address this is through the transformation of the body into an aesthetic form through styling, either in the pursuit of freedom—political or personal—and/or after the achievement of that freedom. Often the same genre of garment, textile, hairstyle or accessory works effectively in both situations. Crucially, it is the "dynamic adaptation" (Fromm 2004 [1942]: 11–12), the use of an object in the styling of the body, that makes the critical aesthetic of freedom. For me the aproned body of the African-Jamaican higgler of 1880 to 1907 reflected freedom. It symbolized the women's ability and right to work, and their movement from one place to another. I say this in contrast to Sipila's thinking on the meaning of the apron for Finnish working women and housewives in the early twentieth century. In this context, the apron posed limitations on the movement of Finnish women to work away from the home (Sipila 2012: vi–vii). As mentioned above, the aproned body of the African-Jamaican female working class tied them as a group. To focus on one section of that group, the aproned body of the African-Jamaican higgler, is to identify a particular practice within that community. Poignantly, the apron absorbed the detritus of the work associated with the higgler; the transport, display and selling of food produce that harbor the soil of Jamaica. Therefore, the aproned body of the African-Jamaican higgler tied her and her trade to the soil of emancipated Jamaica, that had vestiges of enslaved intense labor, subjugation and misery, mingled with the hope of autonomy.

Aston W. Gardner

In contrast to the higgler, Aston W. Gardner possessed the social advantages and economic acumen to effect change on the colonial tangram which underpinned the complex identity of modern Jamaica.[50] Gardner was born in Jamaica in 1854 and died in Kingston in 1916. He was the eldest son of the Reverend William J. Gardner (1825–74) who migrated to Jamaica from England in 1849. Gardner senior became the minister of the self-supporting and influential North Street Congregational Church in 1856 and was the author of *A History of Jamaica: From its Discovery by Christopher Columbus to the Year 1872*. Aston Gardner added an introduction to the 1889 and 1909 editions.

Gardner's business ventures were extensive. He was proprietor of a stationers, printers and book selling business. His company, Aston W. Gardner & Co., was at 127 Harbour Street, one of the main thoroughfares of Kingston, with another branch in Montego Bay. It was a tourist agency and stocked books, stationery supplies and a variety of goods such as tea from Ceylon, wicker furniture, tennis and cricket supplies and "small negro dolls, 2 in a box" (Johnson 1903; Robertson 1985: 14).[51] Gardner also exported fruit, specializing in mangoes, pineapples, oranges and grapefruit, and he was credited with being the pioneer in the export of citrus fruits to Britain, "undertaking to deliver to any address in London" (Johnson 1903; Robertson 1985: 14). In 1899, his presence on Harbour Street doubled with the opening of his restaurant, "The Oleanders" at number 129. In later life, Gardner was director of the Victoria Mutual Building Society[52] and was a member of the Kingston General Commissioners from 1908–12. His cultural interests extended to the collection of art and mahogany furniture.

Jamaica's fledgling tourist industry owed much to Gardner's business acumen. He operated a tourist agency from Harbour Street and was the Jamaican agent for the Eastman Kodak Company. In the postcard culture of the island, Gardner pioneered the production of private postcards for foreign correspondence. The official government postcards, which featured no image, were available on the island from 1877, and were subject to a surcharge if sent abroad, only they benefitted from the postcard rate if sent inland. "Any other cards will be surcharged at letter rates" (*Handbook of Jamaica 1878–1899*). This system was in operation until October 1899. On 15 March 1899, Aston W. Gardner & Co advertised in *The Gleaner* newspaper: "The new Jamaican postcard for foreign correspondence is now ready. Price 1/- per dozen." Glory Robertson believes this to be the earliest indication of a new style of correspondence on the island, but there is no indication whether it had an image or not (1985: 14). With the lifting of the restrictions in October 1899, the public could purchase privately produced postcards (which originated in the United States c. 1869) and place their own stamp on it, which was commercially viable for publishers such as Gardner. Robertson's study of Gardner states that he was obviously attune to the postcard collecting craze through the production of a series of postcards as in the "Jamaica Proverb Series," the "Gardner's Jamaica Alphabet Series," and the "Jamaican Household Series" (1985: 14). "A Jamaica Lady" was part of the "Gardner's Series," which concentrated on photographic scenes of the island.

In the field of literature and the expansion of knowledge about Jamaica, Gardner continued some of the work his father began. Gardner's first edition of a *Handy Guide to Jamaica,* 1889 was the launch of a run of annual pocket-sized guides published in January. The guide is a problematic publication as it is full of contradictions that mirror the collective state of mind in Jamaica as to how it should be defined by its inhabitants and their place in that definition, and most poignantly, how Anglo-Jamaicans defined African Jamaicans. The guide does not have an accredited author. The introduction is signed "Aston W. Gardner & Co.," and therein, Gardner declares responsibility for the contents. Gardner used the introduction of the book as a platform to vehemently defend the identity of Jamaica and its inhabitants, and any criticism levelled at them, regardless of skin color or class. The guide was submitted as a symbol of the progress being made in Jamaica: "The reproach of standing still has often been urged against Jamaicans. While this edition has been passing through the press, the publishers have had reason to believe that this reproach is unfounded." A third edition of the book,[53] under the section "Historical Sketch to Jamaica" is given over to a survey of the history of Jamaica from the Arawaks to British rule and slavery, and to the emancipation of "the new Jamaica" (Gardner 1889: unpagenated). Gardner refers to slavery as "the vile system . . . [and the] Traffic in human flesh . . . a cruel system can only be worked by cruel men and enforced by cruel laws . . . the inequities which were being perpetrated under the protection of the British flag" (Gardner 1889: xix–xxi). Up to this point, Gardner sounds like his father in his book *A History of Jamaica: From its Discovery by Christopher Columbus to the Year 1872*: "The Free use of the whip was perfectly legal. The slave code was cruel in the extreme, it gave the master almost unlimited power and sanctioned some of the most horrid enormities ever tolerated by law" (Gardner [1873] 1971: 177). Although in the next breadth Gardner junior extols that the import of thousands of slaves was a necessary act to invigorate the expansion of sugar plantations and to counter balance the high mortality rate amongst the slaves. The legacy of slavery on the island are the descendents of the system, "Africa West Indians" and the "bitter feelings inherited from a bitter past, are rapidly dying away" (Gardner 1889: xx).

The guide categorizes the descendants of the enslaved as "children" in their faults and virtues, the latter being "docility, affection, simplicity, but who will say these will not grow into the virtues of a man?" (Gardner 1889: xxix). These "children" whose beginnings, following emancipation, was "heavily handicapped with the vices which had come down to them from the days of African Heathenism of their race, or which were incidental to their condition as slaves" (Gardner 1889: xxix–xxx). Effectively, Gardner placed the descendants of Africa, born in Jamaica, as civilized and therefore higher than their "Heathen African" forefathers. Gardner marvels at the rapid development of the African-Jamaicans, that in the fifty years since emancipation, these "West Indian British Negroes" (1889: xxix) have progressed into a reputable, civilized Christian group to be found in all realms of society from lawyers and doctors, to merchants and peasants. This "leap" into civilization is due, Gardner explains, to the exposure of these "children" to the 'English' system of culture that has shaped their engagement with civilization (Gardner 1889: xxx): "African by descent, but British subjects by birth, speaking the English langauge, enjoying English institutions, and English literature and English laws, loyally bound by ties both of gratitude and of expediency to the English throne" (Gardner 1889: xxxi). He advocates that these "Africo-British" should be seen as part of British civilization and if not, then it is "proof of the inferiority of the race which cannot claim them as its own, and of its incapacity to absorb the blessings of that civilistion of which they are alike the pride and the ornament" (Gardner 1889: xxi–xxxii).

Gardner's guide states clearly that to deny African-Jamaicans a place in Jamaica is a sign of a nation's own inferiority and a lack of humanity, which is indicative of a lack of pride in one's self and the achievements of the British Empire in the civilising process of black Jamaicans. He vehemently denied that their African heritage had any part to play in their present progress. This is due to their status as British colonial subjects and the acculturation into Englishness. An identity he indexes with the "ethnicity" of "West Indian British Negroes." An identity that is disconcertingly placeless, yet factual of their historical acclimatazation to Jamaica, the West Indies and British colonialism. The medley of names employed by Gardner to mark African-Jamaicans reappeared in his postcard collections. In the "Gardner's Series," for example, a young girl with a meagre headtie and wearing an unassuming blouse and skirt, as generically "A Negro Girl, Jamaica." In the same series, a higgler dressed in full occupational regalia is captioned "A Jamaica Lady." Both are given a geographical status, the noun "lady" fixes the higgler as being of higher status in the peasant community than an "ordinary negro girl." It is this anomaly in the naming of different sections of Jamaica's peasant class by Gardner that drives *Angel in the Marketplace*, a title chosen to prompt the consideration of black women from Jamaica's working class as having a respected cultural position.

The combination of Gardner's business interests and social engagements, the cultivation of his artistic sensibilities, and his ethnic origins as the son of an eminent English clergyman and historian, placed Gardner amongst Jamaica's white elite. I suggest that Gardner is symbolic of Anne McClintock's notion that members of the middle-class need to create its own discourse of legitimacy:

> Moreover, the heroics of a transcendent, illuminated, self-generating consciousness, unaided by anything but an emancipatory will to self-creation and an aesthetics of metamorphosis, is historically a nineteenth-century middle class idea fabricated by a class anxious to create its own discourse of legitimacy without being able to resort to the idea of history or tradition (which was either a lower- or upper-class preserve). The middle class had to assert the freedom to create its being from its own self-generating energy.
>
> **McCLINTOCK** 1995: 96

Beasts of burden

Herein lies the relationship between the African-Jamaican higgler and Gardner, and the connection with their respective social groups. Both emerged from, and were shaped by, Jamaica's history and consequently its prejudices and its liberality. The confluence of these representatives of opposed and simultaneously intertwined social groups on one postcard, an object now made more problematic and intoxicating, throws up the social and political mire that framed and infused the British colony since the seventeenth century. The analogy "Beasts of Burden" is apt here. The African-Jamaican higgler and Gardner carried the burden of Jamaica's history and imperialism, in differing context, into the future—each burden impacting on the other, one more powerful than the other: "The white man in the West Indies is the master, it being out of the question for him to perform field labor and he must depend upon his intellect for supremacy" (Bradford 1902: 35). This declaratory statement by the American travel writer Mary Bradford negates the fact that there was a white working class on the island, but the sentiment is correct for the period. Jamaica's white community may have been the third largest group on the island, the other being the African-Jamaicans and East Indians, nonetheless they controlled its socio-economic power.

The burden of history borne by the African-Jamaican higgler as featured in the colonial postcard "A Jamaica Lady" was visibly far more pernicious. A collective reading of English and American travel writers' references to the African-Jamaican higgler effectively classified her as an angelic beast of burden (Carpenter-Smith 1901: 68; Bullen 1905: 191–2). Primarily, the burden referenced was the goods she transported on her head from homestead to market, always in angelic white clothing:

> The ride up to Constant Spring is a charming one, and the crowds of negresses in spotless white, bearing burdens on their heads, with an easy swinging gait, are an interesting study, but they lead to a deepening of the impression that in these islands the women do most of the heavy labour. It is natural, I suppose, and without it the labour problem out here would become very acute, but it grates unpleasantly upon our senses as a kind of topsy-turvy idea—a remnant of savagery.
>
> **BULLEN** 1905: 191

This reference to the "topsy-turvy idea" of women working reflects the statement made in nineteenth century travel guides that professed Jamaica's labor problems were caused solely by black men (Willis 1897: 31, Froude 1888: 210–12). In their eyes the whiteness of the African-Jamaican higgler's style was symbolic of her place as an economic savior on the island, and viewed as the antidote to the "lazy men folk." The English travel writer, James Anthony Froude, believed the peasant women to be more intelligent than their men folk, and urged that "if there is to be a black constitution I would give the vote only to the women" (1888: 210–212). Therefore her other burden was also a metaphorical emasculation of the black male, carrying the weight of Jamaica's prosperity and future on her head.

To categorize the African-Jamaican higgler as the Angel in the Marketplace is to set these various facets of the burden that plagued her existence since slavery into a metaphysical context. The decision to represent the African-Jamaican higgler in profile on the colonial postcard "A Jamaica Lady," and in light of the above, illustrates Benjamin's celebrated quote on the angel of history:

> This is how one pictures the angel of history. His [her] face is turned toward the past. Where we perceive a chain of events, he [she] sees on single catastrophe which keeps piling wreckage upon wreckage and hurls it in front of his [her] feet. The angel would like to stay, awaken the dead, and make whole what has been smashed. But a storm is blowing from Paradise; it has got caught in his [her] wings with such violence that the angel can no longer close them. This storm irresistibly propels him [her] into the future to which his [her] back is turned, while the pile of debris before him [her] grows skyward. This storm is what we call progress.
>
> 1992 [1973]: 249

Sigrid Weigel encourages us to consider Benjamin's "Thesis on the Philosophy of History" (Benjamin 1992 [1973]: 245) as a dialectical image and that "the Angel of History" is a thought image (Weigel 1996: 55). Therefore, I want to argue that the African-Jamaican higgler, as featured on Gardner's postcard, was the angel of Jamaica's history. She originated from the "single catastrophe" that was slavery, the detritus of which filtered continually through the decades over the lives of the inhabits of the island. The "storm" in the narration of the angel in the marketplace is emancipation which continued on into the future to construct a pile of debris out of colonialism and imperialism, and the resultant representation of the peasantry by white- and non-Jamaicans. This illustrates Oguibe's proposition that portraiture can be "a marker of memory" and "anticipation" (Oguibe 2004: 82).

An angel is the embodiment of supreme power, "the personification of the numinous, the incomprehensible, the mysterious and the mythic" (Knapp 1995: 7), the messenger and a mediator between differing worlds and stratospheres. Malcolm Godwin in *Angels: An Endangered Species* clarifies the formidable linking mechanism the angel possesses, that is generally between heaven and earth, and between God and his subjects: "One transcendental realm of the sacred and the profane dualistic world of space and time. These convictions range from belief in the power of ancestors, spirits of nature or fairy beings from the 'other world.'" (Godwin 1990: 7). An angel can be created in the likeness of a human form often witnessed by another human being (Knapp 1999: 7–10). The need to confirm the sighting of such a powerful spiritual being creates a bond between the angel and the witness, for in order to have seen the angel and to recognize the being as that, means that the witness had to believe in it to have seen it, in order to identify it, and therefore provide proof of its existence in the visualization of it in some form as in a postcard; "It is impossible to separate the observer from the observed. To question the truth of the angel is to question the truthfulness of the witness" (Godwin 1990: 8). Most poignantly, in the attempt to traverse the vagaries of what or who an angel is, Gottfried Knapp's summation is simply that "The study of angels is in fact the study of human beings" (1999: 8).

To read the caption "A Jamaica Lady" with the portrait of the aproned African-Jamaican higgler in profile, carrying a bankra basket on her head, effectively becoming the halo of the African-Jamaican higgler, and her spotless white clothing, her angelic robes professes godliness and goodness, surreptitiously announces the might of the African-Jamaican higgler as the "image(s) of female power, but they are specifically memory traces of female working-class power and are rooted in class divisions and historical mutability" (McClintock 1995: 96).

The higgler was an angelic beast of burden based on two levels. Politically, her burden lay in the integral part she played in the peasant community's struggle to be identified as an autonomous group since slavery. Visually, the picturesque quality of her styled body in weekday clothing conferred upon her by non-black observers, to some extent hampered this pursuit and placed the higgler, the peasant community and their ethnic difference as a touristic spectacle, whether as a touristic site or captured on a postcard.

The styled African-Jamaican higgler: a graphic symbol of colonial discourse

The visual presentation of the African-Jamaican higgler on postcards during the late nineteenth and early twentieth century was a symbol of historical continuity, perpetuated through the ritual communication of African-Jamaican higgler style as they travelled to and worked at markets. She was a reminder of the slave past and of a level of power lost to the British, as the higgler was no longer a chattel. The styled body of the African-Jamaican higgler, therefore, was a graphic symbol of that history: a ghost of the past, of the slave plantation work and regime, that haunted the present imperial regime and Britains's continued strength as overseer. The commodification of her as outlined above achieved what Joanne Eicher sees as "The past is frozen in time for a specific purpose" (Eicher 1995: 4).

If the higgler is designated as a graphic symbol of the colonial discourse of the British colony of Jamaica, as immortalized in the colonial postcard "A Jamaica Lady," the higgler stands between ideology and materiality, and she tests the boundaries between "reality" and "falseness" (Loomba 1998: 26). As a primary representative of the peasant community her trade and styled body became a language of autonomy, of an autonomous black world whilst technically functioning as a colonial subject and all that it entails:

> Thus, language is not a nomenclature, or a way of naming things, which already exists, but a system of signs, whose meaning is relational. Only a social group can produce signs, because only a specific social usage gives a sign any meaning ... The sign, or words, need a community with shared assumptions to confer them with meaning; conversely, a social group needs signs in order to know itself as a community. On this basis, we can think of language as ideological rather than as objective.
>
> **LOOMBA** 1998: 35

The graphic symbol of colonial discourse featured in the colonial postcard entitled "A Jamaica Lady" tests the theory that there is a disconnection between the sign and what it signifies, as is the case for text, "Meaning ... is not self-present in the sign, or in text, but is the result of this gap, slippage or what Derrida calls 'différance'" (Loomba 1998: 36). Hence my original contestation of Quentin Bell's argument that: "The antithetical figure is the workman, the socially useful person, but the dignity of labor is a concept for which we cannot easily find a graphic symbol, because the workman is not socially reputable and therefore has no place in the mythology of art" (1976: 33). I suggest that Gardner managed to produce a portrait that found a graphic symbol for the dignity of labor in the "socially reputable" African-Jamaican higgler.

The image of the African-Jamaican higgler depicted on the postcard "A Jamaica Lady," was not an act of stereotyping as it depicted the constitutive elements of African-Jamaican higgler style and trade. Nonetheless, this form of classification of a member of Jamaica's lower ranks in the early twentieth century also enabled the "self-definition of the middle class ... for the distance along the path of progress travelled by some portions of humanity could be measured only by the distance others lagged behind" (McClintock 1995: 46). Homi Bhabha, in his summation on stereotyping in colonial discourse, refers to those in power, generally the colonizer, as those who apply stereotyping techniques as a mark of difference. This was also done by the subaltern who colludes with the ideas of colonialism and imperialism and reduces the system to separation:

> separation—*between* races, cultures, histories, *within* histories—a separation between *before* and *after* that repeats obsessively the mythical moment of disjunction. Despite the structural similarities with the play of need and desire in primal fantasies, the colonial fantasy does not try to cover up that moment of separation. It is more ambivalent. On the one hand, it proposes a teleology—

under certain conditions of colonial domination and control the native is progressively reformable. On the other, however, it effectively displays the "separation", makes it more visible. It is the visibility of this separation which, in denying the colonised the capacities of self-government, independence, western modes of civility, lends authority to the official version and mission of colonial power.

BHABHA 1994: 118

Thus visibility within the context of colonial discourse is a double-edged sword: making visible the classic, if to some extent stereotyped, image of the styled body of the African-Jamaican higgler portrayed in colonial picture postcards, for example, as a one-dimensional image of the black female peasantry of Jamaica. The example produced by Gardner discussed here does not deny the higgler her own place of importance in Jamaica—the "elevated" trade of *being* an African-Jamaican higgler. Simultaneously, the colonial discourse and imperial thinking of the period amongst the colonizer and its collaborators conspired to deny the African-Jamaican female peasantry the visible space to engage with modernity through style-fashion-dress and to present herself as an individualized self, to celebrate the visibility of independent thought. Yet as part of her legacy, the African-Jamaican higgler possesses an historical authority that is arrested in the occupational workwear that has resulted in a specific styled body accredited to her which empowered this particular colonized body.

At the close of this chapter I ask myself again, why am I drawn to the postcard "A Jamaica Lady"? It is the postcard's uncanny ability to evoke my need to explore a narrative of presence, to seek that "presence in absence." To return to Prosser, the postcard "tell[s] my story as much as they tell their story. They tell the story of the place, of the feeling, and they speak of desire, fantasy, dream and reality. Some postcards speak of the return to origins . . . The postcard encapsulates the search; a journey that is more than the simple tourist journey" (Prosser 2011: 223). The journey taken here was to gauge an understanding of how the style narratives of the African-Jamaican higgler, as mentioned in the introduction to this book, a woman who is part of my own maternal familial heritage, has immense historical, cultural and style narrative value.

2 "WE ALSO SHOULD WALK IN THE NEWNESS OF LIFE":[1] INDIVIDUALIZED HARLEM STYLE OF THE 1930s

With the visual arts of the 1920s and 1930s anchored by black peoples, we can recollect and reimagine this twentieth-century moment when Harlem was not only "in vogue", or "on the minds" of a complacent few, but also a geo-political metaphor for modernity and an icon for an increasingly complex black diasporal presence in the world.

RICHARD J. POWELL 1997: 18

This chapter focuses on two portraits: the photograph *A Couple in Harlem*,[2] taken in 1932 by James VanDerZee (1886–1983) (figure 2.1), and the painting *Self-portrait: Myself at Work* produced by Malvin Gray Johnson (1896–1934) in 1934 (plate 5). These images are examples of the influential African-American visual arts of the inter-war years that Richard J. Powell refers to above. *A Couple in Harlem* is a favored image amongst scholars, particularly black cultural critics, as it is viewed as the embodiment of black modernity during inter-war American and African diasporic history.[3] Yet such an important visual statement on this cultural issue has not undergone detailed examination as to why *A Couple in Harlem* has been earmarked as being so iconic. This is undoubtedly a polished image that unashamedly revels in symbols of wealth—the Cadillac car, raccoon fur coats, the well-maintained Brownstone houses as the backdrop to these luxurious items, and the incredible beauty of the couple themselves, heightened by the glamor that envelops them. What did it mean then, and now, for an African-American[4] couple

FIGURE 2.1 "Harlem couple wearing raccoon coats," 1932, Harlem, New York by James VanDerZee. © The Granger Collection, New York/TopFoto.

to wear similar fur coats as part of a photographic poem on black glamor and modernity? Were these raccoon fur coats being worn by the couple's white contemporaries? How much cultural significance did the raccoon fur coat and the Cadillac automobile have in 1932?

With regard to the self-portrait by Gray Johnson,[5] I was originally drawn to the work when it was on display in the 1997 exhibition "Rhapsodies in Black: Art of the Harlem Renaissance"[6] held at the Hayward Gallery, London. Although VanDerZee's *Couple in Harlem* was also displayed at the show, I was already well acquainted with the photograph. Gray Johnson's self-portrait was another matter. I recall being mesmerized by *Self-portrait: Myself at Work*, it seemed that the longer I looked at the painting, the larger it became; for me it was *the* "object of contemplation" (Berger 2009: 61). This was partly due to the fact that I viewed, and continue to view, Gray Johnson's painting as an incredibly beautiful and sensitive portrait that invites the viewer to *see* him. On *seeing* Gray Johnson I was drawn to his striped polo-neck sweater. Ken Wilder believes in the reciprocity between the viewer and a painting. The position of the the beholder and their "seeing-in" and imagination applied to a painting "expand what can be experienced in a painting in terms of the implied reciprocity between viewer and work" (Wilder 2008: 275).

The reciprocity between *Self-portrait: Myself at Work* and me tugged at my desire to understand what drove Gray Johnson to project his sense of self in a striped polo-neck jumper as the dominating feature of this painting? How popular was the striped sweater in 1934? Why did Gray Johnson represent himself styled casually in a striped polo-neck sweater, when portraits of other black male artists, intellectuals and writers of the Harlem Renaissance featured in the exhibition were represented in the more "respectable" ensemble of a suit, shirt and a tie? An exception in the exhibition was the artist William H. Johnson in his *Self-portrait with Bandana* (c. 1935–38). In this work, Johnson fixates on a marked reference to the plain orange detail of a large expanse of fabric wrapped around his neck and tucked into what appears to be a black jacket. But it is Gray Johnson's self-portrait that keeps pulling me in through his bold rendition of his striped polo-neck sweater. What was Gray Johnson saying about his "self" at this time of his life? A prime aim of this chapter is to consider how the individualized style choices made by black men and women in Harlem during the 1930s was a comment on their pursuit of modernity. Gray Johnson's seemingly bohemian appearance affords an alternative concept to the equally valid polished glamor performed by VanDerZee's couple in Harlem.

The glamor of this couple is a distinct note. It is glamor as hypnosis that draws one in, that enchants and enraptures the wearer and viewer about some of the good things that can contribute to a life, most accurately here, to a black life. I was inspired to study *A Couple in Harlem* because of this hypnotic quality, a trait that has been seen as a definition of Harlem's draw during the inter-war years, that has reverberated on through the decades to the present (Massood 2013: 1–2). A key reference is the novel *Jazz* by Toni Morrison, a literary portrait of Harlem and its inhabitants in 1926:

> The woman who churned a man's blood as she leaned all alone on a fence by a country road might not expect even to catch his eye in the City. But if she is clipping quickly down the big-city street in heels, swinging her purse, or sitting on a stoop with a cool beer in her hand, dangling her shoe from the toes of her foot, the man, reacting to her posture, to soft skin on stone, the weight of the building stressing the delicate, dangling shoe, is captured. And he'd think it was the woman he wanted, and not some combination of curved stone, and a swinging, high-heeled shoe moving in and out of sunlight. He would know right away the deception, the trick of the shapes and light and movement, but it wouldn't matter at all because the deception was part of it too.
>
> **MORRISON** 1992: 34

In this excerpt, Morrison encapsulates the seduction of the city and its inhabitants. Together the architecture, the very fabric of the city—the bodies and the objects used to create the seductive city dweller—work together to stir and hold desire. For this to have effect, Morrison suggests that the city dweller and the surrounding architecture are inseparable. They become each other's backdrop in the painting of deception and intoxication that is the hard romance of city life. Morrison evokes how a woman can take ownership and manage the enormity of the city and take control of her presence in such an environment. In this environment, generally defined as masculine, the man in Morrison's excerpt is an important player in the performance of the city and is no less safe from urban beguilement. Details, affects and observations made real by VanDerZee in his photograph *A Couple in Harlem* that summarizes his photographic ideology during the inter-war period. With its exhibition of wealth, VanDerZee meticulously captured an image confirming how black people in Harlem pursued a better quality of life than the one generally prescribed them by the segregation culture in America, whilst simultaneously being a deft portraitist of Harlemites (Willis-Braithwaite 1993: 8–25; Mercer 2003: 3–15). His photographs were conscious affirmations of the transformations of people who had migrated from the South of America to the North, or emigrated from the Caribbean to the United States to settle in this area of New York, and who embraced a cosmopolitan outlook with the intent of leaving behind old traditions associated with slavery and subordination (Tulloch 2006: 122).

I therefore see both these portraits as "energy symbols" (Haworth-Booth 1978) of black aesthetic power of a particular geographical space and time—Harlem of the early 1930s. Similarly, the unabashed forceful directness of both images arrests the viewer to ponder, study and decipher the combinations of Harlem life and style as a specific form of black modernity forged alongside the ideals of the Harlem Renaissance movement that helped to underwrite the hypnotic quality of Harlem.

The Harlem Renaissance: a retelling of newness

As mentioned above, both portraits featured in the touring exhibition "Rhapsodies in Black: Art of the Harlem Renaissance." The show was seminal in its endeavor to "challenge conventional representations of the Harlem Renaissance and to provoke new readings of the period" (Bailey 1997: 11). Powell and David A. Bailey, the curators of the exhibition, defined the impact of the Harlem Renaissance as: "a cultural and psychological watershed, an era in which black people were perceived as having finally liberated themselves from a past fraught with self-doubt and surrendered instead to an unprecedented optimism . . . a cultural confidence that stretched beyond the borders of Harlem to other black communities in the Western World" (Powell 1997 (b): 16). In their endeavor to encourage new readings of the Harlem Renaissance, the curators argued that the movement was not fixed in the decade of 1919 to 1929, as generally believed, but that the work of Harlem Renaissance contributors continued through the 1930s and reverberated into the present. This is in line with an earlier argument raised by Houston A. Baker, that the Black Aesthetics movement in America began in the 1920s, coalescing in the Harlem Renaissance movement, and on through to the political activities of Malcolm X, the Black Power Movement and beyond. Baker defines black aesthetics as a process of reclamation and invention, a form of black expression "which the 'special character and imperatives of black experience' had always been developed, articulated, and analyzed. For the black expressive domain has produced stunning entrances into national life for blacks—even during the bleakest moments of the race's entrapment in an economics of slavery" (Baker 1988: 62).

Additionally, in the historiography of the Harlem Renaissance many of the visual arts connected with the movement have been under represented, for example, the styled black body. In my focus on the styled bodies of key images and individuals of the Harlem Renaissance movement, Powell's "reconceptualization" of the term Harlem Renaissance to being "Harlem Re/Naissance . . . Re/Birth" (Powell 1997 (b): 17–18) is useful here. His introduction of the virgule (/), was to "emphasize the concept's original sense of cultural and intellectual renewal and its visual agenda to rediscover and recreate a modern body (in this case a black one)" (Powell 1997(b): 17). Whilst Powell has maintained that a driving force amongst the artists of the Harlem Renaissance was to draw on "black-experience-as-art" (Powell 1997(b): 16) these statements lead one to consider the Harlemites discussed here as three dimensional representations of the black-experience-as-art.

This study takes the baton from "Rhapsodies in Black" to consider the visual arts of different forms of portraiture produced in the early 1930s by African-Americans as a visual narrative on the making of self through the styled black body.[7] In the spirit of a "reconceptualization" of the Harlem Renaissance as Re/Birth, the issue of newness—the state, fact and quality of being new—through self-definition is an important addition to this investigative framework. Homi Bhabha's explanation of newness encourages an embrace of the past to forge new paths, and simultaneously "renews the past" through the performative power of cultural translation "refiguring it as a contingent 'in-between' space, that innovates and interrupts the performance of the present. The past-present becomes part of the necessity . . . of living" (Bhabha 1994: 7). The concept of newness used here incorporates the ideologies of the "New Negro." The term has had a variety of meanings with relation to the complex presence of black people in America, and their cultural and political negotiations with the dominant American ideologies to unravel that complexity and confront the systems, which fed the situation to mark out the legitimate position and presence of black people in America. During the period of enslavement in the United States, "New Negro" referenced the arrival of African men and women to America. In the post-emancipation period, "New Negro" equated with new directions within the arts, education and status amongst, and by, African-Americans. Essentially "New Negro" was about group determination, self-pride and the right to be an American citizen.[8] The term's most celebrated association was with the Harlem Renaissance Movement. Alain Locke, one of the architect's of the movement, refined the meaning of what the "New Negro" was as being an "intelligent Negro" (Locke 1925 (a): 632) who was aware of the social imbalances towards her or himself and raised above this through concerted cultural and critical methods such as painting, literature and music. This view was outlined in the special edition of the periodical *Survey Graphic* "Harlem, Mecca of the New Negro," published in 1925. Locke explained that "the Negro is being carefully studied, not just talked about and discussed. In art and letters, instead of being wholly caricatured, he is being seriously portrayed and painted. To all of this the 'New Negro' is keenly responsive as an augury of a new democracy in American Culture. He [and she] is contributing his [and her] share to the new social understanding" (Locke 1925 (a): 632).

In light of this, *Self-portrait: Myself at Work* and *A Couple in Harlem* are examples of self-telling. The processes of portraits and self-portraits, as Andrew Small explains, "describes the individual at a given moment" which is supported by references in the image (Small 1996: 4, 5). Whilst James Smalls believes the portrait and self-portrait are a particular draw for African-American methods of representation, as they enable control of their own representation to allay the long history of misrepresentation: "from the honing of artistic skill to the recording of identity formation and transformation processes in a history beginning in the Harlem Renaissance of the 1920s and continuing as critical cultural practice into our time" (Smalls 2001: 47). Style-fashion-dress and individual style narratives, of course, play a part in the "exigency of newness" (Adorno 1999: 21–2). As outlined in the introduction to this book, style narratives are a form of agency through the style choices an individual makes to construct their individualized look from various components of garments, accessories and beauty regimes that may be in fashion or not, whilst Elizabeth Wilson reminds us that fashion "*is* change" (Wilson 1985: 3). To be more culturally specific, Van Dyk Lewis has stated that "Black fashion is always open to new trends and modes" (2003: 174) like any other aware and experimental cultural genre, which of course results in a visual discourse that engages with mainstream designs, and when necessary, has used this medium to critique dominant ideologies of place and space. Therefore, *We Should Also Walk in Newness of Life* considers whether the prominent garments of the raccoon coat and the striped polo-neck jumper were mainstream fashionable items in 1932 and 1934 respectively, and if so, then what does this mean when style narratives are led by fashion items? A further consideration was the central role of the black body to address the pressing need for a new cultural and social standing for black people in America during this period, from which the desire for newness—experiences, agency and redefinition—was projected.

This chapter presents case studies on these portraits, zooming in on the elements that comprise the portraits as style narratives of Harlem aesthetics in the first half of the 1930s, and as satellites for place and difference. Equally, *A Couple in Harlem* and *Self-portrait: Myself at Work* are exemplary of, to borrow Fiona Hackney's phrase, "quiet activism" (Hackney 2013). I do so because the portraits were produced before the Harlem Riots of 1935, a reaction to the effects of the Depression as a "race" issue that included job discrimination, as well as police brutality (Fay 1999: 937), actions that established Harlem as a fighting community that would resort to forceful means for their rights (Blair 2007: 1–18). Hackney created the term "quiet activism" to position the historical and cultural importance of the lived experience and practice of domestic crafts—the agency of making things, as well as making the self that is integral to one's autobiography (Tulloch 2010). I use it here to do the same in terms of the historical and cultural, visual and material importance of the making of the black self at a formative moment in African diaspora history. Additionally, to focus on only two images produced in, and about, Harlem during America's Depression also marks a black American trait to raise oneself up above adversity. This was, of course, not always the case or easy to do, but even in dire straights, black Americans attempted to put their best selves forward (see figure 2.2). The portrait of these three artists, VanDerZee's sitters were hoofers (dancers), may place them on a different footing than so-called ordinary lives. Nonetheless, the couple and Gray Johnson bridge the intersection between everyday and "artistic" life, in the performativity of Harlem aesthetics.

FIGURE 2.2 "Wives, Mothers and Daughters of the Unemployed," The Municipal Lodging House, 438 East 25th Street, New York, November 26, 1930. Author's collection.

Couple in Raccoon Coats, with a Cadillac, Taken on West 127th Street, Harlem, New York, 1932

"The Way to Begin a New Wardrobe . . . Start with a Coat . . . for on that hang all the law's of well-planned chic."

AMERICAN VOGUE 1932: 57

The above quote was directed at the female readers of *American Vogue* in 1932 but, as we shall see, it was equally pertinent to male wearers of the raccoon coat. This coat emerged in the early 1900s as part of the trend for more robust fur coats, known as sportswear, to counteract the elements when driving in the open cars of this period[9] (Ewing 1981: 119–120). By the mid-1920s the raccoon coat was not only part of the "fur craze" that seduced America (Weissman Joselit 2002: 149–52), it was also used, Mario Constantino notes, by avant-garde artists, such as Marcel Duchamp as a symbol of "their ideas or individuality" (Constantino 1997: 31), but was also a key player in the definition of American male collegiate style. Deirdre Clemente's[10] extensive study of the style practices of Princeton University between 1900 and the 1930s has led her to view Princeton as the leader and innovator of Ivy League dress (2008: 31) and that it was responsible for the raccoon fur coat craze of the 1920s. Clemente reports that *The Princeton Alumni Weekly* noted on January 16, 1924, "coonskins were almost as thick as flies" which led to it being deemed as "the fur coat devil" (2002: 25). Nonetheless, this fashionable item was a barometer of affluence, not only because it was worn by Princeton's elite collegiate but also in its cost, which Clemente's states ranged from between $200 and $500 (2002: 25).

This trend was not lost on African-American students. For example, the March 1926 issue of the African-American periodical *The Crisis* has a photograph of a young black man wearing a raccoon fur coat. He is kneeling at the center front of three rows of delegates at the Detroit based 18th Annual Convention of the Alpha Phi Alpha, the oldest of the five "Negro Greek letter" fraternities and sororities (*The Crisis* March 1926: 243). The remaining fifty-six gentleman in the photograph, who range from youthful to mature, are dressed in what appear to be plain woollen overcoats, in mid- to dark shades, two of which have large fur collars. The young man in a fine example of a raccoon coat of variegated tones from light to dark with a dark stripe[11] stands out amidst the light, mid and dark shades of smooth woollen coats, worn by the elegant contingent of academics. The bulky transformation of the young man's physique by the density of the raccoon pelt, lends to the rakish air that he projects. Here, within the committed endeavor to discuss future scholarships and "discrimination in Northern Colleges" (*The Crisis* March 1926: 243), a well-planned black male chic had a place in 1926.[12]

Five years later, fur specialist Max Bachrach stated that the raccoon pelt had taken a "strangle hold" on the American collegiate: "[T]he annual football competitions are galaxies of 'coon coats' worn by both sexes to protect them from the crisp, snappy, autumn weather" (1931: 306). This was confirmed by the journals of the fur industry which reported on the popularity of these styles amongst female "fashionable dressers" (*Fur Trade Review* 1932: 15) in attendance at university football games such as Harvard and Yale, which was generally indicative of future trends: "[S]ince what is worn at the football games is an important factor in determining the outdoor fur styles for the season in Greater Boston" (*Fur Trade Review* December 1932: 15). Clemente's illustrates this "short-lived fad" (Mears 2012: 26). By 1930, Princetonians tried to sell or recoup some of the large sums they paid for a raccoon coat (Clemente's 2008: 462–3). These conflicting views of fashionability and rejection continued between 1933 and 1934. There was also contradictory information on the fashionable status of male raccoon furs. For example, in the December 1933 issue of *Men's Wear* magazine the examples worn by more mature spectators at Yale–Princeton football games were considered the object of nostalgia "older grads … with recollection of bygone days when they themselves were the heroes" (December 1933: 24). Whilst the following year, the publication provided reassurance that a raccoon coat remained an attractive and appropriate winter garment for men, as illustrated in the window display of New York's Fifth Avenue emporium, B. Altman and Company (*Men's Wear* December 1934: 46). Alternatively, male shoppers could purchase examples from New York-based raccoon coat specialist S. Robert Zimmerman (*Men's Wear* 1934: 77).

Richard Martin and Harold Koda's historical assessment of the raccoon coat was that it "is the only fur coat ascribed fully to the modern male" (1989: 137) due to its long-term connection with collegiate culture and the persuasive attraction of the "Joe College" persona—the supposedly perfect specimen of the college man. For Martin and Koda, male collegiate dress was the signifier of "the last youthful idyll … [the] wondrously free young man" and sportsmanship, whether as player or spectator, school spirit, the camaraderie and group bonding amongst team or school members (Martin, Koda 1989: 137). Therefore, the wearing of collegiate style on or outside the campus signalled the wearer's inclusion and integration into a particular university— that he belonged and contributed to a distinct educational institution, at a specific time in their respective biographies. To return to Clemente, she argues that collegiate bonding through localized trends on the university campus was about "belonging" (2008: 21). The raccoon coat's contribution to this was to be a bonding mechanism. The color line may have separated black and white university students, but the need to bond with one's peers ran deep on both sides, as illustrated above. In the wrapping of black and white, male and female bodies in a raccoon coat "racial" and gender boundaries were crossed and merged, to have similar relevance to each group within the collegiate context—the pursuit of educational and personal progress.

Raccoon coats also had a strong impact on general fur fashions in America during this period. The coats were produced in lighter weight, shorthaired, "coat stock" peltries, native to North America, and were generally obtained from below the "Mason and Dixon Line".[13] The classic silhouette for women was the "swagger style" that was defined by fullness flowing from the shoulder line, in either single or double-breasted designs. In 1928, *American Fur Style*[14] announced that the double-breasted "youthfully chic" raccoon swagger coat, was "one of the smartest, indispensable fashion staples for motor and general wear."[15] The following year, the *American Furrier and Fur Style* reported that a crucial feature of the new collection of fur coats for women were the "sports fur coats . . . specially designed and stressing new skills in the manipulation of pelts, as well as the new importance of the silhouette. They are designed in the swagger type with fullness from the shoulders; some are belted featuring pockets; collars are convertible and in the high-standing effects, scarf and varied styles now evident in garments of this character. For inexpensive models lapin is widely adopted. For the better class, beaver, gray Persian lamb, shaded krimmer,[16] muskrat and raccoon are used" (Alexander 1929: 6). Another version of the raccoon coat was the "The Tomboy" (figure 2.3)—a double-breasted design with a large "mannish" collar and leather buttons (Alexander 1929: 6). In 1930, "The Tomboy" was deemed to be "the regulation" raccoon coat for sports wear (*American Furrier and Fur Style* May 1930: 20). Between 1931 and 1933, the swagger style raccoon fur continued to be in high demand (*Fur Trade Review* December 1931: 24) and attained a dual fashionable function of being "suitable either to semi-dressy wear or strictly sports types . . . being used for street and sports wear" (*Fur Trade Review* September 1931: 53). By 1932, the swagger style coat in raccoon, Hudson seal and spotted cat, for example, were the best sellers of the year (*Fur Trade Review* December 1932: 7), a style that came to "embody the tempo of the times as regards youth" (*Fur Trade Review* October 1932: 15).

The raccoon fur coat was also available by mail order through the Sears Roebuck catalogue. The fall/winter 1924–5 issue included a raccoon fur coat "made of extra fine grade matched raccoon skins. It also comes in Japanese mink fur for those desiring a more luxurious garment" (71). The coat was available in the swagger style "fashioned in guaranteed, fine quality perfectly matched raccoon skins in one of our most beautiful fur coats in our entire selection" (71). The coat cost $250.00. Raccoon fur coats were still available from the catalogue in the fall/winter 1931–2 edition for $195.00. Once orders were placed, it would take two weeks for delivery, "making this coat especially for you" (33).

A survey of these specialist fur magazines and mail order catalogs did not indicate the intended wearer of the furs, although the women used in the illustrations and photographs to model the designs were "white." The fashion for furs was being mediated to black American women through publications such as *Apex News* founded in 1929 by "Mme Sara Spencer Washington" (*Apex News* June 1929: 13). The paper, which focused primarily on beauty and hair culture, featured photographic news of well-dressed and active members of the black community. In 1929, for example, there were a number of images of young African-American women and men in fur coats, as in "Mrs Verna Wynne Cross, principal of the Apex [beauty] School of New York" in a shawl-collared fur coat and cloche hat (*Apex*

FIGURE 2.3 Tomboy raccoon fur coat, 1930, featured in *American Furrier and Fur Style*.

News July 1929: 6). One could say these were real-life models of style.[17] There is evidence that black women in Harlem had access to fashionable fur coats. During 1931 and 1932, fur coats were being advertised in Harlem's black press, but there is no specific mention of raccoon examples. Readers were directed to new and "[G]enuine fur coats used but a moment for posing in fashion shows" available at Sally's Studio and Hygrade (*Amsterdam News* 1932: 3). Potential customers had the option to pay by instalments over a thirty-week period, a stark reminder of the unfavorable economic climate.

Rebecca Arnold has discussed the "complex process of 'making' American identity" (Arnold 2002: 57). Arnold surmised this through the proliferation of photographs available in the 1930s in publications such as *Life* that "acted as ciphers of the times as well as visual enticements to fantasize and consume" (Arnold 2002: 49). Invariably, due to the entrenched segregation of the country, images such as these "reinforced Americanness as uniformly white, presenting an identity that ignored the nation's ethnic diversity" (Arnold 2002: 59). In contrast to this, VanDerZee's couple, not originally produced for commercial mass public consumption, nonetheless provides today an example of the "making" of black American identity based on high status American commodities, and black aspirational desires for such commodities for personal definition—items that were initially designed and produced specifically to define white American identities that upheld the American trait of "separateness" (Welter and Cunningham 2005: 2). A feature imbued in the acute Americanness of raccoon coats, the pelt of which reflects not only geographical "separateness," being obtained below the Mason and Dixon Line,[18] as mentioned above but also *on* "race" lines. The inclusion of raccoon coats as part of this couple's chic style construction was, I suggest, "a way of laying claim to America" (Weissman Joselit 2002: 2–3) and simultaneously amplified, consciously or not, their projection of African-Americanness.

What, then, is the cultural meaning of the raccoon coat worn by this black couple in Harlem in 1932? The woman is positioned, like the automobile, as a focal point, while the man is partially seen. This position would, quite rightly, place the woman, like the car, as the man's possession. But this assumption cannot be left there. Here is a photographic portrait of a black woman and man in matching raccoon coats. It is difficult to tell if they are identical designs. Both coats have deep cuffs and shawl collars. They are exemplary of a premium raccoon coat that is "undyed, full-furred, with beautifully matched distinctly darker stripes" (Chambers 1951: 454). There is no indication as to what the couple's relationship was—short- or long-term lovers, or married—but the wearing of similar raccoon furs emphasized a bond between them, or what Marie Corbin calls "a unit" whose identity can be regarded as "interchangeable" (Corbin 1978: 13). Corbin's definition of a couple includes the pair acting in a particular way in public: "[T]heir relation is marked off from others, acquiring some degree of exclusivity. Because they define themselves as a 'couple' they may feel that they *ought* to behave in certain ways—to meet, to do things together—and that their relationship should have some precedence over others" (Corbin 1978: 13). This couple in raccoon coats wear a similar item, if primarily for practical reasons to address the climate. Nonetheless, they emphasize their united presence through "[T]he 'visibility' of the relations of ... any couple[s] is important not only in ... urban areas ... but also small-scale rural communities. Sometimes the deliberate demonstration to others in a community that the properties are being observed, the specifically public nature of social interaction, may also be extremely important" (Corbin 1978: 27). Therefore, in this context, I believe this black couple, styled in raccoon coats photographed in Harlem performed a political act of self-expression and self-determination, were "the shibboleth of the 'race' war" (Miller 1925: 711).

Similarly, Katrina Rolley's analysis of lesbian couples who express an emotional or physical bond in public through dress, reiterates Corbin's points. Rolley argues that to dress alike is to raise comment and cause viewers to look again, to emphasize "both their special closeness and their difference from the rest of society" (Rolley 1992: 33). This system of public coupling identification goes beyond surface decoration, but is, as Rolley explains, "[T]he only way to make the mind visible ... through its physical embodiment" (Rolley 1992: 34). Thus, by wearing similar raccoon coats, VanDerZee's Harlem couple could inspire or disturb onlookers (Rolley 1992: 38) through an expression of black prowess, black wealth and black aesthetic power.

The joining of forces and the encouragement of respect across genders was under discussion amongst African-Americans from the mid-1920s. In 1925 Elise Johnson McDougald noted that amongst black male Harlemites there were "modern schools of thought [in a] wholesome attitude of fellowship and freedom towards women" (McDougald 1925: 691),[19] a situation she felt should be championed by young black women "and grasp the proffered comradeship with sincerity" (McDougald 1925: 691). One way of looking at the centrality of this black couple in similar raccoon coats, and their contested place in American society in 1932, can be seen as a continuation of the significance placed on the bond between black male and female relationships that dates back to slavery. Emily West has explained that there was a need for mixed gender slave couples to construct a space of "psychological distance" between themselves and their master (West 2004: 157).[20] West maintains this bonding was sought by the majority of slaves to survive and resist the brutal institution of slavery (West 2004: 1–13). This earlier example of black couples resonates in the intimate portrait of this couple and the poetics of their style that bristled with autonomy. The couple own this space—West 127th Street, Harlem—and to present the woman as the more visible fur-clad figure in the portrait, is to put into context some of the hopes for black women and men during this period of "New Negro" re-construction for:

she is courageously standing erect, developing within herself the moral strength to rise above and conquer false attitudes. She is maintaining her natural beauty and charm and improving her mind and opportunity. She is . . . radiating from Harlem a hope that is cherished by her sisters [and brothers] in less propitious circumstances throughout the land. The wind of the race's destiny stirs more briskly because of her striving.

McDOUGALD 1925: 691

Therefore this black American couple redefined the raccoon coat as "an expressive vehicle" (Olson and Goodnight 1994: 254), of African-Americanness. As a "material signifier" (Emberley 1998: 4–5) these similar-looking raccoon coats act as a yoke— the acknowledgement of cultural and racial connection—as well as a coupler to reinforce the interconnection and interdependence between the African-American men and women as a united front of difference as aesthetic power, thereby a political act.

The automobile featured in the photograph is a Cadillac V-16 two-passenger roadster convertible.[21] It was part of the first generation of "16s" of the 452 or 452A Series produced in 1930 and 1931 respectively. The model featured a rumble seat, known as a "dickey" in Britain, "golf-bag" doors and an enlarged windshield. Only 105 of this body style were produced making it an especially sought-after item at the time, although it was not the rarest of the V-16 styles. The couple's V-16 was not one of the so called "bread and butter" range which was defined, for example, by a styling code which began with the numbers "43" and a raised bonnet (Saunders 2005). The couple's V-16 belonged to a more prestigious price range that had a base price of $5,350 rising to $15,000. Undoubtedly, this car was destined for the wealthy "enjoying the utmost which can be attained in exclusiveness and desirability" (The Cadillac Database 2005: 3). Such luxury embedded in the styling of an automobile at a time of severe financial instability in the USA, had conflicting effects on its citizens. In 1930, the Cadillac V-16 was seen as one of America's powerful cars. Its proficiency extended beyond its speed and mileage performance on the road. The sleek streamlined design was attractive to the stars of Hollywood. In 1931, Douglas Fairbanks Jnr purchased a town car version, and in the same year screen goddess Jean Harlow invested in a Cabriolet (Burness 1970: 30–2). Yet historian James J. Flink viewed the V-16 as a "lesser luxury car," and the luxury car culture as a whole in less glorious terms: "the popular prestige attached in the prosperous twenties to ownership of a unique [car] . . . turned to aspersions in hard times: affluent owners were stoned while driving past breadlines" (Flink 1988: 218). It is difficult to know if such angry reactions were expressed by black Harlemites towards VanDerZee's couple. Yet the dominant feature of the V-16 positioned across the width of the photograph could be read as a constructed critique on the complex relationship black Americans had with automobile companies during the first half of the twentieth century.

In *Driving While Black* (2001), Paul Gilroy suggests that the study of American car culture can be a means of viewing the African-American action against "the indignities of white supremacy" as literally the "movement towards justice" (Gilroy

2001: 100). He recounts that with the introduction of the motorcar to the American public, some companies stipulated that their automobiles should not be sold to black Americans, regardless of their wealth (Gilroy 2001: 93). By the late 1920s these attitudes had changed. According to "corporate legend" the Cadillac was saved from economic demise during the Depression due to the passion wealthy black Americans had for this make of automobile (Gilroy 2001: 97).[22] Two items in *Apex News* illustrate this. The April and June 1929 editions of the paper celebrated the joys of motoring. The owner of *Apex News*, Madame Sara Spencer Washington, was photographed wearing a fur coat, perched on the side of a car bonnet of a convertible roadster, alongside three friends and colleagues, one of whom, Archie J. Morgan, sales manager of the Apex company, is wearing what appears to be a double breasted raccoon fur coat. The caption of the photograph reads: "SPRING MOTORING is quite delightful, especially on beautiful sunny days that has blest New York and Atlantic City very recently" (*Apex News* April 1929: 3). Two months later, *Apex News* reiterated the "delightful vogue" of motoring showing another party of four featured in this pursuit alongside the statement that "the LaSalle roadster supplies a lot of pleasure over the Jersey roads" (*Apex News* June 1929: 16). For Beryl Gilroy "the poetics of transit," the unadulterated pleasure to enjoy "redefined movement and extended sensory experience" was of particular social and cultural significance for black Americans during this period, as it helped to sooth "the particular responses of African-Americans whose histories of confinement and coerced labor must have given them additional receptivity of the pleasures of auto-autonomy as a means of escape, transcendence and perhaps even resistance" (Gilroy 2001: 84). Indeed, for Beryl Gilroy, the ownership of a car by a black person at this time was "a provocative emblem of wealth and status ... [and] one significant means to measure the distance travelled toward political freedoms and public respect" (Gilroy 2001: 94).

In the context of the couple photographed with their Cadillac V-16 roadster convertible, this is writ large. The unapologetic expansive display of the gleaming automobile undermined all the tenets of racial segregation. Like the raccoon coat, this was another high-profile item of white modernity designed originally and primarily for a white clientele. VanDerZee's photographic counter-narrative on this declares the car as being part, and a symbol, of an "alternative modernity" (Gaonkar 2001: 1), a specifically African-American modernity that clearly questioned the present position of black Americans through the "aesthetics of the self" to examine self-exploration and self-realization in Harlem during the Depression. Here in the "life-world" of this couple, defined by their luxurious items of raccoon fur coat and Cadillac V-16 automobile, they "command attention as an autonomous domain of cultural practice" (Gaonkar 2001: 4).

The amalgamation of luxurious cultural objects posed decorously against the backdrop of Harlem's distinctive Brownstone buildings, marked a significant moment of aesthetic articulation for the new black American woman and man.

VanDerZee's portrait reflects and deflects the myths and realities associated with being black in Harlem, which is also about being black in America. In their use of high fashion items to attain self-realization, this couple transgressed the boundaries that defined what the fashionable black American body should be, which should not be on a par with their white counterpart. It is a means of comprehending how black urbanites connected with their space within a black city, within a white country. To reference Filip de Boeck, Harlem and Harlemites "cannot be understood without reflecting upon reflection, upon reflecting realities, mirrors, images, imitation, imagination and (self)representation" (de Boeck 2004: 17). For de Boeck, colonialism is one level of reflection, I would add that the legacies of slavery and segregation are other levels of reflection when one considers the social and spatial position of this couple, as segregated, second-class citizens in their homeland.

I suggest that VanDerZee channelled these layers of reflection through glamor. The *mise en scène* exudes beauty, performance, wealth, dynamism and leisure. It seduces the viewer to worship a perfected version of black life. The image is devoid of flaws, the streets are spotlessly clean, and the couple is faultless in their beauty. VanDerZee achieved the "special aura" of glamor (Wilson 2007: 104). In his language of portraiture, VanDerZee wanted to portray black people as being "a beautiful and informative representation of some portion of the world" (Trachtenberg 1981: 169). To attain this, to capture that "special aura" VanDerZee used "pre-visualisation": "I guess it was just a matter of not being satisfied with what the camera was doing. I wanted the camera to take what I thought should be there, too" (Mercer 2003: 14). I would argue, then, that this special aura, to borrow a contemporary term, is driven by attitude that was charged with the possibilities of black aesthetic power. Therefore *A Couple in Raccoon Coats, with a Cadillac, Taken on West 127th Street, Harlem, New York, 1932* is indeed a photographic portrait that:

> Suggests that the individual [and couple], whatever material context is involved, is given significance, and definition within an everyday world of codes and signifying registers of meaning. In that sense, and for all its limitations, the photographic portrait inscribes into its meaning precisely that play between internal and external worlds ... Above all, the great portrait photographs simultaneously declare identity as they probe the terms of definition.
>
> **CLARKE** 1997: 111

Captured in this moment was the possibility of a particular strand of glamor, black glamor, as cultural critique. The underlying tenets of glamor—knowledge, the forbidden, longing, admiration and aspiration (Wilson 2007: 95–104) helps to fuel, I suggest, the ideologies of the "New Negro." Subsequently, this couple is triumphant, which for me is at the heart of black glamor. As we know, being black in America has never been easy, but for this couple, and as we shall see with Malvin Gray

Johnson below, black aesthetics provided a means to ease the strain to express something new with, and about their bodies.

Malvin Gray Johnson

Self-portraiture is a rhetoric of the self ... [and a] self-portrait is *self-descriptive* because its discourse is auto-referential: the *persona* and events of the text reflect back to the self-portraitist, giving us a window into his or her life and personality.

SMALL 1996: 9

On October 24, 1934, in the same year that he painted *Self-portrait: Myself at Work,* Gray Johnson died. He was thirty-eight. This biographical detail adds autobiographical resonance to the self-portrait. This is further intensified by a moving image representation of Gray Johnson, of just under a minute, in the silent film *A Study of Negro Artists* produced by the Harmon Foundation, and released in 1936.[23] The film is a documentation of black male and female painters, sculptors and textile artists practicing in their studios or showing their work in displays. Harlem is not mentioned directly but through visual clues such as the street sign "Lenox Ave W. 135 Street" that precedes an exterior shot of the New York Public Library division of "Negro Literature, History and Prints" at 135th Street based in Harlem.[24] This is followed by a close-up shot of text on the importance of this institution. As this is a silent film, captions are used to introduce the section on each artist. "The Late Malvin Gray Johnson" is the title of his segment.

The film unintentionally provides close observation of Gray Johnson's styled body, mannerisms and painting practice in action. A seductive quality of film is its ability to make the viewer notice what is being shown, to make all aspects significant (Leslie 2013: 36). Gray Johnson is filmed in his studio that resembles an apartment. He is wearing a striped polo-neck sweater. It is of fine dark and light stripes in a lightweight knit that clings to Gray Johnson's slight frame. He wears the top tucked into the waist of his neat slim cut plain wool trousers. His hair is natural in texture. Gray Johnson's style works. It is modern. The casualness of Gray Johnson's style challenges the respected formality of menswear at the time. He has rejected menswear style conventions of a suit and tie as his contemporary male artists wear in the film. The look is also devoid of the associated ornamentation associated with the suit and tie ensemble. The stripes of the polo neck could be viewed as a form of decoration but are used here as definition of physique and presence, not as surplus comment. The only accessory he adds to his styled self is a pipe. One senses an undeniable air of freedom of expression, the freedom of being by Gray Johnson.

The film also shows Gray Johnson in movement. When he first appears in the documentary, he has an unlit pipe in his mouth. He crosses the screen to walk around the back of his easel to sit down in front of it. He then lights his pipe with a match and works on the oil painting *The Letter*.[25] The camera pans to the center of the screen to focus on the face and torso of the artist. From this position, the viewer can see Gray Johnson's *Self-portrait: Myself at Work*, which hangs on a wall behind him. While he paints, the artist simultaneously draws on his pipe; he then takes it out of his mouth to concentrate on his painting. This film of Gray Johnson at work ends with the artist placing examples of his work on an easel for the viewer to study.

To have these different forms of portraits of Gray Johnson, we see the idea of the man and artist tripled: his self-portrait depicts how he saw himself at a particular moment in his life; the staging of Gray Johnson at work and at ease in his studio on celluloid provides a "real" sense of Gray Johnson; and the painted representation of his self in his self-portrait that loomed visible within the cinematic "real" documentation. What we have here is a series of mirrors and reflections of how Gray Johnson saw himself and how others saw him.[26] Therefore, for Gray Johnson to present himself in two different forms of visual documentation whilst he painted and as a painting, wearing the same styled body ensemble of polo neck and trousers, is an umbilical tie between his sense of self and his practice, of *being* an artist in body and action. What marks these permutations of Gray Johnson is a sense of ease, emphasized by the casual air of his striped polo-neck sweater. This illustrates Michel Foucault's understanding of what a recurring feature means, it is "the arrow that crops up so often ... prescribes the direction that the gaze must follow" (Foucault 1983: 33). Additionally, these arrows point to "the intersection within the same medium, of representation by resemblance and representation by signs" (Foucault 1983: 33–4). The fact that Gray Johnson's self-portrait appears in a celluloid portrait of him, provides an extended space and device to see different facets of him at different moments of his documentation. How does such thinking contribute to what Gray Johnson was trying to portray about himself in *Self-portrait: Myself at Work?*

An alternative reading of *Self-portrait: Myself at Work*

In art historical studies of Gray Johnson's *Self-portrait: Myself at Work* his styled body is ignored. For example, Jacqueline Francis' reading of this work in "Trying To Do What Artists of All Races Do: Malvin Gray Johnson's Modernism" (2002) presents a treatise on masking and disguise, identity and performance. In this frame, Francis focused on the artist's inclusion of two masks positioned close to Gray Johnson's head and surmized that "the masks emblematize the richness of African culture available to African-Americans" (Francis 2002: 78). Francis extends the presence of the masks in the painting to Gray Johnson's face: "Johnson's heavy, mask-like countenance covers and disguises him, permitting the artist to proffer different and mutable identities to his audience" (Francis 2002: 78). For Francis, "there are few signs of the 'artist' and his milieu here" (Francis 2002: 78), due to the fact that what is absent from the portrait is Gray Johnson's studio, or signs of him in the act of painting.

This proposition connects with an understanding that it was a practice amongst black artists of the Harlem Renaissance to place African objects and/or motifs within their work "to indicate an awareness of their ethnicity" (Wardlaw 1990: 146). This was something that Alain Locke raised in the 1925 special issue the journal *Survey Graphic* on Harlem, in which he intimated the importance of "the Art of the Ancestors," African sculpture, as being of importance and possible influence on African-American artists and indicative that they have "inheritance" (Locke 1925: 673). Alvia J. Wardlaw sites Gray Johnson's *Self-portrait: Myself at Work* as an example of this and argues that, "By including in his self-portrait his completed work *Negro Masks* [1932], Johnson indicates that his self-image as a black artist is incomplete without the demonstration of his connection to African culture. In painting these masks, he paints himself" (Wardlaw 1990: 146).

Judith Wragg Chase does not agree. She believed Gray Johnson was not a committed adherent to representations of "the ancestral arts of Africa for inspiration" (1971: 113) but rather followed the path of freedom and experimentation to use art as emancipation to enable "a fresh search for values and ideas in the immediate surroundings" (1971: 115). Wragg Chase further argues that Gray Johnson's practice was in line with the aims of the Harlem Renaissance movement to engage in self-portraiture and self-expression, to revel in and reveal their own culture and overturn stereotyped representations into something contemporary—new definitions of black identities. Therefore, a definition of self-portraiture here is the production of a painting that depicts an individual's sense of self *and* self-portraiture as a biographical representation of a group, in this instance the painting of black America by black Americans. As Shearer West reminds us "all portraits represent ... the soul, character, or virtues of the sitter" (2004: 21). In terms of "self-fashion and self-representation," West sees the use of self-portraiture as a means "to enact roles that declare their aspirations" and express "key moments of a life" (2004: 173, 175). Therefore, Gray Johnson's *Self-portrait: Myself at Work* can be seen as auto/biographical—as an autobiographical presentation of a moment in the artists' life *and* as a contribution to the biography of black American culture and life, art and presence.

The masks do have significance. In *What's in a Mask* (1990), John Picton has outlined various literal and metaphorical meanings of whether a mask is worn or not. Although Picton mainly focuses on their use in Ebira, Nigeria, his thoughts are relevant here. Picton states that masks can be about translation, "dramatic intension," "presence" or "spirit" (1990: 185, 191, 193). That they are not about secrecy but "the source of energy" (1990: 193), and "for many people in a south-western Yoruba community, the efe mask ... serves to establish his [the performer's] everyday place within the community" (Picton 1990: 192). Picton makes reference to "the mask as part of a visual system that is independent of, perhaps alternative to the purposes of the masked performance ... There is, after all, no obvious reason why an artwork must articulate only one system of communication" (1990: 194). I suggest that the "dramatic intension" of the inclusion of the two masks in Gray Johnson's self-portrait was about connection, between Gray Johnson and the masks and their symbolism of another aspect of his descendancy from enslaved Africans; the importance of the masks in the development of modern art practice as a source of reference for Western artists; and as clue in the self-portrait's narrative for the viewer's, simultaneously supports the presence of Gray Johnson's "everyday place in his community" as an artist and African-American. Together this contributed to the aesthetics of presence of Gray Johnson *and* the cultural group he belonged to, African-Americans. But the masks are only one element of Gray Johnson's self-portrait.

In light of the above, Gray Johnson's *Self-portrait: Myself at Work* can be read from an alternative perspective. He lays himself open, which is signified in the broad expanse of his pose. The signs of the "artist" are visible in the autobiographical painted statement which places his self, the styled body of Gray Johnson, at the core of this visual self-writing. The African-American artist and art historian James A. Porter speculated about Gray Johnson's practice, that his portraits of black American male and female sitters "aim directly at the essence of the subject" (Porter 1943: 123), a trait, I suggest, he applied to himself in *Self-portrait: Myself at Work*. Additional support for this idea of Gray Johnson opening himself in the self-portrait is the subtitle of the piece—*Myself at Work*. The noun "myself" is used in apposition with I or me, for emphasis or clarification. "Myself" also means in my own person, for my part, my own very self, and when used reflexively, it means "me" (*Oxford English Dictionary*). Therefore "myself" conjoins "me" and "self." If one considers that "the self-portrait is a kind of metempsychosis, a topography of the individual mind" (Small 1996: 26), then I suggest that in addition to the observations made by Francis and Wardlaw, Gray Johnson was also drawing attention to his styled body in his portrait. I believe that *Self-portrait: Myself at Work* was affirmation of Gray Johnson's declaration of his existence as an individual *and* an artist. Therefore it is a legitimate exercise to focus on and explore the meaning of Gray Johnson's styled body in his self-portrait.

The coverage of Gray Johnson's torso in a terracotta colored polo-neck with numerous horizontal stripes, gives his upper body breadth and strength. This is echoed in his direct gaze at the viewer from the canvas. Gray Johnson holds a hat in one hand, but it is difficult to see what style of hat it is. His dark trousers support the casual tone of what I view as Gray Johnson's bohemian style, as every aspect of the self-portrait resonates the "myth of bohemia" (Wilson 2000: 3), notably his embrace of hybridity (Wilson 2000: 153). James Smethurst has recorded that bohemia was a form of "new poetry" of African-American expressive culture sought by black artists and intellectuals. It was a "countercultural break from the mainstream" that was part of a broader American renaissance of bohemia (Smethurst 2011: 23). So, as the striped polo-neck sweater is the most identifiable garment in his self-portrait, then one needs to address what cultural place did the polo-neck sweater have in the American male wardrobe, regardless of "race" and ethnicity, during the first half of the 1930s. Equally, what contribution did the polo-neck sweater make to the meaning of Gray Johnson's style narrative portrayed in his self-portrait and his sense of self at this point in his life?

That sweater

The various designs of the knitted sweater were a mark of modernity in the early decades of the twentieth century. By the early 1930s, the garment had an overwhelming impact on the sartorial rules of American society, which led *American Vogue* to call the sweater "a scheming little climber that has wangled its way into practically every society, until, in this year 1931, you see sweaters everywhere during the daylight hours—golfing, yes; lunching, yes; sitting about, yes … The sweater has crushed even into later afternoon society" (*American Vogue* March 1931: 65). In 1932, the American journal *Men's Wear* reported the increased interest in the turtleneck, as the polo-neck sweater is known in North America. It encouraged the wearing of this item as being suitable for the country riding set, university undergraduates and film stars (*Men's Wear* July 1932: 43). The periodical reported that there had been a concerted push to promote the garment through major window displays in retail outlets such as Eugene Jacobs of Scranton, Pennsylvania, and Macy's department store in New York (*Men's Wear* November 1932: 62–3).

According to Richard Martin and Harold Koda, the collegiate connection with the turtleneck, like the raccoon coat, began in the early twentieth century. Clemente believes the use of the sweater by the collegiate began in the late nineteenth century. The turtleneck was worn extensively by male students, notably in the form of the "letter sweater," and like the raccoon coat, it "denoted initiation and acceptance as well as individual accomplishment in a sport" (Martin and Koda 1989: 138). Clemente states that "[A]t Princeton, the letterman's sweater took various forms, ranging from the turtleneck to a boat-necked, ribbed cable-knit" (Clemente 2014: 122) which was adopted by women and men on and off the campus as part of the emergent American casual style which was marked by the sweater craze of the World War I era and continued on through the decades. A collegiate trend that fused with the high fashion jersey knits championed by Parisian designers such as Coco Chanel and Jean Patou. This was partly due to its practicality, but also its sense of freedom (Clement 2014: 122–6). This combination of fashion knitwear, ease and leisure was inherent in the emergence of resort wear. Gray Johnson's turtleneck sweater has design traits akin to the narrow and wide "novelty stripes" of the 1930s lightweight polo resort shirt. This genre of garment contributed to a change of direction in resort wear in the United States. Contemporary fashion observers viewed its popularity amongst America's fashionable male plutocrats as a sign of renewed financial vigor following the economic crisis: "Men put on clothes to fit their whims, almost always reflecting ease and comfort" (*Men's Wear* March 1934: 32).

The sport-collegiate-sweater relationship was still present in the early 1930s. For example, in 1933, under the heading "Some Styles You Should be Selling Right Now," *Men's Wear* stated that the turtleneck was a key accessory of the season, and provided evidence in a photograph of a male alumnus photographed wearing a "yellow turtleneck sweater—a sensible garment for such an occasion" at a Yale-Princeton football game (*Men's Wear* December 1933: 21).[27] The presence of this garment at such a prestigious sporting event, *Men's Wear* confirmed that the turtleneck was a good retail buy.

Gray Johnson, then, embraced the growing trend of casual style in America. The sweater, in all its guises, was a definitive marker of that trend. Clement posits that the casual style movement and the wearing of the sweater were helped by the Depression due to the economic practicality of the sweater (Clement 2014: 125). Ultimately it is the inherent quality of the sweater as a symbol of style liberation and as the mark of an individualist (Clement 2014: 2–10) that helps to gain a better understanding of the style narrative of Gray Johnson and its meaning as he re-presented him self in *Self-portrait: Myself at Work*.

Stripes: a trope of meaning

A defining feature of Gray Johnson's sweater is its stripes. The linear pattern has been worn by a host of individuals and cultural groups: from sailors to Edwardian bathers, prisoners to Chanel and Pablo Picasso in their use of the working class striped Breton top. These references are indicative of the contradictory cultural meanings of the stripe. From a positive perspective, the stripe can be about modernity, freedom and the pursuit of happiness through leisure. Alternatively, it is a mark of exclusion through, for example, the possession of or lack of wealth, the label of confinement, "humiliation" and a signifier of difference as in the striped "pyjama" uniform assigned to prisoners incarcerated in Nazi concentration camps in World War II (Pastoureau 2001: 58; Ash 2010: 26). The latter graphic form of categorization marked the wearer as removed from their definition of "normality" into a new sense of everyday life (Highmore 2011: 1–4) one of dehumanization. These elements of positive and negative values of stripes can be invested in one object. For example, the ex-enslaved black American seaman Clement l'On, gave a present to those who had released him from slavery. This was a child's striped blue and white country cloth suit from Liberia[28] (Wragg Chase 1971: 63). These conflicting "good" and "bad" references of the stripe in style-fashion-dress is a pattern that "makes disorder" (Pastoureau 2001: 91) and order. Pastoureau states that the stripe simultaneously conceals and reveals, as well as being "the substance, the finite and the infinite, the part and the whole" (Pastoureau 2001: 91). The stripe, then, marks ideals. And of course a stripe is a line.

Within art practice the expression of the line as force and the strength of the line has been a conscientious pursuit. A line can also trace "an enduring mark let in or on a solid surface by a continuous movement" (Ingold 2010: 15), a connecting system "to strengthen, to reinforce, fortify" (*OED*).

Gray Johnson's rendition of himself in *Self-portrait: Myself at Work* in a striped polo-neck jumper is an autobiographical statement that locks his body, the jumper and his sense of self in an image that projects clarity of consciousness of who he is. Bearing in mind the possible meaning of the stripe, then, the central feature of the polo-neck sweater with its series of lines helps to channel this. Therefore, the striped polo-neck jumper in this self-portrait is "the emblematic function" (Pastoureau 2003: 79) of marking his Harlem Renaissance ideals. In my reading of the striped polo-necked clad upper body of Gray Johnson, it shoots out arrows (Foucault 1988: 83) of resistance to "enclosure within systems" (Pastoureau 2001: 90–1). In addition to defining Gray Johnson as bohemian above, I also view him as an avant-garde artist. Avant-gardism has been defined as an attitude of individuals who engage in "the cult of originality" that has "a belief in progress through exploration of the possible" and its "character" has partly been developed through "borrowing ideas and inspiration" from various sources to create something new (Henderson 1971: 10–13). Gray Johnson positioned himself as an artist who contested the place of black people in America, in his desire for a new cultural and social regime in the USA; a regime Gray Johnson earnestly sought through his practice as an artist, and his affiliation with the Harlem Renaissance Movement.

Therefore, Gray Johnson's *Self-portrait: Myself at Work* is an act of emphasis. If a stripe can also be an underline (*OED*) then, Gray Johnson's portrayal of himself enveloped in the stripes of the casual and fashionable polo neck, marks and confirms the presence of his body. One could say the stripes of his polo-neck sweater in a painting, underlined his rightful presence as an African-American in the USA and his critical expressive self as an artist on this fact.

Malvin Gray Johnson: an underlined presence

Gray Johnson was a trained artist. He pursued this goal from 1912, at the age of sixteen, when he moved to Harlem from his birthplace of Greensboro, North Carolina.[29] The facilities to train professionally were not available to him in the black schools and colleges in Greensboro, nor were the white equivalent open to him. Kenneth G. Rodgers has maintained that the constant threat of racial violence, notoriously executed by the Klu Klux Klan, for example, was a further contributory factor to Gray Johnson's desire to migrate and study under less pressured external tension (Rodgers 2003: 17). Therefore, Gray Johnson was part of the historic migration to the North of America from the South. He lived and worked in Harlem for some twenty-three years until his death in 1934. From 1916, he studied art at the respected National Academy of Design on Amsterdam Avenue and 109th Street, New York. These were part-time classes. A break in his studies there was due to Gray Johnson serving in France during World War I as part of the 184th Brigade, 92nd Division. He resumed his studies at the Academy in 1923 and 1925. His tutors throughout his time at the institution included George Lawrence Nelson, Leon Kroll, Ivan Olinsky, Francis C. Jones and Charles C. Curran.[30]

As an artist resident in Harlem, Gray Johnson documented the urban landscape of this section of New York City—its people and architecture. His delicate drawing, *Strivers' Row* (1925), of the compact overlapping backs of houses that were connected by lines of washing, illustrated James Weldon Johnson's essay "The Making of Harlem" in *Harlem: Mecca of the New Negro,* the ground-breaking special edition of the journal, *Survey Graphic* (1925). This edition was edited by Alain Locke who co-ordinated a portrait of the steady, energetic cultural shifts in all aspects of Harlem life. The publication was effectively a manifesto of the Harlem Renaissance and the "New Negro Movement". The inclusion of Gray Johnson in this issue was recognition of his being part of them.

In terms of the development of Gray Johnson's art practice, the paintings *Swing Low Sweet Chariot* (1928–9) and *Roll, Jordan Roll* (1930) are considered to be two pivotal works. Here he expressed the so-called "Racial Art" and moved from a "naturalist palette" to expressionism, particularly in the latter work. He was also known for depicting "assured black genre subjects." A case in point is his 1934 portrait *Postman.* Here he captured the relaxed confidence of this Harlem dweller and worker, in the way the postman sits on a chair, draping his arm over the back of it. The visible elements of the postman's uniform—a regulated jacket and cap—does not drown the character of the man inside the uniform, he revels in it. What the postman propels from his slouched pose is that his uniformed self is only part of who he is, not the definition of him. In the summer of 1934, Gray Johnson shifted his interest and went to Virginia, in the South, to paint African-American rural life. Other influences on the artist were African art, as mentioned above, the painting philosophies of Paul Cezanne, Impressionism and the work of contemporary artists who exacted "individuality and freshness of view point" (Harmon Foundation 1935: 8). According to Porter, these interests loosened Gray Johnson from his academic training and invigorated "an out-pouring of spirit" (Harmon 1935: 8). With this wide range of references, Gray Johnson's work could not be pigeonholed as that of a "racial artist." His practice was to mix "black" and "white" references to express newness and critique on the legacy of history, black presence and lives in America, as Gray Johnson himself explained in *New York World* in 1930:

A noted American etcher [William Auerbach-Levy] has accused Negroes of imitating their white fellow-workers. No doubt this is true. Not so much from the standpoint that they imitate white artists of this or any other country in as much as they are trying to do what artists of all races do—follow the principles of fine arts technically. We are taught to use lines, forms and color, never being told to look at these things from a racial viewpoint.

The distinguished etcher admits most of these things himself, but says: "While few of the Negro artists used the subject of Negro life the approach is no different than that of the white painters." How can it be? We Americans of both races know and live the same life, except that the Negro encounters racial restrictions.

PORTER 1943: 94

It could be said of Gray Johnson's thinking, above, that he reflected Locke's idea of the "Intelligent Negro," who strived through various means to "know himself and be known for precisely what he is" (Locke 1925: 632).

Porter's obituary of Gray Johnson provides an insightful profile of the artist and the man. Two qualities stand out for Porter: Gray Johnson's position as a "sincere artist," and his "electric quality" (Harmon Foundation 1935: 7). The art historian felt these were debilitating traits to maintain for the modern artist, black or white, who wanted to practice their art and make their mark in contemporary New York. Porter later added that the dichotomy of black artists connected with the "New Negro Movement" was, "what exactly is their heritage—only Africa, or Africa and America" (Porter 1943: 103). *Self-portrait: Myself at Work* emitted the progressive development of the work of modern black American artists as a reflection of the diverse possibilities one could glean and blend. The inclusion of the informal attire of a striped polo-neck sweater that was worn by black and white men, in and outside of the college campus, alongside Gray Johnson's inclusion of African masks, signified his attempt at a definition of the heritage of being "African and American."

Therefore, one could say that *Self-portrait: Myself at Work* is an evocation of sanity (Phillips 2005). I suggest that Gray Johnson's depiction of himself in this self-portrait was to "temper the madness" of the modern city, his contemporary surroundings and racial inequalities faced by practicing black artists, to exact what sanity holds forth "promising the new life" (Phillips 2005: 20). This "new life" for Gray Johnson was the fusion of Africa and America, of modernity and home. With regard to artists and their evocation of sanity, Phillips believes that the artist who does not sacrifice their inner selves, their individuality, to fit in, is a figure of "true sanity" for "[T]rue Sanity transforms the work as it has to make room for the unique vision that each individual person contains inside them" (Phillips 2005: 30). Therefore through *Self-portrait: Myself at Work,* Gray Johnson presented his sincere self as he knew what he was and who knew what he was capable of artistically. This enhances the cool quality that Gray Johnson emits from this painting, and was confirmed in the Harlem Foundation film. bell hooks gives a definition of what she calls black male cool as "individual black males daring to self-define rather than be defined by others" (hooks 2004: 147). It was this quality in Gray Johnson's self-portrait that transfixed me on viewing it for the first time at the Hayward Gallery in 1997.

Malvin Gray Johnson: sincerely himself

It is the ways in which the New Negro artist moved through and from sites of fragmentation and disunity in the production and representation of self that self-portraiture receives its critical relevance and import.

SMALL 2001: 52

I proffer then, that in the production of *Self-portrait: Myself at Work*, Gray Johnson attempted to repair the disjuncture of the African-American self-promulgated in the modern era. The stripes of Gray Johnson's polo-neck sweater signify the unification of the fragmented identities engendered in the diasporic experience of being African-American "to embrace the fragmentation of self (doubling and splitting) which modernity seems to promote" (Gilroy 1993: 188). Rather than being a treatise on a conflicted sense of self, Gray Johnson embraced and collaged the telling of his self in his self-portrait. The projection of newness in *Self-portrait: Myself at Work* was to draw a line between the past and the future. Therefore, for me, the stripes of Gray Johnson's polo-neck sweater act as a segueing mechanism between the desires of the "New Negro" ideology and bohemianism, avant-gardism and the modernity of men's casual style during the first half of the 1930s. Gray Johnson's self-portrait is an example of "alternative modernities" that enable one "to think with a difference—a difference that would destabilise the Universalist idioms" (Gaonkar 2001: 14–15). So in 1934, in the midst of the Depression, here was an example of "the new black man" who "represents . . . new tropes of black masculinity that challenge the most negative stereotypes associated with black masculinity, but more importantly, counter stringently sanitized images of black masculinity" (2006: xx). Gray Johnson's self-portrait was an earnest endeavor by an individualist. Ultimately, he was being sincerely "myself."

Summary: take two portraits about Harlem

The subject of Harlem and its renaissance is vast. It is about the emergence of black modernity in the United States. It is about art and artists, literature, poetry, architecture, jazz, blues, cinema. It is about riches and poverty. It is about the intersections of black lives from different realms within and beyond America. Harlem is about a rhythmic momentum of change by black people in America in spite of the overwhelming categorization of being segregated citizens in the country they call home. To capture all of this in one chapter is not an easy task. The discussion of *A Couple in Harlem* and *Self-portrait: Myself at Work*, which I now view as part of Harlem's DNA, provide some semblance of Harlem's history of cultural intersections and aesthetics, newness, making and reconstruction. Powell sees all black portraiture as "transformative action" (2008: 20) as they are "the products of specific moments and cultural circumstances" and a pursuit of freedom, whether consciously sought or not (Powell 2008: 76). I would add to this that portraits are also a form of self-telling, a form of auto/biography as a "presentation of frozen moments" of a life "rather than ... reflections of it" (West 2004: 180) which is what I have outlined here. Additionally, for Powell, portraits are "cultural benchmarks" (Powell 2008: 17) that portray the real and imagined past/future impact of lives lived and their impact on lives to come, and therefore project the aesthetic of presence. The sign of existence that, in the spirit of the legacy of the Harlem and its renaissance, a presence that contributes to future histories, culture and narratives, as in Geoff Dyer's thinking in, *The Ongoing Moment* (2005). In this treatise, Dyer believes that photography is confirmation of lives lived rather than a "capacity to preserve or bring back the dead" (Dyer 2005: 253). I would extend this to all forms of portraiture, and in the examples discussed here, they suggest that Harlem and its renaissance had a significant pulse during the interwar years of an alternative modernity and aesthetic power, and that this aspect of "Harlem remains" (Massood 2013: 1). Paula J. Massood has argued that there is a nostalgia for the Harlem that was, the culture that made it Harlem that contributes to an abiding definition of Harlem in the twenty-first century (Massood 2013: 1–2).

I first had experience of this legacy whilst conducting research at the Schomburg Center for Research in Black Culture and my return to the apartment of Carol Blank, both in Harlem. I witnessed a living portrait of Harlem aesthetics that radiated the hypnotic draw that reached back to the period of Harlem's history discussed here:

Friday 17th September 1999: About 6.30 p.m. Friday evening and Harlem is jumping. It is home time or out time and the action appears to be along 125th Street/Martin Luther King Jr. Boulevard and across Malcolm X Boulevard/ Lenox Avenue, the intersection there. Three black guys are standing in the middle of Malcolm X Boulevard. They are together but seem to be doing their own thing. The one in the middle fascinates me. He is in a navy loose shirt with a large white floral design as worn by Frank Sinatra in the film *From Here to Eternity*. Gargantuan denim shorts swing low on his hips, stopping mid-calf. Caterpillar boots and white socks. He has big mother ear phones on and listening to something hot, because he can't stop dancing—this does not distract him from communicating verbally with his mate on the right, whose hat, loose short sleeved cream top with sporadic navy stripes and baggy navy trousers put him in the Happy Monday camp rather than booyah. The last of the trio did not get a look in, the other two were just too mesmerising.

TULLOCH 1999[31]

There on the intersection of 125th Street/Martin Luther King Jr. Boulevard and Malcolm X Boulevard/Lenox Avenue was a meeting of past, present and future, myth and memory, icons and performance. The past imposes itself on Harlem from the exteriors and interiors of its homes, studios and businesses, the bricks and mortar of its buildings, the tarmac of its avenues and streets, the performance of style and Harlem aesthetics by its inhabitants that has precedence in the historical portraits of VanDerZee's *A Couple in Harlem* and Gray Johnson's *Self-portrait: Myself at Work*. This is not nostalgia. This is recognition of a moment of black American history that has made its artistic and aesthetic mark.

3 "ALL OF ME": BILLIE HOLIDAY

Music is our witness, and our ally. The beat is the confession which recognises changes and conquers time. Then, history becomes a garment we can wear and share, and not a cloak in which to hide; and time becomes a friend.

JAMES BALDWIN 2011, 1979: 153[1]

Billy Holiday's metier was modernity. She crafted her physical identity into an individualized blend of avant-garde ideology and a range of style-fashion-dress from the beginning of her jazz career in 1933 to her death in 1959. This powerful combination of black music and black style-fashion-dress performed by the African-American female cultural icon Billie Holiday, is exemplary of James Baldwin's statement above. Her musical identity was predicated on innovation which changed irrevocably the relationship between the singing voice and the lyrics of a song, and the emotion elicited by such a performance. The debut of her political identity came with the performance and recording of the protest song *Strange Fruit* in 1939, some twenty years before protest songs became par for the course of political activism. The historical potency of the song, with its graphic imagery of the lynching of black people in the USA, lay partly in the public acceptance of the record by black and white listeners at a time when such horrific, racist targets by specific white Americans, particularly in the south, was still viewed as a birth right.[2] The record's notoriety as a banned item unfit for the listening public of the BBC and many radio stations in America (Margolick 2000: 92–3),[3] augmented the song's sting in the cultural consciousness of white society.

To consider Billie Holiday as a reputable figure of visual and political modernity, from the vantage point of her styled body, and being one of the supreme musical innovators within a distinct counterculture of modernity—black music (Gilroy 1993: 36) is an aspect not generally covered by her biographers and critics. Her

FIGURE 3.1 Billie Holiday poses with band members Ben Webster, and Johnny Russell, New York, 1935. Photo: JP Jazz Archive/Getty Images.

hedonistic decline is the usual narrative. I argue that Billie Holiday used style and music to transform her self into a prism of modernity that facilitates a better understanding of "the panoply of ... the structure and functions of the acts and feelings of the emotional life" (Harré 1997: 112). Therefore this chapter considers Billie Holiday as a black female dandy mediated through garments, accessories and beauty regimes generally associated with hightened femininity.[4]

The chapter refers to tangible material where a sense of Billie Holiday, as she presented her sense of self, can be found as in the photographs and film footage, her records and autobiography (figure 3.1). Each has flaws. In the photographs, for example, they provide only a "split second" (Richard Dyer 1998: xi). Yet this speck of time of the photograph, Dyer notes, encourages the viewer to imagine what was being said, to consider what was going on before and after the shot was taken (Dyer 1998: xi–xii), whilst her autobiography has provoked divided views since its publication in 1956. Yet these documents where Billie Holiday is actually present, are fundamental resources to consider her style narratives.

Lady Sings the Blues: a sincere self

Billie Holiday's autobiography, *Lady Sings the Blues*, which was produced with William Dufty, is generally seen as the revision of a life riddled with half-truths, omissions and elaborations (Clarke 1995: 295–9; Keepnews 1997: 110–114). Others believe it to be a credible document of Billie Holiday's life. David Widgery intimates that it is a document of racial resistance and womanist activity: "one of the most political books ever written by a musician, which insists on going beyond the clichés of jazz tragedy to the economics of the music business and the pressure of Jim Crow" (1989: 83). Stuart Nicholson, when he embarked on his biography of Billie Holiday, believed that the book was a misleading document, but on conducting his own primary research, came to realize that it is factually correct on "major episodes of her life" (Nicolson 1995: 6). From a feminist perspective, Angela Davis views *Lady Sings the Blues* as an authentic personal document. For Davis, when the book is considered alongside Billie Holiday's musical oeuvre, then one gains a feminist "understanding [of] the social contradictions" which she argues are particularly useful for African-American women (1998: 161–97). Davis contends that Billie Holiday achieved this through an "aesthetic dimension that fundamentally historicizes and collectivizes . . . Billie Holiday's work represents a symbiosis, drawing from and contributing to an African-American social and musical history in which women's political agency is nurtured by, and in turn nurtures, aesthetic agency" (Davis 1998: 165).

I am in agreement with Nicholson, Widgery and Davis, and this case study extends their generous reading of *Lady Sings the Blues*. For me, the text is a "sincere" presentation within the context of Lionel Trilling's definition of sincerity. For Trilling sincerity is "the genuine feeling" an individual expresses in an autobiography, the way that an individual wishes to present themselves to the public. Trilling sees this as a presentation of the self "to our community," and the community only feels this presentation is "sincere when we play the role of being ourselves, we sincerely act the part of the sincere person, with the result that a judgment may be passed upon our sincerity" (Trilling 1972: 11, 25, 119). Billie Holiday created a dynamic individuality through her persona as a jazz star using style-fashion-dress, on and off the stage, to harness her cultural role. Individuality and persona are inherent to the semantics of sincerity, and is no more evident, according to Trilling, than in the writing of an autobiography. Through this system of public declaration of what the author of an autobiography believes they have become, then that individuality is ratified (Trilling 1972: 24–5). Billie Holiday saw herself as a "hip kitty" (Holiday 1993: 23):[5] a fashionably sophisticated individual, who informed the persona she created as a jazz singer, and her particular aesthetic engagement with, and articulation of, the culture that encompassed Billie Holiday. Therefore, to unpack this aspect of the jazz artist as a defining feature of who Billie Holiday was, I argue, that *Lady Sings the Blues* is an evocation to the suggestion that Billie Holiday was a female dandy, a central feature of her sincere self.

Billie Holiday: a female dandy

There has been a growing acceptance of this prodigy, women who seek an individualized style that is in keeping with their pursuit of modernity in every aspect of their lives.[6] Shane White and Graham White have identified the presence of the African-American dandizette during the eighteenth and nineteenth century, whilst Susan Fillin-Yeh's anthology *Dandies* maps out new ways of thinking about dandies and identifies different male and female ethnic groups that extend the geographical positioning of the dandy beyond Europe and America since the eighteenth century as being central to an expanded discussion of dandyism. Yet there are no black female dandies in this latter study. A definition of the female dandy is not simply about women who borrow forms and motifs from masculine dress as part of their wardrobe to empower themselves in the public space for the reciprocal action of the gaze. Women can dress in feminine attire and still attain the characteristics of the dandy: "All of these women break into new territory, and their clothing, chosen with care and worn with bravura and panache, is very necessary equipment for their new adventures. Even in adversity" (Fillin-Yeh 2001: 22). Monica L. Miller says that W.E.B. Du Bois, one of Africa-America's leading intellectuals and author of *The Souls of Black Folks* (1903), created the female dandy Sara Andrews in his 1928 novel *Dark Princess*. Miller sees Sara's version of the female dandy as a financially self-reliant, working woman who came from a poor background, whose dandyism "extend[s] beyond her attention to surfaces and her ability to disguise politics as a game in which she always gains the advantage" (Miller 2009: 151). Miller sees the failing of Sara's female dandy was that she did not take advantage of the political possibilities of "the work beauty can do" which in reality her creator, Du Bois, believed in (Miller 2009: 153). Thus beauty, in all its guises, can be a powerful critical allay. An area of interest in this chapter.

Billie Holiday and French fashion designer Coco Chanel share traits of what social and personal traits can inform a female dandy (Evans & Thornton 1989: Steele 1992: 119; Garelick 2001: 35–53, de la Haye 2011). Both came from socially deprived backgrounds and radically adjusted their social positions through a redrafting of their personalities, bodies and careers into a new persona that was suffused with the emotion of being their new selves. For Billie Holiday and Chanel the propulsory factors were modernity and originality. Billie Holiday's edge on her version of dandyism was informed by music and ethnicity which allowed her to weave emotion into her work to enunciate her identity as being black and a woman, a process that inevitably meant that this self-assessment was a cyclical process in the development of her identity and her musical oeuvre. This, in turn, enabled the singer to cultivate the power of self-presentation to subvert existing social forms in an attempt to question cultural "truths."[7]

Billie Holiday: a collage in the making

The feature of Billy Holiday's life that is of concern in this chapter is the aesthetic discourse of the clothing and accessories she wore, the hairstyles and beauty regimes she employed, as strategic agencies with which she extrapolated the emotional intensity of her life—the pleasure and pain of being black in America. To embark on such a study is to enter a fractured composition of who Billie Holiday was and is. She is unquestionably a cultural icon where the idea of her is a blend of an emotionally intense voice; the protest song *Strange Fruit*; her love songs; Lady Day with the gardenia corsage; avant-garde chic with sleeked back pony-tail hairstyle; red lipstick; heavily pencilled eyebrows; clips from songs and lyrics; biographical and critical texts; record sleeves and promotional portraits; photographs of Billie at work and at rest; exquisite evening gowns; fur coats; drugs; street language; television performances; the glimpse of a shoe; posters and playbills. When and where these elements actually fit into her life is often confused, as over time they have been re-positioned and meshed together by her various biographers and reviewers. Effectively what the public has is a collage of Billie Holiday constructed out of key issues and objects associated with her life.

Like jazz, collage was a modernist art form that "makes strange" by gluing together, in an improvised manner, myriad material into new combinations in an "attempt to map some previously inarticulated interior truth" (Douglas 2011: 7). Jazz and collage have the ability to dispense with hierarchy and express "a polyvisual network of images" (Archer-Straw 2000: 109). But collage is also a concept (Brindley 2011: 3). Such thinking supports my decision to write the style narrative of Billie Holiday as a montage through the framework of collage (Brindley 2011: 3), as a collage brings with it political and subversive capital to critical thinking and narrative studies (Douglas 2011: 21). Rachel Farebrother argues that collage is often "a generalized stance of position" (Farebrother 2009: 8–9). Whilst Kobena Mercer situates the concept of collage as an essential element of black culture, black identity constructions and re-presentations of the diasporic experience: "the formal dynamics of collage as especially relevant to the hyphenated character of diaspora identities historically shaped by the unequal interaction of African and European elements" (Mercer 2005: 126).

The limited space of this chapter can only accommodate a few focused studies of Billie Holiday's rich style narratives—the change of her name from Eleanora Harris to Billie Holiday, the performance of the song *Strange Fruit*, her gardenia corsage and her wearing of an exquisitely cut suit, a pair of shoes, her trademark pony-tail hairstyle and twinset knitwear. I have chosen these because they are examples that mark a significant moment in different aspects of her life: her jazz career, her health and of course her style narratives. Sometimes, as in the study of a pair of Billie Holiday's shoes, these elements are combined. My collaged portrait of the jazz artisit is not the telling of an "interior truth," rather, it is to express a sincere sense of the artist. Indeed, the essence of a collage is a composition that comprises clues that are integrated into the work to inform an alternative understanding of the subject. To do this through specific items of clothing, hairstyles and accessories, readers are asked to engage with another technique of collage "the double take, that crucial instant of recognitioin when we realize that a collage is at once a collection of disparate parts and integrated whole" (Farebrother 2009: 8).

As mentioned earlier, in the public collage of Billie Holiday what is tangible are her recordings, photographs, autobiography and to some extent the myth that is Billie Holiday. As Roland Barthes has often been quoted, myth is a representation which, in articulating one set of meanings, silences possible alternatives (Barthes 1993: 109–11).[8] Billie Holiday's myth was formed partly from the eloquence of her singing, her intelligent interpretation of lyrics, and as the consummate jazz artist who worked as part of an equally consummate musical team to create outstanding, often profound, music. Her singing style was modern due to "her ability to reset notes so as to give a phrase completely new musical meaning ... added a conception exclusively her own" (*The Playbill* 1948: 22), and her image contributed to that myth. Photographs of Billie Holiday show different components of her life: her development from a young singer into a major recording star dressed in evening gowns or day wear. These images encapsulate the glamor and subterranean activity that influenced her personal style during and outside of her performances. The majority of the photographs give the impression that Billie Holiday was enjoying the best in life, of having a ball. Essentially, the iconic image of Billie Holiday is a *tableau-objet*: "a built-up, constructed object or entity with a separate life of its own, not echoing or imitating the external world, but re-creating it in an independent way" (Golding 1991: 63).

To consider the aesthetic dimensions of Billie Holiday a balance needs to be reached between the components of her self-construction including the pervasive "dark" stains of drugs and racism, with the self-defining agencies of dandyism that turned her styled body into the "New Black Woman." This composite is discussed within the spectre of modernity Billie Holiday enjoyed, which to an extent placed her as an outsider of Western ideas of what constitutes the feminine ideal, as she consciously ignored in order to create the life she desired.[9] Therefore this chapter reassesses, chronologically, familiar fragments of the Billie Holiday collage. It positions her styled body as a catalyst for her self creation into Billie Holiday, the jazz artist. Such an approach adds materiality to the collage that *is* Billie Holiday and lends a higher degree of certitude. One such confirmation was the considered construction of Billie Holiday by her former self Eleanora Harris.

From Eleanora Harris to Billie Holiday: re-naming and self-creation

[A] change of name will change the way other people regard you and even the way you look at yourself. As in magic, names have the power of metamorphosis.

ASHLEY 1989: 61

"Elinore" Harris was born on April 7, 1915 in Philadelphia to Sarah "Sadie" Harris. "Elinore Harris" was the name Sadie Harris entered on her daughter's birth certificate,[10] although in her autobiography Billie Holiday uses the spelling "Eleanora" (Holiday 1992: 14). Billie Holiday stated that her father was Clarence Holiday (Holiday 1992: 5), which her mother always maintained and Holiday did not deny (Clarke 1995: 11). But on Billie Holiday's birth certificate Frank "DeViese" was entered as her father (Nicholson 1995: 18), Eleanora Harris changed her name to Billie Holiday in about 1930 whilst playing at the Harlem night spot, The Nest. Firstly she changed her surname to Halliday, a version of her father's surname, but she eventually adopted what she believed to be her rightful paternal name Holiday. Her new Christian name came from a number of possible sources. The artist said she was inspired by the actress Billie Dove (Holiday 1992: 13–14), but she also had a close friendship with a one-time singing companion, Billie Haywood. Her father, Clarence, allegedly called her Bill as a child "because I was such a young tomboy" (Holiday 1992: 14). In choosing her own masculine Christian name, Billie Holiday broke away from her past of poverty and abuse, as well as a feminine past as the name Eleanora suggests, that was tied to antiquity and fixed gender roles.

In North America, to change one's name was part of "the American way" to cement one's identity in a land that was built on immigration and complex identities (Ashley 1989: 58). The replacement of her birth name with Billie Holiday was indicative of the renewal of self in progress, which provided the space where Eleanora Harris could present herself afresh to the jazz world: "A change in name indicates a decisive change in a person's life . . . to indicate a radical renewal which he [she] undergoes" (Ware 1974: 20)—a metamorphosis. Consequently, in the case of Billie Holiday, the shift from her "authentic self"—Eleanora Harris, to her "sincere self"—through renaming, posits an indication of a desire for a new direction—the persona that is Billie Holiday. This shift is an expression of Helen Harris Perlman's thoughts on "the merger between the vital social and cultural role of a person that is their mind, body, feelings and the effects of others" (Perlman 1968: 4). The use of her sincere name "Billie Holiday" throughout this chapter imprints the significance of her name change that provided an anchor for the uniqueness of her persona to the styled, the sincere self that Billie Holiday constructed during her jazz career that underpins the definition of Billie Holiday as a female dandy.

The development of Holiday's music career and the richness of her wardrobe assists in an understanding of the creation of the persona that is Billie Holiday. "Billie Holiday" the well-respected jazz recording artist who could transfix an audience and move them emotionally through her individualized interpretation of songs, partially eroded Eleanora Harris, the illegitimate poor daughter of Sadie Harris and Clarence Holiday, the one-time call girl, a profession that enabled her "to buy a few nice things I'd always wanted—my first honest-to-God silk dress and a pair of spike-heeled ten-dollar patent-leather pumps" (Holiday 1992: 24). Singing and the jazz world provided her with a new space to be, to strive for originality and individuality through creativity. Her marginalization as an African-American fired the courage to engage that creativity. This is in keeping with the ideology of dandyism which frees the spirit of its practitioners from the shackles of marginalization to reconstruct oneself on emancipated terms. For Billie Holiday these qualities enabled the appreciation of one's own existence, to make the individual into one that has a fulfilled life. A paramount issue for Billie Holiday was to create her own reality through individualization: "No two people on earth are alike and it's got to be that way in music or it isn't music . . . You can't even be like you once were yourself, let alone like somebody else" (Holiday 1992: 48). Therefore, Billie Holiday trod along the same lines as male and female dandies before her who immersed themselves in the re-invention and commodification of their bodies and persona to create "a new narrative of self" (Garelick 2001: 53) which contributed to the construction of the sincere self as referred to above. This is the vital role an individual contributes to society. This new guise requires an individual to display renewed attitudes in order to attain a satisfying idea of one's self. Thus Billie Holiday's persona was informed by a "subjective experience focusing on self-exploration leading to self-definition" (Maio 1995: 5). She reiterated C.G. Jung's belief that all sides of a person need to be incorporated into the new persona, as an individual's personality is collective (Jung 1917: 466).

It was the considered intention, then, of Eleanora Harris to persuade her potential audience and fans that she was Billie Holiday. Through the subjectivity of being Billie Holiday she constructed and projected another dimension of herself and thus took on the role of creator and being concurrently. The creation of Billie Holiday for her night-time performances and street life was a testament of personal renewal engineered as a "true" presentation of her sincere self. This was achieved through what Susan Kaiser describes as "The spirit of . . . style, truth and subjectivity . . . the process of 'minding appearances . . . an individual can only offer truth claims that must in turn be socially negotiated. In this sense, truth resembles appearance style'" (Kaiser 2001: 79). Kaiser urges that this framework should be incorporated into the study of style and its relationship with the body and the psyche of individuals. By doing so subjectivity and inter-subjectivity, style-fashion-dress, truth and knowledge are intertwined and work on both an individual and collective level. Style-fashion-dress, sincerity and subjectivity meld in the emotional tour de force of Billie Holiday's early performances of the Abel Meerepol's poem *Strange Fruit*, a moment when Billie Holiday was her work.

Strange Fruit: a song, a corsage, an awakening

[T]here is a progressive movement from the language to the poem, from the poem to the song and from the song to its performance.

BARTHES 1977: 186

To wear a corsage is to indicate that there is an occasion. Not only does a corsage add a festive atmosphere but it also gives an air of importance. The choice of flowers, of colors, and design have significance when a corsage has been chosen or made especially for you and just to please you.

REUSCH & NOBLE 1951: ix

An enduring iconic image of Billie Holiday is of her face adorned with a white gardenia corsage (figure 3.2). Within the copious reams of writing on Billie Holiday, and the few references to her styling techniques, the gardenia corsage is posited as being integral to the legend that is Billie Holiday. The lasting relationship between Billie Holiday and her gardenia coiffure corsage continues to be used to signify her historical significance as a leading jazz artist.[11] For Holiday, the wearing of her gardenia corsage became a talisman to ensure the delivery of her musical performance. She recounted in *Lady Sings the Blues* that the white American jazz singer, Peggy Lee, wrote the song *Lady with the Gardenias* "celebrating the gardenia kick I used to be on, when I couldn't sing unless I had flowers in my hair" (Holiday 1995: 154). For others, Billie Holiday's gardenia corsage signified the idea that the perfection of her voice and her dependence on narcotics fuelled the former. For example, in a profile of jazz musicians who had indulged in drug use, Rex Doane suggested that to be an outstanding jazz artist one has to be a heavy dope fiend with a prison record. Billie Holiday was included in his theory:

> Billie Holiday would become arguably the greatest jazz vocalist of all time. She was also one of the music's first widely acknowledged junkies. Holiday turned on to heroin early in life and spent much of her singing career blowing off gigs in search of her next fix and showing up late to recording dates. Early photos of Holiday show a radiant woman of rare beauty often sporting a white orchid in her hair. That an orchid in her hair became a trademark look for Holiday has its own sense of tragic irony. For, in fact, Holiday had adopted the look in a hasty attempt to cover up a nasty burn she had inflicted upon herself after nodding off with a hot curling iron stuck to her head one night backstage.
>
> **DOANE** 1998: 5

FIGURE 3.2 Billie Holiday, New York, 1940s, by Robin Carson. © Gilles Petard/Getty Images.

This statement is a collage of myths about Billie Holiday. Doane says orchid, whereas Billie Holiday always referred to her "gardenia" (Holiday 1992: 154). Here, her corsage takes on the role of a dressing. This is partly true. Bobby Tucker, the jazz pianist and arranger who played for Billie Holiday from 1946 to 1949 and in 1954, said that it was a hat check girl called Ada Kurtz, who came up with the idea of a gardenia corsage for Billie Holiday. The singer Sylvia Syms has said that she devised the headdress, as Billie Holiday had burned her hair with a hot comb in preparation for a performance at the Onyx Club[12] (Gourse 1997: 140–1). Whether this was because Billie was stoned or it was simply a hairdressing accident is unclear; Syms has hinted at both versions (Gourse 1997: 141; Clarke 1994: 207). Rather than dismiss this iconic feature as a signifier of self-abuse, Billie Holiday's gardenia corsage has the potential of being a symbol of black activism. It was a constant feature of her performance of the anti-lynching song *Strange Fruit*, created to draw attention to the relentless lynching of black people in the United States.

There is no consensus on the date when Billie Holiday began to wear her gardenia corsage. One camp has argued that it began in 1937 (Clarke 1994: 207), whilst others date its origin as being when she first performed *Strange Fruit* at the Greenwich Village night club Café Society in 1939.[13] Photographs of Billie Holiday singing at the club during that year confirm she wore a single gardenia. Regardless of when this style was initiated, she was wearing the gardenia corsage as part of her stage style during her long engagement at Café Society. Her devotion to this particular assemblage of hair corsage grew from a single flower to an impressive arrangement of between two and four gardenia blooms by the late 1940s.[14]

During the 1930s and 1940s, the coiffure corsage (Reusche & Noble 1951: 64) was a fashionable style open to all American women. The corsage became part of American vocabulary in the mid-nineteenth century and referred to the creation of a bouquet worn at the waist or the bodice. This predominantly female craft retained a connection with its original French meaning in that the delicate fabric of the corsage—its petals, buds and leaves—were used to emphasize parts of a woman's anatomy and thereby accentuate and caress her femininity. Such intimate properties of the corsage are extended when given as an expression of endearment by a loved one (Reusch & Noble 1951: 3). The style of hair corsage Billie Holiday favored retained the traditions of corsage craft. Her signature preference was for white gardenias arranged in a straight line, possibly constructed through the chain technique which was suitable for hair adornment, where flowers were pushed against one another whilst being secured onto a wire base. Within corsage craft, white flowers were considered one of the best colors for evening wear as it looked exceptional under artificial light (Reusch & Noble 1951: 11–12). Billie Holiday's gardenia corsage was a presiding aesthetic of her stage style which she also included as part of her off-stage wear. She was even photographed wearing her favorite hair corsage whilst in hospital for a course of drug treatment in 1947 (Clarke 1995).[15] If floral decorations in the hair are a "special expression of … personality" (McDowell 1992: 18), how did the gardenia corsage provide Billie Holiday with the confidence to perform her art so spectacularly and similarly help cement her persona as Billie Holiday?

As an accessory, Billie Holiday's gardenia corsage was the hinge between her straightened hair and an immaculately made-up face and emphasized the highly groomed quality of these features. The sensuous quality of the gardenia, its "highly scented showy"[16] white flowers and its glossy dark evergreen shiny foliage enhanced the kinship between Billie Holiday's sleek hair style and immaculately made-up face, and contributed to the beautification of her head. Such properties extended the ability of the gardenia hair corsage to extol its expanding materiality, sensuality and lustre that the gardenia reflected during a performance. Billie Holiday's performance of *Strange Fruit* at Café Society is an enlightening example.

Strange Fruit

Southern trees bear a Strange Fruit,
Blood on the leaves and blood on the root,
Black body swinging in the Southern breeze,
Strange Fruit hanging from the poplar trees.

Pastoral scene of the gallant South,
The bulging eyes and the twisted mouth,
Scent of magnolia sweet and fresh,
And the sudden smell of burning flesh.

Here is a fruit for the crows to pluck,
For the rain to gather, for the wind to suck,
For the sun to rot, for a tree to drop,
Here is a strange and bitter crop.

LADY DAY 1997

The song, originally written as a poem in 1937 by Abel Meerepol, was performed by black and white political and civil rights activists before it reached Billie Holiday.[17] Her first official public performance of *Strange Fruit* was in early 1939[18] at Café Society, which was owned by the former shoe buyer Barney Josephson. It opened on December 28, 1938 (Josephson & Trilling-Josephson 2009: xi)[19] in Greenwich Village, with Billie Holiday as one of its first headliners, and its first female jazz performer. The club was the appropriate venue for the explosive song as Josephson's rationale for opening the club was to subvert the social standing of segregation between black and whites, as its strap line, the "wrong place for the Right people" (Josephson & Trilling-Josephson 2009: xi) suggests. Café Society was open to all, attracting liberals, artists and intellectuals from both sides of the color line.

Billie Holiday was aware of the subliminal meanings of the lyrics of *Strange Fruit*. The subtext being the horrific injustices of racism so suffocatingly present in the restrictive Jim Crow system, tenets which hastened the death of her father in March 1938: "When he [Abel Meerepol] showed me that poem, I dug it right off. It seemed to spell out all the things that had killed pop" (Holiday 1992: 84).[20] Billie Holiday became so connected to the nuances of *Strange Fruit* that her autobiography was originally titled *Bitter Crop*, the closing words of the song. What seems to be in no doubt is the emotional intensity Billie Holiday radiated in what became "the Billie Holiday experience" of her inimitable performance of the song. Her commentators agree, it was the right song performed in the right way to inspire "solidarity not pity" (Davis 1998: 194) about a social evil that had been practised in the United States since slavery. Meerepol's description of her first performance of *Strange Fruit* at Café Society concurs this:

> She gave a startling, most dramatic and effective interpretation,which could jolt an audience out of its complacency anywhere[sic] . . . This was exactly what I wanted the song to do and why I wrote it. Billie Holiday's styling of the song was incomparable and fulfilled the bitterness and shocking quality I had hoped the song would have. The audience gave her a tremendous ovation.
>
> **MARGOLICK** 2000: 46

The visual potency of the lyrics and Billie Holiday's performance of *Strange Fruit* still "packs a punch." Sitting in my living room listening to the opening note of the trumpet and the slow tempo of a funeral-like march leads to the more ominous sound of the piano joining forces with the trumpet to the opening line "Southern trees bear a Strange Fruit."As a piece of prose, each verse is disturbing, but when sung by Billie Holiday they haunt you long after the three minutes and ten seconds of the song are over. Two-and-a-half sections of *Strange Fruit* are dark in their disturbingly melodious presentation, but they do not prepare you, on first hearing the song, for the last two lines: "For the sun to rot, for a tree to drop, Here is a strange and bitter crop." I interpret drop and crop to be the last breath of life and the resulting corpse, respectively, of the victim of a lynching. Holiday takes her voice up to a mournful wail, and sends what seems like the last stabs into the conscience of listeners, begging one to ponder how such barbarous acts continued to take place in the 1930s when the song was written and first performed.[21]

Billie Holiday's voice has long been described as a jazz instrument which earned her the definition of a jazz musician, not a jazz singer: "I [Billie Holiday] don't think I'm singing. I feel like I am playing a horn. I try to improvise like Lester Young, like Louis Armstrong, or someone else I admire. What comes out is what I feel. I hate straight singing. I have to change a tune to my way of doing it." (Crowther & Pinfold 1997: 83). This innovative technique of musical interpretation allowed her the space to master her empathy with the lyrics, which influenced legendary performers such as Frank Sinatra and Ella Fitzgerald, who credited Billie Holiday with being "the first really modern singer . . . we all wanted to be like her" (Crowther & Pinfold 1997: 69). The significance of the supreme musicality of Billie Holiday's voice and her emotional involvement with the lyrics, whether a political or a love song, can be understood within the context of what Barthes calls "the grain of the voice" (Barthes 1977: 179–89)—the innate quality of the voice of a musician and the essence of their work. The grain is the link between the language being communicated and the voice of the singer. Barthes credits the grain with having a central presence, being "the materiality of the body ... almost certainly significance ... the significance it opens cannot better be defined, indeed, than by the very friction between the music and something else, which something else is the particular language (and nowise the message). The song must speak; must write—for what is produced at the level of the genosong is finally writing" (Barthes 1977: 182–5).

The "grain" presented in Billie Holiday's performance of *Strange Fruit* juggled death and hope. Within those tortured lines there is hidden newness and renewal: "blood on the root." Metaphorically, this translates for me that this blood was not shed in vain, but was a continual reminder of the need to oppose inhumanity and pursue civil rights.[22] Of course my interpretation is charged with the knowledge of the dramatic changes of African-American and American history since Billie Holiday's death in 1959, and the African-American's struggle against racism and racist attacks up to and after Billie Holiday's first performance of *Strange Fruit*. What makes it particularly poignant was the song's availability either as an authentic live performance by Billie Holiday, or on a vinyl recording she made on April 20, 1939.[23] Consequently, Billie Holiday and *Strange Fruit* were now an enmeshed feature in the history of African-American struggle. Music and performance allowed her to play with the potential and power of marginalization. Like her dandy predecessors, she capitalized on the culture of creative freedom for those that exist in the margins to engage in a counter discourse to racism through music.

The solemnity of the lyrics engendered in Billie Holiday an individualized stage performance of *Strange Fruit*, choreographed in a way that evoked an intimate wake, as detailed in this recount by Josephson:

> The room was completely blacked out, service stopped—at the bar, everywhere. The waiters were not permitted to take a glass to the table, or even take an order. So everything stopped—and everything was dark except for a little pin spot on her face. That was it. When she sang "Strange Fruit", she never moved. Her hands were down. She didn't even touch the mike. With the little light on her face. The tears never interfered with her voice, but the tears would come and just knock everybody in that house out.
>
> **CLARKE** 1995: 165[24]

In the stage direction engineered for the performance of *Strange Fruit* which closed the three sets Billie Holiday performed each night at Café Society, she and Josephson had created an historical moment which changed the course of Holiday's status as a jazz artist.[25] She was now a consummate performer who could transfix and move her audience through the stark emotional performance of a protest song, and became part of her already famed executions of love songs.

To read the above quote by Josephson, the intensity of the silent backdrop and the darkness of its meaning is injected with familiar images of how Billie Holiday would have been styled when singing *Strange Fruit*. Throughout her engagement she wore a variety of evening gowns, therefore it is impossible to give a definitive image. Yet the stage direction for the *Strange Fruit* number makes her gowns redundant. It is not her body which is the focus, it is her face adorned with a gardenia corsage, shrouded in the ornamental beauty of the flower with a scent that wafts over a great distance and "settles like a memory onto your soul" (Bussell 2005). Apart from being the site of personal identification, the face harbors its own culture. It is a plane that transmits inner feelings (Bobbioni 1999: 123).[26] Those who witness this process of emotional expression by a performer, undergo an intensely intimate moment.

In this instance, the face of Billie Holiday was the idea of change, the possibility of hope. She had come face to face with racism as a child and as an adult.[27] It was an experience wrapped in the paternal connections with Eleanora Harris, as mentioned earlier, which allowed her sincere self, Billie Holiday, to articulate the emotional experiences of her authentic self, Eleanora Harris, through "my personal protest—'Strange Fruit'" (Holiday 1992: 84). A "truth" of life was being expressed as it had been lived by Eleanora Harris/Billie Holiday and other African-Americans. "Truth" is the link between sincerity and authenticity. To return to Trilling, he believed that for an individual to tell the truth they require a mask, or persona. I prefer the term persona in this instance as I do not believe Eleanora Harris was hidden, rather her persona—Billie Holiday— provided Eleanora Harris with articulation. If this is applied to the persona that is Billie Holiday acting on behalf of Eleanora Harris, then, the performance of *Strange Fruit*, as Holiday recounted in *Lady Sings the Blues*, was charged with the emotions and lived experience of Eleanora Harris. It is here, in the performance of the song, that the authentic and sincere self fused. The tears which flowed during the performance of the song rolled down and seeped into the body of Eleanora Harris.

Perlman believes that personal change can be indicated by a moment (Perlman 1968: 12). I suggest that this significant moment was Billie Holiday's performance of *Strange Fruit* in 1939 at Café Society whilst wearing a gardenia coiffure corsage. Thus the lasting kinship between Billie Holiday's white gardenia corsage and her performance of *Strange Fruit* is an expanded reading of African-American culture during the 1930s and 1940s—a metaphor for the political aesthetic dimensions of racial and ethnic difference. Billie Holiday's use of a white gardenia hair corsage demonstrates possibilities of materiality and luminosity as enlightenment, as an integral dynamic of a performance. The iconic image of Billie Holiday of just her face and hair, her head thrown back singing, and the whole composition heightened by the petals and leaves of a gardenia carries something deeper. It is interesting to note that the gardenia is named after the Scottish-born physician and botanist, Dr Alexander Garden, who first grew the flower in Charleston, South Carolina, following the gardenia's discovery in England in 1758 by John Eliis, an acquaintance of Garden's, whilst the magnolia tree, identified as the instrument of torture in *Strange Fruit*, is a symbol of white southernness. In 1900, the magnolia became the state flower of Mississippi and Louisiana, and in 1938, it became the state tree of Mississippi.[28] These two flowers of the south, the gardenia and the magnolia, in the performance by Billie Holiday, the innocence of nature represented two segregated sides of America, black and white respectively. Therefore, in Holiday's claim of the gardenia as a definition of her sense of self, her African-American self, through this use it could be said that the gardenia was a sign of remembrance of those murdered through lynching, as flowers "often figure prominently in the emotional moments in our lives . . . a token of comfort and compassion on sad occasions" (Pryke 1998: 8).[29]

Undoubtedly, music is part of social and cultural issues. Within black culture this is an inextricable bond that dates back to the Atlantic slave trade. James Baldwin believed that music, and for him jazz in particular, channels the horrific, mangled history of black subjugation and survival in the United States. The determined acts to "own," segregate and marginalize black people in America since, as Baldwin puts it, "the auction block" of slavery, was where "[T]his music begins" (Baldwin 2011: 152). Those who understand this, who challenge it and try to survive this, get "the beat which is the key of music and the key to life" (Baldwin 2011: 153). An understanding that is embedded in black music. Paul Gilroy sees this "condition of being in pain" as being a legacy of slavery "and a related ontological state" for black people (Gilroy 1993: 203). But this same notion of the beat being connected with the story of black American experience can be, and has been, used to disengage from this sorrowful inheritance and shift the tempo of history to a new black beat. A beat that is not only about syncopation and tempo, but also includes the internal and outward expressions of individualized emotional response to such concerns. Therefore, the necessary consideration of music within the context of Billie Holiday and her styled body, in this instance her styled head, is to consider emotion as form, thereby perpetuating the idea of the black body, and in this case the adorned black head, is "the quintessential subversive object as sign" (Hendrickson 1996: 15; Fillin-Yeh 2001: 8).

My reading of Billie Holiday at this moment in her life places her at the vanguard of female black dandyism as protest. Her musical performance of *Strange Fruit*, in her own style of eveningwear, used music as a vehicle to relocate and define her persona as a consummate performer with political integrity—a black woman unafraid to confront cultural "truths" and wrongs. The sting in this scenario was the innocence of her coiffure corsage to subtly subvert the triviality of this ultra-feminine accessory. The effect was to confound and emotionally stir her audience by the radicalism of a political act in the performance of *Strange Fruit* whilst elegantly attired. As a consequence, Billie Holiday enacted a tenet of dandyism generally attributed to the male dandy: "Dandyism fused the social and the aesthetic in men's dress, and gave form to an ambivalence in relation to the individual to the social world, one of belonging and not belonging, of conformity and rebellion. Dandyism made possible a kind of incognito, an unmistakable yet understated disguise: the possibility of not being what you seem" (Evans & Thornton 1989: 124).

The overwhelming solemnity of *Strange Fruit* is balanced by the underlying hope in its performance, accented by the glaring beauty and symbolic purity of the white gardenia. Shockingly, by the 1950s, when Billie Holiday wrote her autobiography, this charm of emotional ease was one of four white items she believed became the sum of her persona, where whiteness equated erasure that came to define her professional life in the 1940s.

Four colors white

I spent the rest of the war on 52nd Street and a few other streets. I had the white gowns and the white shoes. And every night they'd bring me the white gardenias and the white junk.

HOLIDAY 1992: 116

This quote from *Lady Sings the Blues* carries the symbols of glamor and showmanship, and the markers of her stage style, most notably in the white gardenia hair corsage discussed above. In this period of her career Billie Holiday had achieved star status in America,[30] she was a star of 52nd Street in Harlem, or "The Street," as it was also known, and her reference to 52nd Street was a significant statement. Between 5th and 6th Avenue one could hear "the history of jazz" as every jazz style was available along "The Street." The area was a particular feature in the development of jazz as it was the space in which the modern sound of black jazz, Be-Bop, was being crafted in the early 1940s. Billie Holiday's leading position was inadvertently aided by the government taxes of 20 percent that was levied "on all entertainment except instrument playing." To engage a singer was a costly affair for club owners. Billie Holiday's artistry was so supreme and desired by the public during the early 1940s that she was continuously engaged in clubs along 52nd Street throughout the war (figure 3.3). Billie Holiday's prime position in the jazz world was supported by her popularity abroad. For example in Britain during World War II, Billie Holiday's songs were played on the BBC's Home Service (*Derby Daily Telegraph* 1940: 4) and the Broadcasting Home Service for the Forces (*Gloucester Echo* 1942: 3).

Yet the above quote effuses with emotional intensity the terse self-portrait Billie Holiday describes at this successful period of her career. It feels as if Eleanora

FIGURE 3.3 Billie Holiday, 1940, by William Gottlieb. Photo: William Gottlieb/Getty Images.

Harris, a glimpse of the sincere self, has no control over "Billie Holiday, the jazz singer," at this point in her life, and is resigned to a conveyor-belt-like existence. Billie Holiday feels she only exists through four objects: "white gowns, white shoes, white gardenias, white junk," heroine and cocaine, the first two she possessed, the last two were markers given by others which culminated in the complete package required for her to perform as "Billie Holiday, America's Jazz Artist" (Town Hall Program 1946: 9–13). As black and white photographs of the artist throughout the

1940s indicate, she gave concerts and night club performances in gowns of varying shades other than white. Had the color white become symbolic of how Billie Holiday, the black jazz star, was now so dependent on her gowns, accessories and drugs to perform, that they were the essence of her—but what of her body, what of Eleanora Harris?

The color white can symbolize purity and newness, honesty and goodness, sophistication and glamor, positivity and hope. Billie Holiday's use of the white gardenia, as outlined above, leads one to consider white as representative of awakening, consciousness and activism. Yet the underlying emotion in the above excerpt is a sense of futility. Whiteness used by Billie Holiday in this blanket way, conjoined with what became self-defining objects; "the white junk," her stage gowns and gardenia corsage, are indicative of Billie Holiday's hatred of the all too simplistic binaries of "good" and "evil" in life. This sense of hopelessness undermines Billie Holiday for control of her body and her musical performances, and in her interaction with society. The elements against which she fought and which prevented that control were layered and overlapped. One of these elements was the culture of whiteness as racism, as discussed earlier with regard to the searing anti-racism of the song *Strange Fruit*, the other was her use of the drugs cocaine and heroin.[31]

The dynamism of the "white" quote is that Billie Holiday had produced a collage of herself at a high point in her career. Whiteness had overshadowed her black body, and the essence of her was replaced by symbols of her musical performance glued together by her style of jazz performance and the hedonistic dimension of its culture. Whiteness in this aspect of Billie Holiday's collage represented for her the tangible vestiges of a musical career as a black performer. It had left her in a state of alienation, she had already begun to exist as a ghostly figure, as if her body only came into existence when it was styled correctly and fuelled by drugs. To dwell on her drug addiction is to perpetuate the usual stereotypical representation of Billie Holiday due to her abuse of drugs (and alcohol). Yet it does also advance the discussion of the relationship between the pleasure and pain of being black through her style-fashion-dress and music. To consider Billie Holiday as a weak-willed, tragic woman who did not know what she wanted in life is to patronize her (*Reputations: Billie Holiday* 2001). On the contrary, she was a woman who craved sensations, a strong-willed, street-wise individual who lived her life the way she wanted to. Her own candid admission of drug use throughout her autobiography helped cement the sincerity of the persona she wanted the public to see. As John Levy, Billie Holiday's lover and manager explained: "I think Billie did everything she did because she was Billie Holiday, and that's it" (*Reputations: Billie Holiday* 2001). Drugs were a feature for most of her adult life that she chose to incorporate into her persona. This is no more evident than how it was traced through and onto her body from the 1940s onwards, once Billie Holiday began mainlining heroin earlier in that decade.

"Heroin Chic"(k)

[S]he's the kind of person for whom we should not feel sorry, really, because she was always able to express herself artistically. A lot of people who become drug addicts or alcoholics that's all they are.

STANLEY CROUCH, Reputations: Billie Holiday 2001

In May 1947, Billie Holiday was photographed at the US Commissioner's office in Philadelphia as she waited for the hearing for her first drugs arrest. It is the image of a pristinely styled woman (figure 3.4). The attention to detail was flawless. The three-piece pinstripe skirt suit echoes the severity of the occasion, worn with an ease which Billie Holiday seems to address a potentially serious outcome. The long jacket with broad lapels is thrown over her shoulders, revealing a collarless, V-neck single-breasted jacket and the detail of a center front inverted pleated skirt, all in the same pinstriped suiting. Underneath the V-neck jacket she wears what could be described as a plain, pale-colored T-shirt-like top. The casualness of this feature not only sharpens the masculine edge of her chosen style, but also it projects a

FIGURE 3.4 Billie Holiday, Bobby Tucker (C) and road manager James Asendio (R), US Commissioner's Office, Philadelphia, Pennsylvania, May 20, 1947. Photo: Michael Ochs Archives/Getty Images.

boldness of spirit that is evoked by such glamor. The look is harnessed by an audacious hairstyle of an elaborate hairpiece that is neatly rolled at the front of the head, with a plait on the crown; the sides and the back of her hair are smoothed into a plane. Billie Holiday holds a robust hatbox handbag.

The television documentary *Reputations: Billie Holiday—Sensational Lady* (2001), provides a detailed account of the life and influence of Billy Holiday, and includes interviews with people who knew and worked with her. It makes detailed reference to the photograph of Billy Holiday at the US Commissioner's Office in Philadelphia. Not in relation to her personal style but as evidence of her arrest and addiction. The camera zooms in closer and closer to Billie Holiday's exposed wrist where her arms are crossed, resting on her legs, the lower one holding her handbag, whilst the upper arm reveals, just below the edge of her jacket, a dark mark which the narrator suggests is a memento of the act of mainlining.[32] It is difficult to prove that the mark represented this act. Following this arrest, Billie Holiday was sentenced to one year and a day at the Federal Reformatory for Women in Alderson, West Virginia. She had requested an early trial and hoped to be sent to hospital to cure her drug addiction instead of imprisonment.

The image is one of many photographs which depicts Billie Holiday as being more than just a drug addict. Aesthetically, there were no signs here that drugs had re-made Billie Holiday into a victim. Other photographs suggest that she never failed in her diligence to perfect her style-fashion-dress and her ardor for fashionable clothing which ran in tandem with her desire for drugs in the 1940s. Holiday established another trademark feature of wearing long fingerless gloves that extended to just below the edge of her short-sleeved evening gowns. Some commentators have attributed this to her attempts to hide needle track marks on her arms. Carl Drinkard, her long-term friend and piano player, remarked on these signifiers of Billie Holiday's addiction, and that she also used a chiffon handkerchief, in the color that matched her gown, to hide track marks in her hands (Clarke 1995: 391, Blackburn 2005: 231).

Another indication of drug use was the change in Holiday's body shape. Throughout her career Billie Holiday's figure alternated between full and slender. A feature that is often read as being indicative of her overall decline. By 1959, her weight had dropped to such an extent that she weighed just ninety-five pounds (Nicholson 1995: 222). But in keeping with the statement made by Stanley Crouch in *Reputations*, the management and styling of her body around her drug abuse could be seen as "an intensity of emotion and experience ... [a] counter-social, rebellious act" (Wallerstein 1998: 13) of what a woman can be. It is this train of thought that, for me, links the 1990s fashion industry-related concept of "Heroin Chic" (Wallerstein 1998: 129–50; Arnold 2001: 48–55) with Billie Holiday's experience.

The body aesthetic of heroin chic was named by the former United States president Bill Clinton in 1997. The styling of heroin chic was formulated in dour theatrical staging on the catwalk or dank fashion photographic stories of the late 1990s. These fashion narratives starred supposedly drug-ravaged bodies shrouded in exquisitely crafted garments and accessories. The disturbing visual paradox of destruction and creation, of "being out of it" and simultaneously exhorting the vitality of innovative fashion designs drove such images. Some fifty years previously," Billie Holiday was an authentic predecessor of this form of dark glamor. Obviously, her street clothes were not part of the inaugural appearance of a fashion designer's new collection, but they were being used in the way fashion is intended to be, part of an individual's living wardrobe. Yet the reality of Billie Holiday's heroin-fuelled body dressed so eloquently for a drug hearing in 1947, effectively bandaged by good tailoring, turned her into a female embodiment of hedonistic glamor.

The partnership of the styled body and heroin use accommodates an interpretation of the female form as signification and desire—"she who desires" (Benjamin 1988: 86). The body of Billie Holiday, then, was bathed in sensation. Her astutely chosen, well-designed clothes and accessories, and the equally well-prepared hairstyle could be said to satisfy the desire of Holiday's "aesthetic dimension." Heroin is seen by its users as a life-giving source[33] which uses the internal body as the host, and consequently the traces of heroin "form a body signature, embedded in the tissue: a limit-point of transcendence, a defile of the unity and self-sameness of the image, a corporeal infiltration of the 'real' into the field of representation" (Baert 2001: 21). This African-American woman demonstrated through the different ways she decided to style her body how she wanted to operate in society, opting for the "vitality fantasies ... associated with change, revolution, vigour, freedom and the future" (Brooker 1969: 64) of the jazz culture.

In one example of Billie Holiday's heroin chic(k) styled body, photographed at a US Commissioner's office on May 20, 1947, was effectively a eulogy to the "transgressive aesthetic" (Dollimore 1991: 14). In the pursuit of deviant desire, the act of transgression can lead the transgressor to finding and shaping a new self.[34] Eleanora Harris's pursuit of her sincere self, Billie Holiday, partially sought through a commitment to substance abuse, was perhaps her most dangerous act of self construction. This level of engagement with modernity demands courage, and undoubtedly carries risks. Nonetheless, in the rich tapestry of style mutations that is Billie Holiday, she fused all these components into her fastidious attention to her appearance.

Beauty nonetheless

In 1955, the American photographer Herman Leonard took a portrait of Billie Holiday wearing a pair of ankle-strapped, peep-toe high-heeled shoes (figure 3.5).[35]

FIGURE 3.5 *Lady Sings the Blues* recording session, New York, 1955, by Herman Leonard. © Herman Leonard Photography LLC.

The image was part of a series of photographs taken during a recording session of Holiday's album *Lady Sings the Blues*.[36] The jazz producer and label owner Norman Granz commissioned the photographs. It was hoped that one of these images would be used for the album cover. The photograph was taken on a wide aperture with a shallow depth of field[37] to focus on a detail of one element of the composition, Billie Holiday's left foot. This allows the viewer to study the design of these shoes and consequently the styling practice of Billie Holiday.

The shoe design consists of a studded ankle-strap, its dog collar references enhanced by the fastening at the center back, that emphasize her slender ankle. From the side of the ankle strap two metal chains connect the ankle strap to the main body of the shoe. The shoe has a slender high heel. The design detail of the front of the shoe, the four light-colored triangle inserts encased by a dark frame, again, present Billie Holiday's feet in an attractive light. The heel of her seamed stockings emphasizes the connection between the ankle strap and chain between it and the heel of her shoe. These shoes are achingly modern. They bridge sass and elegance. There is a feeling of going against the grain of acceptable femininity at this time. Although there are sado-masochist references in the prominent design features of the chains and studs, the shoes speak of Billie Holiday's style confidence to wear such sexy shoes.

Leonard's photograph is an expressive detail of her styled body on a particular day in her life. Jean-Paul Roux, has said, that "shoes give precious indications of habits and modes of life ... the shoe is symbolic, ... tied to a crucial moment of existence" (Roux 2004: 7). Leonard's focus on Billie Holiday's legs and the shoes worn at a significant time in her life (*Lady Sings the Blues* was the album that accompanied the release of her autobiography of the same name) invites one to ponder what aspect of Billie Holiday is being expressed here? What contribution does this image make to the collage that is Billie Holiday?

Leonard found this photographic assignment difficult. He has said that Billie Holiday "looked so drawn at this session that I didn't open up my cameras at first" (Houston & Bagert 2006: 18). Leonard, who had first photographed Holiday in 1949, felt he could not capture the woman "he remembers for her beauty and elegance" (Houston & Bagert 2006: 18). This chimed against Leonard's practice to "tell the truth but tell it in terms of beauty" (Houston & Bagert 2006: 18). After encouragement from Granz, Leonard photographed the artist at work. He obviously saw some element of beauty in Holiday's shoes and legs, as the luminosity of the image is testament to this. Consequently he "glamorized the foot" (Steele 1999: 141). In spite of Leonard's concerns, I believe he managed to capture dignity and beauty in the other images he took of Billie Holiday during that 1955 recording session; effectively honor through the lens.

The photographic series includes full-length shots of Holiday. In one image, she is standing at a microphone looking away from Leonard, with her hands behind her back, a cigarette between her fingers. She is wearing a two-piece suit of a single-breasted jacket, buttoned down the center front with a wide, flat collar and a hobble-style mid-calf skirt. Her hair is short, with soft curls, shaped into the nape of her neck and sides of her head, resembling the poodle hairstyle. In another full body shot, Holiday, in a relaxed pose, again looks away from Leonard, sits on a chair, her left arm thrown over the back of it, her legs crossed with her right arm, decorated with a broad pearl bracelet, resting on them as she holds what looks like a plastic beaker. As the photograph of her shoes indicates, Leonard took a number of abstracted photographs of different features of her. Through the dissection of different elements of her styled body, Leonard takes the viewer around Billie Holiday, as any viewer would look at her in reality. One would see the whole body at some point, but one would invariably zoom in on different details that caught our eye: her shoes, how she was standing or sitting at different times, the covered buttons on her jacket, perhaps a drop of ash falling from her cigarette, her make-up etc. In this way, the abstracted study by Leonard was to actually *see* her. The details of the whole are paramount here.

There is a portrait of Billie Holiday's head in profile, shot so darkly that one can only recognize that it is Billie Holiday because of her famous profile. The back lighting on the right-hand side provides a halo-quality to her hair and face. The curls of her hair soften her pensive look. Leonard's photographic signature of cigarette smoke wafts through the air around the artist. A shot of Holiday's hands, held behind her back, provides a close up detail of an open ended four-strand pearl bracelet and a well-smoked cigarette held between her varnished fingers. The photographs show accepted feminine accoutrements of the 1950s, which includes Billie Holiday's strident shoes. Indeed the ankle, as focused upon in Leonard's photograph, maintained the idea lauded in 1947 that the design of a shoe should enhance femininity through "the most flattering line for the ankle" (*Footwear* February 1947 no page number: Wright 1989: 9).

Lee Wright's detailed study of the development of the stiletto heel in the 1950s, as a barometer of femininity during that decade, is useful to position the meaning of Billie Holiday's shoes. The 1950s are seen as a pivotal moment in women's footwear. Wright charts the development of the stiletto heel from 1947. By 1953, a lighter version of a pre-World War II design was introduced; this began with a two-inch thick tapered shape, similar to the heel worn by Billie Holiday. Wright raises the point that the extreme stiletto heel designs of 1957 to 1962 were liberating, it was not about the housewife, it was not about domestication, but about the "new woman's" rejection of convention whilst the earlier versions reflected "traditional values" of "feminine attributes" (Wright 1989: 14–15). Wright's thinking of a shoe design in the 1950s being empowering is also interesting. As discussed earlier, Billie Holiday was very much "the new woman" through her artistry, contribution to the development of jazz, her popularity and earning capacity. She wore these shoes to a recording session, for work, and therefore connects with Wright's "go-getter" argument that some women of the 1950s engaged in away from the domestic space. And to some extent, Billie Holiday's indulgence in drugs was part of this "new woman" profile.

Leonard's retelling of this photographic session in his later life lamented on the loss of a jazz icon, and a particular period of jazz history that he witnessed and contributed to. Indeed, the 1955 photographic session was the last that Leonard did of Billie Holiday. Essentially, the photographs are a form of mourning for Leonard. He has said that he found it difficult to publish photographs from this session but had come to realize that these were of historical and cultural value in the telling of Billie Holiday's life (Houston & Bagert 2006: 18). To mourn is to grieve for something that is lost. Therefore, for Leonard, the photographic session and these photographs were "the process of adjusting slowly and painfully to the reality which tells us that the loved object, place or idea no longer exists—or cannot be regained" (Pollock 1999: 189). The result, then, is a "visual hymnal" to the emotional qualities related to the subject being photographed (Tulloch 2011: 184) and in the example of Billie Holiday's shoes, exemplified how "the shoe can sometimes serve to represent he [she] who has worn it, who has disappeared" (Roux 2004: 7).

What radiates from this photographic portrait of Billie Holiday wearing a pair of shoes is beauty. This is despite Leonard's fear of being disloyal to his photographic practice and to Billie Holiday should he not be able to capture some semblance of the beauty Leonard felt she had lost. It could be said that taking these photographs was a means to abate that sense of loss Leonard's professionalism took over to rediscover his definition of Billie Holiday's beauty. For the photographer Robert Adams, beauty is form: "Beauty is . . . a synonym for the coherence and structure underlying life" (Adams 1996: 24). It is a quality in photography that can open one's eyes and help to overcome life's fears (Adams 1996: 24). The mechanisms of focusing on detail, composition and the dynamics of occupied and unoccupied space of a photograph, leads to the "sense of possibility" of beauty (Adams 1996: 34–5). In the portrait of her shoes, this was the kind of beauty that Leonard equated with Billie Holiday.

Billie Holiday: night and day

As discussed above, the plethora of photographs of Billie Holiday depict how her styled body evolved in synchronicity with her career and its activities. Both on and off the stage, Billie Holiday was undoubtedly a star of the jazz world, and presented herself to the public accordingly. Her autobiography provides no evidence that she dressed with this duty in mind, but her clear desire for, and consumption of good-looking clothes and accessories which she formulated into a meticulous style fulfilled her commitment that she "looked more like a girl who was going somewhere" (Holiday 1992: 101). Her body—rounded or slim—was primed for her life-long articulation of glamor and fashionability in all her style-fashion-dress requirements: from spending two weeks' salary in the late 1930s on "matching shoes and handbag made in green crocodile" (Chilton 1997: 27), to being a patron of the Swedish jewellery designer Torun Bülow-Hübe. Billie Holiday's stage-self was polished. She understood how to provide a satisfying spectacle for audiences who expected to be entertained visually and audibly. The magical vision of Billie Holiday in luxurious gowns used to enhance her performance of songs places her within the genre of the show girl, a woman who "provides a feast for the eye" (Stuart 1996: 5) for men and women. Her wardrobe allowed her to be theatrical with the audience making use of the full range of delicious light-reflective fabrics such as velvet and lamé, beading and sequins. The numerous collections of Billie Holiday photographs, as well of the overwhelming number of images available on the internet, reaffirms how she experimented with diverse stage-styles.

In a publicity photograph taken by M. Smith in 1952, Billie Holiday presented herself as the epitome of demure, chaste womanhood in a light spaghetti-thin strapped full length dress. The gown has a top layer of lace which starts at the bodice, and continues through to the skirt where it trails off into an asymmetrical scalloped-edge curve above brimming reams and layers of what appears to be chiffon. Two years later, Billie Holiday projects another mood to a packed audience in a low-lit night club (figure 3.6). Here she is the cool chanteuse in a figure-hugging dark-colored halter-neck dress. The clean lines of the dress match Billie Holiday's correspondingly short hair style, reminiscent of a man's quiff. This is

FIGURE 3.6 Lady Day, 1954, Charles Hewitt. Photo: Charles Hewitt/Getty Images.

modernity in sharp relief. It is a look that marks Holiday as a woman who did not fear her physical potential. In fact, in this particular shot she appears to relish in subterranean glamor that achieved the dual task of skilfully channelling her sexuality (Bailey 1990: 148) and the ethnic distance between herself and the predominantly white audience of the night club. Glamor here is a concoction of fact and fiction, of being mysteriously exciting, "a visual language of the enticing that seduces through the deployment of image of theatricality, luxury and notoriety" (Buckley & Gundle 2000: 346–7). Although glamor is shrouded in illusion and deception, through the body of this particular black woman, Billie Holiday used it as a candid declaration of the presence of the female African-American self.

Photographs also provide evidence of Billie Holiday's "street clothes" (Holiday 1984: 85), a term she used to describe the clothing she changed into after a performance. The feminine aspects of her persona in this guise is ever present, most notably in her passion for fur coats (figure 3.7). During World War II, she violently retaliated against three white soldiers who used cigarettes to burn her mink coat (Blackburn 2005: 166). In 1956, Billie Holiday was arrested and held in jail on a narcotics charge. She used her blue mink coat as a comforter and protector for herself and her dog Pepi:

> There was nothing in the cell but a toilet and a long plank to lay down on. Pepi is so delicate he would get pneumonia in a minute, so I was busy worrying how to keep him warm. I spread my blue mink coat on the board and used it for a mattress while I cuddled that dog to keep him warm. But it wouldn't work. We were cold on top. So I pulled out my mink and threw it over us. Then we were cold on the bottom. When I wasn't worrying about Pepi, I was worrying about Louis [McKay] on the other side without any topcoat.
>
> **HOLIDAY** 1992: 190–1

The following account of Billie Holiday's blue mink coat does not connect date-wise with the above statement. Drinkard and Billie Holiday were fellow heroin users. In his interview with Linda Kuehl in the early 1970s, Drinkard related numerous stories of going on errands for Billie Holiday to pawn her rings and blue mink coat to raise cash for drugs. Drinkard says the mink coat had an effect on the pawnbrokers as they recognized the owner, as Billie Holiday's name was "stitched on the lining in gold thread." One refused to handle it, and another "almost cried when he saw the beauty of the coat." Apparently the mink raised $3,000 (Blackburn 2005: 237).

Within the genre of street clothing and its associated spaces, Billie Holiday reveals masculine traits. She allows herself to be photographed smoking, albeit with a man lighting her cigarette.[38] During the 1940s, she is photographed in hard-edged skirt suits, the so-called "Man-Tailored Suits" (Skinner 2002: 25). Holiday

FIGURE 3.7 Billie Holiday, 1954, Charles Hewitt. Photo: Charles Hewitt/Getty Images.

goes one step further. Like other high-profile female cultural contributors, such as Chanel, Marlene Dietrich and Katharine Hepburn, Billie Holiday chose to be associated with the more adventurous ensemble of a trouser suit. Circa 1940, Billie Holiday is photographed with Duke Ellington. She wears a dark trouser suit, a light-colored shirt that has "BH" monogrammed near the point of the left collar. Her face is framed by a knitted turban. Her manicured hands, loop earrings and a single plain ring completes the look. Billie Holiday's penchant for "slacks" continued into the 1950s. According to Alice Vrbsky, Billie Holiday's assistant during the last years of her life, "She liked slacks. She had very good wool slacks" (Blackburn 2005: 311) by which time it was not unusual for women to wear trousers, but it was still a challenging social statement for a mature women to make.

"It's my hair; I paid for it"

The range of hairstyles Billie Holiday wore provides another insight into her fastidious crafting of what she demonstrated as being the correct balance for her styled self. Apparently her hair was naturally "soft," rather than the tighter texture associated with black hair. Nonetheless, throughout her adult life Billie Holiday chose to straighten her hair with a pressing comb (Clarke 1995: 355), as was the general practice amongst African-American women during her life time, to achieve the fashionable sleek coiffured styles. As mentioned above, one style option was to wear her hair short. She would also make use of color, sometimes dying her hair red or bleaching parts of it blonde. But to give volume and access to a whole catalog of hairstyles, Billie Holiday was notorious for her use of hairpieces. They were an integral embellishment of her overall look, so much so that in the early 1950s her husband, Louis McKay, feared how the public would react to her cavalier use of them for different sets on the same evening of a night club engagement:

> Lady kept her hair cut short, but she had a hairpiece, a chignon ... She was inconsistent about wearing it, and McKay would say to her, "You know, Lady, people aren't fools. If you come out for one set with your hair long, and the next set with your hair short, and then again with it long, they're going to catch on." She'd just laugh and say, "It's my hair; I paid for it".
>
> **CARL DRINKARD** quoted by **CLARKE** 1995: 355–6

The criticism made by Billie Holiday's husband was between two black people who were aware of the sensitive subtext of black hairstyling practices, an issue that has been in contestation since slavery was introduced to North America. In particular, how African-Americans (and black people of the African diaspora) can and have been read by white people through the quality and grooming of their hair. Yet during the 1940s and 1950s, African-American magazines such as *Sepia* and *Our World* gave extensive advice and carried a wide range of advertisements on how to style and care for black hair, and information on other accessories required to create fashionable styles. Amongst these were a vast array of advertisements for hairpieces which confirmed the demand for "real" hair attachments at this time. The range was extensive from bi-color braids (figure 3.8), a "surprise Chignon" and the "Page Boy" during the 1940s to the "pony-tail" of the 1950s, all hair styles which Billie Holiday wore. The persuasive line amongst suppliers of these hair accessories, such as the New York retailers Howard Tresses and Personality Products Company, was that African-American women should not be ashamed of having short hair, as this length was an ideal base on which to build fashionable "hair-dos" with the use of their "real hair" tresses.[39]

Hair is a signifier of racial origin and ethnicity. The latter is most significant in the consideration of Billie Holiday and her use of long hairpieces. The instantaneous results in the transformation of one's hair and self through color, texture and length in the use of hairpieces or cutting was "[C]aught on the cusp between self and society, nature and culture, the malleability of hair makes it a sensitive area of expression" (Mercer 2000: 114). Billie Holiday's cavalier use of her hairpiece revealed to her jazz audience that she did not have naturally long hair, it was not a sign of inauthenticity. To consider this aspect of her personal styling, and her decision to use a range of hairpieces that would augment her creativity and

FIGURE 3.8 Billie Holiday, studio portrait, 1948 by Gilles Petard. The portrait was taken for the Associated Booking Corp. Joe Glaser was president and manager of Billie Holiday. Photo: Michael Ochs Archives/Getty Images.

individuality is to suggest that Billie Holiday exercised a political aspect to her hair styling practice. This is in light of the fact that she entertained this as an African-American woman who expressed the right, indeed the need to be inauthentic to perform the different sides to her sincere self (Cheddie 2006).

Therefore in light of the comments made by McKay, the idiosyncratic use of hairpieces by Billie Holiday was a critique on an individual's freedom to exercise versatility and be dramatic. She made a statement as to how she had control over one of the "ethnic signifiers" that had determined how she would be defined by society, and in her personal experience, how she might be read by white Americans. She flaunted this kind of categorization by playing with her audience, keeping them guessing as to which Billie Holiday look would emerge on the stage, adding anticipation and intensity to the visual and musical spectacle she would perform. What she did project in this act of hair manipulation was that she was a black woman who could not or would not be pinned down. Billie Holiday, at the expense of inauthenticity, subverted the codes of appropriate grooming and its ultimate goal of glamor and theatricality which peddled in artifice whilst portending reality. The illusion was in danger of being shattered, but it could be argued that Billie Holiday provided another kind of value for her self, the freedom to indulge in visual transformation at will, even if it was a simple a matter of adding or removing a chignon hairpiece.

In the 1950s, Holiday established her sleek fringeless pony-tail hairstyle that became an established feature of her mature self. There are a number of photographs of Billie Holiday from 1949 with her hair slicked back with a side-parting, and a chignon at the nape of her neck, as featured in a notable photograph taken by Carl Van Vechten on March 23, 1949, of Billie Holiday holding a sculpture of an African head (Stewart 1993: 97). This compact hairstyle could be seen as a forerunner of her pony-tail hairstyle that is as integral to the myth of Billie Holiday as her gardenia corsage. Indeed, Malcolm X, in his autobiography, recounts that he knew Billie Holiday and saw her perform at the Onyx Club:[40] "Billie, at the microphone, had just finished a number when she saw Jean and me. Her white gown glittered under the spotlight, her face had that coppery, Indianish look, and her hair was in that trademark pony-tail. For the next number she did the one she knew I always like so: 'You Don't Know What Love Is'" (Malcolm X 1965: 203). Malcolm X lamented that this was the last time he saw Billie Holiday sing live. The recollection of this memory indicates that Malcolm X saw her perform before 1946, as he was imprisoned that year. When he was released from jail in 1952, Malcolm X had become a member of the Nation of Islam and therefore would not have frequented nightclubs. Billie Holiday did perform at the Onyx Club in the 1940s before Malcolm X went to prison (Clarke 1995: 205). This was during the period when Billie Holiday's gardenia corsage was part of her stage style and, as mentioned earlier, it was a talisman for her to give a good performance. What is clear from this recollection by Malcolm X of the last time he saw and spoke with Billie Holiday, was that he produced a montage of her different style features significant to the beauty and essence that constructed the Billie Holiday that Malcolm X remembered, and the pony-tail was key.

Billie Holiday wore the pony-tail hairstyle throughout the 1950s until her death in 1959. During this last phase of her life she wore it as part of her "street clothes" for work at recording sessions, at public performances for promotional photographs and photographs of the artist on album covers. This is exquisitely immortalized on the color cover image of the 1958 album *Lady in Satin*[41] (plate 6). It features a strong head to bust profile of Billie Holiday wearing a pony-tail accessorized with a silver circular clip, starburst earrings and a shoe-lace slim diamanté choker. Her strapless gown does appear to be satin. Her face carries another established Billie Holiday feature, red lipstick, along with her pencilled eyebrows, applied with a softer touch, and eyeliner. This image of her, the album text relayed, reflected a change in fortune for the artist: "everything about her present points to a happier and more successful future. And if you see her, slender and pretty in her glamorous new wardrobe, you'll find it hard to believe trouble has tagged her for so long" (Townsend 1958).

Billie Holiday's popularization of the pony-tail hairstyle joined forces with other hairstyle shifts and cultural luminaries who made the hairstyle a symbol of 1950s modernity, particularly how the lived experience and the styled self was an integrated expression of what it is to be.

On January 7 1952 *Life* magazine reported on the competition between two fashionable hairstyles, the short curly poodle and the long-haired pony-tail (figure 3.9).[42] The front cover image of the weekly magazine featured these two hairstyles. The poodle was a short curly style that required a lengthy styling process,[43] while the pony-tail, or horsetail as it was also known, was easy to create with just a bush and rubber bands. Even so, some pony-tail hairstyles required more attention, as accompanying photographs to the article show a version of the pony-tail with a neat short fringe, which would require regular grooming. *Life* explained that the different camps for the hairstyles were quite clear: the poodle for mature career women and the pony-tail was popular amongst teenagers (*Life* 1952: 65–6).

In 1954 the pony-tail acquired modernist status through a series of paintings and sculptures by Pablo Picasso of the French-English nineteen-year-old Sylvette David[44] in Vallauris, France. The "Sylvette Series" (Jaffé 1980: 63) featured head studies of David's blonde pony-tail, which Picasso depictive as an expressive, seemingly unkempt feature of his sitter. David's pony-tail began at the crown of her head, with her long hair ending at the center of her shoulder blades. David had a shaggy fringe and two delicate ringlets tumbling down the side of her face. David said her pony-tail was inspired by a suggestion made by her French father who had seen a ballet performance of Leslie Caron wearing a pony-tail (Corbett 2013).[45] Picasso's dedicated study of a young unknown woman through drawings, paintings and sculptures had a cultural impact. *Life* magazine called the series Picasso's "pony-tail period," particularly where one painting focused on David's pony-tail and her facial features were barely visible (*Life* 1954: 119–20). These new works marked a new direction for Picasso in defining a hairstyle as a signifier of youth "to demand the discovery of a method for expressing the effect of her particular hair-do to find the place of that head of hair" (Lucas 1955: 202). They were first shown

FIGURE 3.9 "Hair Styles: Poodle vs. Horsetail," *Life* magazine, January 7, 1952. Photo: Nina Leen/Getty Images.

to the public in the 1954 exhibition, "Picasso, Two Periods: 1900–1914 & 1950–1954" at the Maison de la Pensée Française in Paris (Lucas 1955: 198–202). In October 1954, British journalist Mary Dunbar reported in *The Sunday Times*, having viewed the Paris exhibition of the Sylvette paintings that the "predominant feature" of the show was the pony-tail "and already I saw many girls wearing this style, complete with a thick fringe, exactly like Picasso's Sylvette" (Dunbar 1954: 9). Brigitte Bardot also wore the hairstyle. Through Picasso's immortalization of David's version of a dishevelled pony-tail, the hairstyle was recognized as another bold statement of female teenage presence.

Billie Holiday's use of the pony-tail connected with the fashionability of a style that was an unmistakable mark of female youth on both sides of the Atlantic. Through her choice of the neat, minimalist version popular in the USA, Billie Holiday brokered these features and raised it to be a signifier of 1950s sophistication appropriate for the older woman.

In the numerous hairstyles Billie Holiday wore, whether just her own hair or with the addition of a hairpiece or decoration such as a corsage, she reflected Barbara Miller's thinking on hair as being "conceptualised from three angles: individually experienced hair, socially symbolic hair and political hair" (Miller 1998: 281). I would add a fourth for Billie Holiday, the cultural impact of hair.

Billie Holiday: the classic

By the late 1950s, Billie Holiday had established another signature style comprising a plain round-neck twinset of cardigan and jumper, and her fringeless pony-tail discussed above. She was shown wearing this form of casual dress at the recording session[46] of her album *Lady in Satin* (1958), for which she wore a dark twinset (figure 3.10), and the rehearsal of a landmark live CBS television performance, *The Sound of Jazz* at Studio 58 that was aired on December 8, 1957.[47] For this television rehearsal, Billie Holiday wore a pale-colored twinset buttoned at the waist and the sleeves pulled up towards her elbows, checked ankle-length slacks and flat shoes. The film of this rehearsal lasts nine minutes and enables a focused study of Billie Holiday.

As Billie Holiday walks across the studio floor, through the "All Star" jazz performers[48] who surround her, and sits on a stool in front of a microphone she is stunning, she looks healthy and at ease. She is home. The pale color of her twinset supports her central position as the singer of *Fine and Mellow*, a song written and arranged by Billie Holiday.[49] Through the illuminating quality of the pale-colored twinset, Billie Holiday's face is a beacon in the sea of jazz musicians who encircle her. For both sessions, Billie Holiday wore the same pair of dropped-hoop earrings with a solid heart-shaped feature that dangled from the top center of the hoop, and a charm bracelet. In one of the images of the *Lady in Satin* recording, Billie Holiday is singing and holds a cigarette between her painted fingernails, while a key accessory for her at the Studio 58 broadcast is a handkerchief. In my discussion of Billie Holiday's life-long engagement with modernity, it is necessary to assess the cultural currency of the twinset in America in the late 1950s, to show how it provided another aspect of her style narrative in the latter part of her life.

FIGURE 3.10 Billie Holiday recording *Lady in Satin* for Columbia Records, New York, 1957. Photo: Don Hunstein. © Sony Music Entertainment.

The twinset, also referred to as "go togethers"[50] in the USA (Skinner and McCord 2004: 85), is a staple of female style statements, its cultural meaning ranges from functional, sensual and stable. Alistair O'Neil's detailed survey of the development and cultural value of the twinset, from its origins amongst female golfers in the early twentieth-century to its popularization by curvaceous Hollywood screen goddesses in the 1930s and 1940s, who paired it with trousers (O'Neill 2011: 116), to its demise which began in the 1950s when the twinset became a "classic" image of "safe," womanhood amongst the mature female generation in the 1960s (O'Neill 2011: 116) and then to its revival by fashion designers from the 1980s onwards which renewed its "edgy" qualities originally projected in the 1930s and 1940s. This history of the twinset is generally told through its use by young white females. Mediation of this garment through the pages of catalogs such as Sears, and as O'Neill outlines, the twinset's ubiquity in Hollywood films from the 1930s, is testament to this. Consideration of how Billie Holiday used the ensemble is an example of how a set piece of knitwear bridged the racial lines of stringent segregation culture of the United States.

Billie Holiday's assistant, Alice Vrbsky, has said that her earning capacity had declined at this stage of her life (Blackburn 2005: 311).[51] We will never know when Billie Holiday bought these twinsets, and it is difficult to tell what fabric they were made of—cashmere, wool or Orlon, for example. Therefore, to get a sense of the popularity of the twinset in the USA in the mid to late 1950s, a look at the Sears catalog is a useful guide. It is considered as "one of the great and basic documents of US civilization, and deserves the closest critical study wherever the state of the Union is discussed" (Banham 1999: 112). For fall/winter 1956, Sears offered the long sleeved cardigan of a twinset in cashmere for $19.95, wool for $8.98 and Orlon for $6.98; and its matching short-sleeved crew neck for $14.95, $5.98 and $4.98 respectively (Skinner 2002: 84). In Fall/Winter 1959 Sears continued to offer the twinset to younger and older women.

The term "classic" in reference to the twinset worn by Billie Holiday during the rehearsals of songs and recording an album that have themselves become jazz classics, takes the meaning of the twinset during the 1950s into another realm. In both settings, Billie Holiday is not consciously making a glamorous style statement with her black body. The dark and light versions of the twinset provide a frame for Billie Holiday's face. They shroud her body with ease, which takes a secondary, although elegant, place to her head and voice, the source for her role at the rehearsal and recording sessions, to sing jazz. As material support to her practice as a recording artist and performer at work, the twinset, then, was part of Billie Holiday being in her comfort zone, as a jazz musician working with equally passionate consummate jazz artists.

Therefore, Billie Holiday's use of the twinset in these examples can be seen as her preparatory uniform; an item in which she feels comfortable, in order to perform well. This contributes an additional meaning of the twinset in the late

FIGURE 3.11 Jazz at the Plaza party, Billie Holiday and Miles Davis, The Plaza Hotel, New York, 1958. Photo: Don Hunstein. © Sony Music Entertainment.

1950s, at a time when it had become a "classic" in the context of being safe and dependable, as explained by O'Neill. Billie Holiday's use of the twinset rewrites the meaning of classic to be "of the highest rank or importance" (*OED*) and elevates the twinset by its association with one of America's greatest jazz artists as an arbiter of cool.

Summary: existential resonance

In the last year's of Billie Holiday's life, her style narrative had an "existential resonance" (Martin 2013: 50). An individual's freedom to live the life they chose to live is fundamental to the philosophy of existentialism.[52] The freeing nature of existentialism is the belief that an individual is responsible for itself, and by having the freedom to shape their lives by themselves and thereby "to live with authenticity" (Shand 1996: 189) and it is an individual's duty to act on it. "To behave 'authentically' is to understand that we can make and remake ourselves by our actions and thus become what our acts define us as being" (Eyre 2003: ix). Therefore, in my earlier discussion of Billie Holiday's autobiography *Lady Sings the Blues* as a sincere telling of the self, I want to propose an expanded consideration that the styled self of Billie Holiday during the exacting last years of her life, was the culmination of Eleanor Harris's authentic act of being Billie Holiday, by exercising to live the way she wanted to live.[53] Shand summarizes that, "Indeed, only in death can some kind of assessment of what kind of person one was be legitimately made" (Shand 1996: 188) because the process of becoming has ended. Following death, myth pervades, sustained by others, the projection of who they think that individual was, and becomes part of public memory. In the case of Billie Holiday, this was poignantly put into practice very quickly following her death. She lay in state in an open casket from July 19–21, 1959. Her burial robes consisted of a pale-colored gown and double gardenia corsage placed on the right-hand side of her face. This was a gross error to her memory at this sensitive moment of remembrance, as Billie Holiday generally wore her gardenia on the left-hand side of her head. Here was a hauntingly sad reminder of what was no more from all perspectives.

Compatible elements to achieving an authentic life are things. Mary Warnock highlights that "people differ from each other in their reactions to things. But it would also be argued that there is a number of qualities which things have to which we are bound to react in a standard way, simply because they reveal a truth about the nature of the world and our place in it" (Warnock 2003: xv). Warnock is making reference to Jean-Paul Sartre's thinking on the role of the metaphysical purport and metaphysical coefficient of material objects "of all intuitive revelations of being" (Sartre 2003: 624). What is of interest for me are items that Billie Holiday was reliant upon to help her through her professional life, her rehearsals and performances. Specifically, Billie Holiday's ability to create her own style motifs that doubled as reassurance mechanisms.

Therefore, by 1957 Billie Holiday had a professional working uniform that incorporated a pony-tail, twinset and her voice. Some critics have said that her voice by this time no longer had the magic of "the young Holiday" of the 1930s and 1940s (Cook & Morton 1992: 534–6), whilst others feel that in the last years of her life, her voice reflected an honest tone of the impact of her differing life experiences (Ritz 2006: 227–30). I agree with the latter, as Billie Holiday herself said "The things that I sing have to have something to do with me and my life . . . and it has to have a meaning."[54]

In addition, Billie Holiday perpetuated aspects of avant-gardism where the "breaking with tradition becomes its own tradition, that is, the tradition of the new" (Eager 1996: 38–9) continually using fashionable clothing and accessories as a means to project her "intensely personal version of the world" (Murphy 1999: 57). Some of these garments and hairstyles may have had a cultural heritage situated in white counter and sub-cultures that informed the straight, conservative and hegemonic beliefs that fuelled their oppositional discourse. Yet these systems were not lost to the black community which had used similar operations since slavery (White & White 1998; Tulloch 1999; Powell 2001). It can be argued that Billie Holiday used such self-styling details as the pony-tail, trousers and twinset in the formulation of her self as a modernist text on difference and remaining black.

This was in keeping with what Angela Davis calls "Billie Holiday's project—as that of a jazz musician who worked primarily with the idiom of white popular song—consisted largely in transforming already existing material into her own form of modern jazz" (Davis 1998: 165).[55] Something she clearly did with her styled self.

This manifested the developmental strategies of the New Black Woman. Despite being classified as a social outsider due to her hedonistic lifestyle, Billie Holiday carved out a system of how to live, dress and socialize as an independent woman, which loops back to the argument that Billie Holiday was a female dandy. Her ability to flit between masculine lines and hyper-feminine guise, puts her on an equal footing with the black male dandy. Richard J. Powell argues that the latter holds a unique position in that the art of the black dandy is his ability to wear the clothes of the white man with a difference: "'the art of seduction through transgression'... he transforms himself and the world around him into a different place, where black people—and black men in particular—can no longer be reduced to fixed, immovable images of poverty, danger, and negativity" (Powell 2001: 228, 235). Billie Holiday demonstrates that this is not the preserve of the black male. The modern black body of Billie Holiday, styled in a medley of references and meanings to assist in her negotiations of social contradictions of being a black woman, to eventually construct for herself an individualized persona that incorporated style-fashion-dress, jazz and the grain of her voice. In Billie Holiday's female dandy we see an example of how the power of the combination of the components of style-fashion-dress and the critical ally of beauty, discussed earlier, can be used to create a range of style narratives to maintain the "essential self," and consider the historical, political and cultural significance of the New Black Woman.

4 "MY MAN, LET ME PULL YOUR COAT TO SOMETHING"[1]: MALCOLM X

[P]eople are always speculating—why am I as I am? To understand that of any person, his whole life, from birth must be reviewed. All of our experiences fuse into our personality. Everything that ever happened to us is an ingredient.

MALCOLM X 1966: 225

From the eighteenth century to the present, the techniques of verbalization have been reinserted in a different context by the so-called human sciences in order to use them without renunciation of the self but to constitute, positively a new self.

MICHEL FOUCAULT 1988: 49

Epiphany

My reading of the book, *The Autobiography of Malcolm X*[2] (figure 4.1) is as a document that traces the renewal of a self and its spirit, following a series of life experiences and transformations. The tone of the book veers from anger to joy, and is reflective and informative, always couched in passion. This poignant testimony of self-telling was undertaken to counteract in the public mind the apparition of "Malcolm X"[3] as simply "the angriest man in America" divorced of a "true" context. As the opening quote by Malcolmm X clarifies, he wanted the public to gain access to his "whole" life and persona so one could gain a better understanding of "why am I as I am?" (1966: 225), which in turn reflects what Michel Foucault explained as "the techniques of verbalization" as contributing to "a new self" (188: 49).

By publishing his autobiography Malcolm X provided future generations with the contextual material with which he should be considered. So an exercise that focuses on the styled body of Malcolm X, whose hagiographic status increased during the late twentieth century owing to extensive critical and poetic reference to him, is not to reduce his effective and affective cultural currency and political prowess to that of mere style icon, but it is an attempt to augment his iconic status in the presentation of another aspect of him, the styled Malcolm X. I argue that this aspect of Malcolm X was and is constituent to his telling-of-self, a technique he applied to produce a new self out of a life that he explained as "a chronology of changes" (Malcolm X 1966: 418). Alexandra Warwick and Dani Cavallaro have declared that the analysis of an individual through dress can lead to a broader intelligent understanding of that individual:

> [I]t could be argued that it is only by analysing the superficial language of dress that one may arrive at certain, albeit provisional, conclusions regarding both singular and group identities. Ignoring the surface would leave us with no hints as to the cultural and psychological significance of a sign system which is by definition superficial and whose depth lies precisely on the surface ... Dress, in this respect, is a manifestation of the unconscious at work, in that it is a superficial phenomenon, like symbolic language, which, also like language, speaks volumes about submerged dimensions of experience. Clothing, then, does not just operate as a disguising or concealing strategy. In fact, it could be regarded as a *deep surface*, a manifestation of the "unconscious" as a facet of existence which cannot be relegated to the psyche's innermost hidden depths but actually expresses itself through apparently superficial activities.
>
> **WARWICK & CAVALLARO** 1998: xxiii

In my reading of the style narratives of Malcolm X, I want to blend the political and the sartorial aspects of his life and character with his personal reading of himself and hopefully see "the unconscious at work [that] speaks volumes about the submerged dimensions of experience" (Warwick & Cavallaro 1998: xxiii). Malcolm X placed the *whole* of himself centrally in his pursuit for civil and metaphysical rights of equality and pride for the African-American community at the zenith of the Civil Rights and Black Consciousness Movement of the 1960s, and style-fashion-dress played a metaphysical, as well as technical part in this pursuit.

Malcolm X was acutely aware of the powerful poetry of self-adornment. To look at some of the ways he used and analysed his styled body in *The Autobiography of Malcolm X,* is to situate style as a technology of self-telling. This cogent remembering and verbalization of why he was as he was, is peppered with what Foucault called *technologies of the self.* For Foucault, the system is a study of the transition from one state of the self to another, and the necessity to understand the need and process of that transition. Equally, this change can impact on other areas of one's life or the lives of others, whether public, private or political, in this life or the next (Foucault 1988: 19–23). This knowledge and understanding of the self, leads to the caring of the self through concern for the self, which Foucault argued is subject to four types of technology:

> (1) technologies of production, which permit us to produce, transform, or manipulate things; (2) technologies of sign systems, which permit us to use signs, meanings, symbols, or signification; (3) technologies of power, which determine the conduct of individuals and submit them to certain ends or domination, an objectivizing of the subject; (4) technologies of the self, which permit individuals to effect by their own means or with help of others a certain number of operations on their own bodies and souls, thoughts, conduct, *and way of being, so as to transform themselves in order to attain a certain state of happiness, purity, wisdom, perfection, or immortality* ... Each implies certain modes of training and modification of individuals, not only in the obvious sense of acquiring certain skills but also in the sense of acquiring certain attitudes.
>
> **FOUCAULT** 1988: 18, my italics

Though Foucault's treatise is lodged in ancient Western traditions, the "technologies" he presents are nonetheless associated with techniques used by Malcolm X to understand himself in order to care not only for his temporal, physical self but, as a Muslim, his spiritual self. Therefore, Foucault's thoughts act as a guiding principle for this chapter, which is not solely located in the political thinking and activity of Malcolm X, but as an analysis of his process of becoming. The chapter is structured around epiphanies, "turning point moments" that serve as revelations in an individual's life. In an epiphany, an individual's character is revealed during either a crisis or a significant event that is confronted and often leaves marks on lives (Denzin 1989: 70–1).

The autobiographical text materializes the person, "the very self, the body, the figure" (Steedman 1992: 7). This is made more powerful by the representation of the self in photography. I argue that the "autobiographical performance" of Malcolm X expounds the styling of the self as one of the "technologies of the self." To support this, the photographs of Malcolm X from 1961 to his death on February 21, 1965 are another genre of self-telling used by him to compound the issues and aims raised in the *Autobiography of Malcolm X*, which he wanted to communicate to readers.

As early as 1960, the astute Malcolm X put into place counter-strategies to combat such occurrences. He commissioned Robert L. Haggins as his personal photographer, and allowed photographers such as the white American Eve Arnold and the African-American Gordon Parks, to photograph him in public and private. Throughout he remained guarded as to how he was to be presented, always in control.

FIGURE 4.1 *The Autobiography of Malcolm X*, published by Hutchinson 1966. Used by permission of Random House Group Limited.

The photographs visualize the resonance of his memories, his past *lives*, as to how he *became*. When "read" in conjunction with *The Autobiography of Malcolm X*, then another technology of self-telling occurs, another way of telling lives. Early editions of the *Autobiography* carried photographs. For example, the British first edition, published in 1966 (figure 4.1), features eighteen photographs interspersed throughout the book that detail his childhood and family, his zoot-suit teenage years, his time with the Nation of Islam, with his wife Betty Shabazz and his daughters, speaking at rallies and his death. There is no clarification in the publication of who chose these images.

This chapter also considers the projection of Malcolm's various stages of transformation through the written and visual presentation of the styled self as autobiography. The consideration of styling techniques used by Malcolm X in the presentation of himself to the public, as a leading member of the Muslim community and political activist, placed his body, as a "projection surface" (Warwick & Cavallaro 1998: 47) for political aims and his spiritual beliefs.

Reading between the lines

And it might be an interesting question to ask of an autobiography: who is
its implied ideal reader, and what is the catastrophic reading it is trying to avert?
PHILLIPS 1994: 71[4]

Autobiography is a genre of "self-telling." Adam Phillips examined the similarities between psychoanalysis and autobiography. He overrides Freud's theory that an autobiography cannot be successful if the author has not undergone psychoanalysis. Philips deems that can be successful in the sense that the writer has made some kind of recovery and has come to "know themselves and their history" (Phillips 1994: 66). Phillips argues that there are connections between autobiography and psychoanalysis. Both want to uncover the past through the recounting and analysis of memories. They are systems of self-telling that can uncover the past through the recounting and analysis of memories. These methods of self-knowledge also share the methodology of the interpretation of memories through free-association and clarification of the results. In the case of the production of the Autobiography of Malcolm X, a strong relationship was established between the story-teller, Malcolm X and the guide, Alex Haley[5], to unlock and interpret "screen-memories," "as a way of putting us closer to the truth" (Phillips 1994: 67).[6] An individual's life is not one life, but a multiplicity of lives. Therein lies the problematics of autobiography. How does one get at the "real," the "truth"?; "the autobiographer is always having to manage the fact that too many autobiographies make a life; that one's autobiography might be different at every moment" (Phillips 1994: 75).

The elusive quality of the "real" and the "whole truth," does not deter, in the example of Malcolm X, the reader from being guided through the series of transformations that shaped his life by varying discourses of power and resistance. The autobiography can help us to understand the operations of power and resistance, namely the two different systems of power: that of White America, and the Nation of Islam. Power and resistance are so pervasive in the very existence and interaction with these systems that they become who Malcolm X *is*. Power and resistance, then, feature in the self-imaging of Malcolm X. But what I want to foreground in this study is the importance of the transformation in the making of Malcolm X, and the pivotal part played by style-fashion-dress in the technology of self to complete the transformation in spite, though often because of, the persistent need to attend to the issues of power and resistance.

There are numerous poetic and critical readings of *The Autobiography of Malcolm X* that augment the different facets of his character and achievements. In her essay "Sitting at the Feet of the Messenger: Remembering Malcolm X," bell hooks focuses on his search for spiritual awakening and the fulfilment borne out of his endurance of the "processes of dehumanization [that] warp, distort, and when successful break the spirit" (hooks 1990: 80). It was his devout religious convictions that liberated his mind and soul, particularly following his pilgrimage to Mecca in 1964, and these provide an insight into the persona that was Malcolm X. The autobiography partially informs a second work by hooks on the reassessment of the expansive critical scholarship on Malcolm X (hooks 1994). On this occasion, she conducts a reading of texts on and by Malcolm X from a feminist perspective to reach a new way of looking at the Muslim political activist to "understand the complexity of his thinking about gender" (hooks 1994: 183). She charts his transition from a misogynist to a progressive in the last few years of his life, when he argued that *all*, not just male, intelligent human beings can fight for freedom (hooks 1994: 193). hooks pleads with the present and future generations to see Malcolm X in the round.

This is in contrast to the views held by Michelle Wallace on the "spectacle of Malcolm X's reification, fetishization, and commodification" (Berger et al 1995: 306). Wallace fears that black youth will latch onto the wrong aspects of Malcolm X and ignore his temperate qualities. Reading between the lines of the final chapter of his book, Malcolm X warns that his life had been governed by, "Such qualities as courage, heroism, militance, aggression, competitiveness, coolness, grace, elegance in battle, rigidity" (Berger *et al.* 1995: 306), qualities that were to lead to his death—but he had produced his book to quell the kind of fears as expressed by Wallace (Malcolm X 1966: 459). The posthumous accreditations to the memory and image of Malcolm X are part of the committed assembling of the history of heroines and heroes of the African diaspora to establish a history that has, until the 1970s, been hidden. To deny the whole life of Malcolm X is to deny the African diaspora the pleasure of having him as (and to understand why he is) a political and cultural icon. Spike Lee's 1992 film portrayal of the life of Malcolm X is also based on *The Autobiography of Malcolm X*, and is one of the key players in the celebration of his life.

Lee produced a poetic rendering of the African-American hero told through the voice and eyes of others. Gamilah Shabazz, the daughter of Malcolm X, believes that the average African-American in her home of Harlem, New York, had forgotten who Malcolm X was and what he stood for until the film *Malcolm X* was released. This film repositioned her father into the hearts and minds of what he himself had called his home town.[7] Malcolm X hysteria did seem to take over black communities in America and elsewhere on release of the film. The London Borough of Hackney, for example, and its thoroughfare of Kingsland High Street, pulsated under the plethora of baseball caps and T-shirts festooned with the grey, silver or white logo "X," on black (and some white) bodies, in the window displays of clothes shops, or the market stalls of Ridley Road Market.

The film opens with a carnivelesque night-time vibe of a boisterous, noisy Boston street with all the glamor of black city life in the early 1940s. In the first five minutes of the opening sequence of the film, Lee captures the heterogeneity of black America, conservatively-dressed men and women, children in appropriate garb, shoe shiners giving a high polish to the shoes of black folks, fashionable youths and zooters, a fraternity out on their own. The teenager Malcolm Little, or "Red" as he was rechristened by fellow street revellers during this period, strides across the screen with his "homie" Shorty in an outlandish, meticulously-styled light blue zoot suit[8] ensemble:

[T]he young salesman picked off a rack a Zoot suit that was just wild: sky-blue pants thirty inches in the knee and angle-narrowed down to twelve inches at the bottom, and a long coat that pinched my waist and flared out below my knees. As a gift, the salesman said, the store would give me a narrow leather belt with my initial "L" on it. Then he said I ought to also buy a hat, and I did—blue, with a feather in the four-inch brim. Then the store gave me another present: a long, thick-lined, gold plated chain that swung down lower than my coat hem.

MALCOLM X 1966: 127

Malcolm X devotes a lengthy part of his autobiography to being "schooled" in the etiquette of zoot suit assemblage. This is followed by the initiation process of the do-it-yourself "conk" to complete the transformation of Malcolm Little into Red (figure 4.2). In recollection, it was his "conked" hair, not the image of himself in the zoot suit that was "my first really big step toward self-degradation . . . I admire any Negro man who has never had himself conked, or who has had the sense to get rid of it—as I finally did" (Malcolm X 1966: 129–30). To go beyond "the natural" hairstyle and to chemically transform one's birth-right and identity as "black," caused Malcolm X pain that extracted from him a lengthy sermon on racial pride.

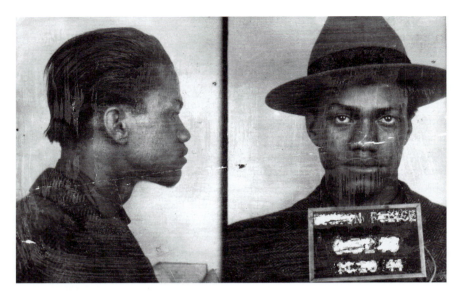

FIGURE 4.2 Police mug shot of 25-year-old Malcolm Little, Roxbury, 1944. Photo: Time Life Pictures/Getty Images.

To wear the zoot suit, on the other hand, and the elaborate accompanying accoutrements of hat and chains, and lindy-hopping at the Roseland Ballroom, was part of being "black." Malcolm X saw the wearing of the zoot suit by black men as staying "real," "being their natural selves," not diluting their identity with "phoney aires" like the "negroes breaking their backs trying to imitate white people" (Malcolm X 1966: 115).

I believe that to straighten one's hair, at this historical moment, and to wear an outlandishly cut and colored suit were both techniques of self-imaging that did not inhabit different degrees of "blackness," but when combined they produced a new, alternative aesthetic of "black" cultural experience. Nonetheless, Malcolm X's adherence to a demarcation of ethnic divide based on an authentic black body aesthetic remained in his analysis of this period of his life. In the opening sequence of the film, Lee tried to capture the quintessence of styling and dressing up amongst young black men in the early 1940s. It was part of the street culture and camaraderie of these youths who revelled in being in the spotlight, and saw themselves as the "connoisseurs of styles," as Malcolm X instructed: "In the ghetto, as in suburbia, it's the same status struggle to stand out in some envied way from the rest" (Malcolm X 1968: 143). When you are sixteen, as Malcolm X was, the styled body, the white girlfriend, and the dancing were the technologies used in this battle for street status amongst one's peers. These were a series of street-life motifs the Black Muslims still referred to in the early 1960s as the signs of a blight on the definition of what it means to be a black man. Dan Burley discussed such issues in the black Muslim newspaper *Muhammad Speaks*:

> the familiar sight in taverns, night clubs and restaurants and interracial parties of blonde, blue-eyed white women in the company of extremely homely black men with heavily greased and "processed" hair, razor or knife scars on their faces, wearing the attire of sidewalk sharpies or "cool cats" ... But no man could be happier than they because they have at last achieved the "lofty" status on their social sphere that can come only when one has won a white woman ... What makes it all the worse is that so-called Negro adults, male and female, have openly admired such conduct and even made semi-heroes out of these black panderers who have made a profession out of living off the prostitution of misguided women, not only white but those of their own race! Subsequently the black man must now work harder than ever to destroy this false picture that is undermining all his efforts towards black solidarity that must come before he achieves full independence and recognition as a man!

> **BURLEY** 1962: 5

Nonetheless, the exuberant and popularist opening of Lee's film into the very serious issue of who Malcolm X was and is, focuses on his immersion into urban style, and being at the center of one of the most radically subversive ensembles. An underlying agenda of the zoot suit was to critique World War II, and to question America's moral stance in its defence of other races from inhumane crimes, when it was guilty itself of such things in its own country, such as lynching and the Jim Crow system against non-whites. To wear such an expanse of fabric as the knee-length, wide-shouldered jacket and voluminous trousers, was to flout the rationing regulations. In the eyes of "right thinking Americans," this caused one to question the patriotism of its wearer (White & White 1998: 249; Alford 2004: 230–2; Pagán 2005: 467). From March 1942, the zoot suit was effectively an illegal ensemble, following a dictate from the War Production Board that "rationed cloth to a twenty-six percent cut-back in the use of fabrics," calling for a more meagre use of cloth in the form of the "streamlined suits by Uncle Sam" (Schoeffler & Gale 1973: 24). Indeed, as Cosgrove put it, "The regulations effectively forbade the manufacture of zoot suits" (Cosgrove 1989: 9). Malcolm X makes no direct reference to these social and political issues in his autobiography. Indirectly, the point is made when "Harlem Red" (the nomenclature signalling his acceptance by Harlemites, that was to become his home) exploits his "clown outfit" to "tom fool" his way out of being drafted into the army and fight for Uncle Sam: "I dragged out the wildest suit in New York. This was 1943 ... The day I went down there, I costumed like an actor. With my wild zoot suit I wore the yellow knob-toe shoes, and I frizzed my hair up into a reddish bush of conk" (Malcolm X 1966: 180). As mentioned above, in his later life the conk may have acquired connotations of denying one's "blackness," but in 1943 it was part of the visual symbols of black self-fashioning, as part of a complete wardrobe that was part of an urban black trend.

The zoot suit was, originally, vehemently un-American, solely entrenched in African-American, Mexican-American, Japanese-American and Filipino cultural groups (Kennedy 1959: 51; Alvarez 2008: 77–106). The zoot suit was also worn by teenage white Americans, who borrowed the style from the non-white groups mentioned above, which Steve Chibnall argues that for this group the zoot "was an integral part of the birth of 'the teenager' as a social category ... to establish an identity and define their relationship to their parent culture. The zoot added the vital element of stylistic rebellion to the other emergent focal concerns of the nascent teenage culture—hedonism, narcissism, faddism, star idolatry and conformity to subcultural codes—but it also highlighted the dependence of that culture on black innovation" (Chibnall 1985: 57). I would add, one also has to remember, that these emergent focal concerns were not only harbored by white American teenage boys, but were also harbored by non-white American teenage boys, because they were also teenagers, who were going through that difficult period all males (and females do) from child to adolescent to adult, and through the zoot suit effected that transformation of having the right to explore this new identity of being a teenager.[9] Their added layer of negotiation was the issue of "race" and ethnic difference. Effectively, in this stage of his life as a zoot-wearing youth from 1942 onwards, Malcolm X was undoubtedly one of "the stewards of something uncomfortable" (Ellison 1947: 381) from the context of engaging in subcultural acts and subversion through style within the framework of "race" and ethnicity. Therefore, the zoot suit was categorized a dangerous ensemble, that became embroiled in racial etiquette of the period, to wear it could have dire effects on the life of a specific ignoble group of non-white American men:

> In many parts of the U.S.A., your race may be judged by the clothes you wear, the way you cut your hair, or the language or accent in which you speak. If you are a white man and wish to avoid the many disabilities and hazards incumbent upon being nonwhite, you should avoid wearing anything suggestive of the so-called zoot-suit, whose distinguishing characteristics are a drape coat and peg trousers. The white community has come to look upon the zoot-suit as a badge of rebellion against its style dictates, and consequently not even a white person may wear one with impunity.
>
> **KENNEDY** 1959: 51

Lee was perhaps right to launch into his filmic biography of Malcolm X with a highly-charged performance of ghetto adornments. The zoot suit was not just about high-rolling and hanging with the "homeboys," it was about the attainment of power and control of the self by the wearer. Here was Black Power some twenty-odd years before the official counter-discourse of the movement of the same name, tailored into a specific style of suit, an attitude in opposition to the White Power constructed in the authoritarian and patriotic garments of the military uniform of the streamlined, rationed suit. One could say that here, in the fabric and cut of three suits—the zoot suit, the "streamlined suit by Uncle Sam" and the military suit of the soldier—the social tension that has marred the texture of American society was played out in the public arena of the actual streets of America or the panoptic plane of the draft board.

Foucault, then, is useful in an attempt to understand the importance of style-fashion-dress in the life of Malcolm X as a political and cultural icon of this panoptic situation. Style for Malcolm X not only provided and linked him with "pleasure and individual freedom [in] the control over the self in one's regulated relations with others" (Lechte 1994: 114), but during his self-construction in his zoot-suit period, and most importantly coupled with the conk hairstyle, he was linked to the extended socio-political meanings of that subcultural dress. This was a successful technology of the self that doubled as a counter-discourse. Clothes, accessories and hairstyles, then, provide the instruments that empower the body to counteract a dominant ideology.

Talking pictures

I was amused recently at an International Center of Photography group show of pictures of Malcolm X. The lead picture was one of mine: a huge smiling profile of him looking smart; hat, gold watch and Masonic ring worn jauntily. A group of young black photographers came over to talk to me. "Thank you," they said, "for making him look like a dude." "It was a collaboration" I said.

ARNOLD 1996: 63

In 1961, four years before the original publication of his autobiography, the white American photographer, Eve Arnold, took this photograph of Malcolm X (figure 4.3). It was part of a series of images Arnold produced on assignment for *Life* magazine to document the Nation of Islam. Thirty five years later, she remembers Malcolm X as an "imaginative professional" who knew how to use the power of photography as an affective tool of positive representation: "He knew his needs, his wants, his best points and how to get me to give him what he required" (Arnold 1996: 63). The question is, what did Malcolm X want out of this portrait? The photograph has become one of the most poetic and iconic portraits of the man who feared in the closing pages of his autobiography, that following his death, the image that would remain engineered by "the white man, in his press" would be one of "a convenient symbol of 'hatred'" (Malcolm X 1966: 462).

Arnold's portrait dominates the front cover of *Malcolm X: The Great Photographs*, an impressive photographic essay of the public life of Malcolm X from 1960 to the

FIGURE 4.3 Malcolm X, meeting of black muslims, Chicago, 1961. Photograph by Eve Arnold. Courtesy of Magnum Photos.

aftermath of his death on February 21, 1965. The profile barely discloses the clean-shaven, facial features of Malcolm X, but there is no denying it is him, the face of Malcolm X is so much a part of the history and ideology of black struggle and black history, black pride and black ideals. The suffusion of his image and ideologies within popular culture per se, is so entrenched that the symbol "X" on a baseball cap or a solitary pair of horn-rimmed brow-line glasses initiates a ricochet of image references, teachings and beliefs that *is* Malcolm X.

Garments and accessories dominate this monochromatic vignette of intimacy and intensity. They are linked to a pivotal period of transformation in a life that "had been a chronology of *changes*" (Malcolm X 1966: 418), that was Malcolm Little, Red (1966: 118), Harlem Red (1966: 155), Detroit Red (1966: 171), Malcolm X, El-Hajj Malik El-Shabazz (1966: 421). Days after his release from prison in August 1952, where he converted to the Nation of Islam, Malcolm X purchased three things:

> I remember well, I bought a better-looking pair of eyeglasses than the pair the prison had issued to me; and I bought a suitcase and a wrist watch. I have thought since, that without fully knowing it, I was preparing for what my life was about to become. Because those are three things I've used more than anything else. My eyeglasses correct the astigmatism that I got from all the reading in prison. I travel so much now that my wife keeps alternate suitcases packed so that, when necessary, I can just grab one. And you won't find anybody more time-conscious than I am. I live by my watch, keeping appointments even when I'm using my car. I drive by my watch, not my speedometer. Time is more important to me than distance.
>
> **MALCOLM X** 1966: 268

What relevance does the prominence of these items have in the photographic portrait of Malcolm X? In his autobiographical voice of self-telling, and in the visualization, through portraiture, of the essence of Malcolm X, his watch and glasses were part of the aesthetic tools that defined him as a man on a spiritual and political mission. This was a "new man" who had come to know himself and took himself seriously enough on leaving prison to enter a new phase of his life. Here, in this example of processing a "screen-memory," Malcolm X shows, as Foucault argued, that "the knowledge of oneself appeared as the consequence of taking care of yourself" (1988: 22). By addressing the importance of the purchase of the spectacles and the watch in his autobiography, and to include their practical and personal meaning of professionalism, Malcolm X could take control of representations, through a skilful blend of memory, dialogue and visual documentation as a route to a kind of "truth." The portrait achieves for Malcolm X and his projected self, what Graham Clarke defines as the possibilities of portraiture, that it is:

not so much a portrait advertising a self as a general idea consumed . . . [but] each slightest difference suggests a distinction which has its place, its meaning, in a context outside the photograph. The result is a complex intertextuality between photographic significance and the social and cultural codes which defines status and power.

CLARKE 1997: 105–12

The trilby, the most overbearing item in the portrait has, in the climate of the persistent Jim Crow etiquette in which this photograph was taken, the most foreboding and subversive communication. During the "racist etiquette" that plagued America during the 1950s and on through the 1960s, writer Stetson Kennedy warned non-white men in 1959 that to wear a hat in the presence of whites could constitute an arrest, and in some extreme cases if they were to wear it when addressing a white woman, it had led to the kind of mob violence "as alleged rape of white women by non-white men" (Kennedy 1959: 220). For a black man to have himself photographed by a white woman wearing his hat, and more conspicuously, for that hat to be worn in the cocksure manner as having it tipped forward and perched sexily on his head, was I suggest, an act of repudiation of the codes of Jim Crow etiquette by Malcolm X, and all it meant in the separation of the races, in the very public flouting of his "uppiteness."

The practicalities of his horn-rimmed spectacles, or the affiliatory marker of the Nation of Islam in a ring, did not prevent Malcolm X from looking as cool as a crooner such as Frank Sinatra, another icon affiliated with the trilby worn by Malcolm X, who affected the same kind of cool pose. The urban aesthetic that the young Malcolm X had cultivated on the streets of Harlem had not been lost to him in his later life, despite the culture of conservative uniformity amongst the brothers of the Nation of Islam. The image suggests the effects of the passage of time on an individual and the results of transition.

Through an analysis of the dress code for men and women of the Nation of Islam in her book *In Retrospect* (1996), Arnold tried to gain some insight into how and why ordinary, working class African-American men and women, who joined the Nation of Islam, had attained an intense aura of dignity and pride, to exact the Nation of Islam's indomitable cultivation of a "collective individuality" (Simmel 1971: 257). Male and female members could purchase smart, formal and casual clothing, as well as accessories from Nation of Islam clothing stores, such as Temple No. 2 Clothing Store, 553, E. 79th Street, New York. Advertisements featured on the women's page of their representative newspaper, *Muhammad Speaks,* offered a service of "CLOTHING MADE INDIVIDUALLY YOURS ANY STYLE OR FASHION TO SUIT YOUR TASTE. TO YOUR MEASURE YOUR CHOICE OF FABRICS IN OUR OWN FACTORY TEMPLE No. 2 CLOTHING FACTORY 453 EAST 79TH STREET" (*Muhammed Speaks* 1962: 31). The uniform distinguished their sense of pride and self-respect given to them as "sons and daughters of Allah," instilling a feeling of belonging and worth, though it segregated men and women through orthodox systems of gendered clothing and color symbolism. An extreme example was the bands of monochrome seating arrangements Arnold photographed, which Malcolm X also described in his autobiography. At a rally of all the Chapters of the Nation of Islam at the Uline Arena in Washington DC, "The balconies and the rear half of the main floor were filled with black people of the general public. Ahead of them were the all-Muslim seating sections—the white-garbed beautiful black sisters, and the dark-suited, white-shirted [and bow tied] brothers" (Malcolm X 1966: 325). In the everyday dress of black Muslims there was no place for ostentation or individual expression, "the men were quietly, tastefully dressed" (Malcolm X 1966: 270). A sense of worth was carved into the close shaven haircut; dignity and pride encircled the frame of the black Muslims, trapped in the buttoning of an inconspicuous single-breasted suit and moderately-shined shoes. Such personal values were reiterated in *Muhammad Speaks*: "TO BE SUCCESSFUL … LOOK SUCCESSFUL BY KEEPING YOUR CLOTHES NEAT … and CLEANED by TEMPLE No. 2 CLEANERS … SUPERIOR CLEANING by EXPERTS PICKUP AND DELIVERY SERVICE WE OPERATE OUR OWN PLANT" (1962: 11). The aesthetic restraints placed upon members of the Nation of Islam narrowed the scope for singular sites of individuality to shine within this "narrow circle." Facets combined to combat any similarity with African-American secular males that threatened to blight the definition of what a black man can be as outlined earlier.

What is expressed in the Malcolm X portrait is the release of emotion, a dimension of an individual amongst the uniformity and orthodoxy of the Nation of Islam.

Dead man walking

To read *The Autobiography of Malcolm X* is to walk with him to his death. The interview process between Alex Haley and Malcolm X began in 1963. On February 21, 1965, Malcolm X was murdered. The emotional intensity of his whole life, up to February 1965, imploded in the last four chapters of the book, as a new phase of his life unfolded and was recorded simultaneously. In December 1963, as documented in chapter sixteen, Malcolm X was suspended for ninety days from the Nation of Islam, the Muslim organization to which he converted in 1947 whilst in prison. He was "silenced" from making any public comments on social issues by the leader of the Nation of Islam, Elijah Mohammed, following the inflammatory comment Malcolm X had made on the death of President John F. Kennedy, "the chickens coming home to roost" (Malcolm X 1966: 379).[10] Malcolm X maintained that this was not the real issue behind the silencing. He believed it was his established status as one of the leading spokespersons on the human rights issue of African-Americans, winning the respect of Muslims and non-Muslims, and his outstanding work in the growth of the Nation of Islam, and the possibility of him replacing Mohammed that had engendered envy amongst members of his own religion. His belief and sense of betrayal at this order from Mohammed, whom Malcolm X had once placed higher than his own life, and the violent repercussions that he believed were to be put in place by the Nation of Islam, were the catalyst for his pilgrimage to Mecca in 1964. The trip was to be a "broadening [of] his knowledge of that religion" (Malcolm X 1966: 397). It came to provide him with the final act to sever his relationship with the Nation of Islam.

The shared documentation of a life as it was experienced by Malcolm X and Haley, the daily witnessing of its roller-coaster ride to its end, attained synchronicity as the interviewer in the forward to *The Autobiography of Malcolm X*, and the interviewee individually documented the period of transformation from Malcolm X into El-Hajj Malik El-Shabazz, particularly through his style. Before his departure to Mecca, Malcolm X was clean shaven, he wore the conservative attire befitting a member of the Nation of Islam of a plain single-breasted suit, shirt and tie and classic unpretentious horn-rimmed spectacles, that combined to form the iconography that *is* Malcolm X. Meeting El-Hajj Malik El-Shabazz on the day he returned from his pilgrimage, Haley can only express the change in Malcolm X through his appearance:

> When the blue Oldsmobile stopped, and I got in, El Hajj Malcolm, broadly beaming, wore a seersucker suit, the red hair needed a barber's attention, and he had grown a beard ... There must have been fifty still and television photographers and reporters jockeying for position, up front, and the rest of the Skyline Ballroom was filling with Negro followers of Malcolm X, or his well-wishers, and the curious ... They picked at his "racist" image. "I'm *not* a racist. I'm not condemning whites for being whites, but for their deeds. I condemn what whites collectively have done to our people collectively." He almost continually flashed about the room the ingratiating boyish smile. He would pick at the new reddish beard. They asked him about that, did he plan to keep it? He said he hadn't decided yet, he would have to see if he could get used to it or not.
>
> **MALCOLM X** 1966: 36

Malcolm X's choice of casual presentation to address a press conference some two hours after arriving in the country was change indeed. In this instance, he had marked his individuality and chronic desire for temporal and spiritual change, to dislocate himself from his recent past as Malcolm X, the minister of New York Muslim Temple No. 7 of the Nation of Islam, into El-Hajj Malik El-Shabazz, the founder of two new organizations in June 1964: Muslim Mosque Inc. and the Organization of Afro-American Unity. The aesthetic codes for men of the National of Islam, in regard to the presentation of the public self, was to be immaculate and unassuming: clean shaven, well-maintained hair, plain conservative suit, well-polished (not highly shined) shoes. Abjection is perhaps the best explanation of this ambiguous self-presentation: "the abject is above all the ambiguous, the in-between what defies boundaries, a composite resistant to unity. Hence, if the subject's identity derives from the unity of its objects, the abject is the threat of unassimilable non-unity; that is, ambiguity. Abjection, therefore, is fundamentally what disturbs identity, system and order" (Lechte 1990: 160, quoted by Warwick & Cavallaro: xvi–xvii).

Could the ambiguity inherent in the identity of Malcolm X be based on his past personas and the new words being spoken, effectively changing much of what had gone before? As a member and leading figure of the Nation of Islam, his immaculate, business-like attire underscored his orthodox Muslim practices, and his stringent views on race and racism—essentially a mistrust of "the white devils" (Malcolm X 1966: 280). In the Hotel Theresa, his views had become more inclusive, no longer the binary struggle between blacks and whites, them and us. His clothing transmitted mixed messages of ease and control, the space for difference and creativity.[11]

In this very public presentation and production of his self, Malcolm X had controlled how he would be visually represented in the media (plate 7). His relaxed attire of unkempt hair, the nonchalant, decorated self in the "blustered" ornamented feature of a seersucker suit, was indicative of the confidence Malcolm X had in himself *to be* himself. The cotton summer suit is a respectable item of the male wardrobe, but not on equal terms as the woolen summer suit, as it is prone to crease and therefore is unable to retain its shape and the smart appearance of the wearer. The aura of elegance is lost. Its ability to keep the wearer cool overrides such sartorial drawbacks (Roetzel 1999: 115–16). A prosaic reading of the seersucker suit would foreground its function as effective summer wear, due to its cool and lightweight properties. In the heated context of a press conference, where El-Hajj Malik El-Shabazz had to explain himself anew on religion, politics and physical appearance, the suit was not only a sign of a new Malcolm X, relaxed yet in control of his future, but also the correct clothing to function in such artificially heated conditions. He kept his cool to be cool. In addition, looking cool in the face of the media, which can so easily show one "looking like a fool" (Malcolm X 1966: 386)[12] was of primary importance to the media wary Malcolm X. It was significant that he should present himself in this way, unpolished and unconventional, voicing new opinions, indeed, he was fully aware that he had "as one asset, . . . an international image. No amount of money could have bought" (Malcolm X: 388), and he wanted to maintain his credibility as a representative in "The American black man's struggle."

That ephemeral quality of cool is generally linked with urban lifestyles, the avant-garde, the unconventional. The exacted expression of cool that Malcolm possessed had the power to entice the generally apolitical self-obsessed "ghetto hustlers" and "ghetto youths"—themselves, connoisseurs of cool—to political issues. After all, by 1964 Malcolm X had amassed such support from black Americans that he was described as "America's only negro who could stop a race riot—or start one" (Malcolm X 1966: 390). He was successful in the construction of a styled image, and a social and political standing, whilst he expressed empathy with *his* people, by "being real" and keeping in touch with his origins had paid off: "The ghetto masses already had entrusted me with an image of leadership among them. I knew the ghetto instinctively extends that trust only to one who had demonstrated that he would never sell them out to the white man" (Malcolm X 1966: 391) (figure 4.4). To be cool then, is not only what Gabriele Mentges defines as part of a modern form of self-construction predicated by street consciousness (Mentges 2000: 27–48), but in the case of Malcolm X, a modern way of political thinking and being, to combine the urban with the intellectual to result in a particular form of pride in being black.

The goatee beard, though, was the fetishized marker of his particular transformation. The decision regarding whether he was or was not going to keep the beard had a profound spiritual meaning for Malcolm X and his experience of the Hajj:

> Standing on Mount Arafat had concluded the essential rites of being a Pilgrim to Mecca. No one who missed it could consider himself a pilgrim. The *Ihram* had ended. We cast the traditional seven stones at the devil. Some had their hair and beards cut. I decided that I was going to let my beard remain. I wondered what my wife Betty, and our little daughters, were going to say when they saw me with a beard, when I got back to New York. New York seemed a million miles away.
>
> **MALCOLM X** 1966: 416

Malcolm X kept the beard until his death in 1965.

The name Malcolm X was already known and unique in the public consciousness. To style himself in this new, easy liberated guise was exacting a personal confirmation of this change in his life, on a course that was more inclusive of other people, of other ideas, political and personal. This relaxed, minimal image was not an original one, as the so-called "Modernists," jazz artists and followers had perfected the look during the 1950s (Marsh 1991: 9; Polhemus 1994: 38–9; Boyer 2012). The image was not far removed from the discreet style he adopted and adapted when he was part of the black Muslims. In this new phase of his styled self, the worldly undertones of his Muslim-style so clearly suffused in the Arnold portrait was foregrounded. This style treatment to individualize the self, in the fine tuning of El-Hajj Malik El-Shabazz, enabled Malcolm X to dissociate himself from the members of the Nation of Islam, break away from being a "Zombie—like all the rest of them" (Parks 1990: 234). Newness in the form of a new self had taken center stage. This particular constellation of body, the self and style provided the

FIGURE 4.4 Malcolm X, black muslim leader, addresses a rally in Harlem in New York City on June 29, 1963. © AP/PA Images.

interface between new directions of his political and religious thinking in order to take care of, and know the self. Therefore Malcolm X had entered into another of Simmel's definitions on individuality, one based on quality: "the single human being distinguishes himself from all others; that is being and conduct—in form, content, or both—suit him alone; and that being different has a positive meaning and value for his life" (Simmel 1971: 271).

The use of style as a metaphor for transformation, to present himself as "El-Hajj Malik El-Shabazz," harked back to the edicts of street culture and philosophy of his time as a "hustler" in Harlem, New York, "that in order to get something you had to look as though you already had something" (Malcolm X 1966: 179). There at the Hotel Theresa, amid people who knew him well (namely his wife and Alex Haley) and people who thought they knew him (in America's press, and through their newspapers and television news articles, all America and beyond), Malcolm X wanted to be accepted for who he was now. The conflation of the visual presentation of himself and the words he spoke, a transformed individual now stood in their presence:

> My pilgrimage broadened my scope. It blessed me with a new insight. In two weeks in the Holy Land, I saw what I never had seen in thirty-nine

years here in America. I saw *races*, all *colors,*—blue-eyed blonds to black-skinned Africans-in *true* brotherhood! in unity! Living as one! Worshipping as one! No segregationists—no liberals ... In the past, yes, I have made sweeping indictments of *all* white people. I never will be guilty of that again—as I know now that some white people *are* truly sincere, that some truly are capable of being brotherly toward a black man. The true Islam has shown me that a blanket indictment of all white people is as wrong as when whites make a blanket indictment against blacks.

MALCOLM X 1966: 441–2

Here in this moment of unveiling a new self, Malcolm X had attained the pride he had longed for. In 1931, following the murder of his father, the Reverend Earl Little, his family had begun to sink under the weight of poverty. The overriding value that Louise Little, his mother, tried to preserve in the midst of all this was pride, but it dissolved. Malcolm X marks 1934 as the year of acceleration of this erosion, ending with the desegmentation of his family, the children sent to different families, and his mother to a mental hospital where she stayed for twenty-six years.

This relaxed image could also be read as Malcolm X placing his style as secondary to his change in political ideologies due to spiritual fulfilment. But I find this hard to entertain. Throughout *The Autobiography of Malcolm X* clothes and accessories, hairstyles and facial hair were at the juncture of change for him. He enters into evocative descriptions of dress as metaphors for pride in oneself or as a combative system in the street or political arena. During his life as a hustler, the gun and the tie were necessary self-defining objects to his character and identity. To function correctly in his chosen environment, to *be* "Red" and to survive on the streets, clothes were a vital component. "As I have said, a gun was as much a part of my dress as a necktie" (Malcolm X 1966: 223). They were the necessary and correct tools to complete a job professionally, more fundamentally, to survive.

The power of clothes, accessories and hairstyles to reveal the internal strengths and weaknesses of an individual were not lost on Malcolm X. Whilst he was in prison, his brother Reginald, who had introduced Malcolm X to the Nation of Islam, was expelled from the organization for transgressing their rules of morality. Reginald visited his incarcerated brother, and now a devout Muslim, Malcolm X believed he saw "the chastisement of Allah—what Christians would call "the curse"—come upon Reginald" (Malcolm X 1966: 263) materialized in the very assemblage of his brother's styled body. "When he had been a Muslim he had been immaculate in his attire. But now he wore things like a T-shirt, shabby-looking trousers and sneakers. I could see him on the way down" (Malcolm X 1966: 262–3). Reginald's easy street style, and Malcolm X's coming out style premiered to the world at the Hotel Theresa, were kindred spirits, though distanced through years and causation. This was an aesthetic statement to demonstrate one's styling capabilities and disdain for convention-making and taking pleasure in the

PLATE 1 Alfred Valentine Tulloch, 1955, Birmingham, England. Author's collection.

PLATE 2 Emmeline Cetira Thomas, 1955, Birmingham, England. Author's collection.

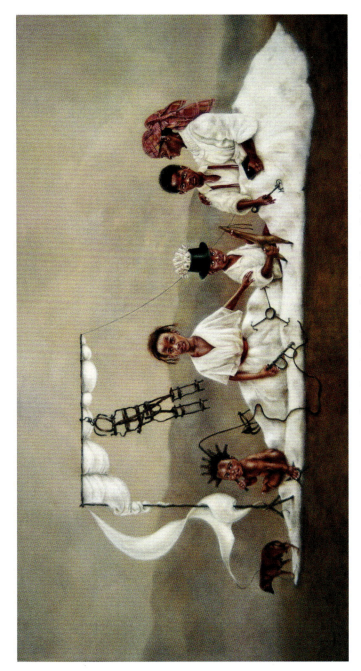

PLATE 3 *Tools of the Trade*, 1996, 50 x 25 inches Oil on linen by Roberta Stoddart. Photo: Abigail Hadeed.

Drawn by James Hakewill.   Engrav'd by Sutherland.

Waterfall on the Windward Road.

near Kingston.

Publish'd Apr. 1.1824. by Hurst, Robinson, & C.º 90. Cheapside. & Lloyd. Harley Street.

PLATE 4 *Waterfall on the Windward Road*, 1820–21. Courtesy of the National Library of Jamaica.

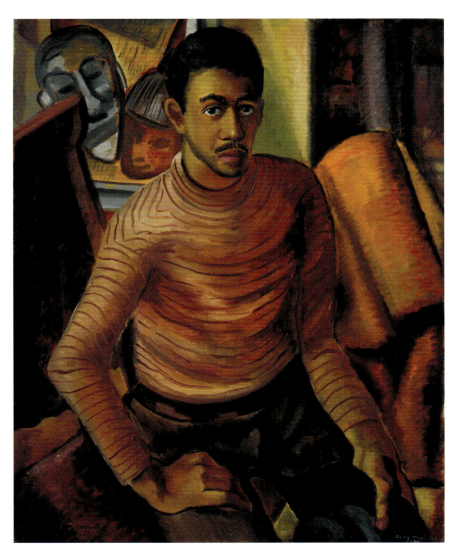

PLATE 5 *Self-portrait: Myself at Work*, 1934 by Malvin Gray Johnson, oil on canvas, 97cm × 76cm. Courtesy of Smithsonian American Art Museum, Gift of the Harmon Foundation.

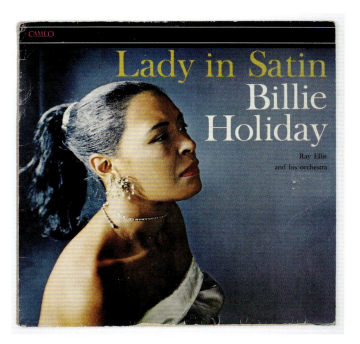

PLATE 6 *Lady in Satin* album, 1958. Photo: Syd Shelton. Courtesy of Sony Music Entertainment.

PLATE 7 Malcolm X, 1964, photographed by Robert Parent. Photo: Robert Parent/Getty Images.

PLATE 8 Steve Biko T-shirt, 2006, Johannesburg, South Africa, designed by Stoned Cherrie. The T-shirt was part of the "South African Designers at Woolworths" campaign. Photograph by Syd Shelton. Author's collection.

PLATE 9 An Outfit worn by Dr Beryl Gilroy following arrival in England in 1951. © Victoria and Albert Museum.

presentation of the new self. This is not to say that Malcolm X did not exercise the latter during his years with the Nation of Islam, the portrait taken by Eve Arnold extols this. He exuded there his maverick character, and his ability to set himself apart with the aid of a hat, a pair of glasses, a watch and a ring.

Summary: Malcolm X, graphically speaking

To style the body in a particular way to meet certain needs places garments and accessories as a metaphor to address issues faced by an individual or group. Of course this is not new, these are observations made by subcultural theorists. What has intrigued me in the case of Malcolm X and his use of clothes and accessories, hairstyles and facial hair, to style his body, to project himself as a legitimate, though unconventional and fiercely autonomous, political leader, is his seersucker suit, for example, which was not so much an object of desire, but rather, part of a new language of self used to signify the desire of his political objectives and activism.

This new language of self was articulated further by Malcolm X in his wearing of a tweed suit, as illustrated in the company of students from the University of Oxford in December 1964 on a trip to England (figure 4.5). He wears a fine checked single-breasted tweed suit with a slim dark tie, and light-colored shirt. This is supported by, the now famous "Malcolm X spectacles." His face is softened by his longer length natural hair, replacing the clean-shaven head that was a rudimentary feature for men of the Nation of Islam, and he has cultivated a neat, full goatee beard. Malcolm X maintains this same look in a photograph taken by Robert L. Haggins on February 18, 1965, three days before his assassination, which is believed to be the last portrait taken of him. Clearly this is a more secular image, a style that was worn by the avant-garde jazz artist Albert Ayler in the same period. It is also a look that was from the same style trajectory of the seersucker suit, both of which were connected to the Ivy League-inspired style developed by jazz artists during the 1950s. G. Bruce Boyer has outlined that jazz artists played at American universities and were drawn to the Ivy League style of students and academic staff. The musicians bought clothes and accessories from campus shops that included Harris Tweed jackets, seersucker, gray flannel sack-cut suits and narrow repp ties button-down shirts, Weejun shoes, Shetland crewneck sweaters and tan balmacaan raincoats (Boyer 2012: 143, 145) then brought the style back to black urban areas where, Boyer believes, the trend was passed on, but he prompts: "That is a dialectic story yet to be told" (Boyer 2012: 145). I suggest that in Malcolm X, here was one example of how the aesthetic of Ivy League, originally a conspicuously white American phenomena, became a powerful visual statement of an aesthetic of black presence, a form of agency that Malcolm X used to continuously punctuate

FIGURE 4.5 The University of Oxford, December 3, 1964. Malcolm X prior to giving a lecture to students on extremism and liberty. Photo: Keystone/Getty Images.

the political world of black and white Americans. Malcolm X mediated through his styled self the "intellectual touch" (Maharaj 2012) of his dogged pursuit for human and civil rights for black Americans to become the embodied "graphic argument" of black activism.

Photographer and graphic designer Syd Shelton refers to the concept of a graphic argument where an image is created by an individual which enables them "to be a subjective witness of the period which could, hopefully, contribute to social change" (Shelton 2008). Shelton is referring to the two-dimensional image of photography, which equally applies to Malcolm X. As outlined above, Malcolm X knew the cultural currency of photography. He had an understanding of the long lasting outreach of newspapers and their accompanying images as evidence and communication. Malcolm X would take photographs himself to support articles he wrote (Malcolm X 1966: 313–14). He produced publications such as the *Messenger Magazine,* which launched in 1959 (Marabel 2011: 163). In 1960, he established the monthly Nation of Islam newspaper *Muhammad Speaks.*[13] This idea of the graphic argument equally applies to Malcolm X in three-dimensional form. Whether speaking on television, at street rallies in Harlem, or at indoor lectures, his black and white audience had the time to "study" the visual, as well as aural, presence of

Malcolm X. Both mediums were channelled into his persuasive arguments.

I have previously used the framework of graphic design, black activism and the composition of related symbols and details (Tulloch 2008), making composition a prime technique in the styling of Malcolm X as a graphic argument for black activism. In his advice on taking photographs, Bruce Barnbaum provides a definition of composition. At a basic level it is "an arrangement of parts" to create "a unified, harmonious whole" (Barnbaum 2010: 15). Ultimately composition is "unified thought ... that all the elements of the photograph work together, i.e., a central concept underlies the photograph" which is achieved when a composition makes clear "your intent" (Barbaum 2010: 18–19).

Consider, for example, the photograph of Malcolm X taken by Gordon Parks in Los Angeles (figure 4.6) in April 1963. Malcolm X had been sent to Los Angeles by Elijah Mohammad to support thirteen Nation of Islam men who had been indicted for a violent encounter between Los Angeles Police Department officers and Muslims on April 27, 1962 where seven unarmed black Muslims had been shot, one of which, Ronald X Stokes, was killed. This aggressive assault on his fellow Muslims had, according to Manning Marable, "shattered" Malcolm. One photograph shows Malcolm X at the center of the image, on the sidewalk, with a white man and woman having just walked past him. The stark yet elegant contrast of his dark sack-like suit and slim tie, with his light-colored cutaway collar shirt, exacerbates the gravity of the issue he addresses to the public in the paper he

FIGURE 4.6 Untitled, Los Angeles, California, 1963, photograph by Gordon Parks. Courtesy and copyright The Gordon Parks Foundation.

distributes with the headline: "EXTRA ... SEVEN UNARMED NEGROES SHOT IN COLD BLOOD BY LOS ANGELES POLICE" (Davis 1993: 78, 81). Although Malcolm X is in a sea of advertising posters that undoubtedly says "America" through its recognizable graphics, and the two members of the public reference "white America," Malcolm X is steadfastly "black America." Here, Malcolm X is a graphic argument of black activism as responsibility to raise awareness and memory of Stokes and his fellow Muslims who had been shot, and for the rights of Muslims on trial. This show of responsibility pre-empted a statement Malcolm X made in the last chapter of his *Autobiography*, "1965," that: "[Y]ou watch. I will be labelled as, at best, an 'irresponsible' black man ... You only get action as a black man if you are regarded by the white man as 'irresponsible' " (Malcolm X 1966: 462). James Baldwin believed the various labels attached to Malcolm X, such as extremist, came from the fact that "What they mean is that Malcolm is an extremist because he makes them uncomfortable and because he argues that not all Negroes are non-violent, which happens to be true.'[14]

In this one example of so many photographs, Malcolm X made sure that people could *see* him. To *see* him was to be constantly reminded of the charge of a new black America. Additionally, "Photography is ... a process of thoughtful consideration of your own point of view overlaid upon the scene. It requires creative thinking, which is not easy" (Barnbaum 2010: 22). Such thinking could be applied to the political aims of Malcolm X. Malcolm X may not have taken the photographs that charted his political activities, but he was complicit in their composition, most powerfully as the stylist of his own activist self.

As the opening quote states categorically, Malcolm X wanted *all* of him, "his whole life" to be reviewed, "from birth ... All of our experiences fuse into our personality. Everything that ever happened to us is an ingredient" (Malcolm X 1966: 225). In this chapter I have tried to blend the political and the sartorial aspects of Malcolm X, as the *whole* of him was placed centrally in his pursuit for the equal rights and the psychological liberation of African-Americans, striving for recognition of their rightful pride of place in the USA. And for Malcolm X that he no longer be resigned to a place in history as just an "angry young man."

5 YOU SHOULD UNDERSTAND, IT'S A FREEDOM THING: THE STONED CHERRIE–STEVE BIKO T-SHIRT

In the face you can have all kinds of political landscapes
MARLENE RUSHTON 2015: 166[1]

In July 2006 I bought a Stoned Cherrie T-shirt. It features a portrait of Stephen Bantu Biko, known more generally as Steve Biko, the black South African anti-apartheid activist and Black Conscious movement leader (plate 8). I was invited by the organizers of Sanlam South African Fashion Week (SA) in Johannesburg to present a paper at the Arts and Culture Fashion Seminar programme that complements the fashion shows and the other range of talks, fashion designer stands, workshops and discussions that comprise SA Fashion Week. I was encouraged by several South African fashion designers and the organizers of SA Fashion Week to visit Woolworths Department Store, based in the Sandton shopping center, Johannesburg, to see the new collections produced by South African fashion designers for the retailer. In all honesty, I was not excited about the prospect as I imagined this South African Woolworths was the same as the cheap but cheerful British, high street staple Woolworths, formerly known as F.W. Woolworth, affectionately known as Woolies.[2] It's not. Woolworths at Sandton is a grander affair.

I made my way to the dedicated South African Designers at Woolworths display area.[3] The first thing I saw was a T-shirt on a mannequin, with the face of Steve Biko dominating the front of the garment. It was a blend of the rich color combination of mustard yellow and claret, and the bold image of Steve Biko from the cover of *Drum* magazine that arrested me. I recognized what the South African artist, Marlene Dumas, profoundly observed above as having "all kinds of political landscapes" (2015: 166). As I came face-to-face with the T-shirt, I asked questions: why this image of Steve Biko? What did the many white shoppers milling around Woolworths with me think about this garment? I thought it was brave. I thought it was bold. I *had* to have it. I had to beg the shop assistant to let me buy the T-shirt on the mannequin as this was the last one. It cost 320 Rand.[4] The Woolworths panel that supported the display of Stoned Cherrie designs consisted of a slogan from the fashion company: "Subscribe to yourself." The remainder of the panel explained: "Nkensani's designs celebrate South Africa's rich history with an irresistible exuberance and energy. It's fresh, and chic, and giving Afro-urban culture the glamour and prominence it deserves."

This fitted T-shirt is a woman's South African size 14, which is the same as the UK; it is 59cms in length, resting on top of the hips. As mentioned above, the dominant color of the T-shirt is mustard for the body and trim on the edge of the sleeves with a burgundy accent for the sleeves and neckline trim. The garment is made of viscose and Spandex. It has a scooped neckline, three-quarter length sleeves and is fitted at the waist. The embroidered black garment label confirms that the T-shirt is part of the South African Designers at Woolworths range, written in white thread, with Stoned Cherrie embroidered underneath in orange.

The T-shirt carries only one image on its front, the profile portrait of Steve Biko, which appeared on the cover of the African magazine *Drum*, November 1977. The *Drum* cover image is "framed" by a white border. The issue chosen is not an immaculate copy. The screen-printing has picked up the "rubbed" and worn areas of the magazine, but this is of secondary importance. The significance of this particular issue is that it mourned the death of Steve Biko who was murdered by the police on September 12, 1977 whilst in detention without trial.

I have not worn the T-shirt, it was never my intention to. I bought it because I viewed it as a potent cultural object, a black South African object, due to the history and legacy of black South African struggle that it blatantly conveys. It was a marker of the emergent South African fashion design culture I had watched at the South African fashion shows. Fundamentally, the T-shirt connects with other parts of the world in a style narrative telling of African diasporic black activism and cultural history. I had to buy the T-shirt to add to my collection of African diaspora T-shirts. The collection is being developed partly to do with African diaspora fashion design practice, and partly as another gateway into viewing the place of black people in the past-present-future tangram. As Susan Stewart has suggested "a collection offers example rather than sample, metaphor rather than metonymy. The collection does not displace attention to the past; rather, the past is at the service of the collection . . . the past lends authenticity to the collection . . . a form involving the reframing of objects within the world of attention and manipulation of context . . . its function is . . . the creation of a new context" (Stewart 2005: 151–2).

I have looked at the relevance of the T-shirt to the style narratives of the African diaspora before, as the impetus for the reassessment of what the Afro comb means in the twenty-first century. It was the crucial tool that created the Afro, a "natural" hairstyle of the 1960s and 1970s Black Consciousness movement across the African diaspora. I wanted to illustrate how an object can provide a contemporary narrative on a previous pivotal moment in African diaspora political cultural history (Tulloch 2008). I have also looked at the concept of black and post-black T-shirts; that is, the former are T-shirts created as expressions of black consciousness, civil rights and visibility, whilst post-black T-shirts comment on more supposedly enlightened multi-dimensional times where back people have the space to draw on an enormous range of other cultural and historical references beyond blackness. I wanted to consider how they reflect the different style-fashion-dress practices of the African diaspora (Tulloch 2010: 283–91). Bearing in mind Eyal Sivan's thinking on a geographical site as an archive, outlined in the introduction of this book, I want to look at the Stoned Cherrie–Steve Biko T-shirt as being part of an archive of African diaspora style narratives, as well as African diaspora fashion design and style-fashion-dress history.

The contributory components of the Stoned-Cherrie–Steve Biko T-shirt

The T-shirt was designed by Stoned Cherrie, a black South African fashion company based in Johannesburg. It was established there in 2000 by Nkensani Nkosi. In 2001, Stoned Cherrie showed for the first time at Sanlam South African Fashion Week, in the same city. In 2004, ten years after the end of apartheid, Stoned Cherrie released its Woolworths diffusion line, which they launched "to drive accessibility" (Stoned Cherrie 2014). This Steve Biko T-shirt was incredibly successful, selling out quickly despite, Nkosi states, "It was a risky thing for a department store to do to have this t-shirt on display."[5]

Black South African cultural and political heritage is important to Stoned Cherrie. They draw on references such as the lost multi-racial urban cultural dynamic of Johannesburg's township Sophiatown that was well documented by *Drum* magazine in the 1950s. A heritage that is still fuelled by Stoned Cherrie's post-apartheid black consciousness, "of daring to be different and daring to be proud to be African" (Nkosi 2006: 145). This is part of the reason why Nkosi, as the creative director of Stoned Cherrie and who led on their *Drum* campaign, personally selected the image for the Steve Biko T-shirt for it to be "one of the key drivers to bring an awareness of the new Identity of South Africa. I was born at the time when the townships were on fire. I believed that as a contribution to the transformation of the country, we could take some of our heroes and icons out of the dusty books and libraries into pop culture to celebrate the sacrifices they made, and to be part of our popular culture, and bring awareness about who we are."[6] Stoned Cherrie's design concept for the *Drum* campaign and the production of what has become an iconic T-shirt has placed Stoned Cherrie as part of the "Struggle Chic" fashion statement of the early twentieth-first century. This term has been given to T-shirts produced by South African fashion designers who depict "past political heroes, such as Steve Biko and Nelson Mandela, and the African-American former heavyweight boxing world champion Mohammad Ali. This genre of popular culture comes under the fashion term 'Afro Chic'—clothing and accessories produced by black and white South African designers who want to reflect, for themselves and their customers, who they are and their heritage" (Simbao 2007: 66).

The fashion design company is highly thought of in the South African fashion industry. Due to its approach to fashion design for a new South Africa, Stoned Cherrie's ability to translate aspects of black South African heritage into accessible "Afro chic" clothing and present it to a customer age range of sixteen to sixty, forced Dion Chang to claim that "Stoned Cherrie really was the turning point for South African street-wear … Stoned Cherrie was able to speak to everybody" (Chang 2006: 8).

As mentioned above, the image used by Stoned Cherrie is the front cover of the November 1977 issue of *Drum* magazine. This edition carries a feature that acts as a memorial to the killing of Steve Biko on September 12, 1977, and a report on his funeral held on September 25 Steve Biko is buried at Leightonville Cemetery in Ginsberg Township. The sixteen photographs that illustrate the article provide a small fragment of the life and funeral of Steve Biko. Some are of Steve Biko with his youngest son Semora Stere Biko, others are of his wife Nontsikelelo (Ntsiki) Biko (née Mashalaba), whilst the funeral procession, of what *Drum* reports as being 20,000 mourners, is well represented. A photograph of Steve Biko's coffin "that carried Steve to the grave also carried a carving of his face and his organisation's motif" (*Drum* 1977: 27). These were at the head and foot of the casket respectively. The organization referred to was the Black People's Convention that Steve Biko helped to found, and the motif was a pair of handcuffed hands that have broken the chain (*Drum* 1977: 27). A lasting imprint of the struggle for freedom, at any cost, the life of Bantu Stephen Biko.[7]

The text was written by the South African poet, Adam Small. It is a poetic rendering of Steve Biko. Small does not dwell on the horrific beatings and consequent head injuries that contributed to Steve Biko's death, or the degrading fact that he had been stripped and handcuffed as part of this fatal ordeal. Small talks about the Steve Biko who was "a man haunted under this regime. Haunted because his pride was indestructible, because as a black man he walked tall" (Small 1977: 21). He recalled that Steve Biko "had a sense of humour" and was resolute on the need for "black consciousness" (Small 1977: 21) and "that he was one of the initiators in this place and this time, of the black man's walking tall upon the streets of South Africa—walking tall, never to be bent again" (Small 1977: 27). In his repetition of "walking tall" for Steve Biko and his fellow black South Africans, Small insisted on the indelible link between the pursuit of freedom for all and Steve Biko's representation of it in life and death. Small, at this reflective time, felt a legacy of Steve Biko was that his "thinking placed the final stamp of pride, of 'rootedness in one's own being', on blackness here and now: pride that cannot be lost any more" (Small 1977: 27). Small closed his poetic remembering of Steve Biko with the final, restorative line, "Steve Biko is 'not' dead" (Small 1977: 27).

At the same time there was much coverage of Steve Biko's violent death and funeral with outraged responses and repercussions. In November 1977, for example, *Anti-Apartheid News*, the publication of Britain's Anti-Apartheid Movement, covered Steve Biko's death. It listed on the front cover the "Banned!" eighteen anti-apartheid organizations.[8] The paper related that "Steve Biko was the forty-eighth victim of Security Police" (*Anti-Apartheid News* 1977: 7) and the repercussions of his death had gathered momentum in the form of demonstrations in South Africa, vigils in Toronto, Canada and the British television programme *World in Action* "on the circumstances surrounding Steve Biko's death," the South African Embassy in London believed the programme had an "anti-white bias" (*Anti-Apartheid News* 1977: 7). Similarly David Widgery, a white-British Rock Against Racism (RAR) activist and medical general practitioner, wrote the article, "But How Did Biko Die?" for the autumn issue of *Temporary Hoarding*, the official paper of RAR. Widgery related the long torturous murder of Steve Biko as the bloody culmination of a catalogue of protests, demonstrations and the detention of activists that took place in the previous year to Steve Biko's death, which included the Soweto Uprising by school children in 1976. Widgery reported on the great number of people who attended his funeral.[9] Responses to and reporting on the death of Steve Biko led to many arrests of anti-apartheid individuals, an action that led Widgery to summarize "[T]he truth itself is illegal" (Widgery 1977: 4). Widgery's article was driven by a demand for freedom for black South Africans and a plea to people in Britain to do the right thing. That is in line with the British Anti-Apartheid Movement and others worldwide, to campaign against the corporate connections between British industries and the South African apartheid regime. As Widgery implored in bold text at the end of his article: "The State that killed Steve Biko is, despite diplomatic talk, deeply connected to Britain. To help black Africa to freedom, we will have to free ourselves" (Widgery 1977: 4).

The relentless, violent, brutality against anti-apartheid activists that led to imprisonments and killings, detentions and banned organizations, continued for years after Steve Biko's death, but he was not forgotten as being part of the anti-apartheid cause and this violent victimization. For example on September 14, 1984 photographer Paul Mattsson captured a section of a London anti-apartheid demonstration of black and white protestors. A black protestor carried the banner: "NO TO APARTHEID POLICE BRUTALITY," whilst an unseen protestor carried another "REMEMBER—STEVE BIKO—."

It's a mystery: the fashioned T-shirt

First and foremost this Stoned Cherrie–Steve Biko T-shirt is a fashion garment that has been designed by a fashion company for sale in a recognized retail outlet, Woolworths department store. It was displayed on a tailor's dummy as an item for sale and an object of desire. This is the crux of this chapter, that the T-shirt is an object—fashioned and desirable—but nonetheless an object carrying the face of the anti-apartheid martyr Steve Biko. It was the combination of all these elements that drew me to it.

What is the meaning of this Stoned Cherrie–Steve Biko T-shirt? Why read it at all? Mona Choo encourages us to re-engage with the "act of wondering" about objects to fuel possibilities (Choo 2011: 96). Elizabeth Wilson is drawn to the exploration of "the quality of mystery attached to clothing" (Wilson 2011: 188) and suggests an approach to unpack this through the combination of an object's *need* for connection with individuals, the garment as object, the meaning and representation of the garment and the enduring mystery and meaning of clothes (Wilson 2011: 189). Wilson's thinking inspires me to consider the style narratives of the African diaspora written on a garment. That an understanding of a garment does not have to be about the individual's use, the wearing of the garment, it can be about the garment's narration and connection with individuals, a group and culture, in this instance the men, women and children of the African diaspora.

Eileen Hooper-Greenhill has provided a succinct definition of what an object is. I present at here in length as Greenhill's explanation underpins the aims of this case study, as negative responses to the Stoned Cherrie–Steve Biko T-shirt testify, which will be discussed below, that for some, the fashioned object, does not qualify as a valid medium of cultural representation; that such objects are merely the invisible accessory to existence, rather than material contributions to constructions of identities and presence:

> Objects are the inscribed signs of cultural memory. Objects re-used to materialise, concretise, represent, or symbolise ideas and memories, and through these processes objects enable abstract ideas to be grasped, facilitate the verbalisation of thought, and mobilise reflection on experience and knowledge ... objects perpetuate and disseminate social values. Human experiences can be accumulated in artefacts, and because of this objects can be associated with the deepest psychological needs. Objects can become imbued or charged with meaning as significance and emotion are invested in them. This can operate on personal, community and national levels. The self, in its gendered and culture diversity is in large part produced through objects.
>
> Objects have the capacity to carry meanings, and these meanings can be attributed to a number of perspectives. Objects, therefore, have the capacity to

be polysemic, to bear multiple meanings. The meanings of objects emerge within relationships and frameworks, and it is these elements external to the object, drawn together by a meaning-making sensibility, an active mind and body, that anchor the endless play of signification, and make provisional closure possible.

Objects are powerful with both everyday life and within pedagogy; they motivate learning and they become significant beyond their material physical selves. They enable human needs to externalise felt convictions; the need to articulate tacit emotions; to visualise relationships; to picture abstract entities; to make the intangible tangible and therefore graspable.

HOOPER-GREENHILL 2000: 111

In terms of how to get at the meaning of an object, Ian Hodder guides that the meaning of cultural objects "is the effects it has on the world ... the object has meaning because it is part of a code, set or structure. In fact its particular meaning depends on its place within the code ... the historical content of the changing ideas and associations of the object itself, which makes its use non-arbitrary" (Hodder 1994: 12).

Part of the exploration discussed here is what does it mean when our eyes fall upon an object that brings together "events and beliefs in harmony for enquiry"? (Wilson 2011: 192). This has been a driver for my T-shirt collection and why I had to have this Stoned Cherrie–Steve Biko T-shirt, and consequently the study of it in this book. I see this T-shirt as a " 'memory-object' . . . 'memory work' that intervenes and forms a connection" (Gibbons 2007: 6). I would push this further and equate this categorization of the creation of this particular Steve Biko T-shirt as an act of "postmemory" or second memory (Hirsch 1993; Gibbons 2007: 73–95) by Stoned Cherry as "postmemory is the inheritance of past events or experiences that are still being worked through. Postmemory carries an obligation to continue the process of working through or over the event or experience and is not yet a process of reply" (Gibbons 2007: 73). Joan Gibbons explains that "the notion of second memory is not to deny or devalue primary testimony ... but to recognise the struggle that the primary witness has in relying on pre-existing forms of representation which are inadequate to his or her needs ... With the advantage of greater distance, the secondary witness is perhaps better equipped to develop much needed new forms of expression" (Gibbons 2007: 75) as in the fashioned, design concept considered T-shirt by Stoned Cherrie, destined for use in different cultural forums as a development on the T-shirts worn during the 1980s by "political activists at the height of political ferment ... Then, the wearing of Biko's likeness, cheaply reproduced onto mass manufactured ordinary cotton T-shirts, communicated a clear message: defiance of the apartheid regime and political alignment with the ideas and purposes of the black consciousness movement" (Vincent 2007: 82).

The T-shirt is over one hundred years old. It emerged in 1913 as a pure white garment that was part of the regulation uniform of the United States Navy. It has always been about comfort and ease, which encouraged its adoption, in its own right, as part of sportswear in the USA. In 1932, it became the first college football printed T-shirt for the University of Southern California. Two decades later it became a symbol of youthful, alternative presentation of self, as part of the rapid rise of sub- and counter-cultural groups led by teenagers, that was counter to the more conservative look of the older generation. In the 1960s, the patterned T-shirt entered the fray when, for example the British singer Joe Cocker wore a tie-dye T-shirt for his performance at Woodstock in 1969. The T-shirt was the ideal pop art canvas for boutique designers. The successful ways of employing the T-shirt continued, with the addition of it being used for making political statements in the name of anti-racism, feminism, gay liberation, on the back, front, sleeves of one or all these areas. The T-shirt, then, has been a "way of displaying allegiance to subcultures, music, politics" (V&A Publishing 2014).

The wearing of T-shirts has long been associated with heroes, such as the ubiquitous Che Guevara version. During the 1960s, the *New Musical Express* carried an advertisement that offered a service where you could send in an image of your hero and they would print it onto a T-shirt, but the turnaround time for this service would take six months (Tulloch 1994). Things have moved on. The popularity and easy accessibility of T-shirts that feature political heroes, as well as the other myriad representations of messages and images that connects with the T-shirt wearer and becomes part of who they are.[10]

The T-shirt, then, is a symbol of modernity and post-modernity, it can be an activist tool, an advertisement and a technique of subcultural bricolage. T-shirts are pristine or torn, pinned or customized. It is a space of individualized and group experimentation and vocalization. Messages projected from the T-shirt have been used as a space for empowerment to put one's politics out there to the public. One of the most notable fashion designers for this was Katharine Hamnett who saw the T-shirt as the perfect item for "rocking the status quo."[11] She produced a series of oversized "sloganned" anti-war and environmental issue T-shirts in the 1980s. Nigel Fountain, the writer and presenter of the BBC's Radio 4 programme *Your Name Here: The T-Shirt*, likened the message carrying T-shirt being worn by moving bodies, in various locations, as being like a pamphleteer of the seventeenth and eighteenth century distributing pamphlets with particular ideologies, philosophies or ideas for public engagement, as by wearing a T-shirt with a particular image and/or text on it, categorizes the wearer in association with what they are wearing (Fountain 1994) and draws the viewer in to wonder at the meaning of the visual and/or textual message of the T-shirt,[12] which is explored in this chapter.

Multiple readings of the Stoned Cherrie–Steve Biko T-shirt

The Stoned Cherrie–Steve Biko T-shirt campaign and the company's fashion design ideology has garnered much response from South Africans, fuelling positive and negative reassessments, directly or indirectly, of the contemporary meaning and understanding of Steve Biko's activism and his political legacy.[13] In 2004, the same year that Stoned Cherrie launched its first Woolworths collection, Sandile Memela despaired at what he believed to be the lack of respect towards the memory and legacy of Steve Biko in post-apartheid South Africa. Memela included here "Young, gifted and black professionals, who pay allegiance to capitalism, are promoted and sponsored in and through the media to serve their interests" (Memela 2004: 10). Memela said this at a time when the number of black South African designers was growing and their designs explicitly expressed black South African cultural and political references. Memela believes Steve Biko's death has not been vindicated as apartheid still exists in economics not politics (Memela 2004: 11).

In "Steve Biko and Stoned Cherrie: Refashioning the Body Politic in Democratic South Africa" (2007), Louise Vincent responds to the negative comments towards the Stoned Cherrie–Steve Biko T-shirt campaign as being "profane," "disrespectful," "frivolous," "a betrayal," "using the past for profit" (Vincent 2007: 83–8); protestations expressed by Console Tleane, in 2004, with regard to these T-shirts as being "a backward, reductionist and narrow understanding of Steve Biko."[14] Vincent provides a series of readings of what she calls "one particular fashion moment in contemporary South Africa" (Vincent 2007: 80) that she acknowledges that in "post-apartheid South Africa ... the sign is more difficult to read" (Vincent 2007: 82). She concludes that Steve Biko's image has a right to be associated with different readings and meanings in the carving out of a new national identity and individual identities since the end of apartheid in 1994 that "has opened up the space for greater political playfulness which is seen in the use of struggle icons in fashion in ways that would previously have been unthinkable" (Vincent 2007: 92).

Sarah Nuttall does not consider Stoned Cherrie or their Steve Biko T-shirts to be about black consciousness, but "in-your-face" registration of "remixing and recoding of an icon" (Nuttall 2004: 437). This thinking contributed to Nuttall's treatise on the Y generation of Rosebank, "a racially mixed" area of Johannesburg where leading designers sell and fashionistas perform, space where "young people remake the past in very specific ways in the services of the present and the future" that is marked by

> cultural accessorization in the making of their contemporary selfhood ... a practice that represents the new edge of a youth movement that cuts across sonic, sartorial, visual, and textual cultures to produce a dense interconnectivity

among them. This accessorization of identity, including racial identity, through compositional remixing both occupies and delimits zones of translatability. It is decreasingly attached to the transfer of meaning per se but rather inhabits a matrix of transfiguration.

NUTTALL 2004: 432–3

That is, there is growing similarity of style-fashion-dress styles amongst this generation, regardless of skin shade, and that "'taste' is displacing orthodox versions of race and culture as the carrier of social distinctions . . . What is clear is that new youth cultures are superseding the resistance politics of an earlier generation, while still jamming, remixing, and remaking cultural codes and signifiers from the past" (Nuttall 2004: 435–6). As Michaela Alejandra Oberhofer has surmized, "After the end of apartheid fashion as cultural practice and economic force means to take back public spaces like the inner city, to reinterpret history in its own terms and to reoccupy the visual representations of the self" (Oberhofer 2012: 73).

Vincent, Nuttall and Oberhofer offer readings of the Stoned Cherrie–Steve Biko T-shirt within the confines of a specific geographical and national parameter. Additionally, at the time of writing, there has not been an academic case study of the Stoned Cherrie–Steve Biko T-shirt discussed here. I want to offer another reading. On coming upon the T-shirt, I saw it with "outsider," "diasporic eyes," that is I am not South African but a critical thinker of style narratives of the African diaspora, who is also part of this diaspora. I saw immediately the transnational and transcultural connectivity of this Stoned Cherrie–Steve Biko T-shirt.

An alternative reading: the Stoned Cherrie–Steve Biko T-shirt, the centered breath of freedom

Apartheid was a relentlessly violent act, physically as meted out on thousands of men, women and children, psychologically the term conjured up the sustained, vehement effect of this virulent strain of oppressive power of the few over the many:

> I would like to tell you what Apartheid really means to us. It means that instead of our children being educated, they are indoctrinated. It means that our men cannot move from country to town and from one part of town to another without a Pass. Now our women too will be unable to leave their houses without a Pass. It means that 70 percent of my people live below the breadline. It means that in my own province of Natal, 85 percent of our children are suffering from malnutrition. Believe it or not, it means that by law our people cannot aspire to do any work other than ordinary manual labour. It means massive unemployment.

What Apartheid means is a long tale of suffering. In a word, it means the denial of dignity and of ordinary human rights: Chief Albert Luthuli.[15]

As mentioned throughout this chapter, the concept of struggle permeated the life and death of apartheid activism—the women, men and children activists, whether consciously or not—and the apartheid system itself: the struggle that continued before, during and after the death of those who fought against apartheid; the struggle for those who survived the death of fellow anti-apartheid activists; the struggle of those who lived through apartheid, alongside the "born frees,"[16] who struggled for new South African identities. I concentrate on the term struggle as it means, according to the *Oxford English Dictionary*: "[T]he act of struggling, a resolute contest, whether physical or otherwise; a continued effort to resist force or free oneself from constraint; a strong effort under difficulties." Most poignantly struggle is also "a strong effort to continue to breathe." This latter definition evokes a cultural and political purpose of the Stoned Cherrie–Steve Biko T-shirts, and for me this November 1977 *Drum* issue in particular.

My reading of this Stoned Cherrie–Steve Biko T-shirt is not as a communiqué "to struggle on," a phrase that has an air of defeatism. Rather, it communicates how black South Africans claimed their right to live freely in their homeland, to breathe freely. The struggle now is to achieve and maintain the centered breath of freedom.[17] In the post-apartheid "new South Africa" this reflects what Steve Biko himself said, "We want to attain the envisioned self which is a free self" (Biko 1987 [1978]: 49).

Therefore, if one reads this Stoned Cherrie–Steve Biko T-shirt as an art work, being a representation of the political message Stoned Cherrie and its director Nkosi wanted to communicate only twelve years after the end of apartheid, through the image of Steve Biko on the front cover of *Drum* magazine that was a form of memorial to Steve Biko and thereby the associated horrors and concerns, responses and repercussions around his death, then the T-shirt, the base upon which the image is printed, can be defined as a substrate or substratum which has an extensive definition:

> something that supports attributes ... the substance in which qualities inhere ... be or remain fixed or lodged *in* something. To remain or abide *in* something immaterial, as a state or condition; to remain in mystical union with a Divine person. The basis on which an immaterial "structure" is raised ... To exist, abide, or have its being, as an attribute, quality, etc., *in* a subject or thing; to form an element of, or belong to the intrinsic nature of, something. To be vested or inherent *in*, as a right, power, function. To cleave to.
>
> *Oxford English Dictionary*

Dan Sturgis has pushed the possibilities of the substrate as "holding contained theoretical meaning" (Sturgis 2015: 39) as "the foundation of the work, it is a foundation that is practical as well as theoretical. A foundation ... intertwining ideas, of material practice with theoretical and historical considerations. Taken within this context the substrate is like a lens through which work can be seen, a lens which emphasizes the twisting and convoluted relationships that artworks have with their material makeup ... a coming together of the material and the theoretical" (Sturgis 2015: 35). From this perspective, the fact that the image of Steve Biko on the front of the November issue of *Drum* seeps into the fabric of the T-shirt reciprocates the need to "lodge" and "fix" the ideas and critical thinking, the urgency and agency of the long fought anti-apartheid and Black Consciousness Movement in South Africa and by its supporters abroad. The "immaterial structure" of that cause made material on this Stoned Cherrie–Steve Biko T-shirt. Effectively memoria technica. It is a "black consciousness," as outlined by Steve Biko that, on the one hand pays homage to struggle heritage and on the other is empathetic to the needs for the construction of new selves, "a free self" (Biko [1978] 1987: 48–9); freedom which in the new post-apartheid South Africa, includes economic and political, cultural and social, civil rights and equality across the various cultural groups, the erosion of "economic disparities between black and white" (Oberhofer 2012: 70). I argue, then, this Stoned Cherrie–Steve Biko T-shirt reflects and respects the views Steve Biko expressed. The activist warned in an interview, shortly before his death, that "[Y]ou are either alive and proud or you are dead, and when you are dead, you can't care anyway. And your method of death can itself be a politicizing thing" (Biko [1978] 1987: 153). This T-shirt is a relentless politicizing thing.

"Freedom is a road seldom travelled by the multitude"

What freedom means in twenty-first century South Africa is a concern amongst black and white South African cultural practitioners. This was explored in the open-space conference *In the Seams: The Aesthetics of Freedom Expressed* held in 2011 at the Center for Historical Reenactments in Johannesburg. I was fortunate to be invited to contribute a keynote lecture and led a critical practical workshop. The latter event is included here as it expands on what, I believe, Stoned Cherrie was trying to communicate through this Steve Biko T-shirt design.

The event was developed so black and white participants from different parts of South Africa, Germany and the UK could discuss and explore "the ways in which fashion and textiles are used to express different ideas of freedom in Africa and the African diaspora" (Micossé-Aikins, aus dem Moore 2012: 5). The thinking behind the conference, which consisted of keynote lectures and workshops where the participants shared the roles of "actors, researchers, teachers and artists" (Micossé-Aikins, aus dem Moore 2012: 5), was that:

"Freedom" is a concept, or better still an aspiration, that is central to the shared experiences of Africans and people of African descent in the Diaspora. It links together divergent histories, cultures and societies and remains a goal, to be achieved through multiple ongoing struggles spared by the history and present ramifications of slavery, colonialism and apartheid. In a constant process of renegotiation, adaptation and appropriation, the idea of freedom manifests itself within everyday practices just as much as within the realms of the arts, academia and institutional politics. The project *In the Seams* was interested in approaching fashion and styles as a location in which all of these different realms intersect and become accessible to everyone.

MICOSSÉ-AIKINS, AUS DEM MOORE 2012: 5

My thinking on the concept of freedom, as part of my contribution to the event, was that the term "freedom" is part of the soul of the African diaspora experience. The pursuit of freedom, particularly political and personal freedom, across the African diaspora has resulted in a shared experience, in spite of the specific historic cultural and social identities of the different parts of the diaspora. "Freedom" is about the choice of *being* as colonialism, imperialism and racism are tenets of freedom for some, yet were imposed on and crushed the freedom of others (Tulloch 2012: 8).

I co-ordinated the workshop "Freedom is a Road Seldom Travelled by the Multitude." The Rap artist Chuck D of the hip-hop group, Public Enemy, sampled this phrase. It was used in their song *Show 'Em Whatcha Got*. The track featured on their 1988 album *It Takes a Nation of Millions to Hold Us Back*. The phrase "Freedom is a Road Seldom Travelled by the Multitude" was originally spoken by saxophonist Harvey "Joe" Henderson of the Bar-Kays at the landmark Wattstax Festival, held on August 20, 1972. The event was organized to commemorate the seventh anniversary of the Los Angeles Watts Riots in 1965.[18]

I was drawn to this sampled phrase as it evoked the spirit of the conference, and *Show 'Em Whatcha Got* referenced civil rights activists and freedom fighters from different parts of the African diaspora. Pointedly, music is integral to African diaspora culture and, in terms of the aesthetics of freedom, it is often difficult to separate the influences between music and the styled body—the individualized construction of a look through the assemblage of garments, accessories, and beauty regimes that may, or may not, be "in fashion" at the time of use. For example, workshop member 1 (wm)[19] of the pop group Amaule pointed out that Congolese singers have a cultural responsibility to style themselves well. The cost of the components is immaterial, whether of a low or high price, it is the styling that is paramount.[20]

Additionally, my focus on the sampled phrase "Freedom is a Road Seldom Travelled by the Multitude" addressed a subtext of the workshop, to connect the past with the present. Sampling for Chuck D is a response to his African-American and broader African diaspora heritage. Through the incorporation of previously made "black" statements into his work, Chuck D acknowledged black history and simultaneously created something new in order to move forward a technique mirrored in the Stoned Cherrie–Steve Biko T-shirt.

The aim of the workshop was to use music, style and making as exploratory tools for fresh thinking on freedom. The program comprised:

1 A brainstorming session on what freedom meant to the individual participants.

2 A group discussion on music. Participants brought one piece of music that represented freedom to them.

3 The making session. An intuitive expression of freedom through a variety of making techniques—embroidery, sewing, knitting, painting. Workshop members were encouraged to bring items from home, garments, textiles or accessories that were part of their autobiography, which they could work into and use to extend familial heritage, for example.

The brainstorming session, held on October 7, 2011, of what freedom can mean to individual workshop members, took the form of a creative act. The participants lay three sheets of A1 paper on the floor. They all wrote their words or statements at the same time, not in a formalized, list-making system, but in many directions on the sheets. Often the participants were on their knees or stretching over one another. At other times they stood up to view the texts from a distance, to consider and then move closer to the sheets of paper to add another word or phrase, much like an artist. The individualized handwriting reflected the diversity of thought. The words and phrases included:

"Think out loud, don't say a word"	Possibility
Huh!	Should
Expression	Would
Variaty[sic]	Justice
Power	Thoughts
Money	Values
Yours, or mine?	Liberty
Uhuru	Buntu
Rebels	Style
Steve Biko	A is for Anarchy
Mini Skirt	Stance

Once completed, the panels were pinned onto the wall of the center (and remained there for the duration of the open-space conference) for the group to assess and respond to. For example, the workshop member wm2 made an interesting observation: "Nowhere is the word equality." It was something he had considered overnight and pointed this out to me on the second day of the event. I made wm2's statement into a separate panel and placed it next to the three original panels.

The expansive thinking on freedom that I had hoped for emerged in this first exercise. Views expressed ranged from the slippery nature of defining the word freedom: "Freedom is an abstract word. I can't express it in words" (wm3). This was supported by another statement from wm2 that "we have different mind sets at this current time." Workshop members also expressed what they saw as the negative aspects of freedom: "Young people today are tired of the word freedom" (wm1); "Freedom is destruction, it depends on how you look at it in certain points in your life" (wm2).

The music session took place the next morning. The range of musical genres submitted attested to freedom of choice and personal expression. Rock, jazz, reggae, spaza[21] and hip-hop were represented. The songs were played on DVD, CD, mobile phones and a vinyl record and included:

Black Bird by Nina Simone (wm4)
Camagu by Driemanskap (wm2)
Can't We Live Together by Jestofunk (wm3)
Ice Cream Love by Johnny Osborne (wm5)
Show 'Em Watcha Got by Public Enemy (Carol Tulloch)
Iqhawe by Skiohumbuzo Makandula (wm6)
Black Soul by Amaule (wm1).

All contributors were asked to say why they chose their particular piece of music. Some of the reflections included:

"In Congo we can't talk about music without style. A musician is someone who is looked up to, to help people to become something . . . you can be what you want, you can rise above the sea. You have the power to be." (wm1)
"Rituals can be constraining." (wm6)
"Sampling is freedom . . . you create a collage and change the context." (wm7)
"Freedom is an unspoken sound . . . Freedom is the right to blossom." (wm8)
"We need to remember the past and traditions to contribute to the present." (wm4)
" 'Ancestors' has turned into a dirty word." (wm8)

To remind the participants of transnational connections for freedom, the photographer and graphic designer, Syd Shelton,[22] explained how he produced his 4 × 2.5m photographic mural *Anti-Apartheid 1959–1994: Making Hope a Reality* (figure 5.1). This was commissioned in 2000 by Cheryl Carolus, the then South African High Commissioner for the United Kingdom, to mark a new regime. The

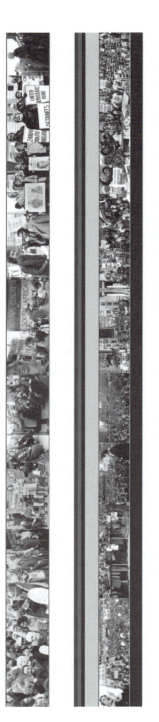

FIGURE 5.1 Anti-Apartheid 1959–94: Making Hope a Reality, 2001, by Syd Shelton. The Anti-Apartheid mural was produced by the Anti-Apartheid Movement Archive Committee. Courtesy of Syd Shelton.

mural is on permanent display at South African House, London. The graphic designer used photographs of the relentless anti-apartheid activity that took place in Trafalgar Square, outside South Africa House, between 1959 and 1994. Shelton presented these as a kaleidoscope of images invisibly seamed together. They were a reminder of the thousands of people who were devoted to the cause, and the various mediums used to evoke protest against the impact of apartheid in South Africa—black and white bodies used themselves as billboards wearing home-made cardboard statements hanging from their necks, their bodies *being* the anti-apartheid statement, or anti-racist texts produced on reams of fabric suspended from buildings. This example, which is visible in the mural, was the unfurling of a 90-foot banner a Steve Biko memorial a year after his death, on September 12, 1978. The banner began with "STEVE BIKO DIED IN DETENTION ON 12.9.77 IN APARTHEID SOUTH AFRICA" (*Anti-Apartheid News* 1978: 10). This was followed by the names of fifty other people known to have died in detention with the dates of their death.

The statements, observations and reflections of the previous sections of the workshop fuelled the making portion of the workshop. This took place in the afternoon on the second day of the event. In that short period of time, the participants engaged whole-heartedly in creating pieces of work, working on their own and collaborated with one another. Relay pieces of work were produced, such as a length of knitting created by different participants knitting in a variety of materials, such as wool and ribbon. An impromptu knitting circle emerged. Male workshop members in particular were incredibly keen to learn to knit; other new skills, notably embroidery, were acquired by all. One example of this was the comment on freedom through cross-stitch embroidery by wm5: "Wud-Kud-Shud"—two of the words he originally contributed to the brain-storming panels—were stitched across the shoulder panel of his denim jacket, thereby extending his personal presence.

The elements of the event: words taken from the keynote papers reflection on and brainstorming about individual interpretations of the word "freedom," the sharing of skills and collaboration on ideas illustrated what positive freedom can achieve for the independent self and we caught a glimpse of the individual from the inside. What we had here, evocatively put by wm7, was "constructive thinking with our hands."[23] A form of thinking expressed through the fashion designed Stoned Cherrie–Steve Biko T-shirt. The proactive workshop "It Takes a Nation of Millions to Hold Us Back" reflected Memela's desire, outlined above, for more critical consciousness in twenty-first century South Africa, adroitly realized in this T-shirt.

Here in this example was a contemporary understanding and interpretation of the past-present-future tangram of the dynamic tension of struggle and freedom in South Africa through the eyes of insiders and outsiders of the region. Expertly summarized, some six years earlier, in the Stoned Cherrie–Steve Biko T-shirt.

The style narrative of Steve Biko's face on a T-shirt

It will always be relevant and powerful, having it as a piece of history. It is still one of the things people comment on the most.

NKENSANI NKOSI 2015[24]

This past-present-future tangram hinges on the portrait of Steve Biko. As Nkosi says in the above quote, having Steve Biko's face on a T-shirt in this way will always be powerful because it connects and transcends time. This portrait on a T-shirt embodies a definition of the photographic portrait which "suggests that the individual, whatever material context is involved, is given significance and definition within an everyday world of codes and signifying registers of meaning. In that sense, and for all its limitations, the photographic portrait inscribes into its meaning precisely that play between internal and external worlds" (Clarke 1997: 111). The simultaneous register of the everydayness of Steve Biko in this portrait of him on the Stoned Cherrie T-shirt is vested with the casualness of his open-neck checked shirt, and the resolutely iconic image of him used to mourn the death and celebrate the life, leadership and activism of Bantu Stephen Biko.[25] Thus, the face of the activist is of paramount significance here. To return to my study of Billie Holiday in chapter 3 and her performance in 1939 of the anti-lynching, anti-racist protest song *Strange Fruit*, which illustrates the connective lineage of African diaspora activism. Like the centrality of Billie Holiday's face in the performance of *Strange Fruit*, Steve Biko's posthumous portrait on the cover of *Drum* magazine, *is* the idea of change, the possibility of hope. As "this image registers a *cut of continuity* rather than rupture as important variation on the same theme ... In this context, photographic portraiture ... facilitated linkage, affiliation, and intense affective attachments" (Campt 2012: 178), in this instance, the solidarity of struggle for freedom through anti-apartheid activism. As the opening quote of this chapter relates, and as illustrative of the Stoned Cherrie–Steve Biko T-shirt, indeed, "In the face you can have all kinds of political landscapes" (Dumas 2015: 166).

I have quoted previously (Tulloch 2008) a defining aspect of graphic design[26] is its intent to persuade, inform or instruct the viewer (Livingston 1998: 90) by "making or choosing marks and arranging them on a surface to convey an idea ... They are signs whose content gives them a unique meaning, and whose positioning of the elements of a graphic design can lend new significance" (Hollis 1997: 7). The latter point, that the positioning of the elements of a graphic design can lend new significance, is a framework applied here to the Stoned Cherrie–Steve Biko T-shirt to unlock the meaning of why Stoned Cherrie's use of Steve Biko's *Drum* November 1977 posthumous portrait on a woman's fitted T-shirt is still an act of black consciousness. For Steve Biko, black consciousness was about self-emancipation, to call oneself black, of "[B]eing black is not a matter of pigmentation—being black is a reflection of a mental attitude" (Biko [1978] 1987: 48). What the Stoned Cherrie–Steve Biko T-shirt achieved was to translate Steve Biko's thinking twice: as it is engrained in his portrait on the cover of the November 1977 issue of *Drum* magazine, two months after his death, and therefore part of the activist momentum that made him a martyr of the Anti-Apartheid Movement; and secondly it is realized again as an intense color print on a woman's fitted T-shirt. As Shelton reminds us that graphic design is "the visualisation of ideas in two dimensional form" (Shelton 2008).

This T-shirt as memory-work is an act of quotation. Significantly, it is quoting from the archive of an historically-relevant black African magazine. To quote, as in this example, is to cite something of importance from the past that has resonance in the present and the future. According to Dick Hebdige, the use of a quotation provides space for experimentation to produce fresh thinking on a subject (Hebdige 1987: 14). For Hebdige, a quotation is "an invocation of someone else's voice to help you say what you want to say. In order to *e*-voke you have to be able to *in*-voke . . . That's the beauty of quotation. The original version takes on a new life and a new meaning in a fresh context" (Hebdige 1987: 14). The new meaning being evoked here is that black South Africans have a history of strength built on black and critical consciousness that can feed into the construction of new selves. The message on the chest of this woman's T-shirt is blatantly made more so, as the scooped neckline emphasizes the chest, an area of the body that is "regarded as the seat of the emotions and passions" (*Oxford English Dictionary*). The unavoidable eye-to-chest encounter of an image on this area of a T-shirt cajoles viewers to question (Tulloch 2010: 290). Indeed, this is what happened to me on first viewing of the Stoned Cherrie–Steve Biko T-shirt on a tailor's dummy in Woolworths at Sandton Shopping Center.

The fact that this quotation was taken from an archive is a salient point. To return to the concept of the substrate, Jo Melvin offers the consideration of the term "substrata" when using and discussing archives as it "conjures and combines various interpretative referents . . . Substrata also suggests the presence of invisible links and layers operating below or beyond what can be seen in the immediate, which may or may not function independently from the surface layer" (2015: 65–6), and thereby fuels the need to evaluate what is presented. And if, according to Melvin, "archives modify meaning because it gives a visualization of how impressions and traces continually revise interpretations of meaning and context" (2015: 68), then the journey of this front cover portrait of Steve Biko from the *Drum* archive that is re-presented as an integral part of a fashion garment, a T-shirt, that then becomes part of a personal archive of African diaspora T-shirts held in England, then the Stoned Cherrie–Steve Biko T-shirt joins the network of African diaspora style-fashion-dress objects that emit the traceable associations of objects-people-geographies-activism-histories that is a network of concerns that connect Africa and its diaspora (Tulloch 2010: 296). Therefore to bring this image of Steve Biko on this Stoned Cherrie T-shirt in line with the history and legacy of the Black Consciousness and Black Power Movements of the 1960s and 1970s across the African diaspora to which it is linked through the face of Steve Biko, reflects a continued meaning of what Steve Biko represented—I am black, therefore I am (Tulloch 2008: 136). Because of the achingly violent act of apartheid that aroused such opposition across the world, Stoned Cherrie subtly reminds us of this through the memory-work of the Stoned Cherrie–Steve Biko T-shirt.

6 HERE: THE HAUNTING JOY OF BEING IN ENGLAND

[T]he past has to be taken apart. Old themes are worn as new details.
JUDITH CLARK 2014: 39

Memory can provide the oil that is poured upon troubled waters, or smoke fires to flame. Memory is a child of the guts and the emotion, of the brain and the heart and the lips. It is the dresser of time—in silks or satins or bruising flax which our forefathers wore during the diaspora. Memory makes us laugh and cry in turn. We cannot escape it.
BERYL GILROY 1998: 233

The post-World War II arrival of Caribbean people in England haunts me. It is the period of history that has been most pivotal to my interest in style-fashion-dress and the construction of black identities.[1] The history of black people in Britain before this moment is not to be forgotten, but the period of migration of British colonial subjects in the 1950s and 1960s has a particular hold on me. As mentioned in the introduction, it is the period in which my parents migrated to England from Jamaica, I say England here because for my parents and their Caribbean contemporaries, it was "England" and "Englishness," not "Britain" they were migrating to. The 1950s was also the decade of my birth. So the 1950s is a particular marker of personal heritage. But such spectres can be of use. As Judith Clark and Beryl Gilroy guide us in the combined opening quotes, the personal experiences and use of the past can invoke a re-evaluation of the past and its meaning in the present and for the future.

For my parents, like many thousands from the Caribbean, as well as Africa India and Pakistan, coming to England was about a new beginning, of taking up residence in the "mother country," to create a home, to nurture a family, in short to secure a future for themselves and their immediate family. What is now our present was that generation's future and although:

Black people in Britain—both as individuals and as confident, vibrant communities—have made a considerable impact on contemporary British culture. This new sense of belonging is not without its problems: racism continues to pervade all levels of social and cultural activity and, ... it is clear that most of the country's institutions have yet to adapt themselves to the demographic realities of the 21st century ... Before we can look forward to a more secure future, Britain has to come to terms with its colonial and imperial past.

History Making: Recovering the Past, Collecting the Future 2001[2]

At the time of writing, this quote unfortunately still rings true[3] and remains part of the spectres of the past which haunt me and many others still, that the sense of belonging in heritage terms is an issue that is constantly being fought for. While this debt is still outstanding, the future in terms of "race relations" remains fragile, a situation the Jamaican-born academic Stuart Hall highlighted nearly fifty years ago, as to the contested "race relations" which hampered the post-World War II settlement of Caribbean migrants (Hall 1967). The above quote was the basis of the study day, "History Making: Recovering the Past, Collecting the Future" held at Victoria and Albert Museum in 2001. It was one of a number of initiatives implemented across Britain in recent years to examine what constitutes "British heritage" in order to provide a more balanced representation of all cultural groups in Britain.[4] For example, the seminal anthology *The Politics of Heritage, The Legacies of "Race"* (2005) promotes the revision of "Britain's island stories to acknowledge their long and intertwined histories with complex patterns of migration and diaspora ... to explore what the possibilities are for progressive practice and activating theory and to open up further discussion on how the legacies of 'race' continue to shape heritage" (Littler 2005: 1, 2).

Jo Littler points out that due to the long history and various references of the term "heritage," it could be viewed as a living, open term, with the capacity to consider often neglected subjects such as the "legacies of race," "gender, disability, age and sex: "What might be extrapolated from the recent mutations in heritage's meanings is that it seems increasingly possible to trace a developed genealogy for heritage as meaning something that is *shared*—amongst and across generations— as well as being able to trace a genealogy of heritage as the inheritance of *individuals,* which in the post-industrial West became most commonly articulated to discourses of superior worth" (Littler 2005: 18 n.5).

Jonathan Rutherford's thoughts in the same publication on "Ghosts: Heritage and the Shape of Things to Come" is useful to understand the burden that the past can have on, for example, people like me, those born in England of Caribbean parents. He states that "England is full of ghosts. They constitute an absence which defines us" (Rutherford 2005: 83). Rutherford adds that as the heritage industry in England persists in focusing on the "glorious myth of England" that harks back to the Victorian era (Rutherford 2005: 83) it forgets other aspects of England's history as, for example during post-1945: "with the birth of youth culture, modern consumerism and New Commonwealth immigration . . . Post-war Englishness has been informed by a mixture of nostalgia and bereavement" (Rutherford 2005: 83, 92). The past, Rutherford reminds, is an ever-present presence and influence on the act of living:

> the past is viewed as a boundary between the living and the dead, presence and absence. Heritage becomes an effort to mitigate its disruptive power, not so much by expelling it, but by attempting to incorporate it into the present . . . we have to remember before forgetting. Such a release transforms our relationship to the past . . . Released from the grip of the past, how might we think historically in a way which helps us to face the future?
>
> **RUTHERFORD** 2005: 83

In essence, to return to the historical past is not to negate its importance and impact on the present, but to confront the ghosts, which in the context of this chapter are the spectres of difference that have marred the possible relationships between cultural groups in England and the wider concept of Britain, so that further social and cultural advances can be made by laying these to rest. Simultaneously to allow the spirit of difference, that is, the possibilities of difference to generate excitement and change in an all encompassing definition of British heritage and thereby a more positive prospect for future social and cultural practice. But how does one deal with this unsettling air of unfinished business left over from the past, which continues to pervade our present? Bill Schwartz has argued for a critical inquiry into the multifarious aspects and differing moments of history that "can activate different pasts to become meaningful in the present" (Schwartz 2005: 221). For me it is a need to revisit the moment of arrival and settlement of British colonial migrants in England, and how their styled selves narrated this life changing experience for them and their descendants, as well as the social, political and cultural landscape of England.

Haunting perspectives

Judith Clark's curatorial and philosophical study *Spectres: When Fashion Turns Back* (2004) considered the relationship between "contemporary fashion, theory and the history of dress" and how "the past haunts and foreshadows the present" (Clark 2004: 19). Clark's thinking applies equally to a need, generally, to look back to understand past-present relationships. As Caroline Evans says, her project was "a monument to ideas" (Evans 2004: 42). Clark encourages us to ask what are the devices one wants to use to consider why does the past haunt, and how to reassess one's version of the past and its impact: "We are always rooted in our point of view, looking from somewhere in particular with a purpose in mind. Looking always transforms what it sees" (Clark 2004: 23). Taking this advice on board to consider the points raised earlier, I need to identify what kind of past haunts me with regards to England. On a personal level, it is the pain of the vestiges of British slavery, imperialism and colonialism experienced by my Jamaican parents in their place of birth, that migrated with them in the 1950s to England, that foreshadowed and haunted their pursuit of a new life here. A haunting that enveloped their descendants through to the twenty-first century. As a critical thinker through style narratives of the African diaspora, this is expanded to include those who migrated to England, particularly British colonial subjects of the diaspora, at this time.

The post-World War II history of migration by British colonial subjects is generally spoken of in the context of a troubled past. Despite the activities and actions of artists and curators, novelists, poets and critical thinkers, politicians and activists who have fought for an enlightened perspective of difference in Britain, there are still "English" commentators who persist in projecting ideas that take Britain back to the dark days of the ideology that fed Britain's color bar system. Examples of this include the British political party the UK Independence Party (UKip) which lays immigration as a problematic blot on the social, economic and medical landscapes of Britain (Williams 2015: 10; Hodges 2014; Withnall 2014) which has resulted in multiculturalism that "encourages division" (Channel 4 News 2015), whilst in 2014, the English novelist Martin Amis professed that support for multiculturalism is a drain on the public purse as

> There is tolerance now and almost a sort of harmonial feeling that in rough areas, it's just as bad as it ever was . . . But a Pakistani in Preston who says "I'm an Englishman"—that statement would raise eyebrows, for the reason that there's meant to be another layer of being English. There are other qualifications, other than being a citizen of the country, and it has to do with white skin and the habits of what is regarded to be civilised society, and recognisable bourgeois society.
>
> **AMIS** 2014[5]

This is an indelible mark on British and African diaspora history that is addressed in this chapter, yet that history also holds evidence of the joys of living and being black in England. This aspect needs to be incorporated into the past-present-future tangram of that experience. To conjoin the legacy of a disturbing past (Clark 2004: 40, Wainwright 2014: 3) and the joys experienced in England is to present a multi-dimensional view of black experiences in England and how the styled black body has been informed by, and has contributed to, this dynamic and perceive another perspective of individualized creativity. This direction could go someway to alleviate the feeling of "strangeness" the diasporic experience engenders.

FIGURE 6.1 Young black woman at a London market, London, 1964, photograph by John Gay. © English Heritage.

A case in point is the photograph of a young black woman at a market in London taken by the German photographer John Gay in 1964 (figure 6.1). Gay came to London in 1939 and saw himself as a "true Londoner." The photograph was included in his book *London Observed* (1964), a project he undertook "to capture the heart of London." There are no details as to where this image was taken. The text that accompanies the image, written by Macdonald Hastings, is what you would expect regarding the presence of black people in England in the early 1960s, coming here to do jobs that "Londoners regard as menial" and that "Inevitably, they have brought social problems with them. Because of the shortage of houses, they tend to herd together. In a new land, they seek each other's company in districts like Notting Hill Gate … Although prejudice is surprisingly small, considering the size and novelty of the invasion, it is still there." Reassuringly Hastings says "the new Londoners are here to stay. Most of London has already accepted them"

(Gay 1964).[6] Hastings affirmed that as many black and white children were attending school together, that "by the time these youngsters grow up integration should be complete" (Gay 1964).

Yet the photograph of this woman jars against its caption. She is modern; the clean lines of her top and hairstyle co-ordinate to let her body take center stage. This is only enhanced by her ornate drop earrings and the expertly applied sweep of eyeliner and lipstick. She is striking. The woman exudes confidence as she commands the center of the image. Her short sleeked natural hairstyle is radical for this time, as it would have been normal to have one's hair straightened within the cottage industry of black hairdressers in London and other cities and towns around the country. There is a sense of joy here as the young woman engages with the market, the joy of simply *being,* in spite of the bemused look of the man, to the left of the photograph, on seeing this black woman.

Joy

The feelings of joy, acceptance and presence in crucial moments of existence are also interior feelings and when recaptured in autobiography they heal and console.

BERYL GILROY 1998: 163

The concept of joy runs through the chapter, as the framework of the emotional experience that Caribbean and African arrivants wanted to achieve in various ways, and I believe was expressed through their styled bodies. For some this goal and emotion was chipped away through the various degrees of adverse reaction to their presence. Through the pursuance of staying in England and fighting for their right to be here, again in various ways, the styled body being one, joy could be achieved as a mark of freedom. Is joy always a tangible emotion, or can it be expressed, measured in other ways? Robert A. Johnson states, that "we cannot say what joy is. We must go the further step and discover its true nature for ourselves" (Johnson 1989: 97).

Although originally written in 1967, *Joy: Expanding Human Awareness* by William C. Schutz still has value. He believed that "Joy is the feeling that comes from the fulfilment of one's potential. Fulfilment brings to an individual the feeling that he can cope with his environment; the sense of confidence in himself as a significant, competent, lovable person who is capable of handling situations as they arise, able to use fully his own capacities, and free to express his feelings. Joy requires a vital, alive body, self-contentment, productive and satisfying relations with others, and a successful relation to society" (Schutz [1967] 1973: 15). When one considers this definition of joy, in light of the excitement of arriving in England and hopes for making a future (Tulloch 2002) and then the gradual erosion of this emotion due to the extended engagement with England, the effect and affect on who one is through the color bar system, through racism, through the realization of what difference and "otherness" means in England, then the dynamic that harbored in the hearts and minds of black people, of the joy and pain of being in England, can be better understood. Therefore, the obstacles put in the way of achieving joy hinders personal development as joy evokes "feelings of renewal" (Schutz [1967] 1973: 188). A case in point I return to Stuart Hall, a leading thinker and prolific writer on being black in Britain, new ethnicities and the value of cultural studies generally. He came to England from Jamaica in 1951 to study at the University of Oxford on a Rhodes Scholarship. Hall has documented that it was in this move, this geographical experience and his difference of being a black Jamaican, that he *became* West Indian in England. Hall stated this during his appearance on *Desert Island Discs*, which I first listened to during its original broadcast in 2000, but on listening to the programme again in 2014, I heard something else in that interview—joy. I omitted this aspect when I first drew on the program for the essay "Strawberries and Cream: the Quintessence of Englishness" (Tulloch 2002). I focused on Hall's political thinking and thoughts on Englishness, devolution and that difference is exciting and modern (Tulloch 2002: 63–4, 74). But on listening to the radio program, I forgot about the songs he chose, how they were markers in his life, that the 1970s were exciting times for him, with the establishment of the Cultural Studies Department at the University of Birmingham and getting married to Catherine Hall, "and what we used to do is dance" (Hall 2000).

More specifically, there is the concept of black joy that Gina Dent and Cornel West see as being in tandem with black pleasure (Dent 1992: 1). West surmised that joy is the domain of "non-market values—love, care, kindness, service, solidarity, the struggle for justice—values that provide the possibility of bringing people together"[7] (Dent 1992: 1). West is hinting that joy is a collective experience here, a collective action, whilst for him pleasure is about the individual. Dent adds to West's thinking and sees joy as knowledge and empowerment that is available to all "and that can lessen the threat of our individual difference" (Dent 1992: 2). The collective experience of black joy is the focus of Dent's introduction to the anthology. But what of the general experience of joy, of new vistas, of new experiences of the black arrivants in a dominant white Mother Country? For Dent, black pleasure and black joy may be mythic and elusive (Dent 1992: 1) but they are nonetheless important to people of the African diaspora in their action of what Dent calls a catharsis and what Michelle Wallis[8] calls a "revolution in vision" (Dent 1992: 18), that is, conduits to being black, to "blackness" and black popular culture. In addition black pleasure and black joy are impetus for change and the acknowledgement of double-consciousness (Dent 1992: 18), of being aware of inhabiting two specific realms of influence and complexities existing in, and coming from, the black and white world.

This "revolution in vision" was, and is, experienced on Britain's streets, particularly its cities since the late 1940s. This vision was not only about the styled black bodies that made a declaration of space in England, Wales and Scotland, it was how those same bodies saw themselves there—through their own and the eyes of others—and adjusted their sense of self based on that revelatory way of seeing. As Dent has argued: "that the move from pleasure to joy takes us from a notion of political agency to an examination of how we come to know, to decide, and to act, we reinvestigate the grounds of consciousness and address not only the subject matter of black life, but also its modes, aesthetic and cultural" (Dent 1992: 11). Thereby for Dent, pleasure and joy are connected. By considering joy, specifically, enables one to see black experiences differently, therefore joy is a form of knowledge (Dent 1992: 18). I heed Dent's warning that to talk of black joy is to conjure up essentialism (Dent 1992: 10) but I am also interested in the individual experience and "individual difference," "personal agency" that black joy can support (Dent 1992: 18) and believe that by presenting individual examples can alleviate the path of essentialism.

Illustrative of this are the photographs taken in the 1960s by the Ghanaian photographer James Barnor. Actually, it was his fashion photograph of Nigerian-born Erlin Ibreck in Trafalgar Square, London (figure 6.2), that inspired me to think along the lines that it is equally valid to think about the joy experienced by black people during this period. Barnor presents the nineteen-year-old Ibreck as a tourist, someone enjoying the tourist attractions of London. The photograph connects with another photograph by Gay taken in 1964 of a young white woman enjoying the pleasures of being in Trafalgar Square (figure 6.3). Barnor had a liberated perspective on black presence in England. As a Ghanaian who came to England two years after his homeland had gained independence from British colonialism in 1957, he had a double-consciousness experience of what it meant to be a newcomer in England, and psychologically freed from colonialism. He was appreciative of the black person's identity and place in their homeland and the possible new identities abroad (figure 6.4).

Barnor calls the image of Ibreck a fashion photograph, although the dress Ibreck wears is her own. As Barnor recalls, "We didn't have clothes to chose from. I wouldn't say it was a photo shoot. We didn't have somewhere where the clothes were packed, to take a picture and go and change . . . Erlin dressed from home" (Barnor 2012). I have argued previously that fashion photography as a communicator of ideas and as a method of social commentary can work as a form of faction, incorporating real events as the basis for the creator's own brand of narrative. This is contentious as the auteur may well feel s/he is conveying some kind of truth. Equally, the notion that the professional photographer is an impartial observer of life cannot be adhered to. The photographer, and this is just as relevant to the fashion photographer, makes an intervention into that milieu and it is that intervention and their observations of daily events which fuel them and the other members of a collaborative team to produce the fashion image they want. Fashion photography contributes to life. As

FIGURE 6.2 *Drum* cover girl Erlin Ibreck at Trafalgar Square, London, 1966. Photograph by James Barnor. Courtesy of Autograph ABP. © James Barnor/Autograph ABP.

another form of communication, another form of story-telling, whether that is truth or fiction, nonetheless there is an attempt to make a point (Tulloch 2002: 1–2). The point being made in this photograph is that Barnor does not position himself or his models as "the foreigner" or "the stranger," as was often the categorization of black arrivants by whites, but as another inquisitive visitor enjoying the vibrant city of London. This example leads one to ask, what of other individualized experiences that straddle time and provide sustained thinking of joy as style narrative in England?

The archival fragment: a vein of history

To return to Clark's question, what device to use to review this moment of the past. One cannot capture the whole past, but we have access to remnants of it held in

FIGURE 6.3 Young woman with pigeons in Trafalgar Square, 1964, photograph by John Gay. © English Heritage.

archives, whether recognized as an archive or not. Such resources, such fragments of lived experiences are, as Clark says "alluring" (Clark 2004: 41). I see archives as the veins of history. They link the present with the past and the past with the future. Archives enable individuals and groups, objects, design and art practices to encourage a narrative of their experiences, achievements and contributions. Archives enable a lived experience to be revived and reassessed time and time again. Such repositories give rise to stories of lives and activities that would often be lost. Significantly, an archive is evidence. Regardless of whether large or small, personal or public, archives are networks of knowledge and of a presence that is now absent.

The archival fragment that this chapter hinges upon is a handwritten letter by Dr Beryl Gilroy (1926–2001) sent to me in 1987 that is part of my personal research

FIGURE 6.4 Mike Eghan at Piccadilly Circus, London, 1967. The Ghanian was a radio broadcaster for the BBC World Service. Photograph by James Barnor. Courtesy of Autograph ABP. © James Barnor/Autograph ABP.

archive. Beryl Gilroy was incredibly supportive of research I undertook for my written dissertation whilst a fashion student. She wrote the letter following a telephone interview I conducted with her on August 9, 1987[9] about a period of history that she had experienced, in terms of style-fashion-dress. Beryl Gilroy came to England in 1951 as a "colonial student" (Gilroy 1998: 193) from her birthplace, Guyana or British Guiana as it was known then. By 1968, Beryl Gilroy was England's first black headmistress. Her letter, which includes hand-drawn illustrations, describes the range of styles she liked to wear during the 1940s and 1950s; as Beryl Gilroy says of herself in the letter, "I was 'bookish' but still a heavy dresser." The letter makes reference to familial style practices in Guyana and of styles of black and white people in England. This is supported by Beryl

Gilroy's book *Leaves in the Wind* (1998). It is a form of life-telling, a collection of writings by Beryl Gilroy about different periods of her life as a student, teacher, writer, psychoanalyst, wife, mother, grandmother and granddaughter. It provides additional thinking about her life in England during this time as I am no longer able to interview her.

I have previously drawn on Beryl Gilroy's memories of being in England and the personal styles she created. These references were effectively short textual and visual quotations from Beryl Gilroy's style practices. I want to revisit those style narratives here as she entrusted me with material about the style practices of her younger self that have not been discussed in detail. Molly Andrews advocates the researcher's desire to revisit data as:

> the more vantage points from which we view phenomena, the richer and more complex our understanding of that which we observe . . . historical changes, as well as changes in our individual life circumstances, provide us with opportunities to see new layers of meaning in our data . . . this characteristic of narrative data as evidence of its resilience and vitality, and of its infinite ability to yield more layers of meaning when examined from yet another lens, as we explore the ongoing changes of the world within and around us.
>
> **ANDREWS** 2008: 87, 98–99

By returning to material, we see new aspects of it lost on an earlier viewing, read in a different context, frame of research and personal experience, as highlighted earlier about my second listening of Hall's interview on *Desert Island Discs*, having heard it fifteen years earlier. Andrews feels that it is not the material that has changed, but the researcher,[10] which inevitably brings, as she says, fresh and "multiple perspectives" (Andrews 2008: 87). In my case, it is the inevitable experience of mourning the loss of family members and friends who were part of the pioneering generation of black travelers from the "British West Indies" to England, whose presence from the late 1940s onwards, though tangible, was rendered invisible because of intolerance and racism. It is my personal and critical need to remember them and their style narratives to contribute to the historical resonance of that period.[11] I come to this piece of "transcultural life-writing" (Baena 2007: vii–x),[12] Beryl Gilroy's letter, as a valuable part of her autobiography. It stands in for the voice it once belonged to, that is no longer audible, but can still be heard through this form of representation.

Rosalia Baena's definition of "transcultural" in relation to the various forms of autobiographical "cultural texts" (Baena 2007: viii), from the written to the visual, is useful here. Transcultural applies itself to the renewed manner of engagement that arises from new forms of perceiving experience, and to the dynamic nature of the resulting narratives stemming from the contact zones produced in the cross-cultural encounters. In the telling of the autobiographical self, or what Janet Varner

Gunn calls "the cultural act of self-reading" (Gunn 1982: 8).[13] Baena says that "what is at stake in autobiographical discourse is not a question of the subject's authentic 'I', but a question of the subject's location in the world through an active interpretation of experiences that one calls one's own in particular "worldly" contexts' (Gunn 1982: 23).[14] What I want to do here, on behalf of Beryl Gilroy, and to paraphrase Baena, is to "wilfully position" her experience of black style-fashion-dress in England "in history and culture" (Baena 2007: viii).

Beryl Gilroy continued her teaching practice that she had started in Guyana, supplementing this with further studies in London in the 1950s. Firstly, her passion for the presentation of self during this period was profound joy of *being* in England that was integral to who she was. That Beryl Gilroy took great pleasure in the fashions of the day and in creating her own styles is evident in her letter, something that was a continuation of style practices she had engaged in in Guyana. Her experiences of difference, and the reactions to her by some factions of the white community, instilled in Beryl Gilroy what she saw as "equality of expectations" (Gilroy 1976: 164).[15]

The academic value of Dr Beryl Gilroy's letter

The letter is a recognized primary resource in dress studies (McDowell 1998: 17, 21, 427; Watt 1999; de la Haye 2013: 10, 62–71). Judith Watt, for example, included letters in the range of literature that expounds the "individual view, of clothes and fashion conditioned by experience and attitude, that adds an often fascinating perception and is a rich source for anyone interested in the history of dress" (Watt 1999: xi). Within narrative studies, particularly under the aegis of auto/biography and life writing, the study of letters, the epistolarity and the epistolarium,[16] has developed into a recognized area of study in the present century[17] because, as Liz Stanley says succinctly, "letters matter because they are connected with real lives" (2004: 223).

I want to position Beryl Gilroy's letter in epistolary theory, as it is an area of study that welcomes an interdisciplinary approach (Cardell and Haggis 2011: 129–33)[18] to clarify that her letter has significance, not only in the style-fashion-dress of the African diaspora, but presents another form of style narrative, the written word. Additionally, the letter has historical significance, as Beryl Gilroy was an important and significant figure in Britain as an educator and novelist. This letter, a minute fragment of Beryl Gilroy's life, nonetheless highlights another aspect of who Beryl Gilroy was. It emits the "presence" of Beryl Gilroy as the author of the letter, and of her younger self in Guyana during the 1940s and in England in the 1950s, as a student and teacher in both countries. The letter also illustrates how a one-off letter—which did not engage in the conventional reciprocity and turn-taking exchange of letter-writing—can engender reciprocity in other ways.

I consider this latter point from the context of Liz Stanley's thinking on letters as a gift (2011), that will be discussed in detail below that Beryl Gilroy's letter and its content was a gift to me that has reverberated on my research on black style in Britain and consequently the African diaspora. Particularly when one considers that reciprocity means: "a state or relationship in which there is mutual action, influence, giving and taking; correspondence, etc., between two parties or things ... mutual action and reaction"; and reciprocal: "Of actions: Alternate, alternating. Existing on both sides: felt or shared by both parties" (Oxford English Dictionary); mutual—me being black British and using the styled black body as way of understanding the world, individuals in it, and their desire to *become* and *be*, and my need to communicate this through publishing and curating. The importance of the visual to Beryl Gilroy and me—her need to draw the clothes; my need to show the objects associated with black style in an exhibition context as evidence.

On re-reading Beryl Gilroy's letter a number of times in the writing of this chapter, I am led primarily by what does this letter mean? What does it mean to have a one-off letter packed with information of personal and wider style-fashion-dress information regarding black and white people in 1950s London, and colonial subjects in 1940s Guyana? What does it mean to have a handwritten letter with drawings of the writer's "wardrobe"? What can one get from this and where exactly can this letter take me? How to use it now in relation to Beryl Gilroy's thinking, particularly from her perspective as an educator and psychologist, on what it meant to be black and female in England and the relevance of such an intensely personal act of styling the self to Beryl Gilroy. I like Janet Gurkin Altman's possibility of epistolarity as "the use of a letter's formal properties to create meaning" (Altman 1982: 4, quoted in Sarah Poustie 2010: 13), which is supported by the fact that "The epistolarium is a heuristic" (Stanley 2011: 137). Therefore, this one-off letter cannot be ignored. Such a letter has a legitimate place in epistolatory studies (Stanley 2004: 209) as it is undoubtedly "a document of life" (Stanley 2004: 202) and part of the documentation of a life.

Beryl Gilroy has packed the letter with information and intentionally or not, offers a challenge to check the historical accuracy of the statements she made and possibly new areas of research to pursue—how accurate is Beryl Gilroy's evocative comment that "[T]win sets and skirts were street wear for teachers." This is a hint at another research project, the style narratives of teachers. Is accuracy important? Beryl Gilroy's energetic text draws a portrait of 1940s Guyana and 1950s London as she remembers them. Yet this reference connects with my earlier comments on the twinset as worn by Billie Holiday in chapter 3. Beryl Gilroy provides another meaning for the twinset here as an item indicative of the woman as educated, as educator and liberated by this. Interestingly, Beryl Gilroy's observation of the twinset and teachers provides another reason why I am interested in this letter. I wrote this chapter after completing the chapter on Billie Holiday. Reading the letter and Beryl Gilroy's thoughts on twinsets was exciting. I had forgotten this observation made by Beryl Gilroy in the letter, as I had not read it for about ten years. As Andrews has mentioned, and outlined above, the ability to revisit research material is a vital aspect of narrative and, of course, style-fashion-dress studies.

The gift of a letter

It is the *acts* of giving and receiving that are most important here: the *objects* are not the main point ... Who gives, and who receives, matters ... thinking about letters in terms of the gift relationship points out that such exchanges occur because they are the material expression of connection and continuing relationship—and this is, of course, the foundation of sociality and the social.

STANLEY 2011: 140–1

On the whole I agree with Stanley as the uninhibited manner in which Beryl Gilroy wrote the letter and drew her wardrobe to communicate more fully her engagement with style-fashion-dress of 1940s Guyana and the 1950s in London, was an act of giving. But the letter as object is also important. I am primarily approaching this letter as a style-fashion-dress specialist where the visual and material is paramount, and as a curator where the object acts as personal and cultural evidence.

With regard to "who gives, and who receives" the gift, Beryl Gilroy was the gift giver as teacher, a sharing of knowledge and experience and an understanding of the importance of the visual regarding style-fashion-dress as worn on the body. In her "making" of the letter—the handwriting, the annotations, the hand-drawn garments and accessories, add to this concept of the letter as gift. Beryl Gilroy and I could not predict the future, but as mentioned above her letter has been part of my research practice, as background information or actual curatorial quotes in projects such as the Victoria and Albert Museum (V&A) exhibition "Streetstyle: From Sidewalk to Catwalk, 1940 to Tomorrow" (1994– 5). As a consultant on the exhibition, focusing on black British styles, I introduced Beryl Gilroy to the curators, who worked closely with her. Beryl Gilroy donated to the exhibition an outfit of a pink suit that she had made in Guyana, a check woolen coat by Krimatex, which she bought when she first arrived in London, a handbag and black hat. Beryl Gilroy donated the outfit to the V&A (plate 9). I used it again in the introduction to the publication *Black Style* (Tulloch 2004: 18) which accompanied the exhibition "Black British Style" (2004–5). The latter focused on the style practices in Britain of black people from the Caribbean, West Africa and Britain from the 1940s to the early 1990s. Beryl Gilroy's outfit featured in the exhibition section "England is the Place for Me" which was about the arrival and "settlement" of black people in post-World War II Britain. The caption was a combination of information that had been gained for the *Streetstyle* exhibition and information Beryl Gilroy had imparted in her letter to me:

> Nat Gaynes Suit, Krimatex Coat, Hat and Chic Handbag
> Guyana and London, c. 1951
> Dr Beryl Gilroy migrated from Guyana to England in 1951 to continue her teaching studies. She had a passion for clothes and remembers that as a student she "dressed up for lectures". In 1968 Dr Beryl Gilroy became London's first black head teacher. This cotton-mix suit was made for Dr Beryl Gilroy by Nat Gaynes, a local dressmaker in Guyana. She purchased the woollen coat and hat in London to keep out the English winter. Museum no. T.132 to 136–1995.
> *Black British Style* 2004

Therefore to return to Stanley's quote, I am expanding on her proposal of "the gift relationship" as an "expression of connection," but continuation was done between Beryl Gilroy and myself, not through epistolary matter, but through curatorial telling of black style practices and the making of the self in England.

"I was 'bookish,' but still a heavy dresser": the letter unpacked

Beryl Gilroy's handwritten letter (figure 6.5), addresses a receiver, "Dear Carole [sic] Tulloch" and is signed by the sender "B.A. Gilroy PhD.," with the imparting of information in between. It covers the first two-and-a-half sides of the (unpaginated) letter. Beryl Gilroy squeezed in as much information as possible, adding lines of negative leading or inserting additional information above a segment of her text as superscript. The following four-and-a-half sides of the letter are more fervent in her desire to impart as much information as possible on the 9in × 7in (22.9cm × 17.8cm) sized sheets of paper. This section follows the close of her letter with "I hope all this helps. B.A. Gilroy PhD.," as if this is a P.S. but without the use of that abbreviation. This section is a combination of handwriting and fourteen drawings, hand-drawn by Beryl Gilroy, of some of the clothes she wore during the 1950s, a period she said "was my time" (Gilroy 1998: 204). For me, these are the most precious elements of the letter, as Beryl Gilroy gives so much of herself here. She states her inability to draw, not as an apology, more as a warning of what is to come: "I am no artist I just try to reconstruct my wardrobe" at the top of the first side of the letter, above her address, in a different colored ink to the main body of the letter. Beryl Gilroy repeats the warning as the encircled text "I am not good at drawing" on side five a packed page of four drawings and detailed captions around each design (figure 6.6). Within this second, longer, section, Beryl Gilroy's tone of

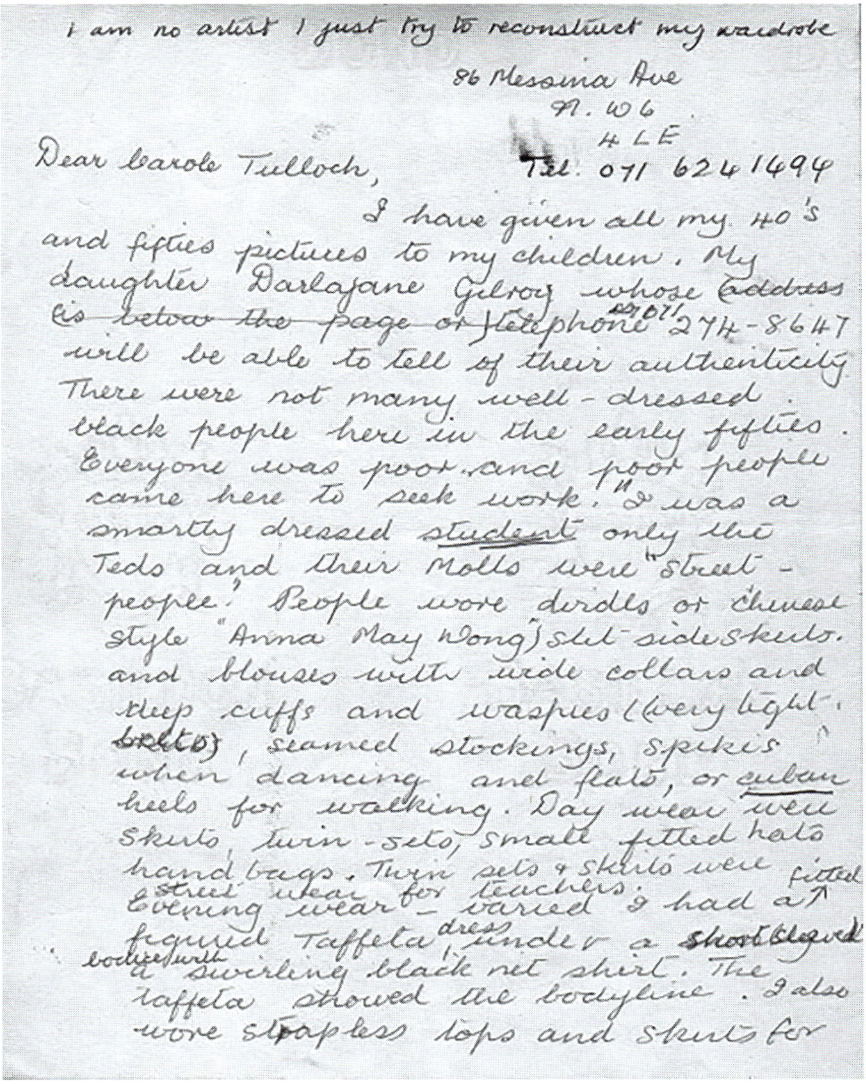

FIGURE 6.5 Letter from Dr Beryl Gilroy, 1987. Author's collection.

information changes. From side four the ink is blacker and the density of the handwritten lines are tighter, whilst sides five to seven are dedicated to Beryl Gilroy's drawings of "my wardrobe."

There is a trusting quality to the writing and drawing of the letter. Beryl Gilroy and I only met a couple of times, and spoke at length once for, about an hour, on the telephone, yet she felt comfortable enough with me to send a letter that had visible corrections and edits, annotations of words and thoughts, and Beryl Gilroy

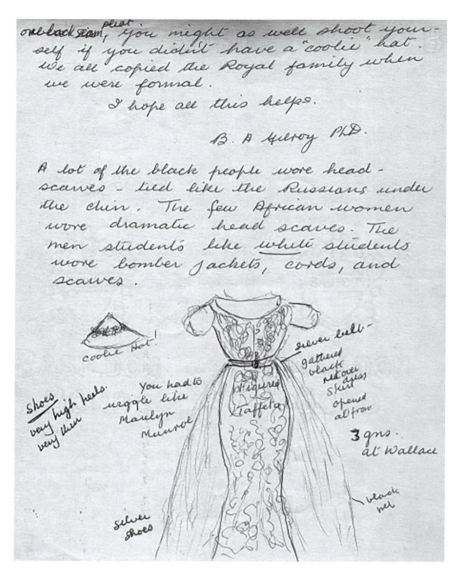

one back seam, pleat, you might as well shoot yourself if you didn't have a "coolie" hat.
We all copied the Royal family when
we were formal.
I hope all this helps.

B. A. Gilroy PhD.

A lot of the black people wore head-
scarves - tied like the Russians under
the chin. The few African women
wore dramatic head scarves. The
men students like _white students_
wore bomber jackets, cords, and
scarves.

coolie Hat!

silver belt

gathered
black
net over
skirt
opened
all from

Shoes
very high heels.
very thin

You had to
wriggle like
Marilyn
Munroe

(figured

Taffeta)

3 gns.
at Wallace

black
net

silver
shoes

FIGURE 6.6 Letter from Dr Beryl Gilroy, 1987. Author's collection.

underlined words she considered to be significant. Therefore, from the time of
receiving the letter in 1987, and the successive times of reading it since, the letter
always feels as if it has come from a friend. More importantly it came from someone
who cared about imparting knowledge.

In the first portion of the letter, which runs for just over two pages, Beryl Gilroy
goes on to define herself and her styled self alongside recollections of the kind of

garments and designs worn primarily by women. The text flips between Beryl Gilroy's description of her wardrobe in the 1950s and with what other women wore regardless of skin color. No specific dates are given, but this segment of the letter focuses on the 1950s, with reference to items that were to be revived in future decades. This first section is revealing in that Beryl Gilroy demarcates fashionable, yet respectable designs, and "daring" garments and accessories. I am presenting the whole text here as I feel it is time to share this incredible document as one woman's insight into, and experience of, style amongst women in London, regardless of skin color in the 1940s and 1950s.

I was a smartly dressed <u>student</u> only the Teds and their Molls were "street people". People wore dirdls [sic] or Chinese style "Anna May Wong" slit side skirts and blouses with wide collars and deep cuffs and waspies (very tight belts), seamed stockings, spikes when dancing and flats, or <u>cuban</u> heels for walking. Day wear were skirts, twin-sets, small fitted hats hand bags. Twin sets [sic] & skirts were street wear for teachers.

Evening wear—varied I had a fitted figured Taffeta dress under a short sleeved bodice with swirling black net skirt. The taffeta [sic] showed the bodyline. I also wore strapless tops and skirts for dancing. I had black crepe-de-chine and also a gingham cocktail dress and a Swirling black and green skirt with wide elastic waist. All had fitted bodices. We wore little marcesete [sic] broaches, earrings and bracelets as well as fake pearls and large round beads. The most daring girls wore ankle-chains. Some wore "short-shorts" (that came back as hot pants) for tennis but we wore Bermuda shorts in the summer with socks, as stockings were scarce. We wore off the shoulder blouses, or blouses with wide necks in the summer. Black people had be respectable. Women were few. As I said I was "bookish" but still a heavy dresser . . .

Coats were A-Line. I did have some pictures but I don't know who has them. A-line coats were full length and the half length coats were loose. I have two good shots of coats which my daughter will show you. I also wore wide striped skirts with the stripes cut on the bias. We wore gloves—little matching ones. I wore gloves winter & summer. I dressed up for lectures.

Everyone wore hats. "Coolie" [sic] hats little suits in grey or brown with 2 skirts were in. One skirt was pleated and the other back seam pleat [sic], you might as well shoot yourself if you didn't have a "coolie" hat. We all copied the Royal family when we were formal.

I hope all this helps.

B.A. Gilroy PhD.

A lot of the black people wore head-scarves—tied like the Russians under the chin. The few African women wore dramatic head scarves. The men students like <u>white</u> students wore bomber jackets, cords, and scarves.

The Forties up [sic] to the time of the McCurran Act most people went to America and were sent clothes from there.

My families [sic] were dressmakers and bought the Weldon Ladies Catalogue and a French one called La Mode which showed current fashions. They made the dresses and cut by looking.

West Indian women were forced during slavery to sew—All used to be able to "cut and stitch". One learned either by "looking" as families sewed or in apprenticeship to dressmakers. All girls dreamt of having a "Singer sewing machine" for sewing & embroidery. We also shopped from catalogues—Damart, Sears, Lennards, and others I've forgotten. My cousins copied styles from True Romances, Ebony, or Jet sent from the U.S. The U.S. had a "black" style. When I came to Britain I wore a plain pink dress with a large white bow and got stared at. People wore sensible colours—Pink got dirty in the grime of the 50's.

Films influenced style. We went to the films and made dresses we saw there you could "read" clothes. My cousins could and copied film-star clothes. In our village an Assyrian man named Mamoud came once a month to sell expensive Silks, taffetas, organdie, crepe-de-chine, georgette and linen. These were used for weddings. Milliners made dress-hats out of plaited crepe-paper, buckram and plaited commercial silky straw—a plastic thing that softened if it got wet. Children wore home made brightly coloured clothes, crocheted socks (white) and very large hair-bows—shoemaker made boots laced up or shoes with ankle strap and one button.

Beryl Gilroy's vibrant recollection of her style-fashion-dress practice and observations during the 1940s and 1950s conveys a belief she discussed twelve years later in *Leaves in the Wind* that: "[C]reativity and identity arrive from a nurtured and nourished in-scape" (Gilroy 1998: 211). As Beryl Gilroy said, the fifties were her time: when she engaged in her teacher training studies that she supplemented with her own "paper chase. Reading to drown myself in books" (Gilroy 1998: 196) alongside the excitement of living in London, drinking espressos at coffee bars, doing the samba at dances, that was shadowed by racism which led to action by Beryl Gilroy, such as being part of a picket line to oppose the sale of Golliwog dolls at a toyshop (Gilroy 1998: 200). This was all part of her feminism in the 1950s, a term she strongly believed should be used in relation to black women in England at this time, due to their independence in light of the "oppression, sedimentation and chronic hostility" of the period (Gilroy 1998: 208–9). Beryl Gilroy believed that "[F]eminism is not what you say it is but what you live." Living and studying in London fed Beryl Gilroy's intellect, and her adventurous and political sides, which helped to formulate her "carefree self" (Gilroy 1998: 211). Beryl Gilroy's wardrobe of fashions of the day and her particular take on styling herself in the 1950s, was part of that period of her wholeness.

"*Leaves in the Wind*"

> It is not easy to define how much of my interior life is defined in my writing.
>
> **GILROY** 1998: 11

Leaves in the Wind (1998) is a collection of writings by Beryl Gilroy. Her first text in the book is titled "I Write Because . . .". It outlines what had inspired the different forms of writing Beryl Gilroy had engaged in—books for children, adolescents and adults. Beryl Gilroy states at the opening of this section: "Creativity includes the element of surprise. I write because there must be time for self-affirmation . . . In my writings, I try to say 'This is the way we are. This is a sample of our life. We are peripheral to your class structures. We are invisible when it doesn't suit you and visible when it does'" (1998: 3, 7). What *Leaves in the Wind* provides is the psychological link between Beryl Gilroy's letter of her past written in 1987 and her expanded thinking on that past some eleven years later. In the book, Beryl Gilroy incorporates a broader outline of herself as an educator, writer and psychologist.

The impact of the reductionist response to black presence in Britain in the 1950s still rankled with Beryl Gilroy in 1998. She clarified in *Leaves in the Wind* that, as one of the colonial students in England, whilst in the colleges you were accepted as it was believed you "would return home," but: "The moment we went further afield, however, we were perceived differently and described, without any categorical doubt, by such words as immigrants, foreigners, natives, spades and other congenitally British/colonial terms of derision. Not only did these names distance us, they also served as filters for our every word and deed" (1998: 3).

With regard to style-fashion-dress, Beryl Gilroy recognized its significance in *Leaves in the Wind* as a marker of belonging as she placed it alongside "language" as "embodying special elements of the British culture with all its encapsulated classisms, ethnocentrisms and prejudices, which, whether incidental or concealed, had to be tolerated by us" (Gilroy 1998: 4). What was reserved for "us," Beryl Gilroy said, was "the stereotype . . . an identity that had been historically constructed for us. This identity bore no relation to our feeling or interior lives, or to our mobile young selves, as against the immutable and attributed selves, through which some of us projected whatever helped us to survive. In effect Black people in a racist society are two people: the façade and the real person who must exist in society" (Gilroy 1998: 4). In support of Beryl Gilroy's position, I have argued for some time that one of the ways black people "projected whatever helped us to survive" was their style practices, their styled selves, of doing this for themselves. This connects with Beryl Gilroy's concept of the "home-made" (Gilroy 1998: 6).

The "home-made" was a skill that had long been part of Beryl Gilroy's life as she recognized the empowering qualities of a doing-it-yourself approach. She outlined this in her letter, about home dressmaking undertaken by her cousins and others, of "reading" films and catalogs for ideas, then cutting out and making clothes. She applied this skill during her teaching practice at primary schools. Beryl Gilroy noticed that the official reading material for her primary school children did not connect with them. Many were from different parts of the world, and so had different cultural and social experiences and values, and for some who were born in England, "some of the children were still talking about and showing the trauma of evacuation. Others had, on returning, been unable to recognise their homes or their streets. For some, close relatives had vanished" (Gilroy 1998: 5–6). Therefore, this time was a new world for the children and, Beryl Gilroy noted, the "perfect world" depicted in children's books such as *Janet and John* was alien to them:

> Quietly I began preparing supplementary reading material . . . I set aside periods of the day for talking. We called this "Problem Time", or "News Time" or "Story Time". "Problem Time" was the most productive because during this period the children talked about what they found problematic in the classroom or on the playground, and what affected them en route to school, or at home, or anywhere in their environment . . . These talks took me into the lives of the children, and in time our home-made books, by reflecting their experiences, became therapeutic and meaningful to the children. They sited themselves in situations in a recognisable world . . . The cultures of the working classes, the Black family, the local Greek family, all needed to be seen as valid cultures. I decided to make this explicit . . . The children had to be helped to understand the psychology of difference by accepting it. Racism in Britain at that time was unacquainted with positive images. Instead, it was trapped in historicist beliefs about the power of Empire.
>
> **GILROY** 1998: 6–7

Racism was a key inspiration for Beryl Gilroy's writing to redress the name calling, the derision, the "false accusations by police, beatings up of innocent people" (Gilroy 1998: 9) as well as the rejection from pubs and public places as Horatio Simpson remembered: "We were young, you know, and had to enjoy ourselves. We had no clubs. Want a drink in the pub and you're told you're not drinking in here. Only two pubs in Brixton you could get a drink—the White Horse, and one other in Atlantic Road" (Tulloch 1988: 15). Beryl Gilroy recounted that "they used their tongues light-heartedly, yet abrasively to strip away any idea of a confident whole or human self" (Gilroy 1998: 10). The rejection projected in so many ways. Beryl Gilroy's reaction to this was that "In my work I try to capture the essential differences between ourselves and other people" (Gilroy 1998: 11).

As illustrated by her letter, Beryl Gilroy is part of her work. Beryl Gilroy was about personal development and existence, "mental and metaphysical" (Gilroy 1998: 33). She advocated existentialism, as "[E]xistentialist is what one becomes in spite of the legacies of colonialism and the body-memories of slavery . . . the key themes of existentialism deal with the here-and-now, as well as problems pertinent to our struggle to survive in time, space and intentionality" (Gilroy 1998: 33). Therefore the past need not be repeated and impact on the present/future: "I consider any creative work depicting the human condition to be existential—coming out of the inner life as emotional rhetoric, to liberate us from fears and nightmares" (Gilroy 1998: 33). Thinking that connects with creative work, the making of the self through style and the narratives they emit to be seen as who one is.

As outlined above, the 1950s was a formative period for Beryl Gilroy, this adds weight to the importance of her letter, and my need to reproduce it here in length to get at some semblance of Beryl Gilroy at this time. Additionally, Joan Anim-Addo underscored the significance of Beryl Gilroy's recollections of her time in 1950s London, as there has been a lack of documentation on "Black women's" experience during this period. (Gilroy & Anim-Addo 1998: 136). Autobiography was an essential form of documentation for Beryl Gilroy, as evidenced by her letter to me and *Leaves in the Wind*. A format that was a means to get at the intangibility of the past, but nonetheless valid, if lives are to be counted as such Beryl Gilroy believed that:

> Autobiography is dependent on memory and on impressions gleaned over time. A time peopled by others, whose individual sensations and intentions, judgements and ideas differ fundamentally from what is acceptable to communities, could leave moments difficult to understand or to classify ... When autobiography is a conscious review of life, there is a time for wandering down the remembered pathways of a past, randomly peopled by ghosts of the past; for within it, experience and time are condensed to become past, present and future where memories of every kind are reassessed. Recollection and interpretation play an integral part in creating new meanings across time that has died, but which must be resurrected if self-history is to lead to greater personal growth.
>
> **GILROY** 1998: 159–60

Beryl Gilroy's letter to me and her book *Leaves in the Wind* are acts of postcolonial life-writing (Moore-Gilbert 2009) that included reflections on her colonial female self of the 1950s in England. These are testimony of a woman who lived, not survived, of her *being* not settling in England amid the contentious frame of what it meant to be different at that time. This form of auto/biographical telling is enhanced by the differing forms of style narratives connected with black lives—as pieces designed around the body or discussed in letters—to traverse racism.

Style as levitation

In consideration of all the above, I propose the idea of the styled black body being a form of levitation. The concept of style as levitation places the styled black body as "invisibly" rising above racism to get on with becoming *and* being. Levitation is the freeing of the body through consciousness, the element of will, of focusing on the self to achieve "states of awareness" (Richards 1980: 109). The resultant levitation is indicative "that something significant is happening" (Richards 1980: 14). Interestingly, Alistair O'Neill has referred to the magic and deception of levitation is likened to the magic and deception of fashion and fashion magazines, that extols one message while by slight of hand subverting the status quo and understanding of the place, and who the wearer of the clothes is (O'Neill 2011: 15–19).

I am not advocating here that the development of black styles and narratives in England is about "deception and illusion" (O'Neill 2011: 16–17), but the "trick," and I am thinking along the lines of a trick as stratagem, the magic, that with one hand draws in viewers to the spectacle of the visual aesthetics of the styled black body, whilst with the other projects the realities of the "uncomfortable truths" (Whitley 2007) of racism, as one of the drivers of this notion of spectacle. Therefore, I use spectacle here, not as the objectification of the black body, but the black body using stylistic skills simultaneously "knowing and transgressive" (O'Neill 2011: 17). The translation of this is the magic of black style and its narratives "for the way we think it says something about us, while it silently discloses something else entirely. This, perhaps, is the true … magic of fashion" (O'Neill 2011: 18), and I would extend to post-World War II black style-fashion-dress in Britain, and across the African diaspora for magic can also be "a very present and awakened state of being" (Shoard 2015: 9). Jane Collins and Andrew Nisbet remind us "our readings of the body are complex and multi-layered. Like the space in which it resides, the body is never neutral, its meanings are subject to interpretations which are themselves the product of ideologies and belief systems rooted in a particular place and moment in time" (Collins & Nisbet 2010: 231).

Therefore, by looking back at this period of arrival and *being* in England and of re-reading this moment through the lens of the spectres of that period of black British and African diaspora history, then the cultural significance of re-reading past style narratives is revealed as magical, for the styling of garments and accessories, hair and makeup that have contributed to the range of style-fashion-dress practices of black people in England, is a making of the self that is "indebted to the staging of magic" (O'Neill 2011: 18).

Mrs Gloria Bennett

An example that illustrates this idea of style as levitation and supports the style narrative examples presented here, is the photograph of Mrs Gloria Bennett (1936–2010) (figure 6.7) that is featured on the front cover of this book. The photograph was taken in 1961, in St Mary's Road, Doncaster, South Yorkshire. For

FIGURE 6.7 Mrs Gloria Bennett, 1961, Doncaster, England. Courtesy of Denise Laurence.

me, the photograph summarizes Gloria Bennett *being* herself. It illustrates how she was *being* herself, a young black Jamaican woman in England. Whilst the social and political context which this photograph is part of, positions her, as Hall mentions above, *becoming* "black in Britain," that is asserting one's presence to deflect racism, and to engage with the various cultures that impacted on her life here. Therefore, I consider the photographic portrait of Gloria Bennett as what Maria Tamboukou calls an "event . . . a continuum wherein past, present and future co-exist, an unfolding time, wherein *events* as forces that effectuate changes, emerge" (Tamboukou 2010: 18). Therefore, what was Gloria Bennett saying in this photograph that has unfolded over time—what it meant at the time in 1961, and what it means now in the twenty-first century?

Gloria Bennett migrated from Jamaica to England, and specifically Doncaster, in 1959 to join her husband, Herman Bennett. I knew her as Aunt G. She was part of my life from 1959 to her death in 2010.[19] At the time the photograph was taken, Gloria Bennett worked as a bus conductor and she was a key figure of the town's Caribbean community as *the* dressmaker and hairdresser. She could also knit, crochet and quilt. Speaking in 1991, Gloria Bennett recalled: "You used to get your styles out of . . . a magazine . . . in Jamaica, and you used to see nice little styles in there . . . I could just sit down and cut out a dress without using a pattern then. I never sewed for anybody back home. I just sewed for myself. When I came here I started to" (Bennett 1991). She also declared her fondness in the 1950s and 1960s for the style of the slim-line dress she wears in the photograph: "when you really made a dress, it was mostly your pencil dress. From the top right down it was tight man . . . and some . . . had a wide frill at the bottom with crinoline under that, fish tail" (Bennett 1991). She learnt hairdressing by watching a hairdresser in Jamaica: "I got so good at it that when I got to the hairdresser, sometimes she was so full, she asked if I could press this [hair] out while she finished, and she would curl it up . . . Then I came over here and I used to have quite a few people" (Bennett 1991). She recalled when she did hairdressing in the early years of her arrival in England cultural references from "home" influenced her hair creations: "if a person had long hair, they had the idea from Jamaica, I used to use tongs to do . . . long curls that looked like bananas. I would curl the hair and let them loose" (Bennett 1991).

Gloria Bennett made the dress she is wearing in the photograph. There are a number of details on this gown: an asymmetrical band of fabric across the bust that leads into a large corsage, in the same fabric as the dress, which extends into a long trail of fabric, symbolic of the stem of a flower. There are stud-like details on the band and corsage. There is ruched draping from the waist to three-quarters of the length of the skirt of the dress. Together they work, particularly as her double strand of what appear to be glass beads, works tonally with the gown. The understated high crown of her hairstyle allows focus on the elaborate detailed styling of her dress. Gloria Bennett's fantail earrings, demure strappy shoes and stockings completes this occasion-wear ensemble.

This *is* Gloria Bennett. The meticulous presentation of self here was a practice Gloria Bennett maintained throughout her life. But what states this, emphatically, is the way Gloria Bennett allows herself to be photographed with a cigarette, a passion she engaged in all her life. Yet the cigarette says something more. It is a declaration of freedom, of black feminine freedom, as does her confidant claim of a Mark II Jaguar car to pose against. This was not her car, nor her husband's, neither of them could drive. But the symbols of the car are right for the sophisticated appearance Gloria Bennett wanted to project. The sleek, streamlined, understated glamor of the Mark II Jaguar was the embodiment of Englishness from the moment it was first produced in 1959, the year Gloria Bennett arrived in England. It exemplified the common sense of good design that incorporated the myth of English heritage and tradition. This was evoked in the tradition of English "craftsmanship" that emitted from the design and detailing of the interior and exterior of the Jaguar. Gloria Bennett embodies a definition of glamor, what Elizabeth Wilson says begins with "magic, developed into a very specific form of individualism . . . The individual imposes himself upon society by means not of power but of beauty and personality, unanchored and divorced from traditional social relations" (Wilson 2007: 97). Wilson is referring to the dandy, the white dandy at that, who perhaps does not *need* the power to be seen. As a black Jamaican woman in England, Gloria Bennett claims the power, as she does the Jaguar car as a prop, together with beauty and personality for her effective performativity that evokes the craftsmanship of self that emits from Gloria Bennett.

Style-fashion-dress as "duppy conqueror"

In summary, Beryl Gilroy's letter and the photographic portrait of Gloria Bennett are illustrative of their response to the cultural and political milieu that left a mark on their lives on arriving and being in England as the women they became.[20] Difference is a key frame of Beryl Gilroy's letter as it references her "otherness" as defined by others and her wilful pursuance to *be* Beryl Gilroy, in England in the 1950s, the student and teacher who was a "heavy dresser." Therefore, style-fashion-dress helped Beryl Gilroy to effectively *levitate* above this, not without responsibility, but in order to maintain self-preservation and determination to *become*. Something that Gloria Bennett also does so eloquently in her portrait in a cocktail dress, a cigarette and her desire to be associated with a categorical statement of Englishness, the Mark II Jaguar.

I refer to the notion of the duppy conqueror in reference to the novel by Ferdinand Dennis (1998) of the same title. A "quest narrative" (Gunning 2010: 25) that is about returning to one's place of birth. The book is built around Marshall Sarjeant's journey from Jamaica, to Britain, Africa and Jamaica to dispel a family curse that originates during slavery. Dave Gunning sees the book as Dennis' exploration of the "burden . . . under which Afro-Caribbeans and black Britons suffer is the sense of a divided self brought about by their unique historical experience" (Gunning 2010: 25). Dennis offers the "duppy conqueror" as the means to address and unite this divided self: "he or she who is able to lay the ghost of history and negotiate an identity free from constraints that past events and discourses have imposed upon him or her" (Gunning 2010: 25). The book *Duppy Conqueror* hints that the only way to do this is by a physical return to the homeland (Gunning 2010: 25). I offer another way, as Beryl Gilroy and Gloria Bennett illustrate, to stay, rise above and claim the right, and use style and develop personalized style narratives to unite the divided self.

CODA

What this research has revealed is that the style narratives of the African diaspora are marked by an aesthetic of presence—to imprint a sense of self on society, culture and history. It has illustrated that to engage in, what is frankly a natural activity of making and defining the self, is not just a counter-narrative to the persistent objectification, marginalization and stereotyping of the black body, but is also the undoubted significance of the "interior dynamic" (Quashie 2012: 6). This was evidenced, for example, in the way that tears ran down the face of Billie Holiday, which was the face of Eleanora Harris, that was framed by her signature gardenia corsage while she sang the protest song *Strange Fruit*; or the joy evinced from Mrs Gloria Bennett's portrait that recorded her wearing a self-made cocktail dress whilst holding a cigarette that was her signature habit. These, along with the other examples discussed here, were self-styled manifestations of inner, personal desires (Quashi 2012: 8), their *need* to live the way they wished to regardless of where they were in the world.

This thinking connects with Kevin Quashie's plea "to restore a broader picture" (2012: 5) of black lives, as he stresses that expression and protest are not the only motivators for their existence. He fears that a continued focus on expression can pull "blackness" into being a concept (Quashie 2012: 4–9). I am in agreement with Quashie in his call for fresh directions, but feel expressiveness still has a part to play. When it is kept in view in the discussions on style narratives as part of black lives and culture, of blackness, then external expression resounds the inner self through the styling of the self. And should that expression be a reaction to racism, then the magic of black style and its narratives, as revealed in this publication, is its ability to trounce the fallout of racism in individualized and group efforts. One could say, then, that the style narratives of the African diaspora have been a quiet revolution.

The examples included here are not aggressive evocations of what it means to be black in specific geographical spaces and time. There are of course more salient style narratives of blackness, the making of a political activist self as an embodied

FIGURE 7.1 Matumbi, Hackney, 1979 London. Photograph by Syd Shelton. Matumbi was a British reggae band that contributed to the Rock Against Racism movement. This was characterized by its profile of black and white participants against racism in Britain. Courtesy of Syd Shelton.

graphic statement of anti-racism—what I call style activism—as in this image of the British reggae band Matumbi taken whilst contributor-participants of the British Rock Against Racism movement of 1976–81 (figure 7.1). But in the *Birth of Cool: Style Narratives of the African Diaspora* I wanted to demonstrate how seemingly innocuous presentations of the styled self can have an equally high octane impact of meaning, as evinced by the understated single-breasted suit worn by Malcolm X. Violence and aggression have been contributory factors in the lives of most of the case studies researched in the book, notably the brutal killing of Steve Biko. Yet these responses to the various forms of fallout towards difference, that at times have been opaque, and at others unequivocal racist statements have been what I call a "cool response," the umbrella term under which a range of cool narratives are explored and expressed. In the examples given here these are: glamor and the everyday, politics and religion, art and design critical perspectives through newness, modernity and the avant-garde.

My concept of a "cool response" is informed by a series of thinkers. Fiona Hackney's term "quiet activism," mentioned in chapter two, as being part of the practice of making conducted in the privacy of one's home, which intimates for me that this private space is where the quiet, pensive focus on the styling and what I see as the *need* to make the self[1] takes place, where one can exercise creativity and autonomy, before crossing the threshold from a private into public space where the ideas that inform the style created is disseminated to perspective viewers. Robert Farris Thompson devised a "concept of cool" that references the "whole of the being" and "whole statement" (Thompson [1974] 2011: 29). For Thompson "dress" plays a part in this through the composition of, that is the styling of, clothing and accessories, hairstyles and makeup into the styled self into what he calls "another kind of bodily incandescence with which to mark . . . for special consciousness . . . the force of reason" (Thompson 2011: 29). Additionally, Thompson listed the myriad meanings of cool in West and Central African languages, that includes the Luo term "mokue" that means "cool, quiet, peaceful" (Thompson 2011: 17). Thirdly, I return to Quashie and his argument for the recognition and consideration of "an aesthetic of quiet", which he views "as a marker of the human individuality of the person who is black" (2012: 4). Finally, Beazley Kanost's consideration of "nonviolent cool" as a cerebral and intellectual endeavor through the "fixity of body and purpose" as in nonviolent civil rights activists in their "refusal to stop protesting" which in the end "defies objectification" (Kanost 2014: 153–62). Kanost has successfully highlighted the power of "[C]ool's stillness thus agitates by disrupting the expectations and assumptions that shape witnesses' mindsets" (Kanost 2014: 151). All of which, for me, underwrites presence.

To merge the concepts of quiet and cool with the styled self brings us back to the essence of the portraits of the individuals discussed in this book. The "cool response" of these examples of black style narratives achieved the twinned mission of strong aesthetic articulation through the quiet persistence of the styled individual's desire and the right to *be,* the right to be seen. The case studies discussed in *The Birth of Cool: Style Narratives of the African Diaspora* are examples of cool as a palpable act of intervention between styled black bodies and the culture around them, as the body can be a philosophical site (Gotschaller 2015: 46), as well as an existentialist plane. This is particularly evidenced in the context of styling as part of the making of the self. Therefore *The Birth of Cool: Style Narratives of the African Diaspora* is a treatise on how the cool response of this genre of style narrative can be a quiet revolution.

When all is said and done, the style narratives discussed here are simply part of the creative, human process of living. But in the realms of what it has meant, and what it continues to mean to be black in the world, the style narratives of the African diaspora deserves to be recognized as an intellectual materialization of reason.

NOTES

Introduction

1   On a research trip to Jamaica in 1996 I met my father's aunt who mentioned how traumatic it was for her to look at this photograph following his death.

2   A consideration that can never be answered is whether the suit was made by my father's stepfather, Horatio Simpson who was a tailor in Jamaica, a trade he hoped to continue in England, but who eventually worked for British Rail until his retirement. Simpson came to England in 1954 and lived in Brixton, and then Stockwell until 1992 when he returned to Jamaica following his wife's (my grandmother Roselyn Agatha) death. He kept his treadle sewing machine in the front room of their London home until he returned to Jamaica where he died in 1999.

3   There has been extensive work to redress the long under representation of this history. In 2015, the exhibition "Staying Power: Photographs of Black British Experience 1950s–1990s" (February 16–May 24), a joint venture between the Victoria and Albert Museum (V&A) and the Black Cultural Archives in London was one example of the ongoing work. They picked up the mantel from Peter Fryer's seminal book *Staying Power: the History of Black People in Britain* (1984) to focus on the visual documentation of this significant moment in history, and to collect these photographs. The work of seventeen black and white male and female photographers, shown concurrently at the two institutions, are now part of the V&A's collection.

4   See Gioia (2010), Hong (2014), Liu (2004), McGuigan (2009), MacAdams (2001), Pountain and Robins (2000), Walker (2012), Rzepka (2013), "American Cool" exhibition, National Portrait Gallery, Smithsonian (2014) http://www.npg.si.edu/ exhibit/exhcool.html.

5   The 2011 re-publication of Thompson's 1973 article "An Aesthetic of the Cool" is an altered version of the original.

6   Eyal Sivan keynote lecture at *Re-Contested Sites/Sights Research Conference,* Chelsea College of Arts, London, March 1, 2012.

7   An excellent example is the article by Lou Taylor, "Beyond Words: An Embroidery in Memory of Anna Binderowska, Married 1864" (2013). Additionally, in 2013, I organized the "Dress as Auto/Biography Workshop" at the V&A Museum. The workshop considered the biographies of lives through dress, dress as an autobiographical statement, the interconnections of auto/biographies and dress, and the inclusion of the academic self in dress studies.

1 Angel in the Market Place

1 See: Mintz 1955; Katzin 1959; Katzin 1960; Edwards 1979; Durrant-Gonzalex 1983; Simmonds 1987; Witter 1989; Mintz 1989 [1974]: 180–224; Boa 1993: 1–3; Wong 1996; Freeman 2002; Ulysse 2007; Brown-Glaude 2011.

2 Prior to the British, the Spanish occupied Jamaica from 1509, under which slavery was established on the island on a smaller scale than that pursued by the British.

3 The number of enslaved women, men and children in Jamaica was vast. Catherine Hall relates that, for example, in 1713 the ratio of black to white people was 8:1, by 1800 nine out of ten people on the island were enslaved, and at the end of the eighteenth-century there were 250,000 enslaved people (Hall 2007: 15).

4 See also "Jamaican Higglers Marketing System and the Future of Kingston (Part I)" (Bertram 2010): http://jamaica-gleaner.com/gleaner/20101031/focus/focus6.html (first accessed November 18, 2014); "Bus Conductor, Higgler in Assault Case" (Burke 2014) http://jamaica-star.com/thestar/20141121/news/news18.html (first accessed January 19, 2015) which not only illustrates the continued practice of higglering amongst women, but also how they include their children, a male in this case, from an early age through to adulthood.

5 This is the date given by the National Library of Jamaica. Krista A. Thompson has raised the issue that some postcard producers used the same image associated with Jamaica for a number of years, but to date there is no evidence of this with "A Jamaica Lady" (Thompson 2006: 257).

6 This publication has no page numbers.

7 I have used the image of "A Jamaica Lady" previously to illustrate the elaborate headtie design that I believe made full use of the meter square madras handkerchief, but without reference to the postcard caption "A Jamaica Lady." I cannot remember if it was my decision to crop this caption or that of the publisher. Yet in my initial unpublished research "Fashioned in Black and White: Women's Dress in Jamaica 1880–1907" the image was used with the postcard caption. See Tulloch 1997: f.42.

8 Email correspondence between Roberta Stoddart and Carol Tulloch, October 12, 2014.

9 Ibid.

10 It is interesting that most images of the higgler at this time, whether photographic or painted postcards depict her at a distance, rarely as a close up as in "A Jamaica Lady".

11 Aston W. Gardner defined the higgler as black in his *Tourist Guide to the Island of Jamaica,* as Gardner states that "the present population of the island is close upon 650,000 persons, of whom eighty percent are black", thereby referring to the Higgler's cultural group (Gardner 1893:1).

12 Edward Lucie-Smith argues that the term "nigger" was primarily used by American photographers for publication in North America (Lucie-Smith 2013: 230).

13 The exhibition was held at Yale Center for British Art, New Haven, Connecticut, 27 September 27–December 30, 2007.

14 John Gilmore states the "Golden Age" of postcard collecting appears to end in 1914, with the period 1900–1914 being the most important for collectors of Caribbean postcards, as the quality of the subjects included was reduced and replaced by the repetitive scenes of sun-sand-and-sea (Gilmore 1995: V11).

15 Gilmore (1995) has called the receptacle for this craze, the postcard album, "the television documentary of its day" (1995: V) as a means of seeing what other countries were like.

16 In Jamaica the publishers included the photographers A. Duperly & Sons, the photographer and travel writer James Johnstone, the Educational Supply Co., the photographer H.S. Duperly, Louis Winkler & Co., England was represented by Raphael Tuck & Sons.

17 Only seven postcards were published outside these dates. My research of the Cousins-Hereward Postcard Collection took place in 1996. More recent research of the collection by Maureen Kerr-Campbell and Frances Salmon has built on Glory Robertson's early research into the collection (1985). They have stipulated that there are 212 picture postcards in the Cousins-Hereward Collection.

18 The exact number of picture postcards of Jamaica published and in circulation has yet to be documented. Gilmore ascertains that between 1900 and 1950 "many thousands" specializing in the Caribbean were published (1995: 144).

19 The photographer Syd Shelton believes the photograph was taken outside, with the use of a backdrop. The indications of this are poor lighting for an interior shot. Had studio lights been used, light would be coming from the camera, and thus more directly at the sitter. In "A Jamaica Lady" the light is coming from above and slightly from the right, but very soft and diffused, so it was probably an overcast day. This is indicated by the fold in the sleeve of the woman's blouse, where it is lighter above than below. Another indicator that the photograph was an outdoor shot is that the basket is lighter on the top than at its base, due to the presence of a soft light source. If the light had shone directly onto the subject, as in a studio setting, then the converse would have happened.

20 The Jamaica International Exhibition ran from January 27–May 2, 1891 in Kingston, and was opened by Prince George of the British royal family. The event was reported in the *Illustrated London News* as a "colonial exhibition" (1891: 111) held in "one of the most beautiful" a purpose built architectures for such exhibition purposes on a site of "unparalled magnificence" (1891: 111). A primary aim of the exhibition was to put Jamaica on the tourist map by inviting visitors and exhibitors from all over the world. An increase in the number of hotels, the improvement of Kingston's roads and pavements to coincide with this event could be seen as the pinnacle of the development of Jamaica's tourism initiative.

21 In the use of "soft" here I reference the Oxford English Dictionary meaning of the production of agreeable or pleasant sensations, to be pleasing to the eye, of pace, progression and movement.

22 See Mintz 1955: 96–7; Durant-Gonzalez 1983: 10; Simmonds 1987; Edwards 1979: 2–3; Le Franc 1989: 99; Bush 1990: 49–50; McDonald 1993: 26; Ulysse 2007: 61; Brown-Glaude 2011: 91–5. In 1955 Sidney Mintz recognized that enslaved women were part of the internal marketing system of Jamaica's period of slavery, drawing on historical documents he later suggests that before the emancipation period of 1838 he does not believe that enslaved women were the prominent marketers, as they were post-emancipation, but that "male marketers may have been more important" (Mintz 1989 [1974]: 216).

23 A market was established, legally, in Spanish Town, Jamaica in 1662. This was a quarterly market (Mintz 1989 [1974]: 195).

24 See also Buckridge 2004: 16–66.

25 Sollas Market is also spelled Solos Market. The spelling used here references the version found in the *Handbook of Jamaica* 1891–2.

26 The legalities of the emancipation act bound the ex-enslaved to complete a four- or six-year apprenticeship with their former masters.

27 East Indians arrived on the island of Jamaica in 1845 as indentured-laborers on a ten-year service contract, five years on contract, five years continuous residence on the island. At the end of their contract the ex-indentured East Indians had the choice to stay in Jamaica, move to a third country or be repatriated free of cost.

28 Veront M. Satchell notes that "Women acquired much less than they transferred . . . In the 1870s they transferred 30,500 acres more than they received, in the 1880s, 64,4000 acres and in the 1890s, 61,000 acres. Women were, indeed, facilitating the growth and expansion of other land-owning classes in society" (Satchell 1995: 227).

29 Eric Hobsbawm's explanation of his thinking on "invented tradition" "includes both "traditions" actually invented, constructed and formally instituted and those emerging in a less easily traceable manner within a brief and dateable period—a matter of a few years perhaps—and establishing themselves with great rapidity" (Hobsbawm 1992 [1983]: 1).

30 Bankra also referenced other basket designs such as a "hamper basket" which was split in two with a handle across the two sections, a "Lady Basket" made of Jippa Jappa and decorated, or the flat "Sandwich Bankra" used for picnics and generally aimed at gentlemen. See Educational Supply Company 1901: 3; Senior 1983: 15.

31 I have looked at the headtie previously, in which I explain the headtie connects with black women, and men, in other parts of the African diaspora from slavery through to periods of migration and settlement from the Caribbean to Britain. See Tulloch 1999.

32 During slavery the cutting of the cotta in half signified "voluntary" divorce between an enslaved couple. Edward Long observed that the wife and husband took a half each and he surmised that "as the circle was a symbol of eternity, and the ring of perpetual love or fidelity, so this ceremony, perhaps, is meant to express the eternal severance of their mutual affections" (Long 1774: 413).

33 In a previous study I outlined the range of headtie styles that were worn between 1880 and 1907. For example, in one headtie style the cloth was tied, with a smooth crown, above the ears with an elaborate knot at the back of the neck, the ends of the tie hanging down to the center of the woman's back. Another version was a looser tie, covering the ears with the ties crossing the name of the neck secured by a loose knot with shorter ends falling across the neck into the area of the collar bone. Another is a gele-style headwrap. Some designs have a deep fold at the front of the headtie which covered all of the forehead, and the overall detail hanging over the eyes, with the fold extending to the top of the forehead where the cloth becomes smooth over the crown of the head and into a full tie at the nape of the neck as worn by a young woman on her way to market riding side saddle on a donkey with paniers (Tulloch 1999: 63–78).

34 This was outlined in the exhibition "Tartan: Its Journey Through the African Diaspora," August 5–30, 2014, Craft Central, London, http://exhibition.ciad.org.uk/ (first accessed December 27, 2014).

35 The use of the madras check as a headtie fabric was worn across the black peasantry, for work and leisure. I have argued that this blanket use bound them together in the adoption of an accessory, and more specifically in the use of the real madras handkerchief whose history dates back to slavery. It is impressive that this apparently humble object can possess such a complex historical narrative and broad cultural influence. The headtie symbolized the tie between African-Jamaican women, and the emergent tie between African-Jamaican women and Indian women as "other," despite the vast cultural and linguistic gulf that divided them. In the headtie itself, its various designs had also developed a relationship "between masses, areas, forms, lines and colours". (Teague 1946: 151). In its longevity of use, the headtie acquired an aura of simplicity that embodied a community relationship based on shared historical roots, colonialism, and difference (Tulloch 1999: 71–2).

36 This bracelet design is similar to one passed down to me from my grandmother who explained, in her usual understated way, "this is an old time bracelet."

37 Alma Oakes and Margaret Hamilton state that the apron was a definition of English countrywomen, "as long as rural costume was worn the apron formed part of it" (1970: 162).

38 In *Black Edwardians: Black People in Britain 1901–1914*, Jeffrey Green does not explain why the choir's name was changed, nor why they had to wear two kinds of clothes, "native costume" and evening dress.

39 The *Jamaican Memories* is a collection of essays produced in response to a competition held by the Jamaican newspaper *The Daily Gleaner* in 1959. People over the age of sixty were invited to recall their memories of the island from the late nineteenth century. Entries were submitted from women and men from different classes, living in Jamaica and abroad.

40 Buckridge likens the design of the apron to the "cover cloths" worn by East and West African women (Buckridge 2004: 164).

41 To date, my research has identified the pinafore version of the apron as being part of the uniform of domestic servants at this time.

42 The reference to Emmeline Pankhurst is a photograph of her with her daughter, Christabel Pankhurst, in "Prison Dress" as a form of protest that includes an apron. The images have no page number. See also Mabel Capper and Patricia Woodlock, Suffragettes wearing "propagandist news-sheets as aprons" about a public meeting to take place in Heaton Park, Manchester, July 19, 1908 http://www.museumoflondonprints.com/image/385242/womens-social-and-political-union-two-suffragettes-mabel-capper-and-patricia-woodlock-1908 (first accessed December 16, 2014).

43 This statement was positioned by "A Practical Nurse, Though a Graduate. New Jersey" in a "Letter to the Editor" of *The American Journal of Nursing* 13, 4: 302–3.

44 See also Jack Higgins, "White Aprons, Black Hands: Aboriginal Women Domestic Servants in Queensland" (1995).

45 Hellis & Sons was established by Robert Hellis in 1870 with his first studio Silver Street, High Street, Notting Hill, Kensington. The "head studios" were 211 and 213 Regent Street, London. Hellis Senior and his sons managed some twenty-four studios across London between 1870 and 1933. See Hellis, Robert http://www.photolondon.org.uk/pages/details.asp?pid=3694.

46 Mary Sibande in interview with Elisabeth Wellershaus in "Sophie Is Not the Only Strong Woman Populating Our Art Scene at the Moment," http://www.contemporaryand.com/blog/magazines/sophieis-not-the-only-strong-woman-populating-our-art-scene-at-the-moment/ (first accessed April 9, 2015).

47 Ibid.

48 This thinking is also informed by personal experience of wearing an apron. When I engage in baking in my kitchen, or making artworks in my studio, the first thing I do is to put on the relevant apron—clean for the former, an extremely "art stained" one for the latter—and the process centers my time to make.

49 This view is taken from "'It Takes a Nation of Millions to Hold Us Back': Freedom and the Dynamics of the African Diaspora," in *In the Seams: The Aesthetics of Freedom Expressed* (Tulloch 2012: 9–10).

50 During the last decade of the nineteenth century several articles were published on the state and possible development of Jamaica. The Jamaican-born Herbert George De Lisser forged the view that it was the role of all Jamaicans, and not the "Mother Country," to "resuscitate" Jamaica and was adamant that to consider such an issue is impossible without the inclusion of Jamaica's black peasantry (De Lisser 1900). The consensus amongst such supporters was that Jamaica remained a jewel to be enjoyed by long- or short-stay travellers. But in order for it to develop, Jamaica was in need of new blood, money, and ideas to migrate to the island. The possibilities of progress to be made on the island could be monitored by the economic and cultural progress made by the descendants of the enslaved since manumission (Blake 1890: 539–42). Within the spirit of such views, Gardner demonstrated his relationship with his place of birth through his entrepreneurial endeavors in Jamaica, which conversely spurred on its economic and cultural development.

51 Aston W. Gardner was one of a number of Jamaican companies whose businesses were featured in Jas. Johnson's tourist-centered publication *Jamaica, The New Riviera*. These advertisements were placed at the back of the book with no page numbers.

52 Reverend Gardner founded the first building society on the island in 1864 for the benefit of the working class. By the end of the nineteenth century the lucrative business no longer concentrated on this group, but the upper classes.

53 The remainder of the guide provides suggestions for excursions in and around Kingston. It includes fourteen pages of Jamaican proverbs, in patois, the language of Jamaica's black working class community. The proverbs are a legacy from the work of Reverend William Gardner, who had collected them during his life.

2 "We Also Should Walk in the Newness of Life"

1 Holy Bible, Romans 6:4, King James Version.

2 There are a number of differing titles given to this photograph which highlight various aspects of the portrait, for example: "Harlem, New York, 1932" (Lurie 1992: 125); "A couple wearing raccoon coats with a Cadillac, taken on West 127th Street, 1932" (Willis-Braithwaite 1993: 12); "Couple wearing raccoon coats with a Cadillac, taken on West 127th Street, Harlem, New York, 1932" (Powell 1997: 53); "Couple, Harlem, 1932" (Skipworth 1997: 131); "Couple with a Cadillac, 1932" (Patton 1998: 115); "Couple in raccoon coats, 1932" (Mercer 2003: 76). These captions are the inspiration for the different section headings of this chapter.

3 See Laurie 1992: 125; Patton 1998: 115; Willis 2000: 38, 43; Hall and Sealey 2001: 6; Finley 2004: 45–51. More recently the portrait was the inspiration for the photograph "Couple in raccoon coats, 2002" which featured in the *Vibe* magazine fashion spread "Harlem Renaissance: Vintage Uptown Cool." This contemporary version was taken by African-American photographer Barron Claiborne, and was styled by Emil Wilbekin. In this version a black woman and man, wearing mink and sable furs, pose alongside a 2003 Mercedes SL500 Coupe. Cheryl Finley's study of this restaging of VanDerZee's photograph suggests that the profound message of the former: "urged a second renaissance of black ownership and pride in the community" (Finley 2004: 45).

4 Throughout this chapter I will alternate between the terms black American and African-Americn in reference to VanDerZee's couple and Malvin Gray Johnson. I use the term black here in the context of Paul Goodwin's thinking of black and blackness as a creative tool, an interface and navigational strategy (Goodwin 2013). Systems that the subjects under study used. The use of African-American applies clearly to Gray Johnson as he was born in America. There is no evidence that VanDerZee's couple were born in America. They are just as likely to be part of the thousands of black people that emmigrated to America from the Caribbean—5,000 during the 1890s and by 1930 54,754 black Caribbeans lived in New York "39,833 of whom resided in Manhattan" (Osofsky 1966: 131). But to also call them African-American is to recognize the African diasporic reality of being a descendent of Africa based in America. The only biographical information that is known to date of this couple is that they were "hoofers," dancers (Mussenden VanDerZee 2005).

5 For the remainder of the chapter I will use the nomenclature Gray Johnson rather than Johnson as other writers have done. Malvin Gray Johnson signed a number of his works "Gray Johnson." For example, in 1934 this included: *Southern Landscape, Postman, Snow Scene, The Old Mill, The Bakers, Fallen Trees*. More personally the artist sent: "Greetings for the Yuletide and coming year Mr & Mrs M Gray Johnson" on an undated Christmas card he painted (Rodgers 2002: 196).

6 The exhibition "Rhapsodies in Black: Art of the Harlem Renaissance" was "devised and selected" by Richard J. Powell and David A. Bailey, and organized by Roger Malbert. The London exhibition was part of an international tour which included the Arnolfini in Bristol, Mead Gallery, University of Warwick, M.H. de Young Memorial Museum, San Francisco, and the Corcoran Gallery of Art, Washington DC.

7 The styled bodies of black people represented in the exhibition "Rhapsodies in Black: Art of the Harlem Renaissance," were not discussed in detail in the show or its catalogue of the same name. The author was invited by the events organizer of the exhibition to produce a workshop on dress and the Harlem Renaissance.

8 See Mordeca 1860: 350; Wintz 1996: 31; Gates 1988: 142.

9 In 1896, Henri Toulouse Lautrec produced the lithograph *L'Automobiliste*, which featured his cousin Dr Gabriel Tapie de Celeyran driving a topless car wearing a bulky fur coat. Arkansas Art Center, Little Rock, Arkansas, http://www.aacwebkiosk.com/Obj1751$%7BClientIP%7D. The fur trend included wool, bear and sheep skins.

10 I would like to thank Geraldine Biddle-Perry for bringing Deirdre Clemente to my attention.

11 The quality of raccoon skins is marked by the silver, iron grey to dark brown tones with a dark stripe, and the darker of these combinations, the better the pelt. See Chambers 1951: 454 and Callan 1998: 196.

12 The importance of a stylish wardrobe amongst black collegiates was integral to the holistic experience of attending university. For example, in 1925 a black female student of Howard University believed that one could manage on $30 for textbooks and the remainder of one's allowance on one's college wardrobe as "no girl will think of coming to Howard without a wardrobe costing $455 at a minimum" (Wolters 1975: 72).

13 This type of raccoon pelt was particularly suitable for coats as the short-haired feature covers all the sections of the animal, without any "wooliness" (Bachrach 1931: 306–8).

14 In 1928 the journal *Album of Fur Novelties* changed its name to *American Fur Style*. The publication described itself as presenting "the vanguard of fur fashions, describing them clearly and concisely" (*Fur Style* February 1928: 7).

15 These descriptions fall in line with the general style predictions of fur coat designs for the season: "The most pronounced feature of the fur fashions developed for fall and winter 1928–29, is the increased style element displayed in the new coats. This importance is stressed in all varieties of furs, whether for formal, daytime or sportswear, and it is believed that this more-than-usual emphasis placed upon styling will be the keynote for a more successful season" (*Fur Style* October 1928: 10).

16 A krimmer is the pelt of the Circassian lamb. This is generally of a silvery white wool with a bluish cast. The name krimmer is given to reflect the Crimea peninsula where the best examples were believed to be found (Bachrach 1931: 485).

17 See *Apex News*, June 1929: 16.

18 The Mason-Dixon Line, as it is also known, is most notable for being the line that separated the slave states of the South and the supposedly free states in the North. It is named after the English astronomer Charles Mason, and his fellow countryman the surveyor Jeremiah Dixon. They created the line between 1763 and 1767 to settle a dispute of where "the boundary between southern Pennsylvania and northern Maryland" should be.

19 Elise Johnson McDougald was a New Yorker of a white mother and African-American father. As a teacher, social investigator and writer, and supervisor of the Women's Trade Union League, McDougald contributed to African-American culture and social issues (Locke 1997: 419).

20 Emily West's book *Chains of Love* charts the struggle for autonomy amongst slave couples, who "would go to great lengths in their desire to love, support, and protect their spouses, their families and their communities" (2004: 13).

21 I am indebted to Yann Saunders at the Museum and Research Center of the Cadillac-Lasalle Club, Inc., and The (new) Cadillac Database (http://www.car-nection.com/yann/Dbas_txt/V16_ndx.htm) for this information. Saunders, as compiler of the database, has included James VanDerZee's photograph *Couple* as it is a fine example of the V-16. The is known as a V-16 due to the cubic displacement of its sixteen-cylinder motor which was developed by the engineer Owen Nacker, and was introduced to the public in late 1929. Production of this make of automobile ceased in 1940. See http://www.car-nection.com/yann/Dbas_txt/V16_ndx.htm.

22 Additional details of this are to be found in Rose 1987: 104.

23 The director of the film is Evelyn S. Brown and the director of photography is Jules V.D. Bucher, and he is credited with working on the Harmon Foundation production in 1935. (Horak 1995: 364). See also. http://www.tubmaninstitute.ca/the_harmon_ foundation_film.

24 The "Negro Literature, History and Prints" division of the New York Public Library is now known as the Schomburg Center for Research in Black Culture. The Puerto Rican-born Arturo Alfonso Schomburg, also known as Arthur Schomburg, is credited with founding the New York Public Library division of Negro Literature, History and Prints in 1925 as "a special collection of the 135th Street Branch Library to meet the needs of a changing community." In 1926 Schomburg's personal collection of some "5,000 books, 2,000 manuscripts, 2,000 etchings and paintings; and several thousand pamphlets" was added to the division. Schomburg was curator of the library from 1932 until his death in 1938. The institution was renamed the Schomburg Collection of Negro Literature, History and Prints in 1940: http://www.nypl.org/about/locations/ schomburg (first accessed May 9, 2015).

25 See Rodgers 2002: 190.

26 Shearer West has discussed how a self-portrait is the creation of a "double" of the artist, "objectifying their own body" whilst for the viewer "looking at a metaphorical mirror that reflects . . . the artist who produced the portrait" (West 2004: 165).

27 The journal *Men's Wear* did not feature the turtle-neck sweater in 1934.

28 Clement l'On was the captain of an early ship that travelled between the United States and Liberia (Wragg Chase 1971: 63). The child's suit was held in the collection of the Old Slave Mart Museum based in Charleston. It was run by Judith Wragg Chase and her sister Louise Alison Graves from 1964 until 1987 when the museum closed. I would like to thank Jenni Arboine for bringing this item to my attention.

29 Gray Johnson's interest in art began around 1905, by the age of eleven he was contributing work to art exhibitions at the Central Carolina Fair in Greensboro, and won first place in exhibitions at the same fair from 1908 to 1911. See Rodgers 2002: 176.

30 The National Academy of Design enrolled black students as early as 1869. Gray Johnson funded his studies at the Academy through various jobs such as janitor, shipping and stock clerk. In 1925 Gray Johnson secured enough funding to attend day classes (Rodgers 2002: 18–20).

31 During this period of research of five weeks I kept a journal. I did not consciously make journal entries everyday, I only wrote things that moved me.

3 "All of Me"

1 I first came across this quote in *The Black Atlantic: Modernity and Double Consciousness* by Paul Gilroy, where he referred to the quote as being particularly indicative of the relevance between music and "distinct conceptions of time that have a special political and philosophical significance" (1993: 203). The quotation used here has *beat* in italics as Baldwin intended, rather than "beat" as used by Randall Kenan, editor of James Baldwin's *The Cross of Redemption: Uncollected Writings.* James Campbell clarifies the importance of the original use of *beat* in italics by Baldwin, as the article was first commissioned by Campbell, see http://www.nytimes.com/2010/09/12/books/review/Campbell-t.html?_r=0&pagewanted=print (first accessed August 6, 2013), and Campbell 1991: 260.

2   See "Without Sanctuary: Lynching Photography in America" in *Autograph ABP Newspaper*, 2011; and the exhibition "Without Sanctuary: Lynching Photography in America," May 27–July 20, 2011, Rivington Place, London.

3   See also http://www.bbc.co.uk/radio2/soldonsong/songlibrary/indepth/strangefruit.shtml (accessed August 5, 2013).

4   Alphonso D. McClendon's study of Billie Holiday's style focuses on "key periods of fashion in Holiday's time" and her style as "a significant record of evolutionary fashion images and silhouettes that continue to resonate" (2015: 115).

5   Billie Holiday used the term "hip kitty" to describe herself when she found her mother had rented a room for her in a brothel. Billie Holiday believed she had arrived at the place that would give her the source to the good things in life. All around her in the house of her madam, Florence Williams, she saw the token of a good life, a "fancy telephone. I had seen those funny-looking telephones in the movies—the ones you answer lying in bed instead of the old-time wall jobs. From the moment I saw them I knew that was for me. Not just any kind, though. It had to be a white telephone. And that's what I had at Florence's place" (Holiday 1993: 23). To be hip is to be "sophisticated, independent, and wise; in fashion, alert, and courageous; a hipcat is wise, intelligent, informed." *Juba to Jive: A Dictionary of African-American Slang.*

6   See Moers 1960; Evans and Thornton 1989; Rolley 1992; Feldman 1993; Tester 1994; White and White 1998; Fillin-Yeh 2001; Cicolini 2004; O'Connor 2005; Gill 2007; Miller 2009: 151–3; Peng 2010. Jessica R. Feldman's study of the modernist literature which addresses the subject of the dandy, argues that it is a terrain equally trod by men and women, of which there is "no essential time, place, or figure of dandyism" (Feldman 1993: 270). She believes that in spite of the adoption of reactionary or revolutionary clothing, the dandy remains a rebellious figure, opposed to accepted beliefs, who has discovered the power of self-presentation to subvert existing social forms through leisure, not industry; solitary passivity rather than group cooperation, "'consumption' of form and style rather than goods and services . . ." (Feldman 1993: 271). Whilst Elizabeth Wilson has defined the classic nineteenth-century male dandies such as Oscar Wilde and Aubrey Beardsley, who were committed members of the Aesthetic Movement, to dress in a manner that expressed their conflict with and distaste for a society that shied away from cultural "truths," as "'rebel[s], déclassé, disgusted, disenchanted', who attempt to create a new aristocracy of genius, or at least of talent . . . a man of the past and the future" (Wilson 1985: 182–3).

7   See Feldman 1993: 270–1 and Wilson 1985: 182–3.

8   Some biographies have tried to present "possible alternatives" to the myth that is Billie Holiday. For example *in Lady Day: The Many Faces of Billie Holiday*, Robert O'Meally called this work a "biographical essay" that focused on Billie Holiday "as an artist" and how she crafted her musical talent (O'Meally 1991: 10) rather than the usual concentration on her addictions and complex love life. In *Wishing on the Moon: The Life and Times of Billie Holiday*, author Donald Clarke admits in the coda to the book that Billie Holiday "became and remained an icon without any hype" (Clarke 1994: 451). The icon Clarke references is from a religious perspective, as his reasoning for Billie Holiday becoming an icon "a real icon, an image of something

sacred . . . because she was granted Grace" (457). Julia Blackburn's concern for the destructive nature of the myths around Billie Holiday was the goal of her book *With Billie* (2001). Blackburn references Billie Holiday, who in 1959, explained her struggle with the many versions of her that were already out in the world: "Every time I do a show I'm up against everything that's ever been written about me. I have to fight the whole scene to get people to listen to their own ears and believe in me again" (Blackburn 2001: 11). Interestingly all these publications built their studies on research undertaken by Linda Kuehl in the early 1970s. She conducted some 150 interviews with people who knew Billie Holiday and collected contextual material. She had planned to write a book of her own on the jazz artist, but died in 1978. References to garments and accessories, make-up and hairstyles are made in these publications.

 9 Billie Holiday was noted for her nocturnal lifestyle, of being aware of the nightclubs to go to, regardless of where she was in the United States. This ran alongside her ability to be a good cook, and in 1949 she was even photographed dressed in an apron preparing a steak for her beloved dog.

10 Eleanora Harris was also known as Eleanora Fagan, the family name of her mother Sadie Harris. It was the name she used on May 3, 1929 when she was arrested for vagrancy and prostitution alongside her mother (Nicholson 1995: 34). Sadie Harris called herself this at the time of Billie Holiday's birth. Later in her life, Sadie changed her name to Fagan, linking herself with her paternal family. Billie Holiday was not especially close to the Fagans, with most affection going to her great grandmother who was born into slavery and was the mistress of her owner, Charles Fagan. In adulthood she rejected the Fagan family as they had rejected Billie Holiday and her mother.

11 For example Donald Clarke used a studio portrait of Billie Holiday with a double bloom gardenia corsage for the cover of *Wishing on the Moon: The Life and Times of Billie Holiday* (1995). It was taken in the 1940s by the New York society photographer Robin Carson. The session was organized by Greer Johnson, a life-long friend of Billie Holiday and promoter of her talent. According to Johnson, he wanted "someone who would be able to capture her serious qualities as an artist" (Blackburn 2005: 161). Johnson relates that, to get at who Billie Holiday is into the photographs, Johnson encouraged her to sing *Strange Fruit* (Blackburn 2005: 161–2); whilst another close up image of Billie Holiday's face, her eyes closed while singing, and wearing an ornate three blossom gardenia corsage has been used to illustrate Cable in the Class Room's online teaching pack *Masters of American Music: Billie Holiday* and the book *Strange Fruit: Billie Holiday, Café Society, and an Early Cry for Civil Rights* (Margolick 2000). Such use of Billie Holiday's face and headdress embalms this period of her life.

12 A hot comb is also known as a pressing comb: a metal comb that is heated on a stove, and then used to comb through the hair to straighten it. A very popular means of straightening black hair at this time.

13 A studio photograph of Billie Holiday as a child, aged about two shows her wearing, with a floral corsage in her hair compliments her formal dress.

14 Generally known for wearing gardenias, Holiday did use other types of flower corsages. For example on March 27, 1948 Billie Holiday's husband Jim Monroe gave her a giant orchid corsage before her performance at Carnegie Hall. The concert was the first following her release from imprisonment (Our World 1948: 36). She was also known to use artificial gardenia corsages (Greer 2005: 162).

15 This was illustrated in a photograph by Bobby Tucker featured in *Wishing on the Moon: The Life and Times of Billie Holiday* by Donald Clarke. No page reference.

16 See The Royal Horticultural Society https://www.rhs.org.uk/advice/profile?PID=367 (accessed May 27, 2015).

17 Abel Meerepol wrote *Strange Fruit* in response to contemporary photographs of lynchings he had seen. He also wrote the music which turned the work into a song. Meerepol, who later changed his name to Lewis Allan, was a Jewish communist school teacher.

18 David Margolick intimates that Billie Holiday did a practice performance of *Strange Fruit* in late 1938 at a party in Harlem (Margolick 2000: 45).

19 Stuart Nicholson places the opening night as Friday December 30. It was due to open earlier, but there was a delay in securing the liquor and cabaret licence. Billie Holiday performed on that Friday night (Nicholson 1995: 110–11).

20 Barney Josephson has said that Billie Holiday did not immediately connect with the song.

21 In 1998 and 1999 I played *Strange Fruit* to first-year fashion and textile students at Central Saint Martins College of Art. A deathly silence rang from the group at the end of the song, as if there was a united, yet unsolicited pause of respect for the dead and reflection on the content.

22 For example, during the 1930s Professor William Edward Du Bois, founder of the National Association for the Advancement of Colored People (NAACP), would unfurl a banner stating "Another Lynching Today" (Margolick 2000: 35).

23 Billie Holiday also recorded *Fine and Mellow*, for which she wrote the lyrics and music.

24 In Barney Josephson's autobiography, he provides a longer version of this art direction and performance, but nonetheless corroborates this earlier telling (Josephson and Trilling-Josephson 2011: 47–9). Josephson also states how important *Strange Fruit* was to the first nightclub he opened, and how it made Billie Holiday into a star. Josephson does not relate in detail the stage setting for Billie Holiday's performance of *Strange Fruit* as he did for Donald Clarke in *Wishing on the Moon*, but Josephson maintains that *Strange Fruit* was the last song she performed in her three-song set.

25 *Time* magazine featured Billie Holiday and the song *Strange Fruit* in the June 12, 1939 edition. This included a photograph of Billie Holiday. http://www.time.com/time/magazine/article/0,9171,762422,00.html (first accessed 15 August, 2013).

26 See also D. Labas 1999: 80–1.

27 Before beginning her engagement at Café Society in early January 1939, Billie Holiday had been on tour with Artie Shaw's white Swing Band. They toured the South and then onto New York, where she finally left the band. The stories abound of racial confrontation about where Billie Holiday could eat or sleep, whether she could perform on stage with other white men whilst in the South. Whilst in New York, she was asked to go to her room in the freight elevator as Maria Kramer, the owner of the Lincoln Hotel in which the band was staying, did not want the public to know she had a black women staying in the guest rooms.

28 See "Mississippi state flower" http://www.50states.com/flower/mississippi.htm#.VWW_KZjB--9 (accessed May 27, 2015) and "Louisiana State Flower" http://

www.50states.com/flower/louisiana.htm#.VWW8aJjB--8 (accessed May 27, 2015). I am grateful to Gen Doy for this train of thought.

29 I am grateful to Alistair O'Neill for raising this point of remembrance with regards to Billie Holiday's use of the gardenia corsage whilst performing *Strange Fruit.*

30 On February 16, 1946, for example, Billie Holiday made her debut solo concert appearance at the Town Hall, New York, which was a phenomenally successful event. The programme included a performance of *Lover Man* which had been a national hit in May 1945, and three other songs became new record releases (Town Hall Program 1946: 9–13).

31 Further on in *Lady Sings the Blues*, Billie Holiday splices two thoughts together where she wants to have control over her life and the way she performs her act by having her own nightclub. She was evidently tired of trying to attain perfection and of being watched. In effect, she wanted freedom within the patriarchal music world. "I'm not supposed to get a toothache, I'm not supposed to get nervous; I can't throw up or get sick to my stomach: I'm not supposed to get the flu or have a sore throat. I'm supposed to go out there and look pretty and sing good and smile and I'd just better. Why? Because I'm Billie Holiday and I've been in trouble" (Holiday 1992: 170). Billie Holiday felt she was being punished because of who she was and what she had achieved. She follows this quote directly with an incident on an aeroplane where a white man sitting next to her second husband, Louis McKay, and herself acts in a racial manner, "I didn't pay any attention. This has happened to me too many times" (Holiday 1992: 171).

32 Another photograph of Billie Holiday in a more casual atmosphere shows her arms covered in the same marks (Clarke 1995 unpaginated).

33 Andrew Preston's explanation of the general effect of heroin acts as a plastic life-giving force and protector: "rushing through their body bringing a very powerful, pleasant, relaxing effect, with a sensation of deep inner warmth, complete emotional insulation and safety from all of life's problems" (Preston 2000).

34 See Dollimore 1991: 3–18. I am indebted to Caroline Evans for bringing this work to my attention. See also Richard J. Powell "Sartor Africanus" in *Dandies: Fashion and Finesse in Art and Culture* (2001).

35 In 1948, Herman Leonard began working with Norman Granz who founded, amongst others, the Verve record label, a relationship that continued until 1965 (Houston and Bagert 2006: 235). Leonard had photographed leading jazz artists since the late 1940s following the opening of his studio in New York in 1948. He was respected by the industry for his empathic portrayal of jazz musicians, gaining "in depth knowledge of the nuances of their music. He knew their personal quirks, their likes and dislikes, their good and bad habits, as well as their dreams" (Houston and Bagert 2006: 18). His reputation within the history of jazz has garnered him the position as the "objective witness of jazz" (Leonard 1989: 13).

36 Herman Leonard has dated this session as 1955. The album *Lady Sings the Blues* was recorded between 1954 and 1956, see Holiday 1992: 200, Cook and Morton 1994: 534.

37 I am incredibly grateful to Syd Shelton for the photographic technical advice (and demonstrations) of shallow depth of field using a wide aperture on a camera.

38 Photograph by Leigh Wiener taken while Billie Holiday was in Berlin in 1954, part of Leonard Feather's "Jazz Club USA" European tour.

39 It could be argued that when black women unite false hair with their biological hair they authenticated what Kobena Mercer calls the "socialization of hair": "making it the medium of significant statements about self and society and the codes of value that bind them, or do not. In this way hair is merely a raw material, constantly processed by cultural practices which thus invest it with meaning and value" (Mercer 1999: 112).

40 The Onyx Club was one of the nightclubs that defined the notorious 52nd Street in Harlem.

41 The cover image of *Lady in Satin* is used as in the 125-year timeline of the history of Columbia Records. http://www.columbiarecords.com/timeline/#!date=1899-06-17_09: 12:20 (first accessed September 5, 2013).

42 In November 1950, *Life* magazine carried the fashion article on "ready made lines" of false hair for pony-tails and chignons.

43 Production of the poodle hairstyle required the use of some 125 curlers, as well as fortnightly visits to the salon and additional visits every eight weeks for women with straight hair who would require a permanent.

44 Sylvette David has changed her name to Lydia Corbett. Due to the context of the period in which Corbett wore her pony-tail and reproduced by Pablo Picasso, I will use her birth name of Sylvette David in the main text.

45 Lydia Corbett (Sylvette David) in a telephone conversation with Carol Tulloch August 21, 2013.

46 Photographic credits for photographs of Billie Holiday wearing her dark twinset at this time, connected with the *Lady in Satin* recording session, are Don Hunstein's photograph dated December 1957, http://www.peterfetterman.com/artists/don-hunstein/. Hunstein was the chief staff photographer for Columbia Records.

47 See http://www.youtube.com/watch?v=SThGnrorGW8

48 The group of all-male musicians gathered for *The Sound of Jazz* live television performance included: Danny Baker, Doc Cheatham, Vic Dickenson, Roy Eldridge, Colman Hawkins, Milt Hinton, Osie Johnson, Gerry Mulligan, Mal Waldron, Ben Webster, Lester Young.

49 Billie Holiday first recorded *Fine and Mellow* in 1939 at the same time as *Strange Fruit*.

50 Seers Roebuck Catalog Fall/Winter 1946–1947.

51 See also Nicholson 1995: 216, 217–26.

52 As existentialist Juliette Gréco expressed in 1957 "Whatever you do you become" (*The Guardian*, 1957: 6).

53 On her death bed, in a letter to Milt Shaw of Shaw Artists Inc., Billie Holiday signed it "Eleanora Fagan McKay (Billie Holiday)" (Nicholson 1995: 226).

54 Recorded interview with Billie Holiday, undated http://www.youtube.com/watch?v=88 x5vdh8nQY&list=RD02SThGnrorGW8 (first accessed August 28, 2013).

55 Billie Holiday's dress practice was also in step with the modernist advances that were being made in her chosen musical form of expression, jazz. Jazz was the music of modern America (Wollen 1993: 109, Brooker 1996: 184–200; Rogers [1925] 1997: 216–24) that was to assist black and white American artists from various fields to define themselves and their work as an alternative voice to that heard from Europe in the case of white Americans (Wollen 1993: 109) and white America for black American artists. For the latter, from the Harlem Renaissance Movement onwards, jazz was integral to the cultural advancements of African-Americans. It assisted in their communication of all aspects of African-American life, their "authenticity" as modern African-Americans, their significance as African-Americans in their own right as well as cultural contributors to America.

4 "My Man, Let Me Pull Your Coat to Something"

1 (Malcolm X 1966: 275). Malcolm X used this street phrase as a metaphor to go "fishing" for new converts as part of his recruitment drive for the Muslim organization the Nation of Islam.

2 *The Autobiography of Malcolm X* was originally published in the United States of America in 1965.

3 Malcolm X had various names throughout his life, only one of which he chose himself, El-Hajj Malik El-Shabazz. They all equated with different stages of his life. The other names were: his family name Malcolm Little, Red (1966: 118), Harlem Red (1966: 155), Detroit Red (1966: 171). El-Hajj Malik El-Shabazz will be used only to signify a specific historical moment. "Malcolm X" is used primarily throughout the chapter to acknowledge the fundamental juncture of transformation from his past life as "Street Hustler" to Muslim and political activist.

4 I am grateful to Paul Antick for bringing this work to my attention.

5 In the foreword to the *Autobiography of Malcolm X*, Alex Haley recounts how at the beginning of their relationship, Malcolm X only trusted him 20 percent. Towards the end of his life it had increased to 70 percent (1966: 16, 25).

6 The weekly interview sessions between Malcolm X and Haley processed what Freud called a "screen-memory, a waking dream of the past" in order for it to be realized as a memory. The trusting relationship that developed between Malcolm X and Haley helped Malcolm X to retrace his past, with prompting from Haley to encourage associations—free or structured—to make sense and build a narrative of the life of Malcolm X. This is all very speculative on my part, but Malcolm X's blending of current events with the past encourages such assumptions.

7 Discussion held with Gamilah Shabazz at her home in Harlem, New York, September 1999.

8 Eduardo Pagán has listed the various names the zoot suit was known as in the USA. It was known as "root suit," "suit suit," and "zoot suit" in the Northeast, "killer diller," "drape shape" in the West, "el tacuche" (the wardrobe) in Spanish. (Pagán 2005: 466: "Zoot Suit" in *Encyclopedia of Clothing and Fashion*).

9 For example, as outlined in Chapter 3, Malcolm X was a fan of Billie Holiday, as well as enjoying listening and dancing to other popular jazz artists of his youth.

10 Malcolm X explains in his autobiography that he was referencing the damage that can be caused by hate, if "spread unchecked" as it was in America at this time.

11 This was more marked in Malcolm X wearing the opulent accessory of an astrakhan hat (Parks 1990: 233).

12 Malcolm X was referring to how he should present himself as a member of the audience at the Cassius Clay (Mohammed Ali) and Sonny Liston boxing heavy weight championship of the world in Miami in1964.

13 Malcolm X was inspired to establish a newspaper for then Nation of Islam having observed how one was produced, through what he called his ability for "Quick 'picking up'" (Malcolm X 1968: 338) whilst working on the Los Angeles *Herald Dispatch*.

14 James Baldwin quoted in an article by Brian Glanville for his piece on Malcolm X for the *New Statesman* in 1964. http://www.newstatesman.com/world-affairs/2013/04/when-ns-met-malcolm-x

5 You should understand, it's a freedom thing

1 A Pull quote by Marlene Dumas taken from the feature article, "Queen of the Canvas," by Susie Rushton in which the journalist was in cenversation with the South African born artist that appeared in the February 2015 issue of British *Vogue*.

2 Woolworths of South Africa opened its first store in Cape Town in 1931. It is not linked to the British high street chain Woolworths, formerly known as F.W. Woolworths, which folded in 2008. Woolworths of South Africa has an identity more in keeping with Britain's Marks and Spencer stores. Indeed connection between the companies dates back to 1947 when Marks and Spencer took an interest in Woolworths that was equal to rather more than a 10 percent of its issued share capital (MacMillan 2005: 210).

3 The other designers that featured in South African Designers at Woolworths in July 2006 were the white South African designers Maya Prass and Stephen Quatember.

4 This was £17.53 at May 5, 2015.

5 Nkensani Nkosi in a telephone conversation with Carol Tulloch, May 5, 2015.

6 Ibid.

7 I use this version of Stephen Biko's name here, as this is how it appears on his headstone.

8 These organizations were: Association for Educational and Cultural Advancement, Black Community Programmes, Black Parents Association, Black People's Convention, Black Women's Federation, Border Youth Organization, Christian Institute of Southern Africa, Eastern Cape Youth Organization, Medupe Writers Association, Natal Youth Organization, National Youth Organization, South African Student Movement, South African Students' Organization, Soweto Students Representative Council, Transvaal Youth Organization, Union of Black Journalists, Western Cape Youth Organization, Zimele Trust Fund. (*Anti Apartheid News* November 1977: 1).

9 There does not seem to be a consensus on the number of mourners. David Widgery reported 15,000. *Anti Apartheid News* reported that it was over 18,000 (November 1977: 6–7), whilst *Drum* magazine reported that there were 20,000 mourners (*Drum* 1977: 26).

10 In the 1970s I would see heavy metal kids in Doncaster walking round in their long coats, with their long hair, carrying an album under their arm. You always knew which band they were into because the cover image was clearly visible for all to see. In the

1990s CDs era the T-shirt with details of musicians on them replaced that practice of visible affiliation, as the former is too small. Therefore music fans were wearing the band (Tulloch 1994).

11 Katherine Hamnett in interview with Nigel Fountain on the Radio 4 program *Your Name Here: The T-Shirt,* 1994.

12 In the 1990s I saw a man wear a black T-shirt with the following in white text on the front, "You wouldn't Understand," as I passed him and looked at the back of the T-shirt it read "It's a Black thang."

13 See Memela 2004; Nuttall 2004: 436–7; Rogerson 2006: 45–7; Kirkham Simboa 2007: 66–7; Vincent 2007; Oberhofer 2012: 70–3.

14 See http://ccs.ukzn.ac.za/files/Console.pdf (first accessed January 27, 2015). Console Tleane states that the paper "Shifting Sands: Steve Biko's Legacy, Efforts to Commercialise Him and the Foundation" is a work-in-progress, but should be seen "as a reflection of my approach to the project and as a further reflection of the direction adopted in the debate that prompted me to write it."

15 "Forward to Freedom: The History of the British Anti-Apartheid Movement 1959–1994," http://www.aamarchives.org/history/apartheid.html (first accessed January 25, 2015).

16 "'Born-Free' South Africans are those who were born after 1994 when the first fully democratic elections were held in South Africa, and have grown up without apartheid and the struggles of South Africa's older generation" http://www.bbc.co.uk/news/world-africa-27146976

17 In my use of the term "centered breath," I am drawing on advice about the importance of breath in vocal and holistic practice, of what centered breath can alleviate and achieve. "A centred breath will give rise to a supported, resonant, confident sounding voice, making us feel more confident ... Centring the breath gives us the opportunity to function more effectively ... to control nerves, anxiety and self-doubt and to replace them with a more positive frame of mind which enables us to function from the most capable side of ourselves. Breath is not just the life force, it is also quintessential in shaping the very way we live our lives" (Weir Ouston 2009: 96).

18 http://www.wattstax.com/backstory/production.html, 1972 Production Notes (accessed October 1, 2011). The music festival was a showcase of African-American culture.

19 The alias wm1, wm2 etc will be used to replace the real names of some workshop members.

20 Workshop member 1 outlined this during the music session on October 8, 2011, Center for Historical Reenactments, Johannesburg.

21 Workshop members 9 and 2 explained during the music session of the workshop "Freedom is a Road Seldom Travelled by the Multitude" that Spaza is a South African form of hip hop. Due to South Africa's vast range of vernaculars, different provinces came up with their own versions of hip hop to suit their languages. The isiXhosa version was named "Spaza." Spaza/hip hop references "moments of resistance." One of the founding members of the Spaza Movement, Driemanskap of Cape Town, who blend isiXhosa, with English and Cape Flats slang, understands that hip hop, more than any other musical art form, is about addressing important issues and representing where you're from (http://pioneerunit. com/driemanskap/). "'Spaza' means 'hidden' in Zulu." The term gained cultural significance when Spaza shops emerged during the

Apartheid era to boycott white shops, and opposed the restrictions that were placed on black people to run their own businesses. Spaza outlets were, and still are, small shops found in the townships of South Africa. Some operate in homes, others as separate spaces (Bear et al. 2005: 9). Residents can buy commodities such as bread, milk, rice, paraffin, sugar, etc., without having to go to the retail stores in town (wm2 in email correspondence with Carol Tulloch, November 29, 2011).

22 Syd Shelton was asked by the conference organizers to photograph the event and to contribute a short presentation.

23 Workshop member 7 in conversation with Carol Tulloch, October 8, 2011, Center for Historical Reenactments, Johannesburg.

24 Nkensani Nkosi in telephone conversation with Carol Tulloch, May 5, 2015.

25 It is interesting that the profile of Steve Biko on South African History Online includes the *Drum* November 1977 Biko cover as one of the four images to represent him on its header http://www.sahistory.org.za/people/stephen-bantu-biko. First accessed January 26, 2015.

26 As I have raised previously with regard to the image of a Black Power fist Afro Comb and the word beautiful on a viridian green T-shirt (Tulloch 2008).

6 Here

1 See Tulloch 1992: 84–98; Tulloch 1998: 378–9; "Black British Style Exhibition" 2004–5.

2 I co-ordinated this event in 2001 with Baroness Lola Young as part of the project initiative of the Archive and Museum of Black Heritage (AMBH).

3 This quote is used as evidence of the racial violence in Britain at the time, when the brutal murder of black teenager Anthony Walker had been committed in Liverpool, and the Greater London Authority, under the auspices of Ken Livingstone, Mayor of London, published the report *Delivering Shared Heritage: The Mayor's Commission on African and Asian Heritage* (2005).

4 See Arts Council of England 1999; Boswell and Evans 1999.

5 See also Lea and Halliday 2014: 5. Martin Amis declared in the film *Martin Amis; England* how shocked he was to see his first black person when he was a child, a Rhodesian academic introduced to him by his father. His reaction was to cry at the sight of a black man, and said "you have a black face." He knew it was "an awful thing to do and say, but it was such a shock to my small system" (Amis 2014).

6 The book has no page numbers.

7 This quote was a response given by Cornel West in the "Questions and Answers Session" of the *Discussions in Contemporary Culture Conference*, New York 1991.

8 Michele Wallace devised the project *Black Popular Culture* for which Gina Dent edited the book of the same name. The project began with a three-day conference held in New York at the Studio Museum in Harlem and at Dia's space to discuss "the growing presence of politicized popular culture" (Wright 1992: vii).

9 Unfortunately Beryl Gilroy did not date the letter.

10 In the case of Molly Andrews, it was becoming a mother and, inevitably, getting older (Andrews 2008).

11 Novelist David Eagleman has written that "There are three deaths: the first is when the body ceases to function. The second is when the body is consigned to the grave. The third is that moment, sometime in the future, when your name is spoken for the last time" (Eagleman). The quote is taken from his book of fiction *Sum: Forty Tales From the Afterlives* (2009). I first came across Eagleman's quote in writing the memorial for my mother in June 2010.

12 I am grateful to Linda Sandino for bringing this book to my attention.

13 Quoted by Baena 2007: viii.

14 Quoted by Baena 2007: viii.

15 Beryl Gilroy outlined in her autobiographical book *Black Teacher* that she became fascinated by schools filled with multiculturalism. When Dr Beryl Gilroy returned to full-time teaching in 1965 she noted that there were some 20 nationalities registered including Americans, Germans, Russians, Africans, Greek, Caribbean, Irish, Indians, Israelis, Austrians, Danish. With such a scenario Beryl Gilroy insisted that "equality of expectations at school, or in the world outside, meant taking equal responsibility" (Gilroy 1976: 164). See also Braithwaite 1993 [1959] and Vaizey 1962: 13.

16 Liz Stanley, a leading auto/biographer has provided an extensive definition of the epistolarium. Its overarching meaning is a collection of an individual's "surviving" letters held in a public and/or private archive or library. Stanley has expanded on this to outline 4 ways of considering an epistolarium:

- the epistolary record of what remains and is available for present-day scrutiny, the "surviving letters" written by somebody;
- the entirety of the letter-writing that a particular person ever wrote, that is, as the totality of every letter, postcard and so on they ever penned and so encompassing those written but which now no longer exist, because destroyed, lost or otherwise missing;
- not only all of somebody's letters, but also including all the replies to these which were received to every single one of their letters from every single one of their correspondents; and
- encompassing the "ur-letters", the shadow-letter forms which are produced through transcribing and publishing printed versions of manuscript letters and which result from the posterior activities of later editing by a third party. (http://www.oliveschreinerletters.ed.ac.uk/Schreiner%27sLetters-ProjectOverview.html#4._The_Schreiner_Epistolarium (first accessed January 10, 2015).

Stanley has considered the epistolarium further as gift giving (2011).

17 At the beginning of the twenty-first century some academics within the social sciences were wary of the value in the study of letters. See Plummer 2001: 54–5, quoted in Stanley 2004: 202. For clarification of the increased use of epistolarity in the social sciences see 3. Letters in social science perspective in http://www.oliveschreinerletters.ed.ac.uk/Schreiner%27sLetters-ProjectOverview.html#4._The_Schreiner_Epistolarium (first accessed January 10, 2015).

18 Kylie Cardell and Jane Haggis are the editors of "To the Letter" a special issue of the journal *Life Writing* (2011).

19 Mrs Gloria Bennett and her husband Herman "CB" Bennett were life-long friends of my parents. They shared a house together on Saint Mary's Road, Doncaster. They were part of the Doncaster Caribbean community who socialized regularly and shared the care of each other's children. I was one of them. My mother commissioned Gloria Bennett to make clothes for her daughters and to press, that is straighten, their hair. "Aunt G", also made gifts for us. I remember a pale green crocheted sleeveless top that I wore with jeans in the 1960s. I was chief bridesmaid at their only daughter, Denise's, wedding. The two families remain very close.

20 See Tamboukou 2010: 26 who discusses the opposite with regards to the paintings and letters produced by Gwen John.

Coda

1 I have discussed the *need* to make previously in the exhibition *Handmade Tales: Women and Domestic Crafts* (2010–11), and my own *need* to make through my textile art practice, see: http://www.caroltulloch.co.uk/.

BIBLIOGRAPHY

A Study of Negro Artists (1936) [film], New York: Harmon Foundation.

Adams, R. (1994), *Why People Photograph*, New York: Aperture.

Adams, R. (1996), *Beauty in Photography*, New York: Aperture.

Adorno, T. (1986), "What Does Coming to Terms with the Past Mean?" in G.H. Hartman (ed.), *Bitburg in Moral and Political Perspective*, Bloomington: Indiana University Press.

Adorno, T. (1999), *Aesthetic Theory*, London: The Athlone Press.

Alexander, C.W. (1929), "Fur Fashion Developments," *American Furrier and Fur Style*, October: 1, 6.

Alford, H. (2004), "The Zoot Suit: Its History and Influence," *Fashion Theory: The Journal of Dress, Body & Culture*, 8(2): 225–36.

Allen, J. & M. Sealy (2011), "Without Sanctuary: Lynching Photography in America," *Autograph ABP Newspaper*.

Alloula, M. (1986), *The Colonial Harem*, Minneapolis: University of Minnesota Press.

Altman, J.A. (1982), *Epistolarity: Approaches to a Form*, Ohio: Ohio State University Press.

Alvarez, L. (2008), *The Power of the Zoot: Youth Culture and Resistance During World War II*, Berkley, Los Angeles, London: University of California Press.

"American Cool" (2014) [exhibition], National Portrait Gallery, Smithsonian Institution, February 7–September 7.

American Furrier and Fur Style, "Sports Fur Coats Specially Designed" (1929), October, 6.

American Furrier and Fur Style, "IPA News—Schedule of Fur Congress" (1930), May, 20.

American Journal of Nursing, "Letter to the Editor" (1913), January 13(4): 302–3.

Anderson, B. (1991), *Imagined Communities Reflections on the Origin and Spread of Nationalism*, London, New York: Verso.

Anderson, L. (2011), *Autobiography,* London, New York: Routledge.

Andrews, M. (2008), "Never the Last Word: Revisiting Data," in M. Andrews, C. Squire, M. Tamboukou (eds), *Doing Narrative Research*, London, California, New Delhi, Singapore: Sage Publications Ltd.

Angelou, M. (1986), *And Still I Rise,* Virago: London.

Anti Apartheid News, November 1977.

Apex News, 1929, April 1 (5): 3.

Apex News, 1929, June 1 (7): 13.

Apex News, 1929, July 1 (8): 6.

Appadurai, A. (1986), *The Social Life of Things: Commodities in Cultural Perspective*, Cambridge, London, New York, New Rochelle, Melbourne, Sydney: Cambridge University Press.

Archer, P. (2010), "Accessories/Accessaries: Or, What's in Your Closet?," *Small Axe*, 14(2): 97–110, June.

Archer-Straw, P. (2000), *Negrophilia: Avant-Garde Paris and Black Culture in the 1920s*, London: Thames & Hudson.

Arnold, E. (1996), *In Retrospect*, London: Sinclair-Stevens.

Arnold, R. (2001), *Fashion, Desire and Anxiety: Image and Morality in the 20th Century*, London, New York: I.B. Tauris.

Arnold, R. (2002), "Looking American: Louise Dahl-Wolfe's Fashion Photographs of the 1930s and 1940s," *Fashion Theory: the Journal of Dress, Body and Culture*, 6 (10): 45–60.

Arts Council of England (2000), *Whose Heritage? The Impact of Cultural Diversity on Britain's Living Heritage*, London: Arts Council of England.

Ash, J. (1996), "Memory and Objects," in P. Kirkham (ed.), *The Gendered Object*, 219–24, Manchester, New York: Manchester University Press.

Ash, J. (2010), *Dress Behind Bars: Prison Clothing as Criminality*, London, New York: I.B. Tauris.

Ashley, R.M. (1989), *What's in a Name? Everything You Wanted to Know*, Baltimore: Genealogical Publishing Co. Inc.

Attfield, J. (2000), *Wild Things, The Material Culture of Everyday Life*, Oxford: Berg.

Bachrach, M. (1931), *Fur A Practical Treatise*, London, Melbourne, Toronto, New York: Sir Isaac Pitman & Sons Ltd.

Baena, R. (2007), *Transculturing Auto/Biography: Forms of Life Writing*, London, New York: Routledge.

Baert, R. (2001), "The Dress: Bodies and Boundaries," in J. Jeffries (ed.), *Reinventing Textiles: Gender and Identity 2*, Winchester: Telos Art Publishing: 11–22.

Bailey A. P. and E. J. Slade (1986), *Harlem Today: A Cultural and Visitor's Guide*, New York; Gumbs and Thomas Publishers.

Bailey, D.A. (1997), "Introduction," in J. Skipworth (ed.), *Rhapsodies in Black: Art of the Harlem Renaissance,* London: Hayward Gallery, 11–12.

Bailey, D.A., I. Baucom and S. Boyce (eds), (2005), *Shades of Black: Assembling Black Arts in 1980s Britain*, Durham and London: Duke University Press.

Bailey, P. (1990), "Parasexuality and Glamour: The Victorian Barmaid as Cultural Prototype," *Gender and History*, 2(2): 148–72.

Baker, H.A. (1988), *Afro-American Poetics: Revisions of Harlem and the Black Aesthetic*, Madison, Wisconsin: University of Wisconsin Press.

Bakerman, J. (1978), "The Seams Can't Show: An Interview with Toni Morrison," *Black American Literature Forum*, 12(2): 56–60.

Bakhtin, M. (1968), *Rabelais and His World*, Massachusetts: The Massachusetts Institute of Technology.

Baldwin, J. ([1979] 2011), "Of the Sorrow Songs: The Cross of Redemption," in R. Kenan (ed.), *James Baldwin: The Cross of Redemption Uncollected Writings*, New York: Vintage Books, 145–53.

Balibar, É. (1998), "Violence, Ideality, and Cruelty," *New Formations*, London: Lawrence & Wishart, 35: 7–18.

Banham, R. (1999), "The Great Gizmo," in M. Banham, P. Barker, S. Lyall, and C. Price, *A Critic Writes: Essays by Reyner Banham*, Berkeley, Los Angeles, London: University of California Press, 109–18.

Barnbaum, B. (2010), *The Art of Photography: An Approach to Personal Expression*, Santa Barbara: Rockynook Inc.

Barnes, A.C. ([1925]1997), "Negro Art in America," in *The New Negro: Voices of the Harlem Renaissance*, New York: Touchstone.

Barnor, J. (2012), interview with Carol Tulloch, Brentford, May 2.

Barranger, N. (2005), "Casket Case," *The Independent Magazine*, May 7: 30–3.

Barringer, T. (2007), "Picturesque Prospects and the Labor of the Enslaved," in T. Barringer, G. Forrester, B. Martinez-Ruiz (eds), *Art and Emancipation in Jamaica: Isaac Mendes Belisario and His Worlds*, New Haven, London: Yale Center For British Art and Yale University Press, 41–63.

Barringer, T., G. Forrester and B. Martinez-Ruiz (eds), (2007), *Art and Emancipation in Jamaica: Isaac Mendes Belisario and His Worlds*, New Haven, London: Yale Center For British Art and Yale University Press.

Barthes, R. (1977), *Image, Music, Text*, London: Fontana Press.

Barthes, R. (1993), *Camera Lucida*, London: Vintage.

Barthes, R. (1993), *Mythologies*, London: Vintage.

Bauböck, R. and T. Faist (eds), (2010), *Diaspora and Transnationalism: Concepts, Theories and Methods*, Amsterdam: Amsterdam University Press.

Baxandall, M. (1991), "Exhibiting Intention: Some Preconditions of the Visual Display of Culturally Purposeful Objects," in I. Karp and S.D. Lavine (eds), *Exhibiting Cultures: The Poetics and Politics of Museum Display*, Washington, London: Smithsonian Institution Press, 33–41.

BBC News, "South Africa's 'born-free' Generation" (2014). Available online: http://www. bbc.co.uk/news/world-africa-27146976 (accessed January 25, 2015).

Becker, C. (1932), "Everyman His Own Historian," *The American Historical Review*, 37(2): 221–36.

Beckett, M. (1949), "The First Professor in Fashion," *Picture Post*, February 19, 23–6

Beckles, H. (1998), "Historicizing Slavery in West Indian Feminisms," *Feminist Review*, 59 (Summer), 34–56.

Beckwith, M.W. (1929), *Black Roadways: A Study of Jamaican Folk Life*, Chapel Hill: University of North Carolina Press.

Belisario, I.M. (1838), *Sketches of Character, In Illustration of the Habits, Occupation and Costume of the Negro Population in the Island of Jamaica*, Kingston: J.R. De Cordova.

Bell, Q. (1992), *On Human Finery*, London: Allison & Busby.

Bellows, C. (1907), *In Fair Jamaica*, Kingston: The Educational Supply Company.

Bender, S. (2015a), "A Brief History of the Gardenia," *Southern Living*. Available online: http://www.southernliving.com/home-garden/gardens/southern-gardening-gardenia-history (accessed May 27, 2015).

Bender, S. (2015b), "Magnolia: Essential Southern Plant," *Southern Living*. Available online: http://www.southernliving.com/home-garden/gardens/magnolia-trees (accessed May 27, 2015).

Benjamin, J. (1988), *The Bonds of Love, Psychoanalysis, Feminism, and the Problem of Domination*, New York: Pantheon Books.

Benjamin, W. ([1970] 1992), *Illuminations*, London: Fontana Press.

Benn, A. (1893), *Memoranda Book* (unpublished), January 1–May 3.

Benn, A (1897), *Memoranda Book* (unpublished).

Bennett, G. (1991), interview with C. Tulloch, Doncaster, July 18.

Berger, D. (2009), *Kant's Aesthetic Theory: The Beauty and Agreeable*, London, New York: Continuum.

Berger, M., B. Wallis and S. Watson (eds), (1995), *Constructing Masculinity*, London, New York: Routledge.

Berger, R and J. Mohn (1982), *Another Way of Telling*, London, New York: Writers and Readers Publishers Cooperative Society Ltd.

Bertram, A. (2010), "Jamaican Higglers' Marketing System and the Future of Kingston (Part I)," *The Gleaner*, October 31. Available online: http://jamaica-gleaner.com/gleaner/20101031/focus/focus6.html (accessed November 18 2014).

Besson, J. (1993), "Reputation and Respectability Reconsidered: A New Perspective on Afro-Caribbean Peasant Women," in J. H. Momsen (ed.), *Women and Change in the Caribbean: A Pan-Caribbean Perspective*, Kingston: Ian Randle, 15–37.

Bhabha, H. (1994), *The Location of Culture*, London, New York: Routledge.

Bhabha, H. (1999), "The Other Question: The Stereotype and Colonial Discourse," in J. Evans and S. Hall (eds), *Visual Culture: The Reader*, London, Thousands Oaks, New Delhi: Sage, 370–8.

Bickell, R. (1825), *The West Indies as they are: or, a real picture of slavery: but more particularly as it exists in the Island of Jamaica,* London: J. Hatchard & Son.

Bidouzo-Coudray, J. (2014), "Mary Sigande—Poking at Power Relations in Post-Apartheid South Africa," *The Guardian*, January 7. Available online: http://www.theguardian.com/world/2014/jan/07/mary-sibande-south-africa-art (accessed April 9, 2015).

Biko, S. ([1978] 1987), *I Write What I Like*, Oxford, Johannesburg: Heinemann.

Black, C.V. (1994), *The History of Jamaica*, Harlow: Longman.

"Black British Style (2004–2005)" [exhibition], Victoria and Albert Museum, London, October 7–January 16.

Blair, S. (2007), *Harlem Crossroads: Black Writers and the Photograph in the Twentieth Century*, Princeton, Woodstock: Princeton University Press.

Blake, H.A. (1890), "The Awakening of Jamaica," *The Nineteenth Century,* 22 (October): 534–44.

Blackburn, J. (2005), *With Billie*, London: Jonathan Cape.

Boa, S. (1993), "Free Black and Coloured Women: Jamaica 1760–1834," *Jamaican Historical Review* 18: 1–6.

Bobbioni, M. (1999), "The Face as a Locus of Speech," in D. Bartlett, (ed.), *Body in Transition*, Zagreb: University of Zagreb, 121–7.

Booker, C. (1992), *The Neophiliacs: The Revolution in English Life in the Fifties and Sixties*, Pimlico: London.

Boone, S.A. (1986), *Radiance from the Waters: Ideals of Feminine Beauty in Mende Art*, New Haven, London: Yale University Press.

Boston, J., and R. Cook (eds), (2009), *Breath in Action: The Art of Breath in Vocal and Holistic Practice*, London, Philadelphia: Jessica Kingsley.

Boxer, D. (2013), "The Photographers: The Duperly's and Their Contemporaries," in D. Boxer and E. Lucie-Smith (eds), *Jamaica in Black and White: Photography in Jamaica c. 1845–c. 1920, The David Boxer Collection*, Oxford: Macmillan, 10–21.

Boyer, G.B. (2012), "A Riff: Jazz Men Take on Ivy," in P. Mears (ed.), *Ivy Style: Radical Conformist,* New Haven: Yale University Press; 137–45.

Bradford, M.F. (1902), *Side Trips to Jamaica*, Boston, New York: Sherwood Publishing Company.

Bradley Foster, H. (1997), *"New Raiments of Self"*: *African American Clothing in the Antebellum South*, Oxford, New York: Berg.

Braithwaite, E.R., ([1959] 1993), *To Sir, With Love*, London: Hodder and Stoughton/Coronet Books.

Breward, C. (2004), *Fashioning London: Clothing and the Modern Metropolis*, Oxford, New York: Berg.

Brilliant, R. (1991), *Portraiture*, London: Reaktion Books.

Brindley, K. (2011), "Foreword," in *Transmitter/Receiver: The Persistence of Collage*, London: Hayward Gallery Publishing, 3–4

Brooker, P. (1996), *New York Fictions: Modernity, Postmodernism, the New Modern*, London, New York: Longman.

Brown-Glaude, W. (2011), *Higglers in Kingston: Women's Informal Work in Jamaica*, Nashville: Vanderbilt University Press.

Bryan, R. (1991), *The Jamaican People 1880–1902: Race, Class and Social Control*, London: MacMillan Education.

Buckley, R.C.V. and S. Gundle (2000a), "Flash Trash: Gianni Versace and the Theory and Practice of Glamour," in S. Bruzzi and P. Church-Gibson (eds), *Fashion Cultures: Theories, Explorations and Analysis*, London, New York: Routledge.

Buckley, R.C.V. and S. Gundle, S. (2000b), "Fashion and Glamour," in *The Fashion Business: Theory, Practice, Image,* N. White and I. Griffiths (eds), Oxford and New York: Berg, 37–54.

Buckridge, S.O. (2004), *The Language of Dress: Resistance and Accommodation in Jamaica 1760–1890*, Jamaica, Barbados, Trinidad and Tobago: University of the West Indies Press.

Bullen, F.T. (1905), "Kingston, Jamaica," *The Cornhill Magazine*, xviii, January–June, 188–207.

Burke, B. (2014), "Bus Conductor, Higgler in Assault Case," *The Jamaica Star*, November 21. Available online: http://jamaica-star.com/thestar/20141121/news/news18.html (accessed January 19, 2015).

Burke, P. (1997), "Representations of the Self From Petrarch to Descartes," in R. Porter (ed.), *Rewriting the Self: Histories from the Renaissance to the Present*, London, New York: Routledge, 17–28,

Burley, D. (1962), "No Room in White Society for 'Negroes'," *Muhammad Speaks* March: 5.

Burman, B. (2002), "'What a Deal of Work There is in a Dress!' Englishness and Home Dressmaking in the Life of the Sewing Machine," in C. Breward, B. Conekin and C. Cox (eds), *The Englishness of English Dress*, Oxford and New York, Berg, 79–96.

Burman, D. and S. Denbo (2007), *Pockets of History: The Secret Life of an Everyday Object*, Bath: Museum of Costume Bath.

Burness, T. (1970), *Cars of the Early 1930s*, Philadelphia, New York, London: Chilton Book Company.

Bush, B. (1990), *Slave Women in Caribbean Society, 1650–1838*, Kingston: Heinemann Publishers; Bloomington and Indianapolis: Indiana University Press; London: James Currey.

Bussell, G.B. (2005), "Gardenias: A Fragrance that Captivates," *Southern Living*, June. Available online: http://www.southernliving.com/home-garden/gardens/gardenias-fragrance-captivates (accessed May 27, 2015).

Butcher, T.B. (1902), *A Peep at Jamaica and Its People*, London: Charles H. Kelly.

Caffin, M.B. (1899), *A Jamaica Outing*, Boston: The Sherwood Publishing Company.

Callan, G.O. (1998), *Dictionary of Fashion and Fashion Designers*, London: Thames and Hudson.

Campbell, J. (1991), *Talking at the Gates: A Life of James Baldwin*, London, Boston: Faber & Faber.

Campbell, J. and J. Harbord (eds), (2002), *Temporalities, Autobiography and Everyday Life*, Manchester: Manchester University Press.

Campt, T.M. (2012), *Image Matters: Archive, Photography, and the African Diaspora in Europe*, Durham, London: Duke University.

Cardell, K. and J. Haggis (2011), "Contemporary Perspectives on Epistolarity," *Life Writing Journal*, 8(2): 129–33.

Carlyle, T. (1837), *Sartor Resartus*, Boston: James Monroe & Co.

Carpenter Smith, T. (1901), *Three Weeks in Jamaica or What Do I Know About the Tropics?* unpublished diary, Jamaica Archives.

Carr, E.H. (1964), *What is History?*, Middlesex, Victoria: Pelican.

Census of Jamaica and its Dependencies (1892), Kingston: Government Printing Office.

Chamberlain, M. (1995), "Gender and Memory: Oral History and Women's History," in V. Shepherd, B. Breereton and B. Bailey (eds), *Engendering History: Caribbean Women in Historical Perspective*, London: James Currey; Kingston: Ian Randle, 94–110.

Chambers, B.G. (1951), *Color and Design: Fashion in Men's and Women's Clothing and Home Furnishings*, New York: Prentice-Hall Inc.

Chambers, E. (2014), *Black Artists in British Art: A History Since the 1950s*, London, New York: I.B. Tauris.

Chang, D. (2006), "Conversations with Dion Chang," in A. Tischhauser (ed.), *10 x SA Fashion Week: Voices and Images from Ten Years of South African Fashion Week*, Johannesburg: Channel F Publishing, 7–12.

Channel 4 News (2015), "Nigel Farage on Paris Attack and failure of Multiculturalism," January 7. Available online: https://www.youtube.com/watch?v=-4yi8ZUwQB8 (accessed January 8, 2015).

Chase. E.W. and I. Chase (1954), *Always in Vogue*, London: Victor Gollancz Ltd.

Cheddie, J. (2006), "What is Black . . . Authenticity and Gender Performance?" at "Should Art . . . Be Authentic?" debate, Victoria and Albert Museum, November 3.

Chen, K. (1996), "The Formation of a Diasporic Intellectual: An Interview with Stuart Hall," in D. Morley and K. Chen (eds), *Stuart Hall: Critical Dialogues in Cultural Studies*, London, New York: Routledge, 486–503.

Chenoune, F. (1993), *A History of Men's Fashion*, Paris: Flammarion.

Chibnall, S. (1985), "Whistle and Zoot: The Changing Meaning of a Suit of Clothes," *History Workshop*, 20 (Autumn): 56–81.

Chilton, J. (1997), "Billie at Cafe Society," in L. Gourse (ed.), *The Billie Holiday Companion: Seven Decades of Commentary*, London, New York. Sydney: Omnibus Press, 21–9.

Choo, M. (2011), "Measuring Soul: On the Extrasensory Perception of Clothes," *Vestoj*, 2 (Winter): 92–7.

Clark, J. (2004), *Spectres: When Fashion Turns Back*, London: V&A Publications.

Clarke, D. (1995), *Wishing on the Moon: The Life and Times of Billie Holiday*, Harmondsworth, Penguin.

Clarke, E. (1966), *My Mother Who Fathered Me*, London: Allen & Unwin.

Clarke, G. (1997), *The Photograph*, Oxford, New York: Oxford University Press.

Clemente, D. (2008a), "Caps, Canes, and Coonskins: Princeton and the Evolution of Collegiate Clothing, 1900–1930," *The Journal of American Culture*, 31(1): 20–33.

Clemente, D. (2008b), "Showing Your Stripes: Student Culture and the Significance of Clothing at Princeton, 1910–1933," *Princeton University Library Chronicle*, 69(3): 437–64.

Clemente, D. (2014), *Dress Casual: How College Students Redefined American Style*, Chapel Hill: The University of North Carolina Press.

Collins, J. and A. Nisbet (2010), *Theatre and Performance Design: A Reader in Scenography*, London, New York: Routledge.

Conover, W. ([1957] 1997), "The Willis Conover Interview with Billie Holiday," in L. Gourse (ed.), *The Billie Holiday Companion*, 62–7, London, New York, Sydney: Omnibus Press.

Constantino, M. (1997), *Men's Fashion in the Twentieth Century: From Frock Coats to Intelligent Fibres*, London: B.T. Batsford Ltd.

Cooke, R. and B. Morton (1992), *The Penguin Guide to Jazz on CD, LP and Cassette*, Harmondsworth, Penguin.

Coquelin. C. (1894), *L'Art du Comedien*, Paris: Ollendorf.

Corbett, L. (2013), telephone conversation with Carol Tulloch, August 21.

Corbin, M. (1978), *The Couple*, Harmondsworth, Penguin.

Cosgrove, S. (1989), "The Zoot Suit and Style Warfare," in A. McRobbie (ed), *Zoot Suits and Second-hand Dresses: An Anthology of Fashion and Music*, London: MacMillan, 3–22.

Crowther, B. and M. Pinfold (1997), *Singing Jazz: The Singers and Their Styles*, London: Blandford.

Crill, R. (2015), "Local and Global: Patronage and Use" in R. Crill (ed.) *The Fabric of India*, 78–179, London: V&A Publications.

Curtis, B. and C. Pajaczkowska (1994), "'Getting There': Travel, Time and Narrative" in G. Robertson, M. Mash, L. Tickner, J. Bird, B. Curtis, and T. Putnam (eds), *Travellers' Tales: Narrative of Home and Displacement*, 199–215, London, New York: Routledge.

Daily Gleaner, The (1959), Kingston, Jamaica.

Dalzell, T. (2010), *Flappers 2 Rappers: American Youth Slang*, Mineola, New York: Dover Publications, Inc.

Davis, A.Y. (1998), *Blues Legacies and Black Feminism: Gertrude "MA" Rainey, Bessie Smith and Billie Holiday*, New York: Pantheon.

Davis, T. (1993), *Malcolm X: The Great Photographs*, New York: Stewart, Tabori & Chang.

de Boeck, F. and M.-F. Plissart (2004), *Kinshasa: Tales of the Invisible City*, Amsterdam: Ludion.

de la Haye, A. (2011), *Chanel*, London, New York: V&A Publishing.

de la Haye, A. (2013), *Coco Chanel: A New Portrait by Marion Pike, Paris 1967–1971*, London: London College of Fashion.

de Lisser, H.G. (1900), "The Negro as a Factor in the Future of the West Indies" in *The New Century Review*, January, 7 (37): 1–6.

Debord, G. (1983), *Society of the Spectacle*, Detroit: Black & Red.

Dennis, F. (1998), *Duppy Conqueror*, London: Flamingo.

Dent, G. (1992), "Black Pleasure, Black Joy: An Introduction," in G. Dent (ed.), *Black Popular Culture*, Seattle: Bay Press, 1–19.

Denzin, N.K. (1989), *Interpretive Biography*, London, California, New Delhi: Sage.

Derby Daily Telegraph (1940), "To-morrow Home Service," May 4: 10.

Derrida, J. ([1980] 1987), *The Post Card From Socrates to Freud and Beyond*, Chicago, London: University of Chicago Press.

Doane, R. (1998), "Blown Away," *The Guide: The Guardian*, May 9–15: 4–6.

Dollimore, J. (1991), *Sexual Dissidence: Augustine to Wilde, Freud to Foucault*, Oxford, New York: Oxford University Press.

Douglas, C. (2011), *Transmitter/Receiver: The Persistence of Collage*, London: Hayward Gallery Publishing.

Drum (1977), November.

Dunbar, M. (1954), "Curious Eating Habits," *The Sunday Times*, October 24: 9.

Durant-Gonzalez, V. (1983), "The Occupation of Higglering," *Jamaica Journal*, 16 (3): 2–12.

Dyer, G. (1996), *But Beautiful*, London: Abacus.

Dyer, G. (2007), *The Ongoing Moment*, London: Abacus.

Dyson, M.E., (1995), *Making Malcolm: The Myth and Meaning of Malcolm X*, New York, Oxford: Oxford University Press.

Eager, G. (1996), "Avant-garde," in M. Payne, (ed.), *A Dictionary of Cultural and Critical Theory*, Oxford, Massachusetts: Blackwell.

Eagleman, D. "Metamorphosis," *David Eagleman Website*. Available online: http://www.eagleman.com/sum/excerpt (accessed January 8, 2015).

Eastlake, Lady E. (1857), "Photography," *London Quarterly Review*, April, 202: 241–55. Available online: https://books.google.co.uk/books?id=yJ0pAAAAYAAJ&pg=PA241&dq'it+is ow ore+than+fifteen+years+ago+that+specimens+of+a ew+and mysterious +art'&hl=en&sa=X&ved=0CBQQ6AEwAGoVChMI2qHW14OzxwIV5pzbCh04DAh4 #v=onepage&q'it%20is%20now%20more%20than%20fifteen%20years%20ago%20 that%20specimens%20of%20a%20new%20and%20mysterious%20art'&f=false (accessed August 18, 2015).

Educational Supply Company, The (1901a), *The Bulletin of the Educational Supply Company*, 1 (14), Kingston.

Educational Supply Company, The (1901b), *The Bulletin of the Educational Supply Company*, 1 (22), Kingston.

Edwards, B. (1798), *The History, Civil and Commercial, of the British Colonies in the West Indies*, London: B. Crosby.

Edwards, E. (1999), "Photographs as Objects of Memory," in M. Kwint, C. Breward and J. Aynsley (eds), *Material Memories: Design and Evocation,* Oxford and New York: Berg, 221–36,

Edwards, E. (2001), *Raw Histories: Photographs, Anthropology and Museums*, Oxford, New York: Berg.

Edwards, E. (2004), "Little Theatres of Self Thinking About the Social," in T. Phillips (ed.), *We Are the People Postcards from the Collection of Tom Phillips*, London: National Portrait Gallery, 26–37.

Edwards, E. (2014), "Watching and Being: One Image in the Magnum Archive," in *Magnum Photos: One Archive, Three Views*, Bexhill-on-Sea: De La Warr Pavilion, [no page numbers].

Edwards, M.R. (1979), *Jamaican Higglers: Their Significance and Potential,* Swansea: Centre for Development Studies, University College of Swansea.

Edwards, T. (1946), "What Should I Do About My Hair?," *Our World,* 1(1): April: 32–3.

Eicher, J.B. (ed.) (1995), *Dress and Ethnicity*, Oxford, Washington DC: Berg.

Ellison, Ralph ([1952] 1965) *Invisible Man*, Harmondsworth, New York: Penguin.

Emberley, J.V. (1981), *Venus and Furs: The Cultural Politics of Fur*, London: I.B. Taurus.

Entwistle, J. (2000), *The Fashioned Body: Fashion, Dress and Modern Social Theory*, Cambridge, Malden: Polity Press.

Entwistle, J. (2001), "The Dressed Body," in J. Entwistle and E. Wilson (ed.), *Body Dressing*, Oxford, London: Berg, 33–58,

Ettinger, R. (1998), *Fifties Forever: Popular Fashions for Men, Women, Boys and Girls*, Atglen, Pa: Schiffer Publishing.

Evans, C. (2004), "A Monument to Ideas," in J. Clark (ed.), *Spectres: When Fashion Turns Back,* London: V&A Publications, 42–7.

Evans, C. and M. Thornton (1989), *Women and Fashion: A New Look*, London, New York: Quartet.

Evenson, S.L. (1994), *A History of Indian Madras Manufacture and Trade: Shifting Patterns of Exchange* (PhD Thesis), Minneapolis: University of Minnesota.

Ewing, E. (1981), *Fur in Dress*, London: B.T. Batsford Ltd.

Eyre, R. (2003), "Preface," in J.P. Sartre, *Being and Nothingness*, viii–x, London, New York: Routledge.

Fabian, J. (1983), *Time and the Other: How Anthropology Makes its Object*, New York: Columbia University Press.

Faist, T. (2010), "Diaspora and Transnationalism: What kind of dance partners?," in R. Bauböck and T. Faist (eds), *Diaspora and Transnationalism: Concepts, Theories and Methods*, Amsterdam: Amsterdam University Press, 9–34.

Fanon, F. (1965), *A Dying Colonialism*, Harmondsworth, Penguin.

Fanon, F. (1986), *Black Skin, White Masks*, London: Pluto Press.

Farebrother, R. (2009), *The Collage Aesthetic in the Harlem Renaissance*, Farnham: Ashgate.

Fawcett, H. (2002), "'Doon the Toon': Young Women, Fashion and Sexuality," in C. Buckley and H. Fawcett (eds), *Fashioning the Feminine: Representation and Women's Fashion from the Fin de Siecle to the Present*, London: I.B. Tauris, 122–49,

Fay, R. (1999), "Harlem Riots of 1935," in K.A. Appiah and H.L. Gates Jr. (eds), *Africana: The Encyclopedia of the African and African American Experience*, New York: Basic Civitas Books, 937.

Feather, L. (1997), "Lady Day," in L. Gourse (ed.), *The Billie Holiday Companion: Seven Decades of Commentary,* London, New York, Sydney: Omnibus Press, 57–62.

Feldman, J.R. (1993), *Gender on the Divide: The Dandy in Modernist Literature,* Ithaca, London: Cornell University Press.

Fillin-Yeh, S. (2001), *Dandies: Fashion and Finesse in Art and Culture*, New York, London: New York University Press.

Finley, C. (2004), "Harlem Sites of Memory," in T. Golden (ed.), *Harlemworld: Metropolis as Metaphor*, New York: The Studio Museum in Harlem, 45–51.

Flink, J.J. (1988), *The Automobile Age*, Cambridge, Massachusetts: MIT Press.

Fortunati, V., R. Monticelli and M. Ascari (eds), (2001), *Travel Writing and the Female Imaginary*, Bologna: Patron Editore.

Foster, M. (2002), "Using Call-and-Response to Facilitate Language Mastery and Literacy Acquisition Among African American Students," *Eric Digest*, July. Available online: http://www.cal.org/content/search?SearchText=call+and+response (accessed May 22, 2015).

Foucault, M. (1983), *This is Not a Pipe*, Berkeley, Los Angeles, London: University of California Press.

Fountain, N. (1994), "Your Name Here: The T-Shirt," *Magic Moments* [radio program], BBC Radio 4, November 25.

Fox News (2004), *Black South African Designers Shine at Fashion Week,* July 31. Available online: http://www.foxnews.com/story/2004/07/31/black-south-african-designers-shine-at-fashion-week/(accessed January 22, 2015).

Francis, J. (2002), "Trying To Do What Artists Of All Races Do: Malvin Gray Johnson's Modernism," in K.G. Rodgers (ed.), *Climbing up the Mountain: The Modern Art of Malvin Gray Johnson*, Durham: North Carolina University Art Museum, 52–80.

Freeman, C. (2002), "Mobility, Rootedness, and the Caribbean Higgler: Production, Consumption and Transnational Livelihoods," in N. Nyberg Sorensen and K. Fog Olwig (eds), *Work and Migration: Life and Livelihoods in a Globalizing World*, London, New York: Routledge, 61–81.

Fromm, E. ([1942] 2001), *The Fear of Freedom*, London: Routledge.

Frostick, M. ([1973] 1977), *The Jaguar Tradition*, London: Dalton Watson Ltd.

Froude, J. A. (1888), *The English in the West Indies*, London: Longmans, Green & Co.

Fryer, P. (1984), *Staying Power: The History of Black People in Britain*, London, Concord: Pluto Press.

Furlong, R. (2014), *Pinnies from Heaven: An Exploration and Celebration of the Apron from Adam and Eve to the Present Day*, Cardiff Bay: Makers Guild in Wales.

Fur Trade Review (1931), "College Crowd Buys Raccoon" December: 27–8.

Fur Trade Review (1931), "Conservative Styles Sell Best in Boston," December: 24–5.

Fur Trade Review (1932a), "Fashions in Furs: A Series of New Designs by the Greenstein Fur Modes, New York," June: 37.

Fur Trade Review (1932b), "Swagger Coats and Capes the Vogue," October: 15.

Fur Trade Review (1932c), "The Best Sellers," December: 7.

Fur Trade Review (1932d), "New England Goes in for Jackets and 'Swaggers'," December: 15.

Gaines, J. (1990), "Costume and Narrative: How Dress Tells the Woman's Story," in J. Gaines and C. Herzog (eds), *Fabrications: Costume and the Female Body*, New York, London: Routledge, 180–211.

Gamman, L. (2001), "Self-fashioning, Gender Display and Sexy Girl Shoes: What's at Stake—Female Fetishism or Narcissism?," in S. Benstock and S. Ferris (eds), *Footnotes on Shoes,* New Brunswick, New Jersey, London: Rutgers University Press, 93–115.

Gaonkar, D.P. (ed.), (2001), *Alternative Modernities*, Durham, London: Duke University Press.

Gardner, A.W. (1889), *Gardner's Handy Guide to Jamaica*, Kingston: Aston W. Gardner & Co.

Gardner, A. W. (1893), *Tourist Guide to the Island of Jamaica*, Kingston: Aston W. Gardner & Co.

Gardner, W.J. ([1873] 1971), *A History of Jamaica: From its Discovery by Christopher Columbus to the Year 1872*, London: Frank Cass & Co. Ltd.

Garelick, R.K. (2001), "The Layered Look: Coco Chanel and Contagious Celebrity" in *Dandies: Fashion and Finesse in Art and Culture,* S. Fillin-Yeh (ed.), New York, London: New York University Press, 35–58.

Gates Jr, H.L. (1988), "The Trope of the New Negro and the Reconstruction of the Image of the Black," in *Representations*, 24: Autumn, 129–55.

Gau, C. (2011), "Conventional Work Dress," in J.B. Eicher, *Berg Encyclopedia of World Dress and Fashion: Global Perspectives,* Oxford, New York: Berg, 10, 85–96.

Gay, J. (1964), *London Observed*, London: Michael Joseph.

Gibbons, J. (2007), *Contemporary Art and Memory: Images of Recollection and Remembrance*, London, New York: I.B. Tauris.

Gilmore, J. (1995), *Glimpses of Our Past: A Social History of the Caribbean in Postcards*, Jamaica: Ian Randle Publishers.

Gilot, F. and C. Lake (1965), *Life with Picasso*, London: Nelson.

Gilroy, B. (1976), *Black Teacher*, London: Cassell.

Gilroy, B. and J. Anim-Addo (ed.), (1998), *Leaves in the Wind: Collected Writings*, London: Mango Publishing.

Gilroy, P. (1993), *The Black Atlantic: Modernity and Double Consciousness,* London, New York: Verso.

Gilroy, P. (2001), "Driving While Black," in *Car Cultures*, D. Miller (ed.), Oxford, New York: Berg, 81–104.

Gioia, T. (1997), *The History of Jazz,* New York, Oxford: Oxford University Press.

Gioia, T. (2009), *The Birth (and Death) of the Cool*, Golden: Speck Press.

Glanville, B. (1964), "When the NS Met Malcolm X," *New Statesman*, June 12. Available online: http://www.newstatesman.com/world-affairs/2013/04/when-ns-met-malcolm-x (accessed July 28, 2013).

Glass, R. (1960), *Newcomers: The West Indians in London*, London: Centre for Urban Studies and George Allen & Unwin Ltd.

Gloucester Echo (1942), "Broadcasting Home Service for the Forces," May 3: 14.

Godwin, M. (1990), *Angels: An Endangered Species*, London: Boxtree.

Golden, T. (2004), *Harlemworld: Metropolis as Metaphor*, New York: The Studio Museum in Harlem.

Golding, J. ([1981] 1991). "Cubism," in N. Stangos (ed.), *Concepts of Modern Art: From Fauvism to Postmodernism*, London: Thames & Hudson, 50–78.

Goldsmith, L. (1997), "A Picture Postcard of St. Paul's Cathedral," in *One-Off*, London: V&A/RCA, 83–101.

Goodwin, P. (2013), "Curating Beyond the Canon? Paul Goodwin in Conversation with Dr David Dibosa," TrAIN Open Lecture Series, University of the Arts London, April 24.

Gotschaller, R. (2015), "Dig, Slash and Stitch: Contemporary Artists and Their Substrates," in D. Sturgis (ed.), *Bright Light: Thinking the Substrate* 2: 43–51.

Goulbourne, H. (2002), *Caribbean Transnational Experience*, London, Sterling: Pluto Press.

Gourse, L. (1997), *The Billie Holiday Companion: Seven Decades of Commentary*, London, New York, Sydney: Omnibus Press.

Governor's Report on the Blue Book and Departmental Records 1881 (1882), Kingston: Government Printing Establishment.

Green, J. (1998), *Black Edwardians: Black People in Britain 1901–1914*, London: Frank Cass Publishers.

Greer, B. (2004). "Don't mean a thing if it ain't got that bling," *The Times*. Available online: http://thetime.co.uk/tto/arts/article2399292.ece (accessed July 29, 2015).

Gunn, J.V. (1982), *Autobiography: Toward a Poetics of Experience*, Philadelphia, PA: University of Pennsylvania Press.

Gunning, D. (2010), *Race and Antiracism in Black British and British Asian Literature*, Liverpool: Liverpool University Press.

Hackney, F. (2013), "Quiet Activism and the New Amateur: The Power of Home and Hobby Crafts," *Design and Culture*, 5(2): 169–93.

Hakewill, J. (1825), *A Picturesque Tour of Jamaica. From Drawings Made in the Years 1820 and 1821*, London: Hurst & Robinson.

Hall, C. (1992), *White, Male and Middle Class: Explorations in Feminism and History*, Cambridge: Polity Press.

Hall, C. (2007), "Britain, Jamaica, and Empire in the Era of Emancipation," in T. Barringer, G. Forrester and B. Martinez-Ruiz (eds.), *Art and Emancipation in Jamaica: Isaac Mendes Belisario and His Worlds*, New Haven, London: Yale Center For British Art and Yale University Press, 9–25.

Hall, S. (1967), *The Young Englanders*, London: National Committee for Commonwealth Immigrants.

Hall, S. (1972), "The Social Eye of Picture Post," *Working Papers in Cultural Studies* 2, Birmingham: University of Birmingham, 71–120.

Hall, S. (1984), "Reconstruction Work," *Ten.8*, 2–9.

Hall, S. (1993), "Minimal Selves," in A. Gray and J. McGuigan (eds), *Studying Culture: An Introductory Reader*, London, New York, Melbourne, Auckland: Edward Arnold, 134–8.

Hall, S. (1999–2000), "Whose Heritage? Un-Settling 'The Heritage', Re-imagining the Post-nation," *Third Text*, 13(49): 3–13.

Hall, S. (2000), *Desert Island Discs* [radio programme], February 13. Available online: http://www.bbc.co.uk/programmes/p0094b6r (accessed January 6, 2015).

Hall, S. (2001), "Constituting an Archive," *Third Text*, 15(54): 89–92.

Hall, S. and D. Scott (2012), "Hospitality's Others: A Conversation," in P. Domela and S. Tallant (eds), *The Unexpected Guest: Art, Writing and Thinking on Hospitality*, London: Art Books, 291–304.

Hallnäs, L. and J. Redström (2002), "From Use to Presence: On the Expressions and Aesthetics of Everyday Computational Things," *ACM Transactions on Computer-Human Interaction*, 9(2): 106–24.

Hardwick, E. (1997), "Billie Holiday: Sleepless Nights," in L. Gourse (ed.), *The Billie Holiday Companion: Seven Decades of Commentary*, Omnibus Press: London, New York, Sydney, 160–8.

Harmon Foundation (1935), *Negro Artists: An Illustrated Review of Their Achievements*, New York: Harmon Foundation.

Harré, R. (1997). "Emotion in Music," in M. Hjort and S. Laver (eds), *Emotion and the Arts*, New York, Oxford: Oxford University Press.

Harrison, A. (1978), *Making and Thinking: A Study of Intelligent Activities*, Sussex: Harvester Press.

Hartman, G.H. (ed.), (1986), *Bitburg in Moral and Political Perspective*, Bloomington: Indiana University Press.

Hatt, M. (1999), "Race, Ritual and Responsibility: Performativity and the Southern Lynching," in A. Jones and A. Stephenson (eds), *Performing the Body, Performing the Text*, London, New York: Routledge, 71–82.

Haworth-Booth, M. (1978), *Cars, Photographs by Langdon Clay* [exhibition leaflet], V&A, London.

Hebdige, D. (1987), *Cut 'n' Mix: Culture, Identity and Caribbean Music*, London, New York: Comedia.

Hellis, R. (2015), *photo London*: gateway to London's public photographic collections. Database of 19th Century Photographers and Allied Trades in London 1841–1901. Available online: http://www.photolondon.org.uk/pages/details.asp?pid=3694 (accessed May 25, 2015).

Henderson, J.A. (1971), *The First Avant-Garde (1887–1894): Sources of the Modern French Theatre*, London, Toronto, Wellington, Sydney: George G. Harrap & Co. Ltd.

Hendrickson, H. (ed.), (1996), *Clothing and Difference: Embodied Identities in Colonial and Post-colonial Africa*, Durham, London: Duke University Press.

Hezekiah, G.A. (2012), "The Interior Life of Painting: Lebenswelt and Subjectivity in the Work of Roberta Stoddart," *Small Axe*, 16(2): 139–52.

Higgins, J. (1995), "White Aprons, Black Hands: Aboriginal Women Domestic Servants in Queensland," *Labour History*, 69: 188–95.

Highmore, B. (2011), *Ordinary Lives: Studies in the Everyday*, London, New York: Routledge.

History Making: Recovering the Past, Collecting the Future (2003), Study Day Programme, London: Victoria and Albert Museum and Archives and Museum of Black Heritage, October 13, 2003.

Hobsbawm, E. ([1983] 1992), "Introduction: Inventing Traditions," in E. Hobsbawm and T. Ranger (eds), *The Invention of Tradition*, Cambridge, New York, Melbourne: University of Cambridge, 1–14.

Hobsbawm, E. (1999), *Uncommon People: Resistance, Rebellion and Jazz*, London: Abacus.

Hodder, I. (1994), "The Contextual Analysis of Symbolic Meaning," in S.M. Pearce (ed.), *Interpreting Objects and Collections*, London, New York: Routledge, 12.

Hodges, D. (2014), "Time for the Main Parties to Stand Up to Ukip Over Immigration," *The Telegraph*, November 24. Available online: http://www.telegraph.co.uk/news/politics/ukip/11249979/Time-for-the-main-parties-to-stand-up-to-Ukip-over-immigration.html (accessed January 7, 2015).

Holiday, B. ([1956] 1992), *Lady Sings the Blues*, Harmondsworth: Penguin.

"Holiday on Broadway" (1948), *The Playbill for the Mansfield Theatre*, New York: Playbill Incorporated, 1–24.

Hollander, A. (1975), *Seeing Through Clothes*, New York: Avon.

Holy Bible: *King James Version* (1819), Glasgow: HarperCollins.

Hong, E. (2014), *The Birth of Korean Cool: How One Nation is Conquering the World Through Pop*, London: Simon & Schuster UK Ltd.

hooks, bell (1990a), "Marginality as Site of Resistance," in R. Ferguson, M. Gever, T.T. Minh-ha and West C. (eds), *Out There: Maginalization and Contemporary Cultures*, New York: The New Museum of Contemporary Art, 341–4.

hooks, bell (1990b), *Yearning: Race, Gender and Cultural Politics*, New York, London: Routlege.

hooks, bell (1994), *Outlaw Culture: Resisting Representations*, New York, London: Routledge.

hooks, bell (2004), *We Real Cool: Black Men and Masculinity*, New York, London: Routledge.

hooks, bell (2009), *Belonging: A Culture of Place*, New York, London: Routledge.

Hooper-Greenhill, E. (2000), *Museums and the Interpretation of Visual Culture*, London, New York: Routledge.

Hopkins, T. (1955), "Are We Building up to A British Colour Conflict?," *Picture Post*, 66(4): 29–32, 41. January 22.

Hoskins, J. (1998), *Biographical Objects: How Things Tell the Stories of People's Lives*, New York, London: Routledge.

Hoskinson, G.E. (1891), "Jamaica as a Winter Residence for Northern People: A Letter from the United States Consul at Kingston," *Report of the International Exhibition Jamaica, 1891*, London, 31–6.

Houston, D. and J. Bagert (eds), (2006), *Jazz, Giants and Journeys: The Photography of Herman Leonard*, London: Scala.

Hughes, G. (1998), "Tourisim and the Semiological Realization of Space," G. Ringer (ed.), *Destinations: Cultural Landscapes of Tourism*, London, New York: Routledge, 17–32.

Hull Daily Mail (1942), "Broadcasting Home Service for the Forces," May 3: 14.

Il Pai, H. (2013), "Staging 'Koreana' for the Tourist Gaze: Imperialist Nostalgia and the Circulation of Picture Postcards," *History of Photography*, 37(3): 302–11.

Illustrated London News, "The Jamaica Exhibition" (1891), January: 111.

Ingold, T. (2010), "Transformations of the Line: Traces, Threads and Surfaces," *Textile: The Journal of Cloth and Culture*, 8(1): 10–32.

Jaffé, H.L.C. (1980), *Picasso*, London: Book Club Associates.

James, A. (1996), interview with the author January 1995.

Jefferson, T. (1993), "Cultural Responses to the Teds," in S. Hall and T. Jefferson, *Resistance Through Rituals: Youth Subcultures in Post-war Britain*, London, New York: Routledge.

Jeffrey-Smith, D.E. (1959), *Jamaican Memories: 7/12/261*, unpublished essay, Jamaica Archives and Records Department, Jamaica.

Jenkins, K. (1994), *Re-thinking History*, London, New York: Routledge.

Johnson, C. (1988), *Being and Race: Black Writing Since 1970*, London: Serpent's Tail.

Johnson, J. (1903), *Jamaica: The New Riviera*, London: Cassell & Company Ltd.

Johnson, J.W. ([1925] 1997), "Harlem: The Cultural Capital," in A. Locke (ed.), *The New Negro: Voices of the Harlem Renaissance*, New York: Touchstone, 301–11.

Johnson, R.A. (1989), *Ecstasy: Understanding the Psychology of Joy*, London, New York: HarperCollins.

Jones, D. (1998). "A Biographical Approach to the History of Education: Nineteenth Century Nonconformist Lives and Educational Expansion," in M. Erben (ed.), *Biography and Education: A Reader*, London: Falmer Press, 130–48.

Josephson, B. and T. Trilling-Josephson (2009), *Café Society: The Wrong Place for the Right People*, Urbana, Chicago: University of Illinois Press.

Jung, C.G. (1917), *Collected Papers on Analytical Psychology*, London: Bailliére, Tindall & Cox.

Kaiser, S. (2001), "Minding Appearances: Style, Truth and Subjectivity," in J. Enwistle and E. Wilson (eds), *Body Dressing*, Oxford, New York: Berg, 79–102.

Kanneh, K. (1995), "Feminism and the Colonial Body," in B. Ashcroft, G. Griffiths and H. Tiffin, *The Post-Colonial Studies Reader*, London, New York: Routledge, 346–8.

Kanost, B. (2014), "The Agitating Power of Nonviolent Cool in 'Going to Meet the Man,'" in S. Henderson and P.L. Thomas (eds), *James Baldwin: Challenging Authors*, Rotterdam, Boston, Taipei: Sense Publishers, 149–63.

Katzin, M. (1959), "The Jamaican Country Higgler," *Social and Economic Studies*, 8(4): 421–40.

Katzin, M.F. (1960), "The Business of Higglering in Jamaica," *Social and Economic Studies*, 9 (3): 207–331.

Keepnews. O. ([1988] 1997), "Lady Sings the Blues," in L. Gourse (ed.), *The Billie Holiday Companion: Seven Decades of Commentary*, London, New York, Paris: Omnibus Press, 110–14.

Kennard, P. (1980), "Postcards as Intervention," *Camerawork*, 17 (January/February): 13.

Kennedy, S. (1959), *Jim Crow Guide to the USA: The Laws, Customs and Etiquette Governing the Conduct of Non-Whites and Other Minorities as Second-Class Citizens*, London: Lawrence & Wishart Ltd.

Kerr-Campbell M. and F. Salmon (2013), "Constitution and Enrichment of the Cousins Hereward Postcard Collection at the University of the West Indies Mona Library: Lessons Learned," *Journal of Electronic Resources Librarianship*, 25(3): 192–200.

Knapp, G. (1999), *Angel, Archangels and All the Company of Heaven*, Munich, New York: Prestel.

Kopytoff, I. (1986), "The Cultural Biography of Things: Commoditization as Process," in A. Appadurai (ed.), *The Social Life of Things: Commodities in Cultural Perspective*, Cambridge, London, New York, New Rochelle, Melbourne, Sydney: Cambridge University Press, 64–9.

Krauss, R. (1992), "In the Name of Picasso," in F. Francina and J. Harris (eds), *Art and Modern Culture: An Anthology of Critical Texts*, London: Phaidon and The Open University, 210–21.

Labas, D. (1999), "Nonverbal Communication: The Body as an Extension of the Soul," in D. Bartlett (ed.), *Body in Transition*, Zagreb: University of Zagreb.

Lady Day: The Very Best of Billie Holiday, 1997 [vinyl record], Sony Music Entertainment (UK) Ltd.

Lambert, S. (1993), *Form Follows Function? Design in the 20th Century*, London: V&A Publishing.

Le Franc, E. (1989), "Petty Trading and Labour Mobility: Higglers in the Kingston Metropolitan Area," in K. Hart (ed.), *Women and the Sexual Division of Labour in the Caribbean*, Kingston: The Consortium Graduate School of Social Sciences, 105–40.

Lea, R. and J. Halliday (2014), "White Skin Still Seen as Key Attribute of Being English, Claims Amis," *The Guardian*, March 18: 5.

Lechte, J. (1994), *Fifty Key Contemporary Thinkers: From Structuralism to Postmodernity*, London, New York: Routledge.

Leslie, E. (2013), "Dreams for Sale" in M. Uhlirova, *Birds of Paradise: Costume as Cinematic Spectacle*, London: Koenig Books, 29–40.

Lester, K.M. and B.V. Oerke ([1940] 2004), *Accessories of Dress: An Illustrated Encyclopedia*, Mineola, New York: Dover Publications Inc.

Levitt, S. (1991), "Bristol Clothing Trades and Exports in the Georgian Period," in E. Ricerche (ed.), *Per una Storia Della Moda Pronta Problemi,* Firenze: Edifir, 29–41.

Lewis L.D. (1999), "Harlem Renaissance," in K.A. Appiah and H.L. Gates, Jr (eds), *Africana: The Encyclopedia of the African and African American Experience,* New York: Basic Civitas Books, 926–36.

Life Magazine (1954), "The Ponytail Period," November 8: 119–120.

Lindsey, E. (2004), "Subtler Shades of Black," *The Observer,* October 10. Available online: http://www.theguardian.com/artanddesign/2004/oct/10/art2 (accessed May 24, 2015).

Littler, J. (2005), "Introduction: British Heritage and the Legacies of 'Race,'" in J. Littler and R. Naidoo (eds), *The Politics of Heritage: The Legacies of Race,* London and New York: Routledge, 1–19.

Liu, A. (2004), *The Laws of Cool: Knowledge Work and the Culture of Information,* Chicago, London: University of Chicago Press.

Livingston, A. and I. Livingston (1998), *Dictionary of Graphic Design and Designers,* London: Thames and Hudson.

Locke, A. (1925a), "Enter the New Negro," *Survey Graphic* 5(6): 631–4.

Locke, A. (1925b), "Harlem," *Survey Graphic* 5(6): 629–30.

Locke, A. (1925c), "The Art of the Ancestors," *Survey Graphic* 5(6): 673.

Locke, A. ([1925] 1997), *The New Negro: Voices of the Harlem Renaissance,* New York, Touchstone Louisiana, Baton Rouge, London: Louisiana State University.

Long, E. (1774), *History of Jamaica or General Survey of the Ancient and Modern State of that Island, Volume II,* London: T. Lowndes.

Loomba, A., (1998), *Colonialism/Postcolonialism,* London, New York: Routledge.

"Louisiana State Flower: Magnolia" (2015), *50 States.com.* Available online: http://www.50states.com/flower/louisiana.htm#.V W XylZjB--9 (accessed May 27, 2015).

Low, D. (1958), "Problem For the Welfare State", cartoon in *The Manchester Guardian,* September 8: 9.

Loxley, J. (2007), *Performativity,* Oxon, New York: Routledge.

Lucas, J. (1955), "Picasso: Bright Light in a Gray Season," *College Art Journal,* Spring, 14(3), 196–203. Available online: http://www.jstor.org/stable/772411 (accessed August 17, 2015).

Lucie-Smith, E. (2013), "Picturesque Otherness: A Question of Race . . .," in D. Boxer and E. Lucie-Smith (eds), *Jamaica in Black and White: Photography in Jamaica c. 1845– c. 1920, The David Boxer Collection,* Oxford: Macmillan, 230–53.

MacAdams, L. (2001), *Birth of the Cool: Beat, Bebop, and the American Avant-Garde,* New York, London, Toronto, Sydney, Singapore: The Free Press.

MacCannell, D. (1976), *The Tourist: A New Theory of the Leisure Class,* London: Macmillan.

MacCannell, D. (1992), *Empty Grounds: The Tourist Papers,* London, New York: Routledge.

MacCannell, J.F. (1998), "Perversion in Public Places," *New Formations,* 35 (Autumn), London: Lawrence & Wishart, 43–59.

MacKenzie, J.M. (1984), *Propoganda and Empire. The Manipulation of British Public Opinion 1880–1960,* Manchester, New York: Manchester University Press.

Macmillan, H. (2005), *An African Trading Empire: The Story of the Susman Brothers and Wulfsohn 1901–2005,* London: I.B. Tauris.

Maio, S. (1995), *Creating Another Self: Voice in Modern American Personal Poetry,* Kirksville: Thomas Jefferson University Press.

Major, C. (1994), *Juba to Jive: A Dictionary of African-American Slang,* Harmondsworth: Penguin.

Makers Guild in Wales (2014), *Pinnies from Heaven: An Exploration and Celebration of the Apron from Adam and Eve to the Present Day,* Cardiff Bay: Makers Guild in Wales.

Malcolm X (1966), *The Autobiography of Malcolm X*, London: Hutchinson & Co. Ltd.

Malcolm X (1992), [film] Dir. Spike Lee, USA: 40 Acres and a Mule, Large International NV, JVC Entertainment Networks.

Marable, M. (2011), *Malcolm X: A Life of Reinvention*, London: Allen Lane.

Marchant, H. (1952), "Breeding a Colour Bar," *Picture Post,* 56(10): 28–31.

Marchant, H. (1956), "Thirty Thousand Coloured Problems," *Picture Post,* 71(10): 28–9, 38.

Margolick, D. (2000), *Strange Fruit: Billie Holiday, Café Society, and An Early Cry for Civil Rights,* Philadelphia, London: Running Press.

Martin Amis's England (2014), [TV program], BBC4, March 23.

Martin, L. H., H. Gutyman and P.H. Hutton (eds), (1988), *Technologies of the Self: A Seminar with Michel Foucault*, London: Tavistock.

Martin, R. and H. Koda (1989), *Jocks and Nerds: Men's Style in the Twentieth Century*, New York: Rizzoli.

Martin, S. (2013), *Eduardo Paolozzi: Collaging Culture*, Chichester: Pallant House Gallery.

Marsh, G. (1991), "No Room For Squares," in G. Marsh, G. Callingham and F. Cromey (eds), *The Cover Art of Blue Note Records*, London: Collins & Brown Ltd.

Massood, P. J. (2013), *Making a Promised Land: Harlem in 20th Century Photography and Film*, New Brunswick, New Jersey, London: Rutgers University Press.

Matlock, J. (1993), "Masquerading Women, Pathologized Men: Cross-dressing, fetishism, and the theory of perversion, 1885–1930," in E.S. Apter and W. Pietz (eds), *Fetishism as Cultural Discourse*, Ithaca, New York: Cornell University Press, 31–61.

McClendon, A.D. (2015), *Fashion and Jazz: Dress, Identity and Subcultural Improvisation*, London, New Delhi, New York, Sydney: Bloomsbury.

McClintock, A. (1995), *Imperial Leather: Race, Gender and Sexuality in the Colonial Past*, New York, London: Routledge.

McDonald, R.A. (1993), *The Economy and Material Culture of Slaves: Goods and Chattels on the Sugar Plantations of Jamaica and Louisiana*, Baton Rouge, London: Louisiana State University Press.

McDougald, E.J. (1925), "The Double Task: The Struggle of Negro Women for Sex and Race Emancipation," *Survey Graphic* 5 (6): 689–91.

McDowell, C. (1992), *Hats, Status, Style and Glamour*, London: Thames & Hudson.

McDowell, C. (ed.), (1998), *The Pimlico Companion to Fashion: A Literary Anthology*, London: Pimlico.

McGuigan, J. (2009), *Cool Capitalism,* London: Pluto Press.

McKay, C. *Harlem Glory*, Schomburg Center of Research in Black Culture, New York, unpublished.

McMillan, M. (2003), "The 'West Indian' Front Room in the African Diaspora," *Fashion Theory: The Journal of Dress, Body & Culture,* 7 (3/4): 397–413.

McPherson, H. (1999), "Sarah Bernhardt: Portrait of the Actress as Spectacle," *Nineteenth Century Contexts,* 20(4): 409–54.

Mead, M. and J. Baldwin (1971), *A Rap on Race*, Philadelphia, New York: J.B. Lippincott Co.

Mears, P. (ed.), (2012), *Ivy Style: Radical Conformists*, New Haven: Yale University Press.

Melvin, J. (2015), "Holes in the Archive—To Fill or to Leave, that is the Question," *Bright Light: Thinking the Substrate,* 2: 65–74.

Memela, S. (2004), "Perverting Black Power," *Rhodes Journalism Review,* 24: 10–11. Available on line: http://www.rjr.ru.ac.za/rjrpdf/rjr_no24/perverting_black_power.pdf (first accessed January 22, 2015).

Men's Wear (1932), September 7, 73 (3).

Men's Wear (1933), December 20, 76 (4).

Men's Wear (1934), S. Robert Zimmerman Advertisement, December 5, 78(3): 77.Mentges, G. (2000), "Cold, Coldness, Coolness: Remarks on the Relationship of Dress Body and Technology," *Fashion Theory: The Journal of Dress, Body and Culture*, 4(1): 27–48.

Mercer, K, (1990), "Black Hair/Style Politics," in R. Ferguson, M. Gever, T.T. Minh-ha and C. West (eds), *Out There: Marginalization and Contemporary Cultures*, Cambridge, London: MIT Press, 247–64.

Mercer, K. (2003), *James VanDerZee*, London, New York: Phaidon.

Mercer, K. (2005), "Romare Bearden, 1964: Collage as Kunstwollen," in K. Mercer, (ed.), *Cosmopolitan Modernisms*, London, Cambridge, Massachusetts: Institute of International Visual Arts/The MIT Press, 124–45.

Micossé-Aikens, aus dem Moore, E. (2012), "Introduction," in A. Diallo and S. Miscossé-Aikins (eds), *In the Seams: The Aethetics of Freedom Expressed*, Stuttgart: Institut für Auslandsbeziehugen e.V, 5–7.

Miller, B. D. (1998), "Afterword: Hair Power," in A. Hiltebeitel and B. D. Miller (eds), *Hair: Its Power and Meaning in Asian Cultures*, Albany, New York: State University of New York Press.

Miller, K. (1925), "The Harvest of Race Prejudice," *Survey Graphic* 5(6): 682–3, 711–12.

Miller, M. L. (2009), *Slaves of Fashion: Black Dandyism and the Styling of Black Diasporic Identity*, Durham, London: Duke University Press.

Minha-ha, T.T. (1994), "Other Than Myself/My Other Self," in G. Robertson, M. Mash, L. Tickner, J. Bird, B. Curtis, and T. Putnam (eds), *Travellers' Tales: Narrative of Home and Displacement*, London, New York: Routledge, 9–26.

Mintz, S.W. (1955), "The Jamaican Internal Marketing Pattern: Some Notes and Hypotheses," *Social and Economic Studies*, 4(1): 95–103.

Mintz, S.W. (1974), *Caribbean Transformations*, Baltimore, London: The John Hopkins University Press.

Mississippi State Flower (2015), *50 States.com*. Available online: http://www.50states.com/flower/mississippi.htm#.VWXzbpjB--9 (accessed May 27, 2015).

Mitchell, V. (1999), "Folding and Unfolding the Textile Membrane: Between Bodies and Architecture," in J. Stair (ed.), *The Body Politic: The Role of the Body and Contemporary Craft*, London: Crafts Council.

Moers, E. ([1960] 1969), *The Dandy: From Brummell to Beerbohm*, London: Secker and Warburg.

Mohammed Speaks (1962) [Newspaper]: March

Mohanram, R. (1999), *Black Body: Women, Colonialism and Space*, Minneapolis, London: University of Minnesota Press.

Moore-Gilbert, B. (2009), *Postcolonial Life-Writing: Culture, Politics and Self-Representation*, London, New York: Routledge.

Moors, A. (2003), "From 'Women's Lib.' to 'Palestinian Women': The Politics of Picture Postcards in Palestine/Israel," in D. Crouch and N. Lübbren (eds), *Visual Culture and Tourism*, Oxford, New York: Berg, 23–39.

Moran, J. (1865), "The Relation of Photography to the Fine Arts," *The Photographic Journal*, 162: 177–9, October 16.

Morrison, T. (1992a), *Jazz*, Chatto & Windus London.

Morrison, T. (1992b), *Playing in the Dark: Whiteness and the Literary Imagination*, Cambridge, Massachusetts, London: Harvard University Press.

Morrow, R.A. and D.D. Brown (1994), *Critical Theory and Methodology*, California, London and New Delhi: Sage Publications.

Munslow, A. (2003), "History and Biography: An Editorial Comment," *Rethinking History*, 7 (1): 1–11.

Murphy, R. (1999), *Theorizing the Avant-Garde: Modernism, Expressionism, and the Problem of Postmodernity*, Cambridge, New York, Melbourne: University of Cambridge.

Nairne, S. (2004), "Foreword," in T. Phillips (ed.), *We Are the People: Postcards from the Collection of Tom Phillips*, London: National Portrait Gallery, 9.

Nash, J.M. (1974), *Cubism, Futurism and Constructivism*, Thames & Hudson: London.

Neal, M.A. (2006), *New Black Man*, New York, London: Routledge.

Neely, D.T., (2008), "Haul and Pull up: History, 'Mento' and the eBay Age," *Caribbean Studies*, 36(2): 95–120.

Nicholson, S. (1995), *Billie Holiday*, London: Indigo.

Nicolson, G. (1995), *Footsucker: A Novel*, London: Gollancz.

Nkosi, N. (2006), "Stoned Cherrie," in A. Tischhauser (ed.), *10 x SA Fashion Week: Voices and Images from Ten Years of South African Fashion Week*, Johannesburg: Channel F Publishing, 143–6.

Nkosi, N. (2015), telephone conversation with Carol Tulloch, May 5.

Nora, P. (1989), "Between Memory and History: Les Lieux des Mémoire," *Representations* 26 (Spring): 7–24.

Nougayréde, N. (2015), "Amnesia is the problem, not immigration," *The Guardian,* January 7, 35.

Nuttall, S. (2004), "Stylizing the Self: The Y Generation in Rosebank, Johannesburg," *Public Culture,* 16(3): 430–52.

Oakes, A. and M. Hamilton Hill (1970), *Rural Costume: Its Origin and Development in Western Europe and the British Isles,* London: Batsford.

Oberhofer, M.A. (2012), "Fashioning African Cities: The Case of Johannesburg, Lagos and Douala," *Streetnotes*, 20: 65–89. Available online: https://escholarship.org/uc/item/4dv2g2n9 (accessed January 22, 2015).

Oguibe, O. (2004), *The Culture Game*, Minneapolis, London: University of Minnesota Press.

Olson, K. M. and G.T. Goodnight (1994), "Entanglements of Consumption, Cruelty, Privacy and Fashion: The Social Controversy Over Fur," *The Quarterly Journal of Speech*, 80(3) August: 246–76.

O'Meally, R. (1991), *Lady Day: The Many Faces of Billie Holiday*, Boston, New York: Da Capo Press.

O'Neill, A. (2011a), "Twinset and Match: The Culture of the Twinset," in K. Godtsenhoven and E. Dirix (eds), *Unravel: Knitwear in Fashion*, Tielt: Lannoo, 111–19.

O'Neill, A. (2011b), "'(Here is the Secret! Here is the Trick!)': On the Editorial Magic of Orson Welles," *Vestoj*, 2 (Winter): 15–19.

Pacteau, F. (1994), *The Symptom of Beauty*, London: Reaktion Books.

Pagán, E. (2005), "Zoot Suit," in *Encyclopedia of Clothing and Fashion*, Detroit, London: Thomson Gale, 3: 466–8.

Pankhurst, E. ([1914] 1979), *My Own Story: The Autobiography of Emmeline Pankhurst*, London: Virago.

Parks, G. (1990), *Gordon Parks: Voices in the Mirror, an Autobiography*, London, New York, Toronto, Sydney, Auckland: Doubleday.

Partridge, E. (1989), *A Dictionary of the Underworld*, Ware: Wordsworth Editions.

Passerini, L. (2000), "Transforming Biography: From the Claim of Objectivity to Intersubjective Plurality," *Rethinking History* 4(3): 413–16.

Pastoureau, M. (2001), *The Devil's Cloth: A History of Stripes and Striped Fabric*, New York: Columbia University Press.

Patton, S.F. (1998), *African-American Art*, Oxford, New York: Oxford University Press.

Payne, M. (ed.), (1997), *A Dictionary of Cultural and Critical Theory*, Oxford, Massachusetts: Blackwell.

Perlman, H.H. (1968), *Persona: Social Role and Personality*, Chicago, London: University of Chicago Press.

Phillips, A. (1994), *On Flirtation*, London: Boston: Faber & Faber.

Phillips, A. (2005), *Going Sane*, London: Hamish Hamilton.

Phillips, A. (2012), "Beginning With Bags" in J. Clark (ed.), *Handbags: The Making of a Museum*, New Haven, London: Yale University Press, 23–31.

Phillips, M. and T. Phillips (1998), "Black and British," *The Guardian Weekend*, May 16, 38–46.

Picht, H. and J. Draskau (1985), *Terminology: An Introduction*, Guildford: University of Surrey.

Picton, J. (1990), "What's in a Mask," *African Languages and Cultures*, 3(2): 181–202.

Picture Post, "Fashion About the House" (1954), December 18: 39.

Pile, S. (1996), *The Body and the City: Psychoanalysis, Space and Subjectivity*, London, New York: Routledge.

Polhemus, T. (1994), *Streetstyle: From Sidewalk to Catwalk*, London: Thames & Hudson.

Pollock, G. (1999), *Differencing the Canon: Feminist Desire and the Writing of Art's Histories*, Oxon, New York: Routledge.

Porter, J.A. (1943), *Modern Negro Art*, New York: The Dryden Press.

Porter, R. (ed.), (1997). *Rewriting the Self: Histories from the Renaissance to the Present*, London, New York: Routledge.

Porter, P. (1984), *Jaguar: The Complete Illustrated History*, Harmondsworth: Penguin.

Pountain, D. and D. Robins (2000), *Cool Rules: Anatomy of an Attitude*, London: Reaktion Books.

Poustie, S. (2010), "Re-Theorising Letters and 'Letterness'," *Olive Schreiner Letters Project Working Papers on Letters*, Letterness & Epistolary Networks, 1. Available online: http://www.oliveschreinerletters.ed.ac.uk/PoustieWPLetterness.pdf (accessed January 10, 2015).

Powell R.J. (1997(a)), *Black Art and Culture in the 20th Century*, London: Thames & Hudson.

Powell, R.J. (1997(b)), "Re/Birth of a Nation," in J. Skipwith (ed.), *Rhapsodies in Black: Art of the Harlem Renaissance,* London: Hayward Gallery, 14–33.

Powell, R.J. (2008), *Cutting a Figure: Fashioning Black Portraiture,* Chicago, London: University of Chicago Press.

Preston, A. (2000), *Heroin,* Exchange Publications.

Probyn, E. (1993), *Sexing the Self: Gendered Positions in Cultural Studies,* London, New York: Routledge.

Prosser, R. (2011), "The Postcard: The Fragment," *Life Writing*, 8 (2): 219–25.

Pryce, K. (1979), *Endless Pressure: A Study of West Indian Life-styles in Bristol*, Harmondsworth, New York, Auckland: Penguin.

Pryke, P. (1998), *Flower Innovations*, London, Auckland, Singapore, Toronto: Mitchell Beazley.

Quashie, K. (2012), *The Sovereignty of Quiet: Beyond Resistance in Black Culture*, New Brunswick, New Jersey, London: Rutgers University Press.

Rapport, N. and A. Dawson (1998), *Migrants of Identity: Perceptions of Home in a World of Movement,* Oxford, New York: Berg.

Read, H. (1974), *A Concise History of Modern Painting*, London: Thames & Hudson.

Reid, J.H. (1888), "The People of Jamaica Described," in R. Gordon et al. *Jamaica's Jubilee: Or What We Are and What We Hope to Be*, London: Partridge and Co.

Reputations: Billie Holiday—Sensational Lady (2008) [TV program], BBC 4, December 21.

Reusch, G. and M. Noble ([1951] 1960), *Corsage Craft*, Princeton, New Jersey, Toronto, London, New York: D. Van Nostrand Company, Inc.

Ribeiro, A. (2002), "On Englishness in Dress," in C. Breward, B. Conekin and C. Cox (eds), *The Englishness of English Dress*, Oxford and New York: Berg, 15–27.

Richards, S. (1980), *Levitation: What It Is, How It Works, How To Do It*, Wellingborough, Northamptonshire: The Aquarian Press.

Richards, T. (1991), *The Commodity Culture of Victorian England: Advertising and Spectacle 1851–1914*, London, New York: Verso.

Ritz, D. (2006), "A Fan-Friendly Discography," in B. Holiday, *Lady Sings the Blues*, New York: Harlem Moon, Broadway Books.

Roberts, W.A. (1952), *Six Great Jamaicans*, Kingston: The Pioneer Press.

Robertson, G. (1985), "Some Early Jamaican Postcards, Their Photographers and Publishers," *Jamaica Journal*, 18(1): 13–22.

Robertson, G. (1995), "Pictorial Sources for Nineteenth-Century Women's History: Dress as a Mirror of Attitudes to Women," in V. Shepherd, B. Brereton, B. Bailey (eds), *Engendering History: Caribbean Women in Historical Perspective*, Kingston: Ian Randle Publishers, 111–24.

Robinson, L.C. (1999), "Locke, Alain Leroy," in K.A. Appiah and H.L. Gates Jr (eds), *Africana: The Encyclopedia of the African and African American Experience*, New York: Basic Civitas Books, 1189–90.

Rodgers, K.G. (ed.) (2002), *Climbing Up the Mountain: The Modern Art of Malvin Gray Johnson*, Durham: North Carolina Central University Art Museum.

Roetzel, B. (1999), *Gentleman: A Timeless Fashion*, Cologne: Köneman.

Rogers, J.A. ([1925] 1997), "Jazz at Home," in A. Locke (ed.), *The New Negro: Voices of the Harlem Renaissance*, New York: Touchstone, 216–24.

Rogerson, C.M. (2006), "Fashion and the Growth of 'African' Brands in South Africa," *African Clothing and Footwear Research Network*, Johannesburg: University of the Witwaterstrand, South Africa. Available online: http://repository.brandleadership.com/documents/download/92ef5b88-2133-41b9-b937-30503c17873f (accessed January 3, 2015).

Rolley, K. (1992), "Love, Desire and the Pursuit of the Whole: Dress and the Lesbian Couple," in J. Ash and E. Wilson (eds), *Chic Thrills: A Fashion Reader*, London: Pandora Press, 30–9.

Roux, J. (2004), "Introduction, The Shoe: Object of Civilization and Object of Art," in M-J. Bossan, *The Art of the Shoe*, 7, New York: Parkstone Press Ltd.

Rose, G. (2001), *Visual Methodologies: An Introduction to the Interpretation of Visual Materials*, London, Thousand Oaks, New Dehli: Sage.

Rosenberg, M., "The Mason-Dixon Line Divided the North and South." Available online: http://geography.about.com/od/politicalgeography/a/masondixon.htm (accessed May 16, 2008).

Rowbotham. S. (1999), *Threads Through Time: Writings on History and Autobiography*, Harmondsworth, New York: Penguin.

Runia, E. (2014), *Moved by the Past: Discontinuity and Historical Mutation*, New York: Columbia University Press.

Rushton, S. (2015), "Queen of the Canvas," *Vogue*, February: 164–9.

Rutherford, J. (2005), "Ghosts: Heritage and the Shape of Things to Come," in J. Littler and R. Naidoo (eds), *The Politics of Heritage, the Legacies of Race*, Oxon, New York: Routledge, 82–93.

Ryan, D. (1999), "The Man Who Staged the Empire: Remembering Frank Lascelles in Sibford Gower, 1875–2000," in M. Kwint, C. Breward, J. Aynsley (eds), *Material Memories: Design and Evocation*, Oxford, New York: Berg, 159–79.

Sagan, F. (1988), *With Fondest Regards*, London: Alison & Busby.

Said, E.W. (1995), *Orientalism, Western Conceptions of the Orient*, Harmondsworth, Penguin.

Samuel, R. (1994), *Theatres of Memory Volume 1: Past and Present in Contemporary Culture,* London, New York: Verso.

Sandino, L. (1997), *Gender and Fin-de-Siecle Studies*, unpublished paper.

Sarup, M. (1994), "Home and Identity," in G. Robertson, M. Mash, L. Tickner, J. Bird, B. Curtis, and T. Putnam (eds), *Travellers' Tales: Narrative of Home and Displacement*, London, New York: Routledge, 93–104.

Satchell, V.M. (1995), "Women, Land Transactions and Peasant Development in Jamaica, 1866–1900," in V. Shepherd, B. Brereton and B. Bailey (eds), *Engendering History: Caribbean Women in Historical Perspective*, Kingston: Ian Randle Publishers; London: James Currey Publishers.

Satre, J.P. (1948), *The Psychology of Imagination*, New York: Routledge.

Sartre, J.P. (2003), *Being and Nothingness*, London, New York: Routledge.

Schoeffler O.E. and W. Gale (1973), *Esquire's Encyclopedia of 20th Century Men's Fashions*, New York and London: McGraw-Hill.

Schutz, W.C. ([1967] 1973), *Joy: Expanding Human Awareness*, Middlesex, Victoria: Pelican.

Schwarz, B. (2005), "Afterword 'Strolling Spectators' and 'Practical Londoners': Remembering the Imperial Past," in J. Littler and R. Naidoo (eds), *The Politics of Heritage: The Legacies of Race*, London, New York: Routledge, 216–36.

Schyuler, J. (1927–8), *Diary* (unpublished), Schomberg Center for Research in Black Culture.

Scruton, R. (1983), *The Aesthetic Understanding: Essays in the Philosophy of Art and Culture*, London, New York: St Augustine's Press.

Sellman, J.C. (1999), "Great Depression," in K.A. Appiah and H.L. Gates Jr. (eds), *Africana: The Encyclopedia of the African and African American Experience*, New York: Basic Civitas Books, 867–8.

Senior, O. (1983), *The A–Z of Jamaican Heritage*, Kingston: Heinemann Educational Books Caribbean.

Shabazz, G. (1999), interview with Carol Tulloch, Harlem, New York, September 15th.

Shand, J. (1996), "Existentialism," in M. Payne (ed.), *A Dictionary of Cultural and Critical Theory*, Oxford, Malden: Blackwell, 187–9.

Shelton, S. (2008a), "Syd Shelton," in C. Tulloch (ed.), *A Riot of Our Own*, London: CHELSEA space. (No page numbers.)

Shelton, S. (2008b), Discussion with Carol Tulloch, London April 6th.

Shepherd, V.A. (1999), *Women in Caribbean History: The British Colonised Territories,* Kingston: Ian Randle Publishers; Oxford: James Currey; Princeton: Markus Wiener.

Shepherd, V.A. (2007), "Work, Culture, and Creolization: Slavery and Emancipation in Eighteenth- and Nineteenth-Century Jamaica," in T. Barringer, G. Forrester, B. Martinez-Ruiz (eds), *Art and Emancipation in Jamaica: Isaac Mendes Belisario and*

His Worlds, New Haven, London: Yale Center For British Art and Yale University Press, 27–39.

Shepherd, V., B. Brereton and B. Bailey (eds), (1995), *Engendering History: Caribbean Women in Historical Perspective*, London: James Currey; Kingston: Ian Randle.

Shepperson, G. (1968), "The African Abroad or the African Diaspora" in T.O. Ranger (ed.), *Emerging Themes of African History*, London: Heinemann Educational Books, 152–76.

Simbao, R.K. (2007), "The Thirtieth Anniversary of the Soweto Uprisings: Reading the Shadow in Sam Nzima's Iconic Photograph of Hector Pietersen," *African Arts*, 40(2): 52–69.

Simmel, G. (1971), *On Individuality and Social Forms*, Chicago, London: University of Chicago Press.

Simmonds, L. (1987) "Slave Higglering in Jamaica 1780–1834," *Jamaica Journal*, 20(1): 31–8.

Sipila, O. (2012), *Apron in Temporal Frames—Multitemporal Textile Culture and Representations of Home, Family, Cleanliness and Crafts in Finland in the First Half of the 20th Century*, Joensuu: University of Eastern Finland. Available online: http://epublications.uef.fi/pub/urn_isbn_978-952-61-0985-5/urn_isbn_978-952-61-0985-5.pdf (accessed September 15, 2014).

Skinner, T. (2002), *Fashionable Clothing from the Sears Catalogs: Early 1940s*, Atglen: Schiffer.

Skinner, T. and L. McCord (1985), *Fashion Clothing from the Sears Catalogs: Late 1940s*, Atglen: Schiffer.

Small, A. (1977), "Steve Biko," *Drum*, November, 20–7.

Small, A. (1996), *Essays in Self-Portraiture: A Comparison of Technique in the Self-Portraits of Montaigne and Rembrandt*, New York, Washington DC, San Francisco, Bern, Frankfurt, Berlin, Vienna, Paris: Peter Lang.

Smalls, J. (2001), "African-American Self-Portraiture: Repair, Reclamation, Redemption," *Third Text*, 15(54): 47–62.

Smethurst, J. (2011), *The African American Roots of Modernism: From Reconstruction of the Harlem Renaissance*, Chapel Hill: University of North Carolina Press.

Smith, Z. (2007), "Fail Better," *Review, The Guardian,* January 13. Available online: http://faculty.sunydutchess.edu/oneill/failbetter.htm (accessed August 18, 2015).

South African History Online, "Stephen Bantu Biko" (2015). Available online: http://www.sahistory.org.za/people/stephen-bantu-biko (accessed January 26, 2015).

Sparke, P. (1995), *As Long As it's Pink: The Sexual Politics of Taste*, London: Pandora.

Stanley, L. (1992), *The Auto/biographical I: The Theory and Practice of Feminist Auto/biography,* Manchester, New York: Manchester University Press.

Stanley, L. (2004), "The Epistolarium: On Theorizing Letters and Correspondences," *Auto/Biography* 12: 201–35.

Stanley, L. (2011), "The Epistolary Gift, The Editorial Third-party, Counter-Epistolaria: Rethinking the Epistolarium," *Life Writing*, 8(2): 135–52.

Stax Records (2003) "Wattstax 1972 Production Notes," in *Wattstax: The Living Word*. Available online: http://www.wattstax.com/backstory/production.html (accessed October 1, 2011).

Stearns, P.N. (1994), *American Cool: Constructing a Twentieth-Century Emotional Style*, New York, London: New York University Press.

Steedman, C. (1992), *Past Tenses: Essays on Writing, Autobiography and History*, London: River Oram.

Steele, V. (1992), "Chanel in Context," in J. Ash and E. Wilson (eds), *Chic Thrills: A Fashion Reader,* Pandora Press: London, 118–26.

Steele, V. (1999), "Fashion and Fetishism: The Sex Life of the Foot and Shoe," in D. Bartlett (ed.), *Body in Transition,* Zagreb: University of Zagreb, 135–47.

Stewart, S. ([1993] 2005), *On Longing: Narratives of the Miniature, the Gigantic, the Souvenir, the Collection*, Durham, London: Duke University Press.

Stoned Cherrie Website, Stoned Cherrie (2015). Available online: http://www.stonedcherrie.co.za/background.html (accessed January 22, 2015).

Stuart, A. (1996), *Showgirls*, London: Jonathan Cape.

Sturgis, D. (2015), "Substrate: Leaning Against Medium," *Bright Light: Thinking the Substrate*, 2: 35–9.

Sturken, M. (1999), "The Image as Memorial: Personal Photographs in Cultural Memory," in M. Hirsch (ed.), *The Familial Gaze*, Hanover, London: University Press of New England.

Styles, J. (2007), *The Dress of the People: Everyday Fashion in Eighteenth Century England*, New Haven, London: Yale University Press.

Tagg, J. (1988), *The Burden of Representation: Essays on Photographies and Histories*, London: MacMillan Press Ltd.

Tamboukou, M. (2010), *Nomadic Narratives, Visual Forces: Gwen John's Letters and Paintings*, New York: Peter Lang.

Tarrant, H.P. (undated), *Strawberries and Cream*, Dover: E. Wild.

Taylor, L. (2013), "Beyond Words: An Embroidery in Memory of Anna Binderowska, Married 1864," *Textile: The Journal of Cloth and Culture*, 11 (3): 300–13.

Teague, W.D. (1946), *Design This Day: The Technique of Order in the Machine Age*, London: Studio Publications.

Tennant, E. (1999), *Girlitude: A Memoir of the 50s and 60s*, London: Jonathan Cape.

The Crisis, March 1926.

The (new) Cadillac Database. Available online: http://www.car-nection.com/yann/Dbas_txt/V16_ndx.htm (accessed April 11, 2005).

The Sound of Jazz (1957) [TV program], CBS, December 8. Available online: http://www.youtube.com/watch?v=SThGnrorGW8 (accessed August 6, 2013).

The West Indian Front Room (2005–2006) [exhibition], curated by Michael McMillan at The Geffrye Museum, London, October 18, 2005–February 19, 2006.

Thompson, K.A. (2006), *An Eye for the Tropics: Tourism, Photography, and Framing the Caribbean Picturesque*, Durham, London: Duke University Press.

Thompson, F.R. (1974), "An Introduction to Transatlantic Black Art History: Remarks in Anticipation of a Coming of a Golden Age of Afro-Americana," *Journal of Asian and African Studies*, 9 (3–4): 192–201.

Thompson, F. R. (2011), *Aesthetic of the Cool*, Pittsburgh, New York: Periscope Publishing, Ltd.

Tleane, C. (2004), *Shifting Sands: Steve Biko's Legacy, Efforts to Commercialise Him and the Foundation*. Available online: http://ccs.ukzn.ac.za/files/Console.pdf (accessed January 27, 2015).

Town Hall Program, The (1945–6), New York: Alfred Scott.

Townsend, I. (1958), *Lady in Satin*, London: CBS Inc.

Trachtenberg, A. (1981), *Classic Essays on Photography*, New Haven: Leete's Island Books.

Trilling, L. (1972), *Sincerity and Authenticity*, London: Oxford University Press.

Tulloch, C. (1992), "Rebel Without A Pause: Black Street Style and Black Designers," in J. Ash and E. Wilson (eds), *Chic Thrills: A Fashion Reader*, 84–98, London: Pandora.

Tulloch, C. (1994), "Your Name Here: The T-Shirt," *Magic Moments Series* [radio program], BBC Radio 4, November 25.

Tulloch, C. (1997), *Fashioned in Black and White: Women's Dress in Jamaica, 1880–1907*, unpublished.

Tulloch, C. (1998), "'Out of Many, One People?': The Relativity of Dress, Race and Ethnicity to Jamaica, 1880–1907," *Fashion Theory: The Journal of Dress, Body and Culture* 2 (4): 359–82.

Tulloch, C. (1999), "That Little Magic Touch: The Headtie," in A. de la Haye and E. Wilson (eds), *Defining Dress: Dress as Object, Meaning and Identity*, Manchester, New York: Manchester University Press, 63–78.

Tulloch, C. (2002a), "Strawberries and Cream: Dress, Migration and the Quintessence of Englishness," in C. Breward, B. Conekin and C. Cox (eds), *The Englishness of English Dress*, Oxford, New York: Berg, 61–76.

Tulloch, C. (2002b), "Letter from the Editor," *Fashion Theory: The Journal of Dress, Body and Culture*, 6(1): 1–2.

Tulloch, C. (ed.), (2004), *Black Style*, London: V&A Publishing.

Tulloch, C. (2008), "Resounding Power of the Afro Comb," in G. Biddle-Perry and S. Cheang (eds), *Hair: Styling, Culture and Fashion*, Oxford: Berg, 123–39.

Tulloch, C. (2010), "Style-Fashion-Dress: From Black to Post-Black," *Fashion Theory: The Journal of Dress, Body and Culture*, 14(3): 273–304.

Tulloch, C. (2010–11), "Introduction," in *Handmade Tales: Women and Domestic Crafts* [exhibition], London: Women's Library, October 28–April 20.

Tulloch, C. (2011), "Buffalo: Style with Intent," in G. Adamson and J. Pavitt (eds), *Postmodernism: Style and Subversion, 1970–1990*, London: V&A Publishing, 182–185.

Tulloch, C. (2012), "'It Takes a Nation of Millions to Hold Us Back': Freedom and the Dynamics of the African Diaspora," in A. Diallo and S. Micossé-Aikins (eds), *In The Seams: The Aesthetics of Freedom Expressed*, Stuttgart: Institut für Auslandsbeziehungen e.V., 8–13.

Tulloch, C. (2014a), "'A Riot of Our Own': A Reflection on Agency," *Open Arts Journal*, 3 (Summer): 25–59. Available online: http://openartsjournal.org/issue-3/2014s12ct/ (accessed 31st October 2014).

Tulloch, C. (2014b), "Artist Statement." Available online: http://www.caroltulloch.co.uk/ (accessed May 24, 2015).

Tulloch, C. (2015), "Preface," in M. Sealy and C. Tulloch (eds), *Syd Shelton: Rock Against Racism*, London: Autograph ABP.

Ulysse, G. (2007), *Downtown Ladies: Informal Commercial Importers, a Haitian Anthropologist, and Self-making in Jamaica*, Chicago: University of Chicago Press.

Uncomfortable Truths (2007) [exhibition curated by Zoe Whitley], Victoria and Albert Museum, London, February 20–June 17.

Vaizey, J. (1962), *Britain in the 1960s: Education for Tomorrow*, Harmondsworth: Penguin.

Van Der Zee, M. (2005), In telephone conversation with the author, May 9th.

Van Dyk, L. (2003), "Dilemmas in African Diaspora Fashion," *Fashion Theory: The Journal of Dress, Body and Culture*, 7(2): 163–90.

Van Peer, W. (1997), "Towards a Poetics of Emotion," in M. Hjort M. and S. Laver (eds), *Emotion and the Arts*, New York, Oxford: Oxford University Press, 215–24.

Vincent, L. (2007), "Steve Biko and Stoned Cherrie: Refashioning the Body Politic in Democratic South Africa," *African Sociological Review*, 11(2): 80–93.

Vischer, R., C. Fielder, H. Wolffin, A. Goller, A. Hildebrand and A. Schmarsow (eds), ([1893] 1994), *Empathy, Form, and Space: Problems in German Aesthetics, 1873–1893*, trans. by H. F. Mallgrave and E. Ikonomou, Santa Monica, California: Getty Center for the History of Art and the Humanities.

Vogue, August 1, 1932.

Walker, R. (ed.), (2012), *Black Cool: One Thousand Streams of Blackness*, Berkeley: Soft Skull Press.

Wallerstein, K. (1998), "Thinness and Other Refusals in Contemporary Fashion Advertisements," *Fashion Theory: The Journal of Dress, Body and Culture*, 2(2): 129–50.

Wardlaw, A. J. (1990), "The Legacy," in R.V. Rozelle, A.J. Wardlaw and M.A. McKenna (eds), *Black Art: Ancestral Legacy, The African Impulse in African-American Art*, Dallas, Texas: Dallas Museum of Art, Harry N. Abrams, 142–61.

Ware, B.K. (1974), *The Power of the Name: The Jesus Prayer in Orthodox Spirituality*, London: Marshall Pickering.

Warnock, M. (2003), "Introduction," in J.P. Sartre, *Being and Nothingness*, xi–xxi, London, New York: Routledge.

Warwick, A. and D. Cavallaro (1998), *Fashioning The Frame: Boundaries, Dress and the Body*, Oxford, New York: Berg.

Washington, B. T., N.B. Wood and F.B. Williams (eds), ([1900] 1969), *A New Negro for a New Century: An Accurate and Up-to-date Record of the Upward Struggles of the Negro Race*, Chicago: American Publishing House.

Watt, J. (1999), *The Penguin Book of Twentieth-Century Fashion Writing*, London: Viking.

Weigel, S. (1996), *Body-and Image-Space: Re-Reading Walter Benjamin*, London, New York: Routledge.

Weir Ouston, J. (2009), "The Breathing Mind, the Feeling Voice," in J. Boston and R. Cook (eds), *Breath in Action: The Art of Breath in Vocal and Holistic Practice*, London, Philadelphia: Jessica Kingsley, 87–100.

Weissman Joselit, J. (2002), *A Perfect Fit: Clothes, Character, and the Promise of America*, New York: Henry Holt & Co.

Welter, L. and P.A. Cunningham (2005), *Twentieth-Century American Fashion*, Oxford, New York: Berg.

West, E. (2004), *Chains of Love: Slave Couples in Antebellum South Carolina*, Urbana, Chicago: University of Illinois Press.

West, S. (2004), *Portraiture*, Oxford, New York: Oxford University Press.

Weston, E. (1981), "Seeing Photographically," in A. Trachtenberg (ed.), *Classic Essays on Photography*, New Haven: Leete's Island Books.

"What Was Apartheid?" in *Forward to Freedom: The History of the British Anti-Apartheid Movement 1959–1994* website. Available online: http://www.aamarchives.org/history/apartheid.html (accessed January 25, 2015).

White, S., and G. White (1998), *Stylin': African American Expressive Culture from its Beginnings to the Zoot Suit*, Ithaca, London: Cornell University Press.

Widgery, D. (1977), "But How Did Biko Die?," *Temporary Hoarding*, 4 (Winter): 4.

Widgery, D. (1986), *Beating Time: Riot 'n' Race 'n' Rock 'n' Roll*, London: Chatto & Windus.

Widgery, D. (1989), *Preserving Disorder: Selected Essays 1968–88*, London, Winchester, Mass.: Pluto Press.

Wilder, K. (2008), "The Case for an External Spectator," *British Journal of Aesthetics*, 48(3): 261–77.

Williams, R. (1976), *Communications*, Harmondsworth: Penguin.

Williams, R. (2015), "Do you speak my language?," *G2, The Guardian*, January 7: 10–11.

Willis, C. (1897), *"Buckra" Land: Two Weeks in Jamaica*, Boston: Boston Press Club.

Willis-Braithwaite, D. (1993), *VanDerZee Photographer 1886–1983*, New York: Harry N. Abrams, Inc.

Wilmer, V. (1984), "VanDerZee Harlem Photographer," *Ten.8*, 16, 80–7.

Wilson, E. (1985), *Adorned in Dreams: Fashion and Modernity*, London: Virago.

Wilson, E. (2000), *Bohemians: The Glamorous Outcasts*, London, New York: I.B. Tauris.

Wilson, E. (2005), "Fashion and Modernity," in C. Breward and C. Evans (eds), *Fashion and Modernity*, Oxford, New York: Berg, 9–14.

Wilson, E. (2007), "A Note on Glamour," *Fashion Theory: The Journal of Dress, Body & Culture*, 11(1): 95–108.

Wilson, E. (2011), "Notes on Fashion as Fetish: On the Magical Investment in the Power of Garments," *Vestoj*, 2 (Winter): 186–93.

Wilson, U. (1959), *Jamaican Memories. Life in Jamaica Over Fifty Years Ago*, Spanish Town Archives (unpublished).

Wintz, C.C. (1996), *Black Culture and the Harlem Renaissance*, College State: Texas A&M University Press.

Withnall, A. (2014), "UKIP Says Babies Born to Immigrants in the UK Should Be Classed as Migrants—Which Would Include Nigel Farage's Own Children," *The Independent*, November 26. Available online: http://www.independent.co.uk/news/uk/politics/ukip-says-babies-born-to-immigrants-in-the-uk-should-be-classed-as-migrants--which-would-include-nigel-farages-own-children-9884841.html (accessed January 7, 2015).

Witter, M. (ed.), (1989), *Higglering/Sidewalk Vending/Informal Commercial Trading in the Jamaican Economy: Proceedings of a Symposium*, Jamaica: University of the West Indies Mona, Jamaica, June.

Wong, D.C. (1996), "A Theory of Petty Trading: The Jamaican Higgler," *The Economic Journal*, 106 (435): 507–18.

Woods, B. (1900a), "At the Justices Window," *Jamaica Pamphlets*, 22: 55–65.

Woods, B. (1900b), "In a Mangrove Swamp," *Jamaica Pamphlets*, 22: 162–6.

Wragg Chase, J. (1971), *Afro-American Art and Craft*, New York, Cincinnati, Toronto, London, Melbourne: Van Nostrand Reinhold Company.

Wright, G. (1981), *Building the Dream: A Social History of Housing in America*, New York: Pantheon.

Wright, L. (1989), "Objectifying Gender: The Stiletto Heel," in J. Attfield and P. Kirkham (eds), *A View from the Interior: Feminism, Women and Design*, London: The Women's Press Ltd, 7–19.

Wyndham, H. (1928), "Style Reflections from London: Overcoats for Sports Differ from the New Town Coats in Variety of Colour, Cut and Materials—A Pronounced Vogue Being Felt for Checks," *American Gentleman*, December 18, New York: American Fashion Company.

Yann Saunders (2005), in email correspondence with Carol Tulloch, April 11.

Yencken, D. (1988), "The Creative City," *Meanjin*, 47 (4): 597–608.

"Your Name Here: The T-shirt" (1994), *Magic Moments* [radio program], BBC Radio 4, November 24.

Zemel, C. (2000), "Imaging the Shtetl: Diaspora Culture, Photography and Eastern European Jews," in N. Mirzoeff (ed.), *Diaspora and Visual Culture: Representing Africans and Jews*, London, New York: Routledge, 193–206.

INDEX

Page numbers in *italics* refer to figures.

glasses/spectacles 139, 147
Godwin, M. 54–5
gowns/evening wear 104–5, 112–14, 189
"graphic argument" of black activism
148–9
Gunning, D. 197–8

Hackney, F. 65, 220–1
hairstyles 196
   conk 133, 135, 137
   hairpieces 116–18
   pony-tail 118–21
Haley, A. 141, 142
Hall, S. 2, 29, 31, 172, 177
Harlem Renaissance 77, 81, 82
   retelling of newness 62–5
   see also Couple in Harlem
      (VanDerZee); Self-portrait:
      Myself at Work (Johnson)
Harris, Eleanor see Holiday, Billie
Hastings, M. 175–6
haunting perspectives 173–6
headwear 140, 189
   and head-portage of higgler
      (market trader) 32–6
Hearn, P. 47
Hebdige, D. 169
higgler (market trader): "A Jamaican Lady"
      postcard 9–10
   A.W. Gardner (postcards and guide)
      49–52, 53
   angel of history 54–5
   beasts of burden 53–4
   captions 15, 23–4, 52, 55
      portraiture and "intellectual space"
      18–24
   as colonial symbol 55–7
   critical draw of 10–14
   critical possibilities of 14–18
   historical emergence of market system
      24–31, 25, 28–9
   style 31–49
      apron 38–49
      feet 38
      furbelow 37–8
      garments 36–7
      head-portage 32–4
      headwear 34–6
      jewellery 37

Holiday, Billie 87–8
   beauty nonetheless 108–12
   and Steve Biko 168
   burial robes 125
   classic twinset 121–4
   as collage 90–2
   drug use (heroin chic) 105, 106–8
   existential resonance 124–6
   as female dandy 89–90, 94, 102–3, 126
   gardenia corsage and Strange Fruit
      95–103
   hairstyles 115–21
   Lady Sings the Blues: sincere self 88–9
   mink coat 114
   as New Black Woman 126
   night and day clothes 112–15
   re-naming and self-creation 92–4
   shoes 108–10, 111, 112
   and Thelonius Monk 4
   trouser suit 115
   whiteness (gowns, shoes, gardenias,
      junk) 103–5
Hollywood film industry 43
hooks, b. 83–4, 132
Hooper-Greenhill, E. 156–7
Houston, D. and Bagert, J. 110, 111
Hughes, G. 22–3

Ibreck, E. 178–9
"intellectual space", portraiture and
   18–24
"interior dynamic" 199

Jaguar Mark II 197
Jamaica see higgler (market trader):
      "A Jamaican Lady" postcard
Jazz (Morrison) 61–2
Jeffery-Smith, M. 23
jewellery of higgler (market trader) 37
Johnson, Malvin Gray see Self-portrait:
      Myself at Work
Josephson, B. 98, 100–1
joy 176–9

Kaiser, S. 94
Kanost, B. 201
Kennard, P. 16, 17
Kennedy, S. 136, 140
Knapp, G. 54–5